P
96
.MH
P68
2001

NUMBER COLLEGE LIBRARY

Barcode in Back

D0073631

Media
Literacy
SECOND EDITION

160101

Media Literacy

SECOND EDITION

W. James Potter

Sage Publications
International Educational and Professional Publisher
Thousand Oaks ▪ London ▪ New Delhi

Copyright © 2001 by Sage Publications, Inc.

All rights reserved. No part of this book may be reproduced or utilized in any form or by any means, electronic or mechanical, including photocopying, recording, or by any information storage and retrieval system, without permission in writing from the publisher.

For information:

Sage Publications, Inc.
2455 Teller Road
Thousand Oaks, California 91320
E-mail: order@sagepub.com

Sage Publications Ltd.
6 Bonhill Street
London EC2A 4PU
United Kingdom

Sage Publications India Pvt. Ltd.
M-32 Market
Greater Kailash I
New Delhi 110 048 India

Printed in the United States of America

Library of Congress Cataloging-in-Publication Data

Potter, W. James.
    Media literacy / by W. James Potter.— 2nd ed.
        p.   cm.
Includes bibliographical references and index.
    ISBN 0-7619-2314-4 (cloth: alk. paper)
    ISBN 0-7619-2315-2 (pbk.: alk. paper)
    1. Media literacy. I. Title.
P96.M4P68   2001
302.23—dc21   00-012407

01   02   03   04   05   06   10   9   8   7   6   5   4   3   2

Acquiring Editor:	Margaret H. Seawell
Production Editor:	Claudia A. Hoffman
Typesetter/Designer:	Janelle LeMaster
Copy Editor:	Kristin Bergstad
Indexer:	Molly Hall
Cover Designer:	Michelle Lee

Contents

PART V: Putting It All Together

Preface

We all live in two worlds: the real world and the media world. The real world is where we come in direct contact with other people, locations, and events. Most of us feel that the real world is too limited, that is, we cannot get all the experiences and information we want from just the real world. In order to get those experiences and information, we journey into the media world. For example, you might want to know what songs your favorite musical groups have just written. If these groups are not coming to your town soon, you can enter the media world in order to listen to their songs on the radio, look for their videos on MTV, or buy their latest CDs. Or you might feel that your life is boring and you want to experience some exciting romance. You could read a novel, go to a movie, or watch a television program in order to get this kind of experience. Or you might be curious about whether there were any crimes in your town in the past day. You don't want to wander around town all day looking for crimes that are happening, so you watch the news to be brought up to date on crime.

We are continually entering the media world to get experiences and information we cannot get very well in our real lives. When we find these experiences, we bring them back into our real lives. We are constantly crossing the border between the real world and the media world.

In some places, the border between the two worlds is very clear. Few of us over the age of 3 or 4 have any difficulty knowing that cartoons and farces are clearly in the media world and have no chance of existing in the real world. I say "few of us" because even where the border appears obvious to most of us, there are still some people who have difficulty in perceiving when they have crossed it.

There are many places where the border between the real world and the media world is not so clear. To illustrate this, consider the following question: Is the news real? Some of you may reply, "Of course it is real. It's what happened. Journalists do not make up news stories." But when you expose yourself to the news, aren't you in the media world? Reading a newspaper or watching the evening

In 1964, Sherwood Schwartz produced a show called *Gilligan's Island*. This was a farcical comedy in which seven characters who had been on a pleasure cruise encountered a storm that left them shipwrecked on an island somewhere in the Pacific Ocean. After about six episodes had aired, Schwartz was contacted by the Coast Guard and told they had received several dozen telegrams from people who were complaining that the military should send a ship to rescue these seven people. The telegrams were serious. Schwartz was dumfounded, calling this the "most extreme case of suspension of belief I every heard of." He wondered, "Who did these viewers think was filming the castaways on that island? There was even a laugh track on the show. Who was laughing at the survivors of the wreck of the S.S. Minnow. It boggled the mind" (Schwartz, 1984, p. 2).

news on television means you have left your world of direct experience and crossed over into the media world. If you were present when an event happened, then it happened in your real world. However, if your exposure to the event is via television, you are experiencing the event in the media world—not the real world—and this makes a difference. Often news coverage is very different from the real-world occurrence; if we were at the newsworthy event, then later saw the news story, we could clearly see those differences, and the line between the real world and the media world would be very clear to us. But what if we did not attend the event and have only the news coverage to tell us what happened? In this case, all we have is the media-world account of the real-world event, and we blur the line between the two worlds when we believe that we are being exposed to real-world events when we are not.

Increasingly, the border between our real world and the media world is becoming harder to discern. More and more often, the media do not wait for us to cross over into their world; they bring their messages into our world. Because much of our exposure to media messages is not planned by us, we don't realize how great our media exposure is. Consider the exposure you have to media messages every day in your real world without your being aware of them. For example, there are radio messages coming from other people's cars as you walk down the street in your real world; you pass messages on kiosks, billboards, cars, clothing, and so on. As the media pump messages into our world at an ever increasing rate, the border line becomes blurred. We take almost all of this for granted.

Also contributing to the blurring of the line is the media's presenting many of their messages as "reality" programming. Think about what makes the following programs real, as the media claim: *Cops, America's Funniest Home Videos,*

Who Wants to Be a Millionaire?, *Who Wants to Marry a MultiMillionaire?*, the *Jerry Springer Show*, *Blind Date*, *Monday Night Football*. To what extent do these shows fit into your real world and resonate with your real experiences?

IMPORTANCE OF BEING MEDIA LITERATE ■■

As the media world grows both bigger and more varied, and as the media pump messages into our world without us deciding to cross into the media world to search for experiences, we are in danger of having our sense of reality taken away from us. We can let this happen, or we can take control of our lives.

Taking control is what media literacy is all about. Becoming more media literate gives you a much clearer perspective on the border between your real world and the world manufactured by the media. When you are media literate, you have clear maps to help you navigate better in the media world so that you can get to those experiences and information you want without becoming distracted by things that are harmful to you. You are able to build the life that *you* want rather than letting the media build the life *they* want for you.

Those who fail to develop their literacy in the media will be swept along on a tide of messages. They will have a false sense that they know what is going on in the world simply because they are exposed to so much information. All of this information is superficial unless you analyze it to build a deeper understanding. Learning all the words in a genre of popular music does not translate into expertise about the recording industry or radio broadcasting. This type of learning does not make people more creative or more able to sing. Knowing a lot about current events presented by news organizations does not necessarily mean we know what the problems in the world are—or how to deal with them. The media can give us a false sense that we are knowledgeable.

Our constant exposure to media messages influences the way we think about the world and about ourselves. It influences our beliefs about crime, education, religion, family, and the world in general. If our exposure is mostly passive, then the mundane details in those messages exert their effect without our awareness. From this massive base of misleading or inaccurate images, we infer our beliefs about the world.

We are constantly faced with the challenge of controlling the media's influence on us—the difference between us and the viewers who wrote letters asking the Coast Guard to rescue Gilligan is a matter of degree. All of us must continually decide how closely media messages reflect real life. Sometimes these decisions are relatively easy; it is simple for most of us to realize that there is nothing in real life anything like *Gilligan's Island*. But some of the decisions are harder to make accurately—especially when they are subtly shaped over a long period of time by the accumulation of thousands of journeys into the media world. Over time, we have come to accept much of the media world as the real world. For example, who is the President of the United States? Are you sure? Have you ever met him? If you have not met him, how do you know he really exists? If you have met him, how do you know he is who he says he is? I am not trying to make you paranoid. I am only asking you to consider the degree to which you trust the information and experiences you bring from the media world back into your real world. When encountering some of that information you should have a high degree of skepticism, while other information should be accepted by you with a feeling of trust. Do you know which is which?

This is why being media literate is so important. Media messages are not always what they seem. There are often many layers of meanings. The more you are aware of the layers of meaning in messages, the more you can control the selection of which meanings you want. Being more analytical is the first step toward controlling how the media affect you. If you are unaware of the meanings, then the media stay in control of how you perceive the world.

Everette Dennis, formerly Executive Director of the Freedom Forum Media Studies Center at Columbia University in New York, refers to media illiteracy as "potentially as damaging and poisonous to the human spirit as contaminated water and food is to our physical well-being" (Dennis, 1993, p. 4). The metaphor of pollution is apt. The media industries provide us with many products that we desire—products that are good for us; but these same media industries also produce harmful byproducts and dump them into our culture. If we are not media literate, we don't know the difference and we consume the toxic elements along with the good.

This book shows you how you can become more media literate. It presents a plan of action for you. If you work hard at executing this plan, you will develop your media literacy to a much higher degree. You will acquire a great deal of information about media content, the industries, and their effects on us as individuals and on society. But developing a high degree of media literacy requires more than knowledge; it also requires the development of skills. The more you develop your skills, the more levels of meaning you will be able to perceive in the media. By the end of this book, you should have a highly developed set of skills that will help you elaborate the beginning knowledge structures presented in the heart of this book.

■ ORGANIZATION OF THIS BOOK

This book is composed of 20 chapters that are organized into five parts: Foundations, Content Knowledge Structures, Industry Knowledge Structures, Effects Knowledge Structures, and Putting It All Together.

The four chapters in the Foundations section ask you to confront the questions: *Should* I work on developing my knowledge about the media? Why is this important? And how can I get started? In Chapter 1, I present a definition of media literacy that spreads out across a range of skills and knowledge. Chapter 2 shows that certain media literacy skills grow on their own during childhood along several dimensions: cognitive, emotional, and moral. Growth can still take place during adulthood, but we must work at it in specific ways. Chapter 3 lays out the sets of skills required for media literacy, and Chapter 4 defines what I mean by a "knowledge structure."

Each of the three chapters in Part II helps you build knowledge structures about the content of the media. Chapter 5 focuses on news content, Chapter 6 on entertainment content, and Chapter 7 on advertising content.

The five chapters in Part III deal with important concepts that you can use to build your knowledge structures about media industries. Chapter 8 helps you see the media industries from a historical perspective. Using a life cycle structure, it shows what is behind the innovation and development of the media industries. An economic perspective is used in Chapter 9 in order to show the business foundations of the industries. Chapter 10 shows patterns of ownership and control in the mass media companies. Then in Chapter 11 each of the media industries is profiled to illuminate the historical, economic, and ownership trends. Chapter 12 takes a marketing perspective, as the nature of the audience is presented through the eyes of industry decision makers. The view of the audience has changed drastically from the days of viewing it as a mass.

The five chapters in Part IV deal with the effects of the media. Chapter 13 will help you expand your vision about what constitutes a media effect. Effects are both long term as well as immediate. While they can affect our behavior, they also have profound influences on us cognitively, affectively, and physiologically. And they have positive as well as negative effects.

Chapter 14 lays out the immediate effects, and Chapter 15 lists the long-term effects. The question of how the effects processes work on us is explored in Chapter 16. Those processes are hardly ever simple or direct. More often the media work in concert with many other factors that each serve to increase the probability that an effect may occur. When we take a broader perspective on effects, we can more accurately assess the influence of the media in our lives.

In Chapter 17, the influences of the media are examined in terms of changes in the fundamental institutions of politics, family, religion, and sports. The media, especially television, have forever altered the way these institutions function.

Part V begins with a chapter that illustrates why a broad knowledge of the real world is as important as a thorough knowledge of the media industries. Real-world knowledge helps us check to see if the media are presenting a balanced picture of society. While this chapter cannot present a full inventory of the real-world knowledge a person needs, it presents some examples (such as in the areas of crime, the legal system, government) to illustrate how real-world knowledge is often at odds with the media picture.

The book concludes with two chapters that lay out some key strategies for improving literacy. Chapter 19 synthesizes the findings in the previous 18 chapters to help build your awareness of your own knowledge structures, awareness of how your mind works, and awareness of the key elements in the effects process. This forms the basis for Chapter 20, which presents perspectives to help you develop your own media strategies at three levels: societal, interpersonal, and personal.

As you read each of these chapters, think in terms of developing your knowledge structures. Begin with the thesis statement, the "key idea" of that chapter. Then look at the outline at the beginning of the chapter. It will show you the major branches and each branch's supporting ideas. Then read the text while continually asking yourself: How does this new information fit in with what I already know? How can I use this? After your first reading, close the book and see how much you can recall. Can you recall only an assortment of facts, or an organized structure? Do the exercises. Continue to think about the ideas as you experience the media in your everyday life. Spontaneously work on parts of the exercise, elaborating and extending your answers. And discuss your growing awareness with others.

This book has a "self-help" tone as it presents guidance and practical exercises to help you achieve higher levels of media literacy. It is not sufficient merely to memorize the facts in each chapter. That alone will not help you increase your media literacy by very much. Instead, you need to internalize the information by drawing it into your own experiences. Continually ask yourself: Can I find an example of this in my own life? How can I apply this when I deal with the media? The exercises at the ends of the chapters will help you get started on this. The more you think through the exercises and the more you develop new exercises for yourself, the more you will be internalizing the information and thus making it more a part of the way you think. For example, in the chapter on media effects, I present a rather long list of possible effects. If you simply memorize this list, it may help you a bit on a test, but it won't help you become a more empowered consumer of media messages. To develop such power over the effects process, you need to internalize the knowledge about these effects so you can spot them when they occur and protect yourself from the effects you don't want as well as amplify the effects you do want. The more you practice spotting and naming these effects, the more you will be internalizing the information and acquiring a tool that will be useful for the rest of your life. Thus the concepts are presented as tools to help you achieve more awareness in your everyday life.

In summary, the purpose of this book is to help you develop strong knowledge structures about the media. Will the book provide you with all the information you need? No. That would require too much information to fit in one book; you will need to continue your reading. At the end of most chapters I suggest several books for further reading on the chapter's topic. While some of those books are fairly technical, most are easy to read and very interesting.

This book is an introduction. It is designed to show you the big picture so you can get started efficiently on increasing your own media literacy. It is important to get started now. The world is rapidly changing because of the media. VCRs, computers, the Internet, and other media channels are substantially revising the way the media industries do business and the way we receive information and entertainment.

I hope you will have fun reading this book. And I hope it will expose you to new perspectives from which you can see much more about the media. If it does, you will be gaining new insights into your old habits and interpretations. If this happens, I hope you will share your new insights and "war stories" with me. Much of this book has been written to reflect some of the problems and insights my students have had in the media literacy courses I have taught. I have learned much from them. I'd like to learn even more from you. So let me know what you think and send me a message at: jpotter@ucla.edu.

See you on the journey!

EXERCISE

Becoming Sensitized to Media Message Saturation

PART I: Estimate Your Exposure

Right now, try to estimate how many minutes and hours you spend with each of the following media during a typical week.

_____ Watching television (cable, broadcast, movies played on a VCR, etc.)

_____ Watching films at a theater

_____ Listening to radio (at home, in your car, etc.)

_____ Listening to recordings (CDs and tapes)

_____ Reading newspapers

_____ Reading magazines of all kinds

_____ Reading books (texts for class, novels for pleasure, etc.)

_____ Using computers (games, word processing, surfing the Internet, etc.)

_____ TOTAL

PART II: Track Your Exposures

Keep a Media Exposure Diary for one week. Get a small notebook—one you can carry with you wherever you go for 7 days. Every time you are exposed to a message from the media, either directly or indirectly, make an entry of the time and what the message was.

Direct exposures are those where you come in contact with a medium and experience a message during that contact. For example, if you watch *Friends*, write: "Message: *Friends*; Time: Monday 7:00 to 7:30." Listening to KXXX for 30 minutes in the car is also direct exposure.

Indirect exposures are those where you see a reminder of a media message, such as seeing a title of a movie on the marquee of a bus stop. You don't see the film itself (which would be a direct exposure); you see something that reminds you of it. Also, listen to conversations. If people talk about something they heard from the media, then you have been exposed to that media message indirectly. For example, if you heard your friends talk about *General Hospital*, then write: "Message: Talked with friends about *General Hospital*; Time: Tuesday morning 10-11:30."
If you happened to hear your roommate humming a popular song that is played often on the radio, write: "Message: Roommate hummed X song; Time: Wednesday all day!"

At the end of the week, examine the entries in your diary to answer the following questions:

1. How much total time were you exposed to media messages?
2. How many exposures did you experience during the week?
3. What proportions of the exposures were direct and indirect?
4. What proportion of media exposures were initiated by you (active)? and what proportion just happened (passive)?
5. How do your diary data compare to your estimates from Part I?
6. What kinds of messages were most prevalent?

PART III: Avoiding Exposure

Choose a day as Media Message Avoidance Day. When you get up in the morning, do not turn on your radio, television, or stereo. See how long you can go without exposing yourself to a message from the media. How long can you go without accidently seeing/hearing an actual media message or a reference to a media message?

PART I

FOUNDATIONS

CHAPTER 1

Key Idea: Media literacy is a perspective from which we expose ourselves to the media and interpret the meaning of the messages we encounter. We build our perspective from knowledge structures, which are constructed from information using skills.

What Is
Media Literacy?

Most of us think we are fairly media literate. We know the names of a great many television shows, films, magazines, books, and songs. We recognize the names and faces of celebrities. We know how to read. We can easily follow plots in movies and television shows. We know what flashbacks mean, and we know enough to get scared when the soft background music builds to a shattering crescendo as a character steps into danger. We might even know how to play games on a computer and program a VCR. Clearly we know how to expose ourselves to the media; we know how to absorb information from them; and we know how to be entertained by them.

Are we media literate? Yes, of course. We have acquired a great deal of information and developed remarkable skills. The ability to speak a language, read, and understand photographs are achievements that we too often take for granted.

We should not overlook what we have accomplished. However, it is also important to acknowledge that we all can be *much more* media literate. So while it is good to celebrate the abilities we have developed, we must also recognize that there is considerable room for improvement.

Improvement in what way? A starting place for thinking about improvement is a broad definition of what it means to be media literate.

DEFINING MEDIA LITERACY ▓

In the minds of many people, the term *literacy* is most associated with the print media, so it means the ability to read (Scribner & Cole, 1981; Sinatra, 1986). Some people expand the term to include *visual literacy* as they think about other media such as film and television (Goodwin & Whannel, 1990; Messaris, 1994). Other writers have used the term *computer literacy* (Adams & Hamm, 1989). Reading literacy, visual literacy, and computer literacy are not synonyms for media literacy; instead they are merely components. *Media* literacy includes all these specialized abilities as well as something more. If we don't know how to read, we cannot get much out of the print media. If we have trouble understanding visual and narrative conventions, we cannot get much out of television or film. And if we cannot use a computer, we are cut off from what is growing into the most important medium.

Media literacy is more than these specialized abilities. It is something more general. Here's the definition of media literacy:

Media literacy is a perspective that we actively use when exposing ourselves to the media in order to interpret the meaning of the messages we encounter. We build our perspective from knowledge structures. To build our knowledge structures, we need tools and raw material. The tools are our skills. The raw material is information from the media and from the real world. Active use means that we are aware of the messages and are consciously interacting with them.

What is a perspective? Let's illustrate this with an analogy. Let's say you wanted to learn about the Earth. You could build a 100-foot tall tower, climb up to the top, and use that as your perspective to study the Earth. That would give you a good perspective that would not be blocked by trees so that you could see for perhaps several miles in any direction. If your tower were in a forest, you would conclude that the Earth is covered with trees. But if your tower were in a suburban neighborhood, you would conclude that the Earth is covered with houses, roads, and shopping centers. If your tower were inside the New Orleans Superdome stadium, you would conclude something quite different. Each of these perspectives on Earth would give you a very different set of perceptions. None of these perspectives is better than any other. The key to understanding the Earth is to build lots of these towers so you have many different perspectives in order to enlarge your understanding about what Earth is. And not all of these towers need to be 100 feet tall. Some should be very short so you can better see what is happening between the blades of grass in a lawn. And others should be hundreds of miles away from the surface so that you can tell that the Earth is a sphere and that there are large weather formations constantly churning around the globe.

The same principle of multiple perspectives applies to media literacy. Your "towers" are your knowledge structures. The more knowledge structures you have, the broader your overall perspective. For example, you may have a very large, well-developed knowledge structure about popular music. You may know the names of all the important musical groups (as well as all of their members and managers), all their songs, the dates of those songs, which awards each group has earned, and what the critics have said about every song. If you have all of this information well organized so you can recall any of it at a moment's notice, you have a well-developed knowledge structure about popular music. Your perspective is "above" all the detail; that is, from where you stand, you can see all your information well organized, and it all makes complete sense to you. If some people, for example, were to claim that there were only three members of the Backstreet Boys, you could argue with them and have complete confidence that they were wrong and you were right. Your knowledge structure about popular music prevents you from being misled. Are you media literate? Within the small corner of the media world where popular music resides, you are. But if this were the only knowledge structure you had developed, you would be at a fairly low level of media literacy, because you would have a weak perspective on television, film, books, or any of the other media. You would have little understanding of who owns and controls the media, how the media have developed over time, why certain kinds of content are never seen while other types are continually repeated, and what effects the industries and content may be having on you. Clearly it is much better to have many highly developed knowledge structures in order to have a strong perspective on the media.

How can you construct a strong perspective on the media? The key to doing this is to build a good *set* of knowledge structures. As mentioned previously, to build a knowledge structure, we need tools and raw material. The tools are our skills. The raw material is information from the media and from the real world. If we have a great deal of information but weak skills, we will not be able to make much sense of the information. If we have strong skills but don't expose ourselves to a range of media messages or real-world experiences, our knowledge structures will be very limited and unbalanced.

Importance of Information

Information is the essential ingredient in knowledge structures, but not all information is equally useful when building a knowledge structure. Some information is rather superficial, such as the names of television shows or the melodies of popular music. If all a person has is the recognition of surface information such as lyrics to television show theme songs, names of characters and actors, settings for shows, and the like, he or she is operating at a low level of media literacy, because this kind of information addresses only the question of "What?" The more useful information comes in the form of the answers to the questions of "How?" and "Why?" But remember that you first need to know something about the What before you can delve deeper into the questions of How and Why.

In order to increase your media literacy, you need to get good information, then organize it into useful knowledge structures. In undertaking such an organization, you need to be concerned with depth and breadth of information. As for depth, you need to get below the surface of the media content and look for underlying themes. You need to think about the values that must be operating in a business that would produce such content. You need to be concerned about the effects—positive as well as negative—that are happening all the time all around you.

Your knowledge structures also need breadth. Remember, the more knowledge structures you have, the stronger your overall perspective. What are the most important knowledge structures for building a good media literacy perspective? First, we need knowledge about the message conventions used by media producers and the patterns of content these conventions produce. Second, we need knowledge about the media industries: their origins, patterns of development, economic basis, and structural (ownership patterns and governmental regulation) contexts. Third, and perhaps most important, we need a broader perspective about media effects. This means recognizing long-term as well as immediate effects; recognizing effects on society as well as on individuals; and recognizing that media effects are *not* limited to only our behaviors—those effects can also work on our cognitions, our attitudes, our emotions, and our physiology (bodily functions).

We also need to have strong knowledge structures about the real world—both factual information and social information. Factual information refers to characteristics about the world that are usually not in dispute (not open to individual interpretation). Examples include the size of the population of this country, names of political leaders, final scores of sporting contests, the distances between cities, and so on. In contrast, social information refers to shared understandings about human interactions. Examples include the moral themes within a culture or institution, as well as the way people should behave in certain roles (such as student, romantic partner, friend, stranger, family member, job applicant, athletic team member, etc.).

People who have had a wider range of experiences in the real world have a broader base from which to appreciate and analyze media messages. For example, those who have helped someone run for political office can understand and analyze press coverage of campaigns to a greater depth than those who have not had any real-world experience with political campaigns. People who have played sports will be able to appreciate the athletic accomplishments they see on television to a greater depth than those who have not physically tested themselves on those challenges. People who have had a wide range of relationships and family experiences will have a higher degree of understanding and more in-depth emotional reactions to those portrayals in the media.

Information is the raw material on which our skills work to build knowledge structures. In order to get good raw material, we need to expose ourselves to a wide variety of messages to expand our base. We also need to search out more in-depth information on areas where we have some superficial knowledge so as to deepen our understanding. While most of this information comes from media sources, we also need to search out information from primary sources in real life.

Importance of Skills

Knowledge structures do not occur spontaneously, they must be built with care and precision. They are not just a pile of facts; they are made by carefully crafting pieces of information into an overall design. In order to perform such a task, we rely on a set of skills (see Chapter 3). These skills are the tools. We use these tools to mine the large piles of facts to uncover the particular facts we need and brush away the rest. Once we have selected the facts we need, we shape them into information and carefully fit those pieces of information into their proper places in a structure. The structure helps us see patterns. We use these patterns as maps to tell us where to get more information and also where to go to retrieve information we have previously crafted into our knowledge structure.

SUPPORTING IDEAS ▦

This definition of media literacy rests on three fundamental ideas. Each of these is explained below.

Media Literacy Is a Continuum, Not a Category

Media literacy is not a category—like a box—where you are either in the category or you are not. For example, you are either a high school graduate or you are not; you are either an American citizen or you are not. In contrast, media literacy is best regarded as a continuum—like a thermometer—where there are degrees.

We all occupy some position on the media literacy continuum. There is no point below which we could say that someone was not literate, and there is no point at the high end where we can say that someone is fully literate— there is always room for improvement.

People are positioned along that continuum based on the strength of their overall perspective on the media. The strength of someone's perspective is based on the number and quality of that person's knowledge structures. And the quality of knowledge structures is based on the level of the person's skills and experiences. Because people vary substantially on skills and experiences, they will vary on the number and quality of their knowledge structures. Hence there will be great variation on media literacy across people.

People operating at lower levels of media literacy have weak and limited perspectives on the media. They have smaller, more superficial, and less organized knowledge structures that provide an inadequate perspective for interpreting the meaning of a media message. These people are also habitually reluctant or unwilling to utilize their skills, which remain under developed and therefore more difficult to employ successfully.

Media Literacy Is Multi-Dimensional

When we think of information, we typically think of sets of facts found in a textbook, a newspaper, or a magazine article. But this is only one type of information—cognitive. There are three other types: emotional information, aesthetic information, and moral information. Each of these four focuses on a different domain of understanding. The cognitive domain refers to factual information—dates, names, definitions, and the like. Think of cognitive information as that which resides in the brain.

The emotional domain contains information about feelings, such as love, hate, anger, happiness, frustration, and more. Think of emotional information as that which lives in the heart—remembrances of happy times, moments of fear, instances of embarrassment. Some people have very little ability to experience an emotion during exposure to the media, while others are very sensitive to cues that generate all sorts of feelings in them. It is relatively easy for us to perceive emotional information concerning rage, fear, lust, hate, and other strong emotions. Producers have easy-to-recognize symbols to trigger these, so these emotions do not require a high degree of literacy to perceive and understand. But there are also more subtle emotions, such as ambivalence, confusion, wariness, and so on. Crafting messages about these emotions requires more production skill from writers, directors, and actors. Perceiving these subtle emotions accurately requires a higher degree of literacy from the audience.

The aesthetic domain contains information about how to produce messages. This information gives us the basis for making judgments about who are great writers, photographers, actors, dancers, choreographers, singers, musicians, composers, directors, and other kinds of artists. It also helps us make judgments about other products of creative craftsmanship, such as editing, lighting, set designing, costuming, sound recording, layout, and the like. This appreciation skill is very important to some scholars (Messaris, 1994; Silverblatt, 1995;

Wulff, 1997). For example, Messaris (1994) argues that viewers who are visually literate should have an awareness of artistry and visual manipulation. By this, he means an awareness about the processes by which meaning is created through the visual media. What is expected of sophisticated viewers is some degree of self-consciousness about their role as interpreters. This includes the ability to detect artifice (in staged behavior and editing) and to spot authorial presence (style of the producer/director).

Think of aesthetic information as that which resides in our eyes and ears. Some of us have a good ear for dialog or musical composition. Some of us have a good eye for lighting, photographic composition, or movement. The more information we have from this domain, the finer the discriminations we can make between a great actress and a very good one; between a great song that will endure and a currently popular "flash in the pan"; between a film director's best and very best work; between art and artificiality.

The moral domain contains information about values. Think of moral information as that which resides in the soul or conscience. This type of information provides us with the basis for making judgments about right and wrong. When we see characters make decisions in a story, we judge them on a moral dimension, that is, the characters' goodness or evilness. The more detailed and refined our moral information is, the more deeply we can perceive the values underlying messages in the media and the more sophisticated and reasoned are our judgments about those values. It takes a highly media literate person to perceive moral themes well. You must be able to think past individual characters in order to focus your meaning-making at the overall narrative level. You separate characters from their actions—you might not like a particular character but you like his or her actions in terms of fitting in with (or reinforcing) your values. You do not focus your viewing on only one character's point of view, but try to empathize with many characters so you can vicariously experience the consequences of their actions throughout the course of the narrative.

Strong knowledge structures contain information from all four of these domains. If only one type of information is missing, the knowledge structure is weakened. For example, if you have a knowledge structure without any emotional information, you are able to be highly analytical when you watch a movie and able to quote lots of facts about the history of the genre, the director's point of view, and the underlying theme. But if you cannot evoke an emotional reaction, you are simply going through a dry, academic exercise.

When you have strong knowledge structures that contain information from all four domains, then you can move the focus of deficiencies off yourself and onto the media messages. For example, with strong knowledge structures, you might find yourself hating a movie for manipulating your emotions but really admiring the artistry of the director. Or you might greatly admire the moral position of a book but feel the author was not a good writer, because he was not able to evoke any strong emotions. Whereas if your knowledge structures are weak, you will be much less likely to spot deficiencies in the messages, because the deficiencies are so prevalent within yourself.

The Purpose of Media Literacy Is to Give Us More Control Over Interpretations

All media messages have a surface meaning along with many deeper meanings. People who are at a low level of media literacy are limited to accepting the surface meanings; thus the media are in control, because the media determine the meaning, and those meanings remain unchallenged—even unexamined. With only a limited perspective on the media, these people have smaller, more superficial, and less organized knowledge structures, which provide an inadequate perspective to use in interpreting the meaning of a media message. Thus, low-literacy people are much less able to identify inaccuracies; to sort through controversies; to appreciate irony or satire; or to develop a broad, yet personal view of the world.

People who are less media literate do not realize that all media messages are interpretations. Journalists tell us their interpretation of what is important and who is important. Entertainment storytellers show us their interpretation of what it means to be human, develop relationships, engage in conflict, and achieve happiness. Advertisers try to convince us that we have particular problems and that their products can help us quickly overcome those problems. Also as audience members, we can construct our own interpretations of those messages, but if we are not very media literate, we do not know much about constructing interpretations that are different from what the media present to us, and therefore we are much more likely simply to accept what the media tell us.

In contrast, when we operate at a high level of media literacy, we actively use a set of highly developed interpretive skills to place a media message inside the context of well-elaborated knowledge structures and thereby are able to interpret any message along many different dimensions. This provides us with more choices of meaning. Are all choices of meaning equally good? The answer is no. When we are highly literate, we know how to sort through all the choices of meaning and select the one that is most useful from several points of view—cognitive, emotional, aesthetic, and moral.

When you are more media literate, you have many more options. And these options translate into more power by giving you more control over your beliefs and behaviors. With few or no choices, much of the world is closed, and you are forced to accept unquestioningly the dominant themes, values, beliefs, and interpretations presented in the media.

Operating at a higher level of media literacy also gives you more control over the media. This does not mean that you can change the media themselves; instead it means that you can change *how* you are exposed to the media and the *effects* those exposures have on you. That is a significant amount of control.

In order to gain control over how the media affect us, we need to be able to recognize the full range of media effects and how they exercise their influence on us. This is not an easy task. Most media effects are subtle, they happen very gradually, and most of the effects take a long time to show up. By the time they have attained a high enough profile to be easily recognizable, they have grown deep roots in our subconscious and are very hard to change.

Also, the effects often exert their influence indirectly—through other people or institutions. Even if we somehow avoid all direct exposure to media messages, we would be indirectly influenced by those messages that have influenced our institutions of government, family, education, and religion. The only way to be totally free of all media influence is to remove yourself completely from society and its institutions. But ironically, this might potentially be the greatest media influence of all—to force you to alter your lifestyle radically and to give up all the many benefits of being part of our culture.

The process of media effects continues whether we are aware of it or not. When we can gain greater control over the media (not just through exposure but also through interpretation), we can amplify the effects we want to have and discount those effects we want to avoid.

With greater understanding and control comes appreciation. When you watch a movie, in how many different ways are you able to appreciate the film? For most of us, appreciation is usually focused on the overall plot and the acting. We appreciate the film's ability to keep us interested and excited. We also admire how certain actors are able to project an interesting character. But there are many other things going on in the film, many of which we take for granted unless they seem really unusual. For example, think about the last film you saw. Did you notice the editing—were there dissolves, flashbacks, cuts in dialogue, pacing that excited you in places? Was there music under the entire film or just in places? Can you remember how certain scenes were lighted to change colors or elicit a certain mood? Can you remember how the characters were dressed in all the scenes? How were the rooms furnished to convey information about the background of the action and characters? The more of these questions you can answer in vivid detail, the more media literate you are and the more dimensions you are able to appreciate.

If we consciously choose our media exposures and actively select the most useful information from those exposures, we can build stronger and stronger knowledge structures. With strong knowledge structures and highly developed skills we will be able to increase our appreciation of the media. This is the opposite of the old saying: Ignorance is bliss. When it comes to the media, ignorance limits people to a very narrow range of reactions. In order to expand your range of reactions—cognitive, emotional, aesthetic, and moral —you need to move far away from ignorance. The more media literate you are, the more you understand and hence appreciate the media, their messages, and effects.

■■ CONCLUSION

Media literacy requires a broad perspective. It is not limited to reading or to any other single skill. A broad perspective is built on well-developed knowledge structures. We build these knowledge structures by using our skills to select information. Then we assemble those selections into meaningful designs.

Media literacy is a continuum, not a category. We can all increase our degree of literacy. Media literacy is multi-dimensional. We need to acquire information from the cognitive, emotional, aesthetic, and moral domains in order to build strong knowledge structures. The purpose of media literacy is to increase our understanding of the media and their messages; to increase our control over the interpretive process; and thus to increase our appreciation of the media.

Media-literate people are able to see much more in a given message. They are more aware of the levels of meaning. This enhances understanding. They are more in charge of the processes of meaning-making and selection. This enhances control. They are much more likely to get what they want from the messages. This enhances appreciation. Thus people operating at higher levels of media literacy fulfill the goals of higher understanding, control, and appreciation.

■■ FURTHER READING

Aufderheide, P. (1993). *Media literacy: A report of the National Leadership Conference on Media Literacy*. Washington, DC: The Aspen Institute. (37 pages)

This is a report of a meeting held in December 1992 by several dozen Americans concerned about the need for media literacy to be taught in the nation's public schools. They derived the following definition of media literacy: "It is the ability of a citizen to access, analyze, and produce information for specific outcomes" (p. v). They recommended that "emphases in media literacy training range widely, including informed citizenship, aesthetic appreciation and expression, social advocacy, self-esteem, and consumer competence" (p. 1).

Bianculli, D. (1992). *Teleliteracy: Taking television seriously*. New York: Continuum. (315 pages with indices)

David Bianculli was a TV critic/columnist for 15 years before writing this book, which is a defense of television. Admitting that 90% of TV content is "crap," he feels that there is a great deal of value in television programming. He presents a manifesto of 10 points, all intended to get more respect for TV. The most interesting part of the book is in the first section where he presents a 150-question literacy quiz (75 questions about TV and 75 about classic literature and music). The TV questions are very easy to answer while the other questions are very difficult. His point is that the population is very TV literate. He also presents a fascinating history of criticism of various forms of literature and music dating back to Plato; this clearly shows that there are people who think every new piece of art is bad and every new medium is dangerous.

Gordon, D. R. (1971). *The new literacy*. Toronto: University of Toronto Press. (190 pages with index)

Gordon argues that the Three R's are no longer sufficient for literacy in the new media environment. But in this rather McLuhan-esque book with its changing type faces, odd graphics, and use of white space, he raises issues more than he provides prescriptions or definitions.

Messaris, P. (1994). *Visual "literacy": Image, mind, and reality*. Boulder, CO: Westview. (208 pages)

Paul Messaris, a communications professor at the University of Pennsylvania, argues against some commonly held assumptions about visual literacy. For example, he rejects the notion popular among many scholars that there can be no objective standards to judge the reality of visual images. He says that there are generic cognitive skills that people apply when they experience the pictorial media. His notion of training people to be media literate focuses on helping viewers detect unrealistic visual manipulation.

Metallinos, N. (Ed.). (1994). *Verbo-visual literacy: Understanding and applying new educational communication media technologies*. Montreal, Canada: 3Dmt Research and Information Center. (276 pages)

These 38 chapters are from a symposium of the International Visual Literacy Association. They focus on suggestions about how best to use the emerging new technologies to foster verbal and visual literacy.

Neuman, S. B. (1991). *Literacy in the television age: The myth of the TV effect.* Norwood, NJ: Ablex. (230 pages)

Neuman treats literacy mainly as a print skill, then lays out the arguments posed by four theories—displacement, information processing, short-term gratification, and interest stimulation—that TV has reduced literacy. She shows that the empirical evidence does not support any of these theories; that is, the criticism that the media have hindered literacy is unwarranted.

Silverblatt, A. (1995). *Media literacy: Keys to interpreting media messages.* Westport, CT: Praeger. (340 pages including index)

This mass media book presents some chapters with information about what is needed as far as knowledge about the media. It has the feel of a textbook for an introductory-level course and presents lots of photographs and exercises for students to undertake. The first section of the book, called Keys to Interpreting Media Messages, lays out a method of critically analyzing the process, context, framework, and production values of the mass media. The second section, called Media Formats, presents exercises that show students how to analyze print journalism, advertising, and American political communications. The third section—the smallest at under 40 pages—briefly raises some critical issues, such as violence in the media, children, social change, and global communications.

Sinatra, R. (1986). *Visual literacy connections to thinking, reading and writing.* Springfield, IL: Charles C Thomas. (307 pages)

Richard Sinatra, a Professor in Human Services and Counseling at St. John's University, argues that visual literacy is primary to more developed forms of literacy, such as oral language literacy and written language literacy. Many of the arguments in this book are rather technical. For example, he provides an in-depth treatment of the topic of how the human brain processes verbal and visual information.

CHAPTER

2

Key Idea: Media literacy must be developed. It cannot simply be switched on all of a sudden.

Developing Media Literacy

Two fathers are proudly discussing how smart their children are. One of the fathers says, "Robert, my five-year-old, already knows how to read."

"So does my four-year-old Jeremy," says the other father.

"When I say Robert can read, I don't mean simple pre-school books. I mean he can read books that my older children read in the fourth and fifth grade."

"Jeremy reads at a sixth-grade level."

"Is that so? Well, Robert reads the newspaper—every night, and we discuss the news. He really understands everything."

"We had to get Jeremy a subscription to the *New York Times*. He just pestered us so."

"Well, Robert saved up his own money and bought his own subscriptions to *The Atlantic Monthly* and *Forbes*."

"That's great! Then your Robert must have read the article that my Jeremy had published in *The Atlantic Monthly*—it was only a short article but then Jeremy is only 4 years old."

Sometimes proud parents exaggerate their children's level of development. Proud parents believe that their children can understand and produce much more than they really can. Sometimes adults overestimate their own abilities, especially concerning media literacy. Being an adult does not guarantee that you are highly media literate.

COMPONENTS OF DEVELOPING MEDIA LITERACY ▪

The development of higher levels of media literacy relies on three components. The first component is experience. The more experience we have with the media and with the real world, the greater our potential for developing to a higher level of media literacy. But experience alone is not enough. While we are exposed to messages, we need to be active in applying our skills. Thus the second component is the active application of skills. The third component is maturation—this is readiness. In order to understand how we develop our media literacy, we must consider all three of these components.

Experience

The more experience you have with the media and the real world, the more chance you have to develop your media literacy. More experience can translate into more elaborate knowledge structures. As we age, we acquire more experience with the media and with real life. However, age does not automatically translate into experience. As we move through life, some of us acquire thousands of unique experiences. But others of us have the same experience thousands of times. If we stay entrenched in the same habits and place, we are not moving through life—we are only moving through time.

People who are stuck in one place along life's path (i.e., a repetitive exposure to only one kind of medium, vehicle, or message) are not broadening their experience, so they cannot increase their media literacy. While accumulating a lot of experiences provides us with the potential to build stronger knowledge structures, it does not automatically translate into higher media literacy.

Active Application of Skills

We need to be active in applying certain skills when we encounter the media. Mere exposure or experience will not amount to much if we are not paying attention. We need to apply our skills consciously in order to filter out the messages we evaluate as inaccurate, misleading, or not useful. We need to analyze messages to get below their surface and perceive deeper meanings. We need to compare what we see in media messages with what we know from our knowledge structures. In short, we need to be active in interacting with the media.

If we are passive during our media exposures, we can still pick up a good deal of information in our media-saturated culture, but that information will not be balanced or complete. To illustrate this point, let's say you need 100 facts to have a commanding knowledge base in a particular area. Passive exposure to the media might result in your being exposed to maybe a dozen facts. The mainstream flow of messages from the media will never provide you with the full range of information you might need. The media have a narrow agenda for information and a narrow repertoire for entertainment stories. Passive exposure will not get you outside these limits. If you stay fixed in this passive state, the continual flow of messages will only serve to reinforce a narrow, unbalanced set of information. Unless you actively seek a wider variety of sources of information your knowledge structure will not become stronger, and you will fall into the trap of believing that you are well informed—because of all your exposure—when you are really becoming less informed as the world changes without you being aware of it.

Unless we stay active in processing messages, our position on the media literacy continuum can degrade to lower levels. Without continually practicing skills, those skills will deteriorate. Without continually updating and adjusting our knowledge structures, they quickly become out of date and cluttered with unprocessed information. For example, the ownership, control, economic, and organizational patterns of the media industries change each year; each week brings a flood of new messages; and social scientists conduct hundreds of important studies each year that require us to expand as well as alter the way we think about effects. If we don't keep up, we will slide behind.

Maturation

The third factor is maturation. This factor is especially important during childhood, and this is why children are often treated as a special group when it comes to the media. Our capacities increase as we grow from infancy through adolescence. This is obvious physically, that is, as we age from infancy we are able to run faster, jump higher, and lift heavier objects.

We also mature cognitively. When we are very young, our minds are not developed enough to allow for an understanding of abstract thoughts like those required by mathematical reasoning, for example. A task of reasoning (such as multiplying 4 × 5) is very difficult for us when we are 4 years old but very easy for us a few short years later. We also mature emotionally (Goleman, 1995) and morally (Kohlberg, 1981). As we reach higher levels of maturation intellectually, emotionally, and morally, we are able to perceive more in media messages.

Think of maturation as a series of gates along the path to higher media literacy. When we encounter one of these gates, we must wait behind it until we mature to a certain level, then the gate opens and we can proceed. There are a series of cognitive gates, emotional gates, and moral gates. These gates occur every few years throughout childhood and hold us back in the early stages of media literacy. For example, most humans are not capable of acquiring the skill of reading until they are beyond the age of 4 or 5, because their brains have not matured to a point where such learning is possible. Trying to teach reading to 2-year-olds is very frustrating. No matter how hard you work or how hard the children work, their minds have not matured enough to be able to employ the skills required for reading a book. But once the child's mind matures to the point where he or she can use those skills, the practice of reading begins to pay off.

This is why children's exposure cannot be compared to adults'. Children are not people who differ from adults simply because they have less experience. They also have less capacity to make sense of their experiences. As they mature, children have more capabilities available to them. As they reach adolescence, they pass through the last maturation gates and are capable of applying more advanced skills. Whether they actually do apply these skills or how well they apply them is no longer a matter of maturation—it depends on their experiences and whether they actively use their skills during media exposures.

These three factors work together. For example, a young girl of 7 will be able to read because she has passed through the gate of cognitive maturity where her mind has developed to a point where she can learn to read. If she reads a simple book on gardening, she will be able to recognize most words and be able to recognize how the words are assembled into sentences to convey an idea. She has a rudimentary reading skill. If she also has a good deal of experience in gardening, this experience along with her reading skill will combine to allow her to read the book more quickly and to acquire a good deal more meaning from it than a child who has not had any experience in gardening. As her experience with gardening increases, her need for more information will also increase. She might subscribe to gardening magazines, listen to tapes on gardening, and seek out television programs on the subject. As her knowledge base grows, she will seek out information from related areas—perhaps botany and landscape architecture. If she carefully analyzes the messages as she is exposed to them, she will be developing a better "eye" for the artistry of gardening, and thus her ability to appreciate will be increased. Thus combining experiences from the media with real-life experiences and the conscious application of advanced skills along the way moves her farther down both the gardening path and the media literacy path.

Let's take a closer look at how people develop multi-dimensionally—cognitively, emotionally, and morally.

■■ COGNITIVE DEVELOPMENT

Development During Childhood

In cognitive development, children differ from adults primarily in terms of maturation. The most influential thinker on the topic of cognitive maturation during childhood was the Swiss psychologist, Jean Piaget. From years of research, Piaget found that a child's mind matures from birth to about 12 years of age, during which time it goes through several identifiable stages (Smith & Cowie, 1988). Until age 2, children are in the sensori-motor stage, then advance to the pre-operational stage, from 2 to 7 years of age. Then they progress to the concrete operational stage, and by 12 they move into the formal operational stage, where they are regarded as having matured cognitively into adulthood. In each of these stages, children's minds mature to a point where they can accomplish a new set of cognitive tasks. For example, in the concrete operational stage (ages 7 to 12) children are able to organize objects into series. If you try to teach this skill to a child of age 3, you will fail—no matter how organized and clear your lessons are. Another skill that is developed throughout childhood is conservation, which is the ability to realize that certain attributes of an object are constant, even though that object is transformed in appearance (Pulaski, 1980). For example, ask a child to make two balls of clay exactly the same size. Then roll one of them out into a long, thin shape like a snake, and ask the child which of the two pieces of clay is bigger. The child will say the snake is bigger than the ball, because the snake is longer. The child does not have the ability to understand that the amount of clay has been conserved, only the shape (not the quantity) has been changed. Children's minds have matured enough to understand the idea of conservation by the time they reach about age 7.

Infants and Toddlers. Children begin paying attention to the TV screen as early as 6 months of age (Hollenbeck & Slaby, 1979) and by the age of 3 many children have developed regular patterns of viewing of about an hour or 2 per day (Huston et al., 1983). Their viewing is primarily exploratory. This means they are looking for individual events that stand out because of certain motions, color, music, sound effects, or unusual voices. They look for action, not dialog. They have great difficulty in understanding that individual events are ordered into plots, that characters have motives that influence the action, and that characters change as a result of what happens in the plot (Wartella, 1981). The reason for this is that young children have not developed a very sophisticated understanding of narratives. Until they learn more of the principles of narrative progression, they will have difficulty making sense out of stories longer than a minute or two (Meadowcroft & Reeves, 1989).

Younger Children. By about age 4, children are spending less time in the exploratory mode and more time in a search mode. This means that they begin developing an agenda of what to look for. Their attention does not simply bounce haphazardly around from one high-profile action to another. By kindergarten, a continuous story line holds their attention. They focus their attention on formal features in making their decisions about what is important in the shows. For example, they interpret that a laugh track signals that a program is a comedy.

Also by age 4, children begin trying to distinguish between ads and programs. This is difficult until they develop the skills of perceptual discrimination. During this trial-and-error learning, children either express confusion about the difference or use superficial perceptual or affective cues as the basis for the distinction. With practice, they become more facile at separating ads from program content.

Children must also acquire the knowledge that ads are paid messages that are designed to get them to buy something—or make them ask their parents to buy something. Only 10% of children between 5 and 7 years of age have a clear understanding of the profit-seeking motives of commercials; 55% are totally unaware of the nature of ads and believe commercials are purely for entertainment. For example, Wilson and Weiss (1992) found that compared to older children (7 to 11), younger children (4 to 6) were less able to recognize an ad for a particular toy and comprehend its intent when it was shown in a cartoon program, even when the product "spokesperson" was a character from a different cartoon program.

Disclaimers placed before ads to alert children to the fact that the program is being interrupted and an ad is about to be shown do not generally work well with children younger than 7, because children this young do not fully understand what an ad is. When disclaimers are in both the audio and video tracks, however, children are better able to perceive them. Also, when disclaimers are reworded into the language of children, their comprehension dramatically increases.

By the second or third grade, most children have overcome their difficulty distinguishing between programs and commercials. With the combination of cognitive maturation, experience, and active application of critical skills, children really understand the nature and purpose of ads. This understanding leads to a drop in attention to the ads. Furthermore, attention is inversely related to the knowledge and experience necessary for critical evaluation. By the fourth grade, children have developed a critical and skeptical attitude toward advertising. They are also cynical about the credibility of commercials and begin feeling that they have been lied to by the advertiser in an effort to get them to buy products that are not as desirable as the commercials portray.

Can you remember back to when you were in early elementary school and you saw an ad for some fantastic toy that you "just had to have"? If you are male, the toy was probably a GI Joe or some sort of action toy like a truck or helicopter. In the ad, the thing moved and made action noises and did really cool things. But when you got the toy, it just sat there like the inert piece of plastic that it was. You felt betrayed. This taught you to be skeptical about advertising.

Recall of brand names and product attributes increases with age, especially between kindergarten and third grade. Simplified wording significantly affects comprehension and recall. But even older children still have some difficulty in understanding certain types of claims, such as superlative, comparative, and parity claims. For example, a parity claim is something like, "Buy Brand X, because it is as good as Brand Y." Children are confused by this type of claim if they don't use Brand Y. Also, children get confused about how Brand X and Y can be so similar, unless the ad clearly shows the similarity across brands on the product attributes that are most important to children.

Older Children. By ages 8 to 10, most children have developed a good understanding of fictional plots, how the motives of characters influence plot points, and how characters change as a result of what happens to them. Children of this age are not limited to understanding characters on only their physical traits, but can also infer personality characteristics. Also, they can distinguish among characters along more dimensions.

By ages 10 to 12, children have a well-developed idea of the economic nature of TV, that is, its profit-making motive. And most children this age and older are very skeptical of ads. However, this skepticism is usually limited to their experience with products. For example, the skepticism is high with ads for familiar toys. Presumably, they have had real-world experiences with these toys and have learned that the ads contain exaggerated claims. However, children are much less skeptical of ads for medical or nutritional products; understandably, they have much less technical knowledge about these products and have less of a basis for skepticism.

Development as an Adult

We must not fall into the trap of believing that once we have aged past childhood that we have completed all the development we can and that there is nothing left to do. While we may have completed our maturation, we still have a great deal of potential for development. This potential can be realized by continuing to acquire experience and by actively applying more advanced skills. Our development stops "happening to us" because maturation is over; now we must take over and become more active. But this requires work. And it also requires knowledge about what to do.

Above, we have seen that there are profound changes in cognitive development during childhood as the human mind matures and is capable of a wider range and more sophisticated tasks. The human mind also changes throughout adulthood. For example, research has shown that there are generally two types of intelligence and that these change as adults age. One type of intelligence is called crystalline, which is the ability to memorize facts. With most adults, crystallized intelligence seems to increase throughout the life span, although at a decreasing rate in later years (Sternberg & Berg, 1987). This means that as adults get older, they do better on tests requiring factual knowledge of their world, such as vocabulary and general information. In general, older people can more easily add new information to existing knowledge structures and more easily retrieve that information from those knowledge structures they use most often. For example, pick a topic that is of equal interest to you and your parents (your neighborhood, your family, politics, sports, etc.), then see how much detail your parents remember compared to you.

The other type of intelligence is fluid, which is the ability to be creative and see patterns in complex sets of facts. Fluid intelligence increases in early adulthood but then decreases. This means that there is a decrease in our ability to use abstract symbols, manipulate words and numbers, recognize analogies, and complete number series.

Think back to the kinds of tests you have taken in college and high school. If you are like most students, you have had many tests that measure your crystalline intelligence—that is your ability to memorize lots of facts. You are not likely to have had many tests (besides the Scholastic Aptitude Test or some tests of mathematical or philosophical reasoning) that measure your fluid intelligence. Therefore you have had much more practice at developing your crystalline intelligence and not much at developing your fluid intelligence. It is therefore not surprising that in the general adult population, crystalline intelligence appears to be higher than fluid and it continues to increase with age. We are given little opportunity to develop our fluid intelligence.

The implication of this difference in the development of the two types of intelligence has a direct application to media literacy, where we need to develop both. Highly developed crystalline intelligence gives us the facility to absorb the images, definitions, opinions, and agendas of others. Highly developed fluid intelligence gives us the facility to challenge what we see on the surface, to look deeper and broader, and to recognize new patterns. Both types of intelligence are important and need higher development. Being media literate requires you to develop your crystalline intelligence so as to acquire many facts, but you also need to develop your fluid intelligence to assemble those facts creatively into useful knowledge structures.

Although there is evidence that a person's mind continues to mature throughout adulthood, the substantial gains in media literacy come not so much through maturation but through expanding experience and consciously working on developing higher-order skills. Unfortunately, few people continue to work consciously at expanding their experiences and developing their skills. This can be seen in figures that indicate that most people do not even begin to process most of the information to which they are exposed—rather they screen it out and do not remember it even a short time after exposure. Most people remember only about 40% of what they see and only 10% of what they hear (Adams & Hamm, 1989).

Developing media literacy throughout adulthood requires the continual expansion of one's experiences and knowledge structures through the more sophisticated use of the higher-order skills of analyzing, comparing/contrasting, evaluating, and synthesizing. But not all adults do this. What is the difference between those who do and those who do not? The answer is: a person's cognitive style. A cognitive style is a person's approach to organizing and processing information (Hashway & Duke, 1992). People vary in their cognitive styles along four characteristics: field dependency, tolerance for ambiguity, conceptual differentiation, and impulsivity-reflectivity.

Field Dependency. Think of field dependency as a continuum along which people are arrayed according to their ability to distinguish between signal and noise in any message. Noise is the chaos of symbols and images; signal is the information that emerges from that chaos. People who are highly field dependent get stuck in the field of chaos—seeing all the details but missing the big picture, which is the signal. Field independent people are able to sort quickly through the field to identify the elements of importance and ignore the distracting elements (Witkin & Goodenough, 1977).

For example, when watching a story during a television news show, field independent people will be able to identify the key information of the who, what, when, where, and why of the story. They will quickly sort through what is said, the graphics, and the visuals to focus on the essence of the event being covered. People who are field dependent will perceive the same key elements in the story but also pay attention to how the news anchor is dressed, the hair, the makeup, the color of the graphics, the background people walking around the scene, and so on. To field dependent persons, all of these elements are of equal importance, so they are as likely to remember the trivia as they are to remember the main point of the story.

No one is purely field dependent, that is, no one perceives every micro element in every message and is totally incapable of sorting the signal from the noise. People vary by degrees. To estimate your position on the continuum, try this mini-exercise. Close this book. Then on a piece of paper, jot down the main idea in this chapter and three subsidiary ideas that amplify that main idea. If you were able to do this quickly, you are relatively field independent. You are reading actively and continually asking yourself, "What is most important?" Before reading this chapter, you probably looked carefully at the chapter's first page with its key idea and outline, then you scanned through the chapter to get a feel for its structure and main points. Then with that structure in mind you were able to navigate your way efficiently through the reading—adding detail to your structure at appropriate places. So when I asked you to close the book and write down the main idea, you had a picture of the entire chapter and were able to do this exercise easily. If you instead struggled with this mini-exercise, you are less field independent: You did not have the "big picture" of this chapter clearly in your mind. As you were reading through the chapter, you were giving each sentence and each idea equal weight. So when I asked you to write down the most important ideas, you probably listed the most recent ideas you encountered. Or perhaps you were able to list 10 or 12 points but were not able to decide which were the most important. Or perhaps you could not list any points, in which case you were forcing your eyes over each line of type but your mind was not distinguishing the ideas (signal) from the lines of type (noise). Developing field independent strategies requires a little more work up front when beginning to read a chapter, but it is a much more efficient way to acquire and organize information.

We live in a culture that is highly saturated with media messages. Many of these are noise, that is, they do not provide us with the information or emotional reactions we want. The sheer bulk of all the information makes it more difficult to sort the important from the trivial, so many of us do not bother to sort. Instead we default to a passive state as we float along in this stream of messages. Developing media literacy requires that we take a more active role and consciously sort—and thus become more field independent.

Tolerance for Ambiguity. Every day we encounter people and situations that are unfamiliar to us. To prepare ourselves for such situations, we have developed sets of expectations. What do we do when our expectations are not met and we are surprised? People who have a low tolerance for ambiguity choose to ignore messages that do not meet their expectations and hence appear confusing to them. In contrast, people who are willing to follow situations into unfamiliar territory that go beyond their preconceptions have a high tolerance for ambiguity. A little confusion does not stop them; instead, it motivates them to search harder for clarity.

During media exposures, people with a low tolerance encounter messages on the surface. If the surface meaning fits their preconceptions, then it is filed away and becomes a confirmation (or reinforcement) of those preconceptions. If the surface meaning does not meet a person's preconceptions, the message is ignored. In short, there is no analysis.

People with a high tolerance for ambiguity do not have a barrier to analysis. They are willing to break any message down into components and make comparisons and evaluations in a quest to understand the nature of the message and why their own expectations were wrong. People who consistently attempt to verify their observations and judgments are called scanners, because they are perpetually looking for more information (Gardner, 1968).

Conceptual Differentiation. People who classify objects into a large number of mutually exclusive categories exhibit a high degree of conceptual differentiation (Gardner, 1968). In contrast, people who use a small number of categories have a low degree of conceptual differentiation.

Related to the number of categories is category width (Bruner, Goodnow, & Austin, 1956). People who have few categories into which to classify something usually have broad categories so as to contain all types of messages. For example, if a person has only three categories for all media messages (news, ads, and entertainment), then each of these categories must contain a wide variety of things. In contrast, someone who has a great many categories would be dividing media messages into thinner slices (breaking news, feature news, documentaries, commercial ads, public service announcements, action/adventure shows, sitcoms, game shows, talk shows, cartoons, and reality shows).

When we encounter a new message, we must categorize it by using either a leveling or a sharpening strategy. With the leveling strategy, we look for similarities between the new message and previous messages we have stored away as examples in our categories. We look for the best fit between the new message and one of remembered messages. We will never find a perfect fit because the new message always has slightly different characteristics than our category calls for, but we tend to ignore those differences. In contrast, the sharpening strategy focuses on differences and tries to maintain a high degree of separation between the new message and older messages (Pritchard, 1975). To illustrate this, let's say two people are comparing this year's Super Bowl with last year's Super Bowl. A leveler would argue that the two games were similar and point out all the things the two had in common. The sharpener would disagree and point out all the things the two games did not have in common. Levelers tend to have fewer categories so that many things can fit into the same category, while sharpeners have many, many categories. In our example, the first person would likely have only one category for Super Bowls, feeling that all Super Bowls are the same. A sharpener might have a different category for every Super Bowl, treating each one as unique.

Reflectivity-Impulsivity. This refers to people's cognitive style according to how quickly they make decisions about messages and how accurate those decisions are (Kagan, Rosman, Day, Albert, & Phillips, 1964). People who take a long time and make lots of errors are regarded as slow/inaccurate. This is the worst combination. Those who are quick and make few errors are fast/accurate. This is the best combination.

Typically, there is a trade-off between speed and accuracy, so we are usually either reflective or impulsive. Those who take a long time and make few errors are reflective, and those who are quick and make many errors are impulsive.

Now let's take a look at all five cognitive style characteristics together. If you are one of those people who has depended on maturation for all your development and have not actively worked at increasing your skills, you are likely to be at a low level of media literacy and fit the following profile.

1. Weak on fluid intelligence (problem solving and creative ability), preferring to let things work themselves out on their own; and not much better on crystalline intelligence, although you are able to memorize things when they become very important to you, such as the night before a big exam.

2. Field dependent, that is, you have a lot of trouble discerning what is important in messages. You need someone else to tell you what is important; before each test you ask for a study guide so that the professor will show you what is important in all the material you have covered, rather than feeling confident that you can do this for yourself.

3. Low tolerance for ambiguity, so you are quick to avoid messages that introduce uncertainty or complexity. Over time you narrow your exposure down to fewer messages and experiences so that you always stay with what is familiar and protect yourself from having to expend more mental effort.

4. Weak conceptual differentiation characterized by having few categories for messages and the tendency to use a leveling strategy almost all the time. Rather than work at acknowledging differences and creating new categories, your attitude toward new messages that don't fit your existing categories is simply to throw the new message into the easiest category and justify it by saying, "Whatever!"

5. High impulsivity so that you can make decisions fast. Sacrificing accuracy is a small price to pay for getting away from decisions and on to other things.

Think about where you are on these cognitive style characteristics. You have the potential for improvement. The direction of improvement is to develop your cognitive style characteristics so as to become stronger in both fluid and crystalline intelligence; become more field independent by learning to distinguish better between what is important and what is trivial; cultivate a higher tolerance for ambiguity by being more willing to scan more messages and scan them in more depth; construct knowledge structures with more categories; and move away from making impulsive decisions by spending more time analyzing the messages and trying to achieve more accuracy in interpreting the meanings.

■■ EMOTIONAL DEVELOPMENT

Media messages can arouse emotions in people of all ages. Emotions do not need to be learned in the sense that we learn to recognize words in order to read.

Instead, emotions are hardwired into our brains (Goleman, 1995). Regardless of the culture in which we are raised, we all can recognize in ourselves and others the basic emotions of anger, sadness, fear, enjoyment, love, surprise, disgust, and shame.

We develop higher levels of emotional literacy by gaining experience with emotions and by paying close attention to our feelings as we interact with the media. As we gain greater experience with emotions, we are able to make finer discriminations. For example, we are all familiar with anger because it is one of the basic emotions. But it takes experience with this emotion to be able to tell the difference between hatred, outrage, fury, wrath, animosity, hostility, resentment, indignation, acrimony, annoyance, irritability, and exasperation.

A lack of cognitive development can be a barrier to appropriate emotional reactions. For example, very young children cannot follow the interconnected elements in a continuing plot; instead, they focus on individual elements. Therefore they cannot understand suspense, and without such an understanding they cannot became emotionally aroused as the suspense builds. So a child's ability to have an emotional reaction to media messages is low not because of a lack of ability to feel emotions, but because of a lack of ability to understand what is happening as certain narratives unfold.

By adolescence, children have reached cognitive maturity and all the gates are open to a full understanding of all kinds of narratives. But some adolescents and adults still do not have much of an emotional reaction to media stories. Some people can be very highly developed cognitively but very undeveloped emotionally. Goleman (1995) argues that a person's emotional intelligence interacts with IQ. He says, "we have two brains, two minds— and two different kinds of intelligence: rational and emotional. How we do in life is determined by both—it is not just IQ, but emotional intelligence that matters. Indeed, intellect cannot work at its best without emotional intelligence" (p. 28).

How can we develop our emotional intelligence? Salovey and Mayer (1990) say that we can develop emotional literacy by working in five areas: reading emotions (empathy), emotional self-awareness, harnessing emotions productively, managing emotions, and handling relationships. The first three have relevance to media interactions and how we deal with those messages. First, we need to develop greater empathy, which refers to our ability to see the world from another person's perspective. Second, we also need to be aware of our own emotions as well as understand what causes and alters them. Third, we need to be less impulsive and to exercise more self-control in concentrating on the task at hand rather than becoming distracted by peripheral emotions.

Being emotionally literate requires an understanding of how emotions are evoked by the media and how we can control those effects when we are confronted with different types of messages. We can use the media to achieve the emotional effects we want if we are conscious of what we are doing and aware of how the effects processes work.

When we are unaware of emotional effects the media can exercise unwanted influences, such as reducing our sensitivity to things about which we should care. For example, people who watch a great deal of violence on television become desensitized to the suffering of victims not only on television but also in the real world.

In summary, emotional literacy is tied to cognitive development. Children who cannot read or follow visual narratives will have their emotional reactions limited to reactions to micro-elements in messages. As people mature to a point of mastering the lower-order skills, there is still a range of emotional abilities. Some people are better able to "read" emotions in themselves and others due to having a higher degree of empathy and a greater self-awareness. In contrast, lower literacy people are not able to experience emotions vicariously through characters, and they may be desensitized to many emotions by constant exposure to superficial treatments of news stories and formulaic fictional plots.

■■ MORAL DEVELOPMENT

We can also choose to develop along a moral dimension. We can increase our awareness of moral issues in the media. All media messages have moral implications. These are easy to spot in some documentaries, news stories, or fictional stories that portray difficult choices people must make. But when we look at cartoons, game shows, or sports, it can be harder to understand that these kinds of shows also have moral implications. We need to be sensitive to the character revealed in the people portrayed. We need to look at the implications of the decisions those characters make and judge whether the story is fair in showing them. And we need to dig below the surface action and infer the themes in the stories as well as the values of the industry that produces them.

We are not born with a moral code or a sensitivity to what is right and wrong. We must learn these as young children, and children learn these things in stages. Like Piaget, Lawrence Kohlberg has studied the development of children. While Piaget was concerned with cognitive development, Kohlberg focused on moral development. He suggested there are three levels of moral development: pre-conventional, conventional, and post-conventional. The centerpiece is "conventional," which stands for fair, honest, concerned, and well regarded—characteristics of the typically good person (Kohlberg, 1966, 1981).

The pre-conventional stage begins at about age 2 and runs to about age 7 or 8. This is when the child is dependent on authority, and inner controls are weak. Young children depend on their parents and other adults to tell them what is right and to filter the world for them. A child's conscience is external; that is, children must be told by others what is right. The pre-conventional stage has two sub-stages.

Sub-stage 1: Children are motivated by avoiding punishment and this guides their reasoning. They do not distinguish between accidents and intentional behaviors. So if a child spills milk or steals a cookie and both are punished, both are regarded as equally bad.

Sub-stage 2: Children are guided by self-satisfaction as expressed in the attitude, "You do me a favor and I'll do you one." What brings pleasure to the child is felt as a reward.

During the conventional stage, children develop a conscience for themselves as they internalize what is right and wrong. They distinguish between truth and lies. However, the threat of punishment is still a strong motivator.

Sub-stage 3: The child is motivated to get the approval of others such as peers, parents, and other people. This is the "good-boy, good-girl" orientation.

Sub-stage 4: The motivation shifts to a sense of duty. The child becomes concerned with avoiding the harming of others and avoiding bringing dishonor to him- or herself. There is an orientation toward law and order. Many people stop developing at this point, and it becomes the highest level they ever exhibit.

The post-conventional stage can begin as early as middle adolescence, when some people are able to transcend conventional notions of right and wrong. They tend to focus on fundamental principles. This requires the ability to think abstractly and therefore recognize the ideals behind society's laws. Thus the stages in this level are characterized by the sense that being socially conscious is more important than adhering to legal principles.

Sub-stage 5: In this stage, there is a focus on the social contract. Individuals agree to do certain things even if they do not agree with them. In return, those individuals get to live in a society where things run harmoniously. Correct action is defined by terms of general rights, usually with legalistic or utilitarian underpinnings that are agreed upon by society.

Sub-stage 6: The person is motivated to make ethical decisions according to his or her own conscience. The focus is on universal principles of justice and respect for human dignity. The rules of society are integrated with the person's conscience in the creation of a personal hierarchy of moral values. Thus there are times when the demands of society are most important, while at other times the dictates of one's conscience must be obeyed. To an individual at this stage, external punishments are much less important than the internal feeling of being right.

Kohlberg's (1966, 1981) stages are not fixed steps that everyone follows in sequence. People can move around among the steps, given particular problems and moods. Each stage is very different, however, and they are hierarchically ordered such that the more evolved person is one who is likely to operate most often at higher levels.

Gilligan (1993) has extended Kohlberg's ideas by arguing that there is a gender difference in moral development. Men more typically base their moral judgments on rights and rules, while women tend to think in terms of care and cooperation. So in a conflict situation women are likely to try to preserve relationships. Men will search for a moral rule and try to apply it.

Let's examine these stages with a media example. Bobby is a young child in a family where the television is used as a baby-sitter. Bobby watches a great deal of television unsupervised; he has no parent or authority figure to help him process the messages or to show him alternatives to what is portrayed in the media world. Therefore his moral development during the pre-conventional stages is shaped by the themes in the television messages, mainly cartoons, action/adventure shows, and situation comedies. From his steady exposure to these types of shows and values, Bobby is likely to learn the following moral lessons: Aggression (both physical and verbal) is an acceptable and successful way to solve problems; with a little hard work, everyone can be successful, that is, be wealthy, powerful, and famous; family relationships are full of conflict and deceit but everyone still loves everyone else; and romantic relationships are exciting but superficial and temporary.

As Bobby moves into the conventional stages, much of his behavior will be governed by these moral lessons. He will feel that the best way to get approval from others is to be funny, live dangerously, and have lots of peer relationships filled with conflict—that is, an active, interesting life.

Finally, as Bobby reaches late adolescence and confronts the post-conventional stages, he must begin asking questions such as: How can I live my life so as to benefit society in general? and How can I resolve moral dilemmas so that I don't make decisions on a purely selfish basis? Given Bobby's moral development and the lessons he has learned, it is unlikely that he will be interested by these post-conventional questions. It is probable that he will stay at the conventional stage and continue to make moral decisions based on the principles he learned while watching TV as a preschooler.

■■ CONCLUJION

Media literacy is developed through maturation, experience, and active application of skills. During childhood, maturation can hold up development, but by about age 12 the gaining of experience and the active processing of that experience are the dominant ways we continue our development.

Media literacy is not only developed cognitively, but also emotionally and morally. When we develop along all three dimensions, we are able to build strong knowledge structures and skills. Each of us needs to assess ourselves in terms of where we are in our development. We need to think about our cognitive style on the characteristics of type of intelligence, field dependency, tolerance for ambiguity, conceptual differentiation, and reflectivity-impulsivity. We need to think about our emotional style in terms of the range of emotions we can feel and the degree to which we are aware of and in control of those emotions. We need to consider our moral development to determine if the locus of our judgment-making rests with an outside authority; with our internal, personal conscience; or with our social conscience.

FURTHER READING ■

Goleman, D. (1995). *Emotional intelligence*. New York: Bantam Books. (352 pages with index)

In this very readable best-seller, Goleman argues that there is an emotional IQ, not just an intellectual one. He challenges the long-held belief that a person's intelligence as measured by a narrow IQ test is an adequate predictor of success or ability. First, he broadens the concept of intelligence, then shows how a person's emotional development interacts with a broad range of cognitive abilities. He cites physiological data to show that emotions are part of the brain and are triggered by the capacity of the body.

Kohlberg, L. (1981). *The philosophy of moral development: Moral stages and the idea of justice*. New York: Harper & Row. (441 pages with index)

Kohlberg lays out his moral development scheme of three stages, each with two sub-stages. There are lots of examples relating this structure to how people come to understand the concept of justice.

Pulaski, M. A. S. (1980). *Understanding Piaget: An introduction to children's cognitive development* (Revised and expanded edition). New York: Harper & Row. (248 pages with index)

This is a very clear, well-organized description of most of Piaget's thinking and research. There are lots of drawings to illustrate key concepts.

EXERCISE 2.1

Awareness of Your Development

The Questions

Cognitive

1. Think of your favorite television series, then complete the following two tasks:

   a. Make a list of all important characters and describe each in detail.

   b. Write out a plot for what will happen on a future show.

Emotional

2. All emotions have a range of sub-emotions or sub-types. For example, the emotion of fear has the sub-emotions of terror, panic, fight, dread, consternation, apprehension, anxiety, nervousness, wariness, qualm, edginess, and concern. Each of these is a type of fear, but each indicates a different feeling of fear. How many sub-emotions can you list for love? How many sub-emotions can you list for sadness?

3. Watch a television show and count how many times you see the emotions of fear, love, and sadness.

   a. When you see one of these emotions, can you classify which type (sub-emotion) it is?

   b. Watch several different kinds of television programs and notice which emotions are most prevalent and which emotions are hardly ever portrayed.

Moral

4. Watch several action/adventure television shows or movies in which there is a good deal of anti-social behavior, such as crime, violence, and lying. Notice how the characters justify these acts to themselves and to others. Think about those justifications and try to place those characters on Kohlberg's levels of moral development.

   a. Now think about the show as a whole and try to infer the intentions of the writers and producers. To which moral level of viewers are they trying to appeal?

   b. If you were producing this show and you wanted to appeal to viewers who were several sub-levels *higher*, what would you change in the scripts?

   c. If you were producing this show and you wanted to appeal to viewers who were several sub-levels *lower*, what would you change in the scripts?

Thinking About Your Answers

Cognitive

1. Your answers to the first part (a) reflect your degree of crystalline intelligence. Look at how many characters you listed. For each character, how many adjectives or descriptive phrases did you list? Notice the variety in the descriptors: Were they all physical attributes? Or did you also list other attributes such as personality, dress, career, favorite gestures/mannerisms, and so on? The more detail you have in your answer, the more information you can access about that show.

   Your answers to the second part (b) reflect your degree of fluid intelligence. If you had a difficult time thinking of any plot developments, you are probably low on fluid intelligence. If you wrote down lots of events, look at how your events tie into the past action on the show. Is your plot more of the same events or does your plot really push the characters well beyond where they are now? If you have exhibited a lot of imagination and creativity, you are high on fluid intelligence.

   Compare your performance on (a) and (b). If you did much better on (a), then your profile is more crystalline, and you have a strong ability to gather facts. If you did much better on (b), then your profile is more fluid, and you favor imagination and searching for new perspectives. Developing a high level of media literacy requires you to increase both of these types of intelligence.

Emotional

2. The more sub-emotions you can list, the more you are attuned to subtle variations in emotions and the more emotionally literate your are.

3. It takes skill at empathy to be able to spot emotions in others, especially to make fine distinctions among sub-emotions. Television shows and movies are packed with emotions. Many of these are very easy to spot, but some of the sub-emotions are more difficult to perceive. Were you able to think of examples of the more difficult to perceive emotions? Were you able to see some ways that the expression of emotions (and types of emotions) differ on situation comedies compared to action/adventure shows?

Moral

4. Were you able to make some generalizations about where most television characters are on Kohlberg's levels of moral development? If you can clearly see a pattern and can argue your conclusion with lots of examples, you are fairly morally literate. Also, your moral literacy is high if you can understand how scripts could be changed to appeal to a different level of viewer.

CHAPTER 3

Key Idea: The exercising of high levels of media literacy requires the usage of two sets of skills. The set of rudimentary skills are those acquired during childhood and that bring us up to a functional level of literacy. The advanced skills are those that must be continually exercised so as to expand our understanding and appreciation of media messages.

Introduction
Rudimentary Media Literacy Skills
   Maturation
   Component skills
      Exposure
      Recognizing symbols
      Recognizing patterns
      Matching meaning
Advanced Media Literacy Skills
   Message Focused Sense Making
      Analysis
      Compare/Contrast
      Evaluation
      Abstraction
   Message Extending Sense Making
      Deduction
      Induction
      Synthesis
Conclusion

The Skills of Media Literacy

The setting is a kitchen table where two mothers are having coffee while their 6-year-old sons watch Saturday morning television in the adjoining family room.

"I don't know what I would do without television," says Janet. "I can tell Harley to watch and he is perfectly happy for hours. Meanwhile I get some time to myself."

"But don't you think that all that TV viewing may be hurting him?" Marilyn is wary as she looks into the family room and sees little Harley kneeling in front of the TV set, staring intently, while her son Julian fidgets in a nearby chair.

"It doesn't hurt him a bit, it really doesn't. Look at him. He's perfectly happy." Janet takes a swig of her coffee, burps, and smacks her lips loudly. "Besides it's the only time I can keep him quiet. Otherwise he's all over me wanting me to do stuff with him all the time." She gulps more coffee. "You know, I need a break every now and then. Know what I mean?"

Julian comes into the kitchen, "Mom, I'm bored. Can you read me a book?"

Marilyn reaches into her handbag to pull out a book and thinks, "I'm so glad Julian is not addicted to television and likes to read." Julian snuggles in his mother's lap as Marilyn begins to read to him.

Harley suddenly runs into the kitchen, making car-like noises, screeching around the table, then crashing into his mother. "Mom, I'm watching this really cool show." He precedes to tell her all about the plot and his favorite characters in vivid detail. Janet thinks, "I don't know how he keeps all that action straight in his mind. And so many characters! I ain't able to do nothing like that. It all makes no sense to me."

Harley then spins around to Julian. "What is your story about?"

Julian shrugs his shoulders.

"Hey, Julian. Tell me about your story."

Julian shrugs again and waves Harley away.

"That's not very nice, Julian," says Marilyn. "Tell your friend what this story is about."

"Mom, it's just a story. Read some more."

This short scene illustrates that some of the preconceptions we have about media literacy should be challenged. One preconception is that people who watch a lot of TV are less media literate than those who prefer reading. In the scenario, Harley loves TV and he gets a lot out of it. He follows the plot and characters closely. He remembers the information and can tell others about the show. In contrast, Julian prefers reading, but he is passive and seems to like reading only so he can be held by his mother, apparently getting little information out of the reading.

Another preconception is that all children are lower in media literacy than adults. In the scene above, Harley seems to get more out of the TV messages than his mother. So in some ways it is possible for children to be more media literate than some adults.

As you can see, these preconceptions—as well as many others—are often wrong once we analyze them a bit. Analysis is one of the many skills of media literacy. In this chapter, we'll take a look at the skills of media literacy we have already acquired. Let's call these the rudimentary skills. There are also additional skills that we can develop significantly in order to reach our higher potential of media literacy. We'll call this second set the advanced skills.

▟▙ RUDIMENTARY JKILLJ

The rudimentary skills are the ones we develop throughout our childhood. These include the skills of listening, reading, viewing, and computing. By computing, I do not mean the ability to program a computer or write software for games. Instead, I mean the ability to use the computer to access information and entertainment.

Maturation

The development of these rudimentary skills is influenced by our childhood rates of maturation cognitively, emotionally, and morally. For example, when we are very young, our minds are not mature enough for us to recognize written symbols and associate meaning with them. When our minds mature, we reach a point where we have the potential to read. But we must work to deliver on that potential. Try to think back to when you were about 5 years old and first learning how to read the written word. You would have to expend a good deal of effort to concentrate on each word and recognize its meaning and how it sounded when pronounced. Then you needed to work on putting words together into sentences in order to recognize a larger chunk of meaning. The act of reading a page of a book took a long time and was exhausting. Now after years of practice, you take the skill of reading for granted. Your eyes fly over the words barely "seeing" them. Instead your mind is "seeing" the ideas and images evoked behind the words. The little black lines that form the letters and words are transparent— you see right through them and into the author's meaning.

By early adolescence we are fairly proficient with all of these rudimentary skills and have reached a level of functional literacy; that is, we know how to expose ourselves to all types of media and get information as well as entertainment from them fairly easily. Additional practice continues to improve those skills until their use becomes automatic—we do not need to think consciously as we apply them.

Once we have acquired these rudimentary skills to a point where we are comfortable with them (usually during the early elementary school years), we think we are media literate. We feel very proficient with these skills. Our media exposures are more efficient—we no longer struggle when reading a newspaper article or following a plot in a TV show or film. But the danger in feeling proficient is that we no longer feel we need to concentrate, and this leads to mindless exposure where we accept the surface meanings in the messages. Many people stay on this plateau, practicing these rudimentary skills the rest of their lives. People who do this feel a false sense of literacy, because exposure comes so easily, and they fall into the mindless processing trap, which limits them to accepting the surface meanings in the messages.

Component Skills

The rudimentary skills of listening, reading, viewing, and computing share some generic components. They all require some ability in the areas of exposure, recognizing symbols, recognizing patterns made by the symbols, and matching meaning. With exposure, we need to know what vehicles are available and how we can gain access to them. When we have access, we need to recognize the symbols that are presented. The individual symbols are the micro-units in a message—a word, a figure in a photograph, a note in a melody. When many symbols occur together, which is almost always, we need to see connections among the individual elements. Words form sentences, then paragraphs, chapters, and books. A visual shape is part of the overall composition of a photograph. A musical note played against other notes can be part of a chord; and when the note is played as part of a sequence of notes, it can form the pattern of a melody. Recognizing the meaning of a sentence, a picture, or a melody requires that we can recall the experience of having previously associated that pattern with a meaning. Let's take a closer look at each of these components of rudimentary skills.

Exposure. This is usually regarded in a technological sense, but there is more to it. Let's say you want to find out if the New York Jets football team won its game yesterday. You could turn on your television and tune into the sports station—a skill requiring some technological expertise. But you would need to know the channel of the sports station. You would also need to know if it is football season and if the Jets played a game yesterday. If you tune in the correct sports update show in April, you have the technological expertise for the exposure you want, but your knowledge base is so weak that you don't realize that football season has been over for more than 3 months, and there is no chance for you to be exposed to a score of a Jets game. The technological skill of knowing how to turn on a machine is not sufficient; you also need knowledge structures.

Because your rudimentary skills are highly developed, the technological skills might seem pretty simple to you. You may be able to operate a remote control device (RCD), program your videocassette recorder (VCR), and navigate your computer onto the Internet. But these are things you had to learn, and not everyone has learned them. Unlike the other rudimentary skills, the ability to access technology is not usually higher with children than with adults. Think about the people in your family. Who is more likely to be able to program the VCR or the buttons on the car radio or set up the components of a stereo system—your parents or your younger brothers and sisters?

Deciding what to exposure yourself to is part of this exposure skill, and this judgment grows with experience (DeGaetano & Bander, 1996). For example, who in your family would be more likely to give a better answer to the following questions: Which authors should you read when you want to be entertained by a humorous detective novel? Which magazines have the strongest political orientations? Which television channel presents the most credible news reports?

Notice how the application of this skill, like other skills, relies on good knowledge structures. The more information you have about media channels, vehicles, and messages, the higher potential you have for exercising this skill. However, if this information is not structured effectively, then you will not be able to access it efficiently. So this skill is not the same as information; the skill is your ability to add information to your knowledge structure and access it quickly when you want to make a decision.

Recognizing Symbols. Some symbols are words, so we need to know what a word is compared to a letter, a sentence, a line of type, and so on. Some symbols are elements in pictures, so we need to be able to recognize form, dimension, and perspective. Some symbols are auditory, so we need to be able to recognize voices, music, and sound effects. And some symbols are movements on a screen; we need to be able to recognize a cut, dissolve, pan, zoom in, and so on.

All media users must first go through a process of extracting elements from the mass of stimuli in any message. Without this step in the process, no meaning can be perceived. This point may seem trite to you, but it is enormously important. You have mastered this so well, you take this accomplishment for granted. To help you realize this, do the following short exercise. Turn on your television set and get up very close to the screen so that your nose is touching the glass. Squint your eyes until they are almost closed and try to focus on an area of about one quarter of an inch square. What do you see?

The television screen is really individual dots arranged in a grid of 525 lines, each containing several hundred glowing dots. The hue of those dots is limited to three primary colors, but when you move back a few feet from the screen you can see the blending of those three primary hues into an entire rainbow of colors. Also, you no longer see the dots or even the lines; instead you see images. And while the dots on the screen do not move, it appears that the images of people and objects are moving on the screen. How is this possible? Your mind blends the individual primary colors into combinations. The blinking off and on of different colored dots leads your mind to perceive that there are objects on the screen and that they are moving.

You take this skill for granted, because you have been practicing it so well for so many years. But this is a skill you had to learn as a child. Very young children watch television in an exploratory mode, because they do not have a strong command of symbols and conventions. They attend primarily to perceptually salient formal features (such as loud sounds, unique voices, special effects, etc.) and struggle to figure out what they mean. With cognitive development and additional experience, children are better able to recognize symbols.

With newspapers, young children will look at the front page and will "see" the same thing as an adult but will not be able to extract many elements. They will recognize that certain things are pictures, but they will not be able to extract any of the words or graphics, that is, they will not be able to distinguish the boundaries of the symbols there. With radio, children will "hear" the sounds but not be able to recognize the boundaries between the songs, jingles, stingers, happy chat, serious news, and ads.

Recognizing Patterns. Once you have recognized a symbol, you must put it together with other symbols to make a pattern. Within media messages there are various types of guidance that provide help. For example, with print, the letter or word is the basic symbol unit. These words are not arranged randomly; instead the author arranges the words in a special pattern to evoke a particular meaning in readers. The larger the assortment of symbols, the more interpretation is required. For example, with smaller assortments (such as letters into words and words into sentences) there are fairly accepted formal rules that most people use without thinking. Readers carefully follow the construction rules of grammar and sentence syntax with little interpretation. But as symbol sets become much larger and more complex (such as plot development and narrative conventions), people must exercise much more interpretation.

We also must recognize patterns in the visual media. Messaris (1994) argues that children first need to learn to interpret still images, because of their two dimensionality, lack of color, and reduced detail. Then the issue of literacy moves to the more complex task of interpreting the interplay of pictures, speech, music, graphics, and special effects, such as required by film and television. At each of these levels, a person must know how to spot patterns among the symbols. Production techniques can help us identify these patterns, but we must learn how production techniques cluster into patterns. For example, there are formulas for the way a camera frames an object so as to reveal its image as a coherent object, action, or space through the successive presentation of partial views. We must learn how production techniques tell us what a character is feeling and thinking through the juxtaposition of facial close-ups and contextual cues.

People must also be able to spot patterns in narratives. We must be able to link a character's motives with actions; link actions with consequences; understand the unities of time and place; and infer themes. If we cannot make these linkages, we will not be able to see the patterns among the symbols.

Matching Meaning. After we have isolated a symbol, we must interpret it, that is, match the symbol with a meaning that has been previously learned. For example, we memorize the definitions of words and the conventions of grammar and expression to be able to read. From our experience listening to radio, we know that certain sounds signal the lead-in to news, certain voices convey humor or seriousness, certain sounds convey danger or silliness. With television and film, we learn the meaning of a flashback, an extreme close-up on a character's face, character stereotypes, and what to expect in the unfolding sequence of a detective show. We have learned to connect certain symbols with certain meanings.

The same type of matching process takes place with patterns of symbols, although it is more complex because there are more elements involved. Messaris (1994) says the key task of being visually literate with film and television is the making of meaning from the complex modes of communication involving the interplay of pictures, speech, music, graphics, and special effects. When people attempt to make sense of all these stimuli in media messages, they use two strategies. One strategy is to focus on patterns in *changes across time and/or place;* a montage of scene changes can signal the pattern of time passing. The other strategy focuses on a pattern of *unity of time and place.*

Looking at media literacy only as a set of rudimentary skills tends to over-simplify what is needed in order to be truly literate. For example, let's examine the skill of matching meaning. Cognitive psychologists used to believe that when readers saw the printed word *dog* they automatically associated this three-letter combination with a certain type of four-legged furry animal. Thus, the human mind was regarded as a large dictionary of learned definitions. Every time the mind perceived a symbol, it would work like a machine to match that symbol with its meaning from that mental dictionary.

This simple matching of meaning is too limited an explanation for how people derive meaning from the media. Reading a book requires more than simply recognizing words and matching individual meanings. What if a word in our mental dictionary has more than one meaning? For example, *bad* can mean "not good" but it can also mean "very good." *Cool* can mean a "low temperature," "a chilly demeanor," "a laid back attitude," or "very good." Which meaning do we match? It depends on the context of the sentence in which the word is used. So matching by itself is not enough; we often must understand the meaning of the sentence before we can figure out the meaning of some of the words in the sentence. But how do we understand the meaning of the sentence without first understanding the meaning of the words? Are you beginning to see how complex this task is?

Now consider this. The idea conveyed by a sentence has more to it than the simple sum of the meaning of each word. The arrangement of words and the grammar as well as punctuation are important. For example, if two characters are kissing and one says, "Don't! Stop!!!" that conveys a very different meaning than if the character says, "Don't stop." And the way the sentences are arranged into paragraphs and stories conveys more meaning than the simple sum of ideas conveyed in each sentence. If you read about a mother saying, "You are so smart" to her child, the meaning can change given the overall story. If the mother has just seen her child brag that he can take his bicycle apart and fix it but in the process he destroys it, the mother's comment is sarcastic. But if the mother has just looked at the child's report card and sees all excellent grades, the comment is one of pride and happiness. Determining the meaning of words, sentences, and stories is a complex process.

The above description of rudimentary skills helps us begin to understand how we derive meaning from media messages. But there is much more to the process. We need to examine the set of more advanced skills. We need to get beyond the relatively simple task of matching meanings and get on to the more demanding task of constructing meanings. This requires us to examine a set of more advanced skills.

■■ ADVANCED MEDIA LITERACY SKILLS

The rudimentary skills give us the ability to derive simple meaning from media messages. That meaning rests on the surface of messages and is easy to see. But there are many layers of meaning in media messages. In order to see the range of meanings and gain the control to select the ones most useful to us, we need to employ more advanced skills. The use of advanced skills will provide us with more control over creating our own meaning. Thus the advanced skills give us the power to understand more about the media, their messages, and the effects on us. Also, when we have highly developed advanced skills and use them in a knowledgeable manner, we shift the power of meaning making away from the media and bring it much more under our own control.

The application of advanced skills requires more concentration; we cannot be passive and take our exposure for granted. It also requires a skeptical attitude that the surface meanings might not always be accurate, balanced, or useful for our needs. This skepticism is often referred to as "critical viewing" (Messaris, 1994), or "critical thinking" (Brown, 1991), or just "critical" (McLaren, Hammer, Sholle, & Reilly, 1995; Silverblatt, 1995).

The advanced skills can be grouped as either helping with message focused sense making or helping extend the sense making beyond the messages.

Message Focused Skills

When we stay within the bounds of a message or set of messages, we use four skills to interpret meaning: analysis, compare/contrast, evaluation, and abstraction. Analysis refers to the breaking down of the message into meaningful elements. Once we have the meaningful elements identified, we can compare and contrast those elements to the elements residing in our existing knowledge structure. Where the elements are the same (compare), the new elements reinforce the existing ones. But where there is a difference (contrast), a controversy arises. Which elements are to be given greater credence? We evaluate the new elements from the media message and the old elements in our existing knowledge structure. This process serves to discount certain elements and amplify others. Abstracting is the ability to assemble a brief, clear, accurate description of the media message. Each of these is developed in more detail below.

Analysis. This refers to the breaking down of the message into meaningful elements. It is possible, of course, to read an entire newspaper or watch an entire movie without analyzing it; that is, we could experience it as a monolithic whole. If we treat the message as a whole, we fail to get below the surface and see the parts or layers. Our reaction to such a message can only be of the most general, intuitive sort, such as, "It was good," or "I hated it." Because we did not analyze the message we cannot give a good or insightful reason for our reaction.

Being good at analysis requires highly developed knowledge structures. The more context you have (about narrative forms, industry motives, message conventions, etc.), the more dimensions you will be able to use in the analysis, and the more "in-depth" the analysis can be.

Analysis can help assess the accuracy or usefulness of a message. For example, let's consider a media message that contains percentages. A percentage is an expression of the relationship between two numbers. All of us have probably seen at least one story that reports how high the divorce rate has grown in this country. Often these stories will say the divorce rate is now 50%. But what does this really mean? Let's analyze it. This figure is a percentage, and like all percentages, it is computed from two numbers. What are those numbers? If we compare the number of marriages with the number of divorces in any given year, we get a ratio of 2 to 1. In other words there were twice as many marriages last year as there were divorces, or, expressed another way, the number of divorces last year was 50% of the number of marriages. But this makes it sound like half the married people get divorced each year; this interpretation is wrong. If we change the base number of the comparison, we get a very different number. Let's compare the number of divorces last year with the number of total existing marriages at the beginning of that year. When we make this comparison, we get a figure of about 1%. This means that last year, 1% of all existing marriages ended in divorce by the end of that year. Which is the correct divorce rate: 50% or 1%? They both are. The difference is attributable to a difference in the base of comparison, where both bases of comparison are legitimate. Because the bases are different, they answer different questions. If the question is, "What percentage of existing marriages will end in divorce this year?" the answer is 1%. But if the question is, "What is the ratio of the number of marriages this year to the number of divorces this year?" the answer is 50%. If we don't analyze the claim that the divorce rate is 50%, we can be misled to believe that half of all marriages will end in divorce this year.

See how percentages can be misleading? It is important that you always analyze numbers in media messages to make sure you understand how they were computed. If you do not do this, you are in danger of interpreting the wrong meaning from accurate figures.

At lower levels of media literacy, we accept the claims made in media messages at face value. But often those claims are wrong or misleading. Unless we analyze those claims, we have no way of protecting ourselves from faulty information or opinions. When we do analyze those claims, we need to look for traps in reasoning. Five such traps are illuminated here.

One trap is to become so skeptical of statistics that you don't believe any of them. Not all statistics are equally credible—or faulty. If you know what to look for, you can separate the good from the bad.

A second problem is the ecological fallacy where a message shows you that there is a causal relationship between two things merely because they occur together. For example, in the 1950s it was found that crime rates were the highest in neighborhoods where immigrants were most numerous. Some people used this "co-occurrence" to argue that immigrants were a cause of crime. But a careful analysis of this situation reveals that immigrants were forced to live in neighborhoods where crime rates were high, because they could not afford more expensive housing in safer neighborhoods. Immigrants themselves committed very few of the crimes (Strauss, 1996). Unless you analyze the claim carefully, you can misinterpret the relationship.

A third problem is known as the butterfly effect. This is named after the belief that if a butterfly flaps its wings today in the Amazon basin, it will trigger a chain of events that will eventually lead to rain in your hometown next week. The problem with this "connection" is that there are too many simultaneous effects occurring, any one of which could account for the rain. You would need to analyze each link in the very long causal chain from the Amazon to your house in order to see if there were any faulty links that would invalidate the jumping from a particular cause to a far-removed effect.

A fourth problem is the halo effect: believing someone else's explanation merely because we believe that person is an expert or because we trust him or her. But even experts are sometimes wrong because of faulty reasoning. We must analyze their claims to see if this is one of the times they are right.

A fifth trap is believing false predictors. Economists continually are developing sophisticated mathematical models to predict facets of the stock market or the economy, and meteorologists use supercomputers to predict weather trends, yet both economists and meteorologists are often wrong. At any given time there are many different predictive outcomes, and almost all of them will be wrong. If you accept one of these unquestioningly, you will probably select a wrong one. To protect yourself, carefully look across all the predictions at a given time to see what the majority say. Or look at the history of a particular model to see what its track record is. Some models are better at predicting the performance of certain stocks; however, be careful to understand that better is not perfection. My predictive model may be better than any of the others, because I am right 35% of the time, while everyone else is right only 20% of the time. If you invest with me, it will be better than using other models, but you will still lose money most of the time.

Compare/Contrast. After we have broken a media message down into its component parts, we need to compare those elements with the elements in our existing knowledge structure. Elements that match are compared; elements that differ are contrasted. If some elements are different, then we can add something new to our knowledge structure. If all of the elements match, then the message adds nothing *new* to our existing knowledge structures, but that does not mean that our knowledge structure is not changed. The information can reinforce our existing knowledge structures and add weight to them, thus making them more resistant to change later on.

Let's consider an example. Imagine that I show you three objects: a red ball, a pear, and a knife. Then I ask you which of the three objects is like an apple. You could pick the red ball, saying that both share the same shape and color. Or you could pick the pear, reasoning that both are examples of fruit. Or you could pick the knife, thinking that you use a knife to pare the apple before eating it. Which of these three is correct? They all are, because they all have a reasonable connection to the apple. Making good comparisons is not a rudimentary skill—it is not simply memorizing the one best pairing for every object or concept. Instead, comparisons rely on your ability to see reasonable connections among objects. The more connections you can see and articulate, the stronger is your skill of comparison. Thus you are more media literate when you can see a given object from many different perspectives—each of which relates the object to something else.

On what points can we make comparisons/contrasts with the media? One point of comparison is to look across media. How is a message changed as it is freed from the constraints of one medium and becomes subject to the constraints of another. Some elements do not change, but others do.

Another point of comparison is to look across vehicles. Within any medium there are a variety of vehicles. Making comparisons across vehicles reveals the editorial perspectives, business constraints, and vision of the audience. To see for yourself that not all magazines are alike, compare a non-fiction story in *Newsweek, Cosmopolitan,* and *Soldier of Fortune.*

Other points of comparisons are across episodes of a show to see character development or across performances of a particular artist to assess his or her range. There are many possibilities for points of comparison. Not all of them are equally useful. A key to using these advanced skills is to have an agenda to assess a deeper and broader set of meaning in the messages, then apply the skills consciously in working toward that goal.

Evaluation. Evaluation is making an assessment of the worth of an element. The assessment is made by comparing the element to some criterion. With cognitive information, we identify a fact in a media message and compare it to a fact in our existing knowledge structures. If the fact in the message matches the fact in a knowledge structure, we judge the message fact to be accurate. The criterion here is accuracy. However, if we find an element in a media message that does not conform to our existing knowledge structure, we must decide whether to give high value to the new element and therefore change our knowledge structure or to value more highly our existing knowledge structure and disregard the new element. The criterion here is utility, that is, we determine if the new element is more useful to us than the element in our knowledge structure.

As an example, let's say you hear a very damaging claim against a political candidate that you favor. Your existing knowledge structure has a great deal of positive elements about this candidate. The new claim does not fit into your existing knowledge structure, which is constructed favorably for the candidate. You must decide whether to believe the new claim and incorporate it into your knowledge base, which would require substantial alterations, or to disregard the new claim. There are several strategies you could use to make the evaluation. You could examine the credibility of the claim, that is, who is the source of the accusation and does it seem plausible? Another strategy is a weighting one. If the claim sits out there by itself with no additional people coming forth to support it, then the claim has little weight, especially compared to the weight of favorable knowledge you already have about the candidate.

People who operate at higher levels of media literacy will be more careful, reasonable, diligent, and logical when making evaluative judgments. People at lower levels of media literacy will feel the effort is not worth it and quickly make a judgment based on only superficial intuition.

Making good evaluations requires the use of knowledge structures with well-developed information in many areas: cognitive, emotional, aesthetic, and moral. The more information a person already has, the easier it is to make judgments about new information. For example, if we use a knowledge structure with only cognitive information, we have the basis for undertaking a logical reasoning process. But what happens when this logical process results in several good judgment alternatives? Had we also had some emotional information in that knowledge structure, we could draw on that additional knowledge. Goleman (1995) reminds us that emotions are an important part of evaluation. Unless we factor in how we feel about something, we may become paralyzed and not be able to make a judgment. We need to have enough self-awareness about our emotions to determine where our preferences lie. Goleman says that many decisions "cannot be made well through sheer rationality; they require gut feeling, and the emotional wisdom garnered through past experiences" (p. 53).

There is a difference between using our emotions and letting our emotions use us. When we are highly media literate, we use our emotions—we don't ignore them. If we try to ignore them, they can influence us subconsciously. If our emotions stay at the subconscious level, they can still exert influences on our decisions and behaviors, but they do so without us being aware of it. Even without our awareness decisions are being made, attitudes shaped, and behaviors acted. Goleman reminds us that "as Freud made clear, much of emotional life is unconscious; feelings that stir within us do not always cross the threshold into awareness" (p. 54). Being media literate requires us to develop greater self-awareness about our emotions so we can use them in the evaluation process.

Our knowledge structures are even stronger if they also include aesthetic and moral information in additional to cognitive and emotional information. More information and more different types of information give us a sounder foundation from which to make good judgments.

Abstraction. This is the ability to assemble a brief, clear, accurate description of something. Abstracting is what you do when you tell a friend about a book you have read or a show you have seen. This requires that we first analyze the message and identify its component parts. Then we must evaluate those components to select those that are most important to the message. Finally, we must assemble a short description of the message from the results of our evaluation of the components.

Some of us are able to abstract better than others. For example, let's say you ask your friend to tell you what happened on the last episode of *ER*. Your friend says, "A bunch of doctors helped some sick people." Your friend has captured the essence of the show but has not communicated anything unique about that particular episode. If instead your friend says, "This mugging victim covered with blood was brought in by an ambulance and the medical team went to work checking his vital signs, then Dr. Greene put a tube down his throat so he could breathe," this provides a lot more vivid detail, but it covers only a few minutes of the hour-long show. A good abstract is one that is detailed enough to convey the essence of the important events in the show but also broad enough so that all the essential happenings are covered.

The skill of abstracting relies on some of the other advanced skills discussed so far. Abstracting requires a person to break down the show into parts, evaluate the importance of different elements as to their centrality of the action, then report those most important parts in a narrative that flows without raising any unanswered questions.

Message Extending Skills

The advanced skills described above keep our focus on the messages themselves. But we often want to move beyond the message, and there are three advanced skills that help us do this. First, there is deduction, which is the ability to use general principles to explain particulars. A second message extending skill is induction, which refers to the ability to perceive one or a few concrete examples and use them to construct a conclusion or opinion about a general trend. Third is the skill of synthesis, which is the ability to reassemble elements into a new structure.

Deduction. This is the use of general principles to draw conclusions about a particular case. In a sense, deduction (which moves from general principles to particulars) is rather the opposite of induction (which moves from particulars to general principles).

We use general rules all the time. For example, if you were to walk into your house, your arms and legs would go with you. Also, you would no longer be outside. These conclusions sound silly; they *sound* silly because we are so absolutely sure they are true. But did your parents or teachers specifically tell you these particular things? No, of course not. They taught you some general principles about the importance of keeping your body parts together and the impossibility of being in two places at once. You use these general principles to deduce all kinds of particulars. You have billions of facts like this available to you without ever having memorized them all. If you had to memorize one billion facts, it would take you more than 31 years if you learned one per second of every minute of every day without taking any breaks. As you can see, deduction is a powerful skill if used correctly and if we begin with good general principles.

Deduction is what the fictional detective Sherlock Holmes uses to solve his mysteries. Holmes has acquired many general principles about criminal behavior and about the natural world. He uses his keen powers of observation to focus on key particulars in the case. Then he explains the particulars by using his general principles.

Where do we learn our general principles? We either absorb them through a process of socialization or we induce them ourselves (Berger & Luckmann, 1966).

Induction. Induction is the process of observing a few examples, inferring a pattern among those examples, then constructing a general principle that represents that pattern we inferred. We use induction all the time. For example, let's say you watch a movie where a young child throws a temper tantrum and you find yourself thinking, "All children are so spoiled these days!" You have seen the portrayal of only one child and from this one example you have fashioned a belief about all children. Induction is the inferring of general principles after observing one or a few particular instances.

One key to media literacy is that we make good inductions from our limited contact with messages and not fall into the trap of making faulty inductions. In this trap, people focus on an isolated incident and conclude that it represents the typical. For example, people who read a news story about a criminal who copies an unusual bank robbery depicted in a popular recent movie might conclude that all movies are bad or that certain movies are responsible for the high rate of crime in society. Concluding that all movies are bad because one person copies a particular action in one movie is a faulty induction. No one movie can represent the incredible variety of all movies. Also, concluding that movies alone are responsible for crime in society is also a faulty induction, because this conclusion fails to consider the many factors that can lead a person to commit a crime.

This induction trap is also frequently in evidence when we try to assess risk in our personal lives. Often the media will present a story—as either news or fiction—of an airplane mishap, a stalker, or something that makes us fearful. We then use this one portrayal to over-estimate the risk to ourselves from this type of occurrence while ignoring other things (that the media do not talk about) that may pose a much higher risk to us. For example, in 1987 many news reports told about the danger of asbestos in older school buildings and the risk to children. Fear spread as people induced a belief that all schools had problems and that their children were at risk. Almost overnight the asbestos removal industry more than doubled its revenue. However, the actual risk of a premature death from exposure to asbestos is 1 in 100,000. Compare this to the rate of premature death due to being struck by lightening at 3 in 100,000. There is also a generalized belief by many in the population that exposure to X rays in dentists' and doctors' offices is risky. It does present a small risk, but the risk of premature death due to smoking cigarettes is 2,920 *times* greater than premature death due to exposure to diagnostic X rays (Matthews, 1992). However, many people calmly accept the risk of smoking but feel reckless when a dentist x-rays their teeth once a year.

How can we avoid the trap of making false inductions? There are two strategies. One is to use trustworthy reference materials to find out what the general patterns really are, so we don't have to induce them ourselves, especially when our inference would be nothing more than a wild guess. Look up the actual rates of divorce, government expenditures, health risks, and so on.

Oftentimes we will need to find a general principle that we cannot find in a reliable reference. What do you do when you want to induce the best way to end a romantic relationship? In this situation, you must use another strategy. Try to broaden your observations beyond one or two cases. Don't look at just romantic relationships in the media, look at romantic relationships in real life. If a pattern consistently shows up in many cases, then it is a better bet that the pattern may be common to all instances. Also, in collecting your observations, try to find cases that are able to represent the norm. Don't focus all your attention on how Beavis or Butt-Head would end a romantic relationship. Even if you observe 100 freaks, you still can't use the patterns you see there to make a good induction about how normal people behave.

Synthesis. This is the skill of reassembling all the valuable elements (identified through a process of analysis and evaluation) into new knowledge structures, formulating a better opinion than you had before, or solving a problem. Doing this well requires creativity and a willingness to break the old rules. Unless we use the ability to reassemble emotional, aesthetic, and moral interpretations into a fresh perspective on a film, novel, or television show, we have no option but to accept the insights of others.

As with the other advanced skills, synthesis can be conducted over a range of challenges from a quick micro-level synthesis to a very large-scale creation. For example, on the micro level, when a television program breaks for a commercial, sometimes we reassemble the characters and elements in the plot line to imagine what is coming next or to imagine ourselves in the teleplay. This type of synthesis can take only a few seconds and be more emotionally guided than intellectually complete. On a larger scale, one day we may become inspired to write an episode of our favorite show. In order to do this we need a deep knowledge about all the elements in the previous episodes. We need to know all the quirks of each character and have an intimate sense of what each would do or say in any situation. Then in writing our script, we would need to evaluate the appropriateness of dialog, plotting points, character interactions, and so on. The final product depends on our complete command of all these elements assembled in a new, creative manner.

▌▌ CONCLUSION

There are two families of media literacy skills. The rudimentary skills are those we develop through maturation and practice during the early years of our lives. By adolescence, we have gained a great deal of experience with the media. We have matured cognitively, emotionally, and morally to a point where we have a good facility with exposing ourselves to the media messages we want; recognizing symbols and patterns among symbols; and matching previously learned meaning with those patterns. When we enact these skills in combination, we are able to read, listen, and view media messages fairly easily. Because the application of these skills becomes easy, we often use them without thinking, that is, our minds are often on automatic pilot.

The advanced skills require conscious effort and a critical perspective throughout exposure. They require the active processing of messages through the skills of message focused sense making (analysis, compare/contrast, evaluation, and abstracting), as well as the skills of message extending sense making (deduction, induction, and synthesis).

Operating at higher levels of media literacy requires the active use of these skills. But it also requires a highly developed knowledge base. It is important that the two components of skills and information do not merely co-exist, but

TABLE 3.1   Advanced Skills of Media Literacy

Message-focused sense making

Analysis: the breaking down of a message into meaningful elements

Compare/Contrast: determining which elements are alike in some way; determining which elements are different in some way

Evaluation: judging the value of an element; the judgment is made by comparing it to some criterion

Abstracting: the ability to assemble a brief, clear accurate description of the media message

Message extending sense making

Deduction: using general principles to explain particulars

Induction: inferring general patterns from observation of particulars

Synthesis: the ability to reassemble elements into a new structure

that there is an active interplay between the two. Skills are useful only when they have raw material—information—on which to work. And a knowledge structure is more strongly formulated when it has been constructed with a wide range of highly developed skills.

FURTHER READING

Berger, P. L., & Luckmann, T. (1966). *The social construction of reality*. Garden City, NY: Doubleday. (219 pages with index)

This is a classic book about how people come to know their world. Written by two sociologists, this short but dense book carefully lays out a theory about how certain information gains prominence in a society and how that information is then internalized by members of that society.

Healy, J. M. (1990). *Endangered minds: Why children don't think and what we can do about it*. New York: Simon & Schuster. (382 pages with index)

Healy argues that we are unwittingly rearing a generation of "different brains." Her point is that our brains have changed physiologically due to massive exposure to visual messages in the media, such that what it means to be intelligent has changed. The old skills of reading the written word and mathematical reasoning are much lower than before, because our attention spans are so much lower.

Pinker, Steven. (1997). *How the mind works*. New York: W. W. Norton. (660 pages including index)

This is a long and often technical book, but it is well worth the time to read. Pinker presents many intriguing insights about how our minds work. He argues that our brains come with a great deal of software that programs many specialized tasks—and this programming is very unlike the software of computers. This software has been developed through natural selection and evolution. Thus there are many similarities in humans across all cultures. The difference between Einstein and a high school dropout is negligible compared to the difference between a dropout and a robot or a chimpanzee.

EXERCISE 3.1

Becoming Sensitive to Rudimentary Skills

By the time you have reached college age, you have been practicing rudimentary skills for well over a decade. You are very proficient at using these skills, but you also take them for granted. The purpose of this exercise is to help you experience what it felt like before you were so proficient at these skills.

Exposure

1. Buy a piece of sophisticated electronic equipment and try to hook it up and operate it without any help and without reading the directions.

2. Sit down in front of a computer and try to boot up an application (such as a word processing, spreadsheet, or communications application) that you have never run. Today many of these are very user friendly with lots of menus and help screens. Try to find a program from at least 10 years ago and run that.

3. Try to play a video game you have never played before. These are usually user friendly at the very beginning so you can begin play. But most of them have many challenges that you must figure out on your own. See how long it takes you to progress to various points in the game. Then find a child to play the game and watch how long it takes him or her to learn it.

4. Think of three topics that you know absolutely nothing about. Go to a library. Without using computer searches, the card catalog, or a librarian, see how much information you can find on each topic.

Recognizing Symbols

5. To sensitize yourself to how much you have learned in recognizing patterns, turn on your television set but leave the sound off. Now get very close to the screen so that your nose touches the glass. Try watching television for one minute. Can you recognize any patterns? Probably not—you have not learned how to spot individual symbols that close.

Recognizing Patterns

6. Take a magazine article on something you do not know much about. Cut the article into separate paragraphs and fasten each to a different piece of paper. Randomly order the paragraphs. Now read the newly arranged article and see if you can follow a progression of thought.

Matching Meaning

7. Find a book written in a language you do not understand, such as French, Italian, Spanish, or German. Begin reading aloud. You will be able to recognize individual letters and form the groupings of letters into words, and you probably will be able to pronounce these words, but you will not be able to match any meaning to most of the words.

EXERCISE 3.2

Exercising Advanced Skills

1. Think of some current event of interest to you. Now find a newspaper article on that topic and analyze it—break it down into its main components.

   a. What was the main point of the story?

   b. Where quotations used?

   c. What sources were interviewed?

   d. What are the key facts and figures?

   e. Are there important visuals—graphics or photographs?

2. Find a story in a recent magazine on the same topic and analyze it.

3. Find this story covered on television and videotape it, then analyze it.

4. Compare across the three stories: Which elements appeared in all stories?

5. Contrast the stories: What are the really noticeable differences?

6. Evaluate the set of elements: Which of the elements are the most valuable in terms of informing the audience about the current event?

7. Synthesis: Take the elements you valued highly in No. 6 and assemble them into a magazine story. What information would you present first? What would the sequence of information be? As you assemble the flow, is something missing, that is, do you need to put in something that was not in any of the three stories you analyzed? Why do you need this extra element: to help the balance of the story; to help it flow more smoothly; to help make it more interesting?

8. Synthesis: Repeat the process in No. 7 but instead of assembling the elements for a magazine story, assemble them for a television news story.

CHAPTER

4

> *Key Idea:* We need to be selective in acquiring information and careful in constructing that information into useful knowledge structures.

Importance of Knowledge Structures

Has this ever happened to you? You're sitting in class listening to a professor lecture about the media, and you wonder: How can I memorize all this information? There is so much!

This feeling is a symptom of several problems. First, you want to know what is most important. If you are field independent, this is a minor problem because with a little effort you can sort through the information and decide what is of relatively high, medium, and low importance. Once you have the information rank ordered in importance, the second problem is to decide how much of that information to learn, especially if you feel there is too much information to learn it all.

We have these same two problems every day as we are exposed to information from the media. How can we sort through all this information in terms of importance? And how can we make decisions about how much to retain? These questions become more important every year as the flood of information and images increases.

OVERWHELMED BY INFORMATION ■■

Think about how much information is made available to you by the media. The major media in our culture are newspapers, books, magazines, film, recordings, radio, television (both broadcast and cable), and the computer. Each of these offers an expanding array of *vehicles* to deliver messages of information, entertainment, and persuasion. The *New York Times* is one newspaper vehicle; *USA Today* is another.

Each of these vehicles is driving down the information highway and coming to you. Can you handle the traffic? Let's consider only the book vehicles. Each year there are 68,000 new titles published in the United States. That means that if you wanted to keep up with the vehicles presented in just this one medium, you would have to read about eight books per hour—with no breaks, not even for sleep. At the end of this very intense year of reading, you would have just kept up with the *new* books. You would not have had time to read any book published prior to this year. Also, you would not have time to read any of the 10,000 magazines published this year—that's magazines, not issues. For example *Time* magazine publishes 52 issues a year, and *Sports Illustrated* publishes 12 issues a year. If we were to count issues, the total would be well over 200,000 *per year*. Also, the typical city offers about 500 hours of radio programming and another 1,000 hours of cable television programming *per day*.

Each of these vehicles contains many messages—perhaps in the thousands—and the number of these messages per vehicle is growing. For example, news vehicles present information in the form of sound bytes, which are quotes from people. From 1965 to 1995 the length of the average TV news sound byte shrank from 42.3 seconds to 8.3 seconds. On top of all this, add newspapers, CDs, and especially your computer, where you can access the almost limitless pool of information on the Internet (see Figure 4.1).

The workforce is shifting away from manufacturing goods to manufacturing information. In 1850, 4% of American workers handled information for a living. Now information processing accounts for more than half of the workforce and more than half of the Gross National Product (Shenk, 1997).

Paradox

It is a paradox that as information increases, the public becomes *less* knowledgeable. Shouldn't a richer information environment make us more knowledgeable and smarter? It would appear so. But the opposite seems to be the case. Even though we are flooded with more and more information, it appears that the public knows less and less. For example, in polls of general knowledge, especially political knowledge of our government leaders, Americans score dismally low. In polls where people are asked questions about general knowledge, half the respondents typically cannot answer simple questions (Buzbee, 1995).

Despite more and more contact with the media, people know very little about what the media are and how they operate. "There is the assumption, I think, that people are so immersed in media that they inherently understand them. That, I am convinced, is not the case," says Everette Dennis (1993, p. 9), director at the Freedom Forum:

> I know public curiosity about the media to be fairly high but actual knowledge and information to be minimal. I believe that most people are functional illiterates when it comes to understanding media. They are heavy users of media's equivalents of junk food—that which is sensationalized and superficial—but not well acquainted with a wide range of media con-

Newspapers

- There are 1,700 daily and 9,000 weekly newspapers published in the United States.
- One weekday edition of the *New York Times* now contains more information than the average person in 17th-century England was likely to come across in an entire lifetime.

Books

- Over 68,000 book titles are now published each year, compared with 11,000 in 1950.
- During that time, the number of bookstores has more than doubled, as have per capita book sales and library circulation.

Magazines

- There are more than 10,000 magazine vehicles published regularly in this country.
- About 83% of U.S. households subscribe to at least one magazine, and magazine circulation has been growing faster than the population for the past four decades.

Television

- There are currently about 1,600 broadcast television stations in operation across the country.
- There are about 4,500 cable franchises now connecting almost 70% of all homes. Each cable system has been providing an average of 40 channels for over 6,500 hours of programming available in those homes each week.
- Over 99% of all households in this country have at least one television.
- Even among this country's poor people, 95% have at least one television set and 40% have more than one.
- About 70% of college students have TV sets and 29% have VCRs while they are away at school.
- Four out of every five households have a VCR and 90% have access to cable or satellite TV, although 20% choose not to subscribe.
- The average American watches television for more than 1,500 hours each year, and 75% say they watch every day.

Film

- Hollywood studios release about 350 film vehicles each year, and this does not include the untold thousands of educational and corporate training films.
- 40% of Americans regularly go to theaters to watch movies.

Radio

- There are about 7,000 radio stations currently broadcasting in this country.
- 99% of all households own at least one radio.
- The average household has more than five radios.
- 95% of all automobiles have a radio.
- 61% of all adults have a radio at work.
- Americans listen to an average of 3 hours of radio a day.
- 66% of all American adults listen to radio on an average day.
- 80% of the population listens to radio on the weekend for an average of 5 hours. *(continued)*

Figure 4.1. Information Access

Computers
- The percentage of homes with personal computers is now over 40%, and 97% of the country's schools have computers—one for every 11 students, which is up from one computer for every 63 students just 10 years ago.
- In 83% of households with computers, people say they use their PCs more than 5 hours a week.
- 9.5 million people use the Internet—including more than a million children under 18. The average session lasts about 68 minutes; about two thirds of users look for information weekly, and a quarter search daily.
- In the 1960s, computers were seen as a labor-saving device. Predictions were that soon we would all be working only 4-day weeks, 32-hour weeks, but the work week keeps getting longer—up 3.2 hours per week from the early 1970s. Instead, computers have become task masters, constantly picking up the pace.
- In the United States there are over 12,000 electronic information services offering consumers everything from complex electronic legal libraries to reports on local surfing conditions, and almost everything imaginable in between. These services are offered by hundreds of different providers including newspapers, cable TV companies, broadcasters, database services, and all sorts of start-up entrepreneurs.
- The information superhighway was expected to generate $1 trillion in annual revenue by 2000, making it the largest industrial sector in the world.

Advertising
- In 1971 the average American was targeted with about 560 daily advertising messages; 20 years later the figure had climbed to 3,000 ad messages per day.
- Between 1965 and 1995, the length of the average network TV ad shrunk from 53.1 seconds to 25.4 seconds; the number of ads per network TV minute increased from 1.1 to 2.4. During the 1980s, third class mail grew 13 times faster than the population.
- By 1990 there were 30,000 telemarketing companies employing 18 million Americans and generating $400 billion.
- Advertising spending from 1930 to 1990 increased 2,200%; but recall was in steep decline.

Paper
- Per capita paper consumption in the United States tripled from 1940 to 1980 (from 200 to 600 lbs.), then it tripled again from 1980 to 1990 (1,800 lbs.).

Children
- The average child spends more than 38 hours with the media each week; this does not include media used in school or for homework.
- If we were to search for media in the bedrooms of American children, we would find that 70% have a radio, 64% have a tape player, 53% a TV, 51% a CD player, 33% a video game player, 29% a VCR, and 16% a computer. In 1970, only 6% of sixth graders had a TV in their bedroom; by 1999 that figure had grown to 77%.
- 69% of children live in a home with a computer; 45% of children have access to the Internet on their home computer.

Figure 4.1. Information Access (continued)

SOURCES: A. C. Nielsen, 1990, 1991; Audits & Surveys, 1991; Austin, 1989; Black, 1992; Donnelly, 1986; Intelligence Infocorp, 1996; Jeffres, 1994; Kantrowitz, 1993; Miller, 1989; Newspaper Advertising Bureau, 1988; Radio Advertising Bureau, 1991, 1993; Rideout, Foehr, Roberts, & Brodie, 1999; Shapiro, 1992; Shenk, 1997; Standard & Poor's, 1996, p. L32.

tent options, nor are they well versed about how media function and why. (p. 8)

We have the same situation in the political realm. The media provide us with more information about politics, but we know less about how the political system works. Also, the new media allow us to provide more information to our leaders, but those leaders appear to know less about what we want. Voters use the mail, faxes, and e-mail to send messages to elected officials. In 1970, the members of Congress received a combined total of 15 million messages from the voters. By 1991, the number had grown to 300 million (Shenk, 1997). That means the average congress person received well over 600,000 messages from voters in that year. Compare this to the fact that there are 525,600 minutes in each year. How can any congress person keep up with all these messages? They cannot, yet the number of messages they have to deal with today is 10 times as many as it was a decade ago. Also in 1993, the White House received 84,600 e-mails, and by 1999 it had received 1.1 million ("Hack Attack," 2000).

There is real concern about whether democracy can survive this trend. Democracy and voting require an informed electorate—by informed we mean that voters share a high level of knowledge about the political system. But voters are overwhelmed with too much information. How can they make good voting decisions? Elected officials are overwhelmed by messages from voters. How can they understand what the voters really want? As the sharing of information goes up, the understanding goes down.

Information Fatigue

There is so much information, many of us feel a great deal of stress just thinking about it. In *Data Smog,* a book published in 1997, David Shenk explained that

at a certain level of input, the law of diminishing returns takes effect; the glut of information no longer adds to our quality of life, but instead begins to cultivate stress, confusion, and even ignorance. Information overload threatens our ability to educate ourselves, and leaves us more vulnerable as consumers and less cohesive as a society. For the most part, it actually diminishes our control over our own lives, while those already in power find their positions considerably strengthened. (p. 15)

Shenk says that for the first 100,000 years of human history, people were able to examine and consider information about as quickly as it could be created and circulated. But in the past few decades, the amount of information available doubles each year. Because our ability to process information has not changed, we are left with "permanent processing deficit" (Shenk, 1997, p. 28). Referring to this information overload as "data smog," he says it "crowds out quiet moments, and obstructs much needed contemplation. It spoils conversation, literature, and even entertainment. It thwarts skepticism, rendering us less sophisticated as consumers and citizens. It stresses us out" (p. 31).

We have been feeling fatigued for a long time. In 1970, Stanley Milgram, a prominent social psychologist, began noticing various classic responses to information overload: (a) allocating less time to each input, (b) disregarding low-priority inputs, (c) redrawing boundaries in social interactions so that the overload can be shifted to another person in the exchange, (d) blocking off reception (unlisted phone numbers), (e) diminishing intensity of inputs by filtering, and (f) creating specialized institutions to absorb inputs and thus keep the individual from becoming swamped (Milgram, 1983). All of these behaviors are even more prevalent today.

Shenk argues that this data smog is responsible for three out of four Americans who now say they have chronic stress. Two out of three visits to family doctors are stress related. The top-selling drugs are for ulcers, depression, and hypertension. There has been a 300% increase in depression over the course of this century. More people are also suffering from Attention Deficit Disorder, which keeps people restless and prevents them from concentrating.

■ IMPLICATIONS OF INFORMATION FATIGUE

We live in an information saturated culture, and the rate of information pouring through the media into our culture is accelerating each year. Clearly, it is impossible for any person to keep up with all the new information, images, jingles, music, issues, and more. We must avoid most messages, so we choose to read only several books and a handful of magazine issues each year. But even when we work at avoiding most media messages, there are certain media that are obtrusive and continually break through our barriers of avoidance. We can choose not to read books, newspapers, and magazines; but the obtrusive media of television, radio, CDs, billboards, and so on, are flooding our lives with messages even if we do not consciously choose them. Many messages in the media world do not wait for us to find them; they seek us out in our real lives and create the exposures for us.

What do we do? Most of us simply ride the tide of media information, passively exposing ourselves to whatever comes along. Every now and then we

---

BOX 4.1

You are driving down the street, past billboards with ads for all kinds of products. Your car radio pours out a stream of advertising messages that are briefly interrupted with music now and then. A taxi passes with a reminder to watch a certain television show. At the dentist's office you flip through a magazine. In the background, music from an FM radio station soothes and relaxes you before the sharp objects enter your mouth. As you leave the office, the news of your cavity is already in a computer and moving at the speed of light through fiber-optic cable into your insurance company's database in another city across the country. On your way home you stop at a grocery store where you scan a display of coupons from yesterday's newspaper. In the background, recorded music puts you in an active, spending mood as you walk aisles jammed with 30,000 products that attempt to reach into your mind and stir up memories of their multi-million dollar advertising campaigns. Your shopping cart is covered with ads, as is your cash register receipt. At home, you turn on the TV for company as you put your groceries away. Then you pop a tape in your Walkman and go out for some exercise, wearing clothes emblazoned with logos of sports teams, your college, and several soft drinks. You run by the movie theater and look at its big bright posters of coming attractions. Back home again you pick up the newspaper from the porch and toss it onto the coffee table—noticing a picture of a car wreck and a burning building on the front page.

Suddenly the phone rings and a voice asks you to be part of a survey on media usage habits.

You say, "I really don't have time for the media."

The surveyor asks, "Can you remember any media messages from the last day or so?"

You are peeved. "Like I said, I don't have time to expose myself to the media. I'm so busy."

---

search out a particular exposure—perhaps our favorite television program, a movie by our favorite actor/actress, a book, a magazine or two, a few Web sites, and so on. But our planned exposures are typically far less than our haphazard exposures. Take a look at the scenario in Box 4.1, then reflect on how much information you are being exposed to every day without being aware of it.

Passive Exposure

Much of our exposure to media messages is not planned by us. It happens outside of our control. We will never be able to change this. But there is something we *can* change, and that is the degree to which we actively process this information. Active processing gives us control over what we do with the information and images to which we are exposed. However, most of our unplanned haphazard media exposure is *not* actively processed by us. When it comes to most media information, our minds are on automatic pilot as we let the messages happen to us passively without paying much attention. We keep this exposure in the background while something else (such as a conversation with a friend or thinking about what we need to do this evening) is in the foreground. When a message comes along that we particularly like or particularly hate, it captures our attention and we actively deal with it. Then we return to automatic pilot where we again passively process the messages.

What happens during passive processing? The messages go into our subconscious without us being aware of it. Thus we do not challenge these messages, nor do we think about how we want to link up the new information with the existing information we already have. Instead, the information gets put somewhere in our brains without our thinking about it. For example, did you ever find yourself humming a song or a jingle and wonder what triggered that?

Many people in the media—especially advertisers—prefer that their messages be processed passively rather than actively by you. Advertisers know that when you passively process their messages you have much less control over what you think and their messages have a greater chance of influencing your attitudes. Cognitive psychologists call this explanation the elaboration likelihood model (Petty & Cacioppo, 1986). According to this model, attitudes can be changed by two routes. The central route of information processing involves a thorough consideration of the merits of the arguments given. When people use this central route, they actively process the message by thinking through the arguments and elaborating those arguments by making relevant associations, scrutinizing the evidence, inferring their value, and evaluating the overall message. People must be highly motivated to use this route, because it requires more time and effort to think through all the elements of a message and to carefully evaluate the claims made in the message.

In contrast, when people are passive they do not use the central route of processing but default to a peripheral route. Messages then bypass the person's thinking process and take a peripheral route around the conscious defenses and into a person's subconscious. When people allow information to follow this route, they do not exercise control over the processing of the messages and turn that control over to the designers of the messages.

It is far easier to stay on automatic pilot than it is to exert the mental energy needed to process messages from the media actively. As the information flood overwhelms us, we think it is better to ignore it. But this ignorance comes with a price—a price we are not aware that we are paying.

Faulty Beliefs

There are many examples of faulty beliefs. An interesting place to observe faulty beliefs in the general population is to examine the results of public opinion polls. Often these polls will ask people about issues that would seem to be very important. When we look at the patterns of public beliefs, however, we can see that many people are not really well versed in these seemingly important issues. We can see that these beliefs are clearly faulty, either because they are not accurate reflections of reality or they are logically inconsistent.

In public opinion polls about crime, only 17% of people think crime is a big problem in their own community while 83% of Americans think crime is a big problem in society (Whitman & Loftus, 1996). Thus, most people do not experience crime in their own lives and therefore do not think it is a big problem where they live. However, they are convinced it is a big problem in society. Where could the public get such an idea? From the media's fixation on crime in the news with its ethic of "if it bleeds, it leads." Watching evening newscasts with their highlighting of crime and violence leads us to infer that there must be a high rate of crime and that most of it is violent assaults. But in reality, less than 20% of all crime is violent. More than 80% of all crime is property crime with the victim not even present (*Statistical Abstract of the United States: 1999*, 2000). Furthermore, the rate for violent crime has been declining in this country for the past decade, both in terms of crimes reported to the police as well as in actual victimization rates. Yet in a recent poll only 7% of Americans believed that violent crime had declined in the past 5 years (Whitman & Loftus, 1996). People have remembered a few crime stories and gory images, but they have not taken an active role in finding out what the true crime rates are. They have fashioned their opinions on superficial information that has misled them.

In a wide range of public opinion polls, we find that people not only exaggerate the problems with crime, but they also over-estimate the problems with health care, education, religion, and family—believing that they are all serious, growing problems. For example, with health care, 90% of adults think that the health care system is in crisis, but at the same time, almost 90% feel that their own health care is of good quality. About 63% of people think other people's doctors are too interested in making money, but only 20% think their own doctor is too interested in making money. As for education, 64% give the nation's school's a grade of C or D, but at the same time, 66% give their local public school a grade of A or B. As for religion, 65% say that religion is losing its influence on American life, while 62% said religion is becoming a stronger influence in their own lives. As for responsibility, almost 90% believe that a major problem with society is that people don't live up to their commitments, but more than 75% say they meet their commitments to families, kids, and employers.

Nearly half of the population believes it is impossible for most families to achieve the American dream, while 63% believe they have achieved or are close to the American dream. And 40% to 50% think the nation is currently moving in the wrong direction, while 88% of Americans think their own lives and families are moving in the right direction (Whitman, 1996).

Most people think that the media, especially television, have a very strong effect on other people. They have an unrealistic opinion that the media cause other people to behave violently. There are people who believe that if you allow PSAs (Public Service Announcements) on TV about using condoms that children will learn it is permissible and even a good thing to have sex. This is clearly an over-estimation; the media do not turn people into zombies by taking over their minds and completely transforming their personalities and forcing them to do things against their will.

At the same time, people *under*estimate the influence the media have on them. When they are asked if they think the media have any effect on them personally, only 12% say yes. These people argue that the media are primarily channels of entertainment and diversion so they have no negative effect on them. The people who believe this say that they have watched thousands of hours of crime shows and have never shot anyone or robbed a bank. While this may be true, this argument does not fully support the claim that the media have no effect on them; this argument is based on the false premise that the media trigger only high profile, negative, behavioral effects that are easy to recognize. But there are many more types of effects. When you expand your perspective on what a media effect is, you can see that hardly an hour goes by in your life without your experiencing some kind of media effect. With a broader perspective, you can avoid this prevalent myth that the media "exert no effect on me."

There is a faulty belief in this country that television is to blame for the educational system not being very good. The media often present reports about how poorly this nation's youth do on learning compared to youths in other countries. For example, the Third International Mathematics and Science Study, which is administered to 8th graders in 41 countries, revealed that American students rank 28th in math and 17th in science in the world ("The Learning Lag," 1996). The 1998 National Assessment of Educational Progress, administered nationally by a group established by Congress, reported that one third of high school seniors lack even a basic understanding of how the American government is run, and only 26% of seniors were considered well versed enough in civics to make reasonable, well-informed choices during elections (McQueen, 1999). The National Assessment of Educational Progress (NAEP) reports that only about one quarter of American school children have achieved the proficiency standard in writing (Wildavsky, 1999). Reports like this lead critics to complain that children in this country watch too much television. However, the same report says that students in Japan rank 3rd on both tests although they watch as much television as do American kids, but this bit of information is rarely reported.

Many conscientious parents have accepted the belief that it is bad for their young children to watch television. They believe that TV somehow will make their children's minds lazy, reduce their creativity, and turn them into lethargic entertainment junkies. If this happens, children will not value achievement and will not do well in school.

This belief is faulty because it blames the media, not the child or the parent, for poor academic performance. It also focuses only on the negative effect and gives the media no credit for potentially positive effects.

This is an important issue, but again it is not a simple one. When we look carefully at the research evidence, we can see that the typically reported finding is wrong and that when we look more carefully there are several effects happening simultaneously (see Potter, 1987a). For example, the typically reported finding is that television viewing is negatively related to academic achievement. And there is a fair amount of research that reports this conclusion. What makes this faulty is that this relationship is explained better by something else—IQ. School achievement is overwhelmingly related to IQ. Also, children with lower IQs watch more television. So it is IQ that accounts for lower achievement and higher television viewing. Research analyses that take a child's IQ into account find that there is no overall negative relationship; instead there is a much more interesting pattern. The negative relationship does not show up until the child's viewing has passed the threshold of 30 hours per week. Beyond that 30-hour point, the more television children watch, the lower their academic achievement, and that effect gets stronger with the more hours they watch beyond that threshold. This means that academic achievement goes down only after television viewing starts to cut into study time and sleep. But under 30 hours of viewing per week, there is no negative effect. In fact, at the lowest levels of television viewing, there is actually a positive effect, that is, a child who watches none or only a few hours a week is likely to do less well academically than a child who watches a moderate (around 12 to 15 hours per week) amount. Thus the pattern is as follows: Children who are deprived of the source of information television provides do less well in school than children who watch a moderate amount of television; however, when a child gets to the point where the amount of television viewing cuts into needed study time, academic performance goes down. This conclusion is not so simple as to lend itself easily to a short sound byte or flashy image, so it is not likely to be presented in the obtrusive media. If it is presented, it is not likely to move through the peripheral route as smoothly as shorter info-bits, so it is not likely to be stored accurately or completely in one's subconscious. It is instead much easier for the media to report a negative overall relationship and for people to remember a simple negative relationship.

When we pose the question, "What effect does viewing television have on a child's academic performance?" we could give the simple, popular answer: There is a negative effect. But now you can see that this answer is too simple-minded. It is also misleading, because it reinforces the limited belief that media effects are negative, polarized, and that the media are to blame. Instead, all of us need to build stronger knowledge structures so that we can formulate more accurate, well-reasoned opinions about the media. As long as our beliefs are faulty, we cannot exercise adequate control over their effects on us.

Why the Faulty Beliefs?

Information fatigue leads us to passive exposure where our minds are on automatic pilot and we do not control either our exposures or how the messages get into our minds. This passive exposure increases the probability that the information we receive is inaccurate. By "inaccurate" I do not mean that the media are presenting biased or non-factual information to us—although there is some of this. The condition of inaccurate information is traceable much more to the fact that our information base is filled with partial understandings, facts without context, facts that are out of date, and unsorted impressions where conflicting information resides unresolved in our memories. With this type of information as our base, it is no wonder that many of our beliefs are faulty. As long as we continue with passive exposure, our absorption of more information will not translate into better knowledge; instead it will only increase our stockpile of faulty beliefs. Habitual passive exposure to this constant flow can serve to reduce our literacy if we merely float along in the stream of messages. If we accept unquestioningly the images in these messages, we can end up with faulty beliefs about the world and ourselves.

Our opinions can get started in all sorts of strange ways, and often they are not based on sound reasoning or on in-depth knowledge of a topic. They can spring forth spontaneously, in surveys or conversations, without much thought or foundation. When it comes to the media, we often create opinions on intuition or on partial, anecdotal information. We might look for high-profile anecdotes in the media and in our real lives.

When we are media literate, we are active in our exposures. We analyze the messages and determine for ourselves what is important. We discard that which we judge to be unimportant or faulty. We use the important information to induce good principles for ourselves and not allow the media to give us their principles. When we have good principles, we can deduce explanations for particulars. However, if we have poor skills of induction or deduction, we will end up with faulty principles and we will be led to make inaccurate judgments about how the world works.

We need to monitor our beliefs continually and try to determine why we hold them. If we do not do this, then it is not possible to challenge ourselves to think more deeply about something that has a strong, continual influence on our knowledge, attitudes, and behaviors. When we think more deeply and more systematically about this, we can get control of those influences. If we don't, we will continue to accumulate our knowledge very haphazardly, and put those elements of information together sloppily into opinions that we will come to hold more dearly over time—thus firmly entrenching our faulty beliefs.

SCHEMAS ■

The human brain has not changed much over the past 50,000 years, but scientists have changed their explanations for how the brain works. The prevailing belief used to be that the human mind was a giant computer that stored all our experiences and knowledge. When we needed to solve a problem, our brain would search out all relevant information and systematically sort through it to make logical decisions.

The more we learn about how the brain functions, the more we come to realize that the brain is not a logical computer. In his book *How the Mind Works*, Steven Pinker (1997) contrasts human brains with computers, saying

> computers are serial, doing one thing at a time; brains are parallel, doing millions of things at once. Computers are fast; brains are slow. Computer parts are reliable; brain parts are noisy. Computers have a limited number of connections; brains have trillions. Computers are assembled according to a blueprint; brains must assemble themselves. (p. 26)

This does not mean that computers are superior to the human brain. No. There are things the human brain can do that computers cannot do. We humans are comfortable solving "ill-posed problems," while a computer will freeze when faced with such a problem.

What is an "ill-posed problem?" To illustrate, let's use a mathematical example. If I were to ask you what the product of 4 × 6 was, you would say it is 24. This is a clearly posed problem. It gives you two numbers and asks you to solve for one unknown number. You have enough information to solve the problem easily, and you would be very confident that there was only one right answer. Both you and a computer could solve this problem equally well. But what if I asked you to work backwards from 24. What if I asked you to tell me that 24 is the product of what? You could answer that 24 is the product of 4 × 6. That would be correct. But it would also be correct to say that 24 is the product of 3 × 8, 2 × 12, 1 × 24, 0.5 × 48, and on and on. There are many accurate answers. This is an example of an ill-posed problem, because you are given only one number and asked to solve for two unknowns; there is not enough information and there are too many unknowns. Thus you find that there are many possible alternative answers, and you have no way of determining which of the many possible answers is the best because you do not have enough information.

In our everyday lives, we are constantly faced with ill-posed problems. We solve them by filling in the missing information. What do we use to fill in the missing information? According to the prevailing explanation offered by cognitive psychologists, we use schemas.

What Are Schemas?

Schemas are groupings of facts and experiences that each of us assembles in order to be able to organize the information we hold in our brains (Graesser, Millis, & Long, 1986). Think of schemas as slides in a projector. When we are confronted by something—let's say a dog—we pull up a slide and project it onto the animal. If the animal we see conforms to the sketch on our slide (information in our schema) and we conclude it fits, then we conclude the animal is a dog. If the animal does not fit, we usually look for another schema until we find one where the animal does fit. If we can't find a schema that fits, we either give up and say, "I have no idea what that is!" or we find the schema that fits the closest and modify it, while thinking, "I believe that is a dog, but I have never seen one that color or size before."

The "slides" contain more than just visual information. They contain memories of sound, smell, touch, taste, and how things feel. They also contain memories of emotions. All of these elements are linked together in networks of associations. Some of those links between elements are very strong and others are much weaker. For example, when some people think of dog, their first reaction might be one of fear as they recall being bitten by a dog when they were very young. The next thing they might remember is a visual image of a dog with bared teeth, because that has the strongest link to the fear. Then there might be a link to the sound of the dog barking and the person crying. As we use a schema, we begin with the element that is most salient and work our way to other elements by following the links throughout the network.

We are not born with our schemas. Instead, we must construct them as we experience the world. As we have more experiences, we have more elements to code into our schemas. When we have a lot of experience in one area, we have a very elaborate schema. This is why young children have difficulty understanding many things about their world—their experience has been too limited for them to have developed many schemas. This is also why they are so interested in exploring; they crave experiences that will help them understand how things work so they can elaborate their schemas.

As we grow older, we develop hundreds of schemas to cover all possible people, events, ideas, and things in our experience (see Figure 4.2). We also develop schemas to use with the media. For example, through our exposure to fictional stories in the media, we have developed our narrative schemas, that is, the media storytellers have taught us how stories begin, how they progress, and how they end. We are taught about the elements that generate action, what heightens action and intensifies interest, and how conflict is resolved. We have schemas for flashbacks, dream sequences, and projections into the future. Once we learn these narrative schemas, it is very easy to watch television or film. Simple shows follow these formulas closely, and thus you do not have to think much about the plot. In contrast, more complex shows will signal a recognizable formula early in the program but then break with the formula in order to surprise you emotionally or get you more involved cognitively. This requires you to search continually for new schemas to make sense of the action. When viewers don't want to work that hard, they turn off these complex programs and chose instead to watch the easy formula programs.

Using Schemas

When we encounter a new experience, we look for a schema that fits the experience and can guide us in our interpretation of what that experience means. We use our schema to "fill in the blanks" with what we see in real life. For example, let's say you meet someone and immediately feel a romantic attraction. You pull up your "Romance" schema and project it onto this person. You can make a match on some physical characteristics and some first impression superficial personality characteristics. But you don't stop at this point. You have an ill-defined problem of, "Can I have a romantic relationship with this person?" You don't have nearly enough information to answer this question, but that doesn't stop you from moving forward. So you pull up a lot of information from your "Romance" schema. Some of that information is in the form of an image of a candlelight dinner; some of it about how it would feel to hold that person's hand; some of it might be about how that person's voice would sound during a walk on the beach; some of it is about walking into a party and watching the looks on the faces of your friends. You play these scenarios in your imagination to see if you can fit this person into them. This allows you to come up with a good answer for the ill-defined problem.

In selecting a schema, we are driven by two goals: accuracy and efficiency. Accuracy is the goal to "get it right." When we use the accuracy goal, we keep

Real-World Schemas

Person schema: You have a schema for every person you know. Each of these schema include the physical characteristics and personality traits of that person. For acquaintances, the schemas are very sketchy. But for your closest, long-time friends, the schemas are highly elaborate.

Self-schema: These are all the images you have of yourself. Most people have developed a more elaborate schema about themselves than any other single thing.

Role schema: These are your expectations for how people should behave in certain situations. You have a role schema for behaving as a student in the classroom, one for behavior at a family reunion, one for a job interview, one for a party with friends your age, and so on. Each of these roles is very different, because each has a different goal and requires a different set of attitudes and behaviors.

Event schema: These are expectations you have that unfold over time, and as such they can be regarded as scripts. In the long term, you have a script that tells you what you should be doing in the next few years and what you should be doing in 10 or 20 years with your imagined career and family. In the short term, you have scripts that guide what you should say in conversations; that is, if a person is funny, you respond one way, but if the person is a bore, you respond another way.

Media Schema

Character schema: The media deal in stock characters (i.e., stereotypes) that we can easily recognize. Our character schema are what make it possible for us to have such a sense of recognition.

Narrative schema: These are the storytelling formulas used by the media. They contain elements that cue us as to whether the media message is a fictional story about crime, a news story about crime, a comedy, and so on.

Setting schema: Settings influence our expectations. If an armed robbery takes place in a liquor store in a poor urban neighborhood, the meaning of that crime can be different than if it takes place in the bedroom of an upper-middle-class family home in a small rural community.

Thematic schema: These schemas help us recognize the moral of a story. This is a higher-order knowledge structure than the previous three, because those three are used in inferring this one. Viewers observe how certain characters perform in the quest of their goals, and they observe what happens to those characters. For example, if a bad character is punished for his behavior, the theme is usually that crime doesn't pay or that honesty is the best policy. But if a good character is continually punished, the theme can be something quite different, such as the world is unfair or good guys finish last.

Rhetorical schema: This is the viewer's inference about the purpose of the storyteller. Is the primary contribution of the story to provide information or to entertain? Is the story trying to teach us a moral lesson or provide us with a fantasy escape? Is the story meant to be humorous, and if so, how—slapstick? satire? irony?

Figure 4.2. Types of Schema

searching among our schemas until we find the one that fits the experience. If we cannot find one that fits, we pick the one that fits the closest then modify it until it fits accurately. With the goal of efficiency, we pick the first schema that seems to fit OK, then move on to something else. You can see that the two goals are not usually compatible. Ideally we want to achieve both goals at the same time. But when we find ourselves taking too much time finding the most accurate place for new information, we likely will switch to the efficiency goal so that we can finish more quickly.

Given the massive amount of information flooding our culture, which goal do you think we use more often? If you answered quickly, you most likely said "Efficiency!" Efficiency is more important when we feel we have a lot to do and very little time to do it—this is true of most of us, most of the time. Also, if our thinking skills are not very good, then we typically use the efficiency goal exclusively. The accuracy goal requires more thinking from us as we reformulate a schema by carefully grafting in new information and pruning away inaccurate facts and images.

While we may save time by using the efficiency goal, the danger is that we are too quick to (a) throw away important information, (b) give up searching for elements in an experience, (c) select peripheral rather than important information to put into our schemas, (d) put an element in the wrong schema, or (e) put an element in the correct schema but in the wrong place, such as linking it with the wrong elements. All of these cause problems. If we continue adding to these problems over and over, our schemas will be very superficial or be composed of lots of inaccurate information. When we rely on schemas like these, we will find ourselves arguing for some myths or bad opinions—absolutely convinced that we are right—then get very frustrated that we cannot make others realize that *they* are wrong. It can be a big problem if we do not periodically compare our schemas to accurate information and rework our schemas to remove the old, misleading, and biased information.

Contrasting Media-World Schemas and Real-World Schemas

Another important problem is confusing media-world schemas with real-world schemas. Sometimes we get disoriented between the two worlds and use a media narrative schema in our real world when we should be using an event schema (see Figure 4.2). For example, we go to a party and ignore all of the previous experience we have had at real-world parties and instead expect to participate in a party as it would take place in a Hollywood movie. This can get us into trouble or embarrass us at the party, or at minimum make us feel enormously disappointed when the party turns out not to be as glamorous or intense as expected.

There are three major differences in how schemas are used in the two different worlds. First, the media provide a wider range of messages than does a person's real social life. People need a wider range of schemas to deal with the types of people they see in the media but do not encounter in their interpersonal interactions—people such as national political figures, major entertainers, professional athletes, psychopathic killers, the very rich, and others. People also need a wider range of event schemas to understand what it means to play a sport professionally, to be a person living in Bosnia, to be a Medieval knight looking for the Holy Grail, or to be an astronaut on a futuristic voyage to another galaxy.

Second, the media have a sense of authority about them. Thus when we read something, we feel it has been written by an expert so we should believe the claims in the message. Because cameras have recorded images of actual events presented as news, we are likely to believe those images. Also, the repetitiveness of the messages contributes to this expert effect.

Third, in conversations, the level of involvement is fairly high, but with the media, involvement is usually very low. We are more active in searching for schemas and modifying them in interpersonal situations, because there is usually more of a negotiation process as we can direct conversations and ask the questions that are important to us. As we get answers to our questions, we often need to modify our schemas. When we expose ourselves to the media, we search out schemas that fit the media messages early on in our exposure, then stick with them.

The more consciously we pay attention to our world, the more elements we notice and the more we add to our existing schemas. We are constantly developing our schemas—adding to them and subtracting elements that we find not useful or that belong in other schemas.

▉ KNOWLEDGE STRUCTURES

Knowledge structures differ from schemas in two major ways. The first difference is that schemas are composed of elements that are informally grouped together, usually by expediency. In contrast, knowledge structures are consciously built and maintained with the use of higher-level skills. We can construct a knowledge structure beginning with a schema if we thoroughly examine our schemas and clear out all the inaccurate and irrelevant information, then put in the effort to search out new information to fill in the logical gaps. Schemas are simple tools used to cut corners in an efficient drive to accept some meaning with as little effort as possible, whereas knowledge structures are authoritative maps that provide strong context for helping us work toward the most useful determination of meaning in an accurate manner.

The second difference is that knowledge structures are formal mapping devices with analytical depth, while schemas are loose amalgamations of elements that are connected by simple associations. Schemas can be regarded as two dimensional, with the elements lying on the surface. Knowledge structures require us to break each idea or element down into its component parts. Each part must then be broken down into its components. This can be envisioned as the root system of a tree. We begin with a main idea, which is the trunk of the tree. This is broken down into two or three component ideas, each of which is broken down into its component ideas. The structure moves from the key idea (the trunk) outward and downward in a cone shape. Each element is not just connected to other elements, but each element is nested within a series of other elements. In a schema, it does not matter where an element is located. All that matters is what the element is associated with. In a knowledge structure, location matters a great deal. This is why a knowledge structure is a better mapping tool.

The two also share some commonalities. Both are constructions by individuals; people are not born with these but must build them as they experience life. Both are composed of information that is cognitive, emotional, aesthetic, and moral. Both are used by people to make sense of their world. And both are organic, that is, they are continually in a state of change as people acquire new experiences.

Using Knowledge Structures

Let's return to the two questions that were posed earlier in this chapter when we dealt with the problem of being overwhelmed with information:

1. How can we sort through all this information in terms of its importance?
2. How can we make decisions about how much to retain?

The answer to both of these questions is: Use good knowledge structures. Good knowledge structures will help orient you when you are deciding what is important. Remember, knowledge structures are maps. They show you which are the main branches of knowledge, which are smaller branches, and which are twigs. When you encounter media messages, you can compare the information in those messages to the information you have in your existing knowledge structures. If you already have that information, you do not need to re-learn it. If you do not have that new information but it is relevant to a central branch of knowledge in your structures, then it becomes important that you learn it. If the new information is relevant only at the "twig" level, then you must decide whether you want (and have time) to grow that part of your knowledge structure. If so,

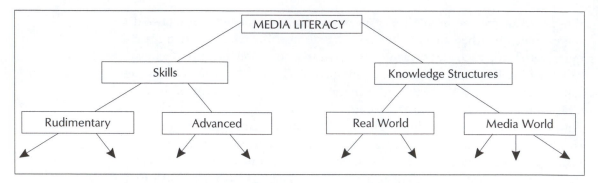

Figure 4.3. Knowledge Structure of Media Literacy

you will need to learn it. But that type of learning will be more efficient, because you already have the context for that bit of information, so you know where and how that new information fits into the overall picture. If instead you do not have time to learn this new "twig"-level information, you know that you still have a firm foundation of learning and that ignoring this new information is not going to harm your knowledge structure much. If you do not have a knowledge structure for some new information, then you have no basis for judging whether this new information is of central importance or whether it is relatively trivial. Making judgments of this nature is the mark of an educated person. It is not how much information you have memorized that makes you educated. Being educated means that you have "maps to the world" and you can use these maps to keep yourself oriented to what is most important, to make good judgments about new information, and to know where to go to get additional accurate information. If you keep your focus on building these maps—these knowledge structures—you will be able to rise above the tidal wave of information that is threatening to drown us in facts and images. Knowledge resides in the structure, not in the information.

The stronger your knowledge structures, the more literate you are. To be media literate, you need to have an in-depth understanding of the media across a broad range of topics, such as production techniques, narrative structures, character patterns, and thematic indicators; knowledge about industry practices, motivations, and perceptions of audiences; knowledge about the full range of media effects; and a self-monitoring awareness about the variety of ways the human mind can process information from the media.

Let's look at an example of a graphic of a knowledge structure (see Figure 4.3). This shows the analysis of the concept Media Literacy. Notice that we begin by breaking the concept down into the two major components of Skills and Knowledge Structures. This is Level 1 in the analysis. Skills can be sub-divided into Rudimentary and Advanced; Knowledge Structures can be sub-divided into Real World and Media World. These four components are Level 2. But notice that it matters where the four Level 2 components are located. For example, it would be incorrect to put Rudimentary under Knowledge Structures, even if it were still at Level 2; Rudimentary not only belongs on Level 2, it belongs under Skills. Location matters.

Notice that this graphic goes down to Level 2. Does that mean there are only two levels of analysis in the Media Literacy concept? The answer is no. There are many more levels. The information that can be used to continue this analysis is contained in the following chapters of this book. Each chapter deals with one of the Level 3 concepts under the Knowledge Structure branch. Keep this graphic in mind as you work through each of the following chapters. Also, each of the following chapters begins with a graphic to show the piece of the Media Literacy knowledge structure that will be examined in that chapter.

As you work your way through this book, stay focused on how this graphic map is growing. If you do this, you will end the course with a clear picture of all the important information and how it all fits together. Then when the course is over, you can use this structure to help you efficiently acquire additional information in all of your future readings and study about the media.

Remember, the more actively you read this book and the more consciously you expose yourself to the media, the more you will perceive. The more you perceive, the more you will be able to elaborate and strengthen your knowledge structures. And the better your knowledge structures, the more media literate you will become.

CONCLUSION ■■

Because the media make so many messages so easily accessible, they give us the impression that we are seeing the world in all its variety. And the more exposure we have, the more we begin to feel in a superior position to understand how the world operates. But are we really learning things of value? Knowing all the words and tunes of a genre of popular music does not translate into expertise about the recording industry or radio broadcasting. Knowing a lot about current events presented by news organizations does not necessarily mean we know what the problems in the world are—or how to deal with them.

Our constant exposure to media messages influences the way we think about the world and ourselves. It influences our beliefs about crime, education, religion, families, and the world in general. If our exposure is mostly passive, then the mundane details in those messages exert their effects without our awareness. We are limited to using this base of misleading and inaccurate images to infer our beliefs about the world. Thus many of our beliefs will be faulty.

Cognitive psychologists have moved beyond simple models and now tend to favor schemas as an explanation for how humans construct meaning from complex messages. People rely on schemas to help them identify symbols and make sense of them. There are many different kinds of schemas for social situations: self, person, role, and event. Also, there are schemas for dealing with media: narrative, character, setting, and thematic. Most of us are not very systematic or thorough in processing information about our world, because we are not always motivated to achieve accuracy. Many times we are more interested in efficiency. Knowledge structures are superior to schemas, because they are more formal; they are stronger maps that we can use in making meaning from our experiences, both from the media world as well as the real world.

▊▊ FURTHER READING

Fiske, S. T., & Taylor, S. E. (1991). *Social cognition* (2nd ed.). New York: McGraw-Hill. (718 pages with index)

This is an excellent book that clearly lays out the cognitive perspective about how the human mind works in social situations. It also serves as a strong reference source, with more than 140 pages of references.

Shenk, D. (1997). *Data smog: Surviving the information glut.* San Francisco: HarperEdge. (250 pages with references and index)

In this trade book, David Shenk argues that we are drowning in information. All this information has not made us more informed; instead, it has made us retreat into niches of interest to try to keep up with the information in that small area. This fragments society and damages the idea of an informed electorate that is needed to make a democratic form of government work. He presents 13 laws of data smog; these include: "Information, once rare and cherished like caviar, is now plentiful and taken for granted like potatoes," and "Too many experts spoil the clarity."

EXERCISE 4.1

Examining How People Make Sense of Their World

I. Test your understanding of models of thinking

1. Next time you are in a conversation with a friend and your friend expresses an opinion, try expressing an opposite opinion. Observe what your friend does. Does your friend ignore the disagreement? Or does your friend try to put things back into balance by either (a) trying to change your mind or (b) changing his or her mind to agree with you?

    How important was that opinion to your friend? Do you think that importance of attitude was related to how your friend reacted? Try this with several friends. Do their reactions vary across different types of people?

2. Find several topics on which your friend does not have an opinion. On one topic, try to get your friend to form an opinion by giving him or her lots of information and a systematic argument —thus forcing the use of the central route to processing information. Later, on another topic, try to get your friend to form an opinion by providing one anecdote or an emotional reason. Several days later, get your friend into a conversation about these topics and see if he or she has an opinion. If so, can your friend remember where the opinion started?

II. Become more sensitive to the way you use schemas

1. Watch an episode of a situation comedy. Take notes about schemas:

    Narrative: Write down the important events in the plot.

    Characters: List each of the important characters and describe each in one sentence.

    Setting: List two things that typically happen in that setting; then list two things that would never happen in that setting.

    Thematic: What is the moral of this story?

    Rhetorical: What is the storyteller's purpose? Is it to provide you with information, to entertain you, or a combination? If the purpose is entertainment, what kind of entertainment?

2. Now watch episodes of several other situation comedies. If you watched *Friends* above, watch something totally different, such as *The Simpsons* or *Drew Carey*. Again, make notes on schemas.

3. How many schematic elements can you list that are common to all of these situation comedies? What elements make the comedies different from one another?

4. Choose another genre (such as action/adventure, comedy cartoons, real-life crime, family drama, etc.) and repeat the exercise.

PART II

KNOWLEDGE STRUCTURES
OF MEDIA CONTENT

CHAPTER

5

Key Idea: News is not a reflection of actual events; it is a construction by news workers who are subjected to many influences and constraints.

What Is News?

In the United States we appear to revere the press. For example, we often quote Thomas Jefferson, who said in 1787, "Were it left to me to decide whether we should have a government without newspapers or newspapers without a government, I should not hesitate a moment to prefer the latter" (quoted in Jensen, 1997, p. 11).

However, we also like to criticize the press. Even Thomas Jefferson, himself, delivered one of the most strident criticisms of the press after he became President and had to deal with it on a daily basis. In 1807 he said, "The man who never looks into a newspaper is better informed than he who reads them" (quoted in Jensen, 1997, p. 11). Jefferson took the position that "he who knows nothing is nearer to truth than he whose mind is filled with falsehoods and errors" (p. 11). Thus Jefferson was arguing that nothing printed in a newspaper could be believed. A few years later, Jefferson added, "I read but one newspaper and that . . . more for its advertisements than its news" (quoted in Jensen, 1997, p. 11).

Jefferson's ambivalence toward the press is reflected in public opinion today. When Americans were asked in a recent survey about their opinion of the press, 46% said they had a favorable opinion, and 45% said they held an unfavorable opinion (Luntz, 2000). This opinion split is also in evidence in exposure patterns. Only about 45% of American adults read newspapers regularly, and only 61% watch television news ("Fewer Adults Reading Newspapers, Watching News," 1995). Furthermore, there is reason to believe that news exposure will continue to decline. A 1998 survey reports that only 38% of young people had read the newspaper the day before, while 69% of seniors had done so (Pew Research Center, 1998). If this trend continues with the younger generation of news avoiders replacing the older generation of news seekers, the rates of news exposure in the general population will continue to drop.

Why are younger people more likely to avoid seeking out news? The answer seems to lie in the larger trend of people feeling overwhelmed by information. We cannot process it all. We feel fatigued and look for ways to reduce the exposure. With news, people do not want to seek out information unless it is relevant to them. For example, Chew and Palmer (1994) conducted a survey and found that people's need for information varies according to how relevant the issue is to them. With low-relevance issues, people are primarily concerned about information about how that issue would affect them. With high-relevance issues, people are more interested in gathering information that will help them form a good opinion, so they want information covering different viewpoints and they want to hear from experts.

Also, many people feel fatigued with bad news. In surveys, most people will complain about the amount of bad or negative news and ask for more good news, saying that is what they prefer (Galician, 1986). They say that bad news is not necessarily more interesting. But the news organizations continue to feature bad news predominantly (such as crime, scandal, and controversy).

The reasons cited above—too much news is irrelevant or bad—are easy explanations for why people are increasing their avoidance of news. But there are deeper, more fundamental problems. When we analyze the situation, we can see that the deeper problem is that people do not really understand what news is. The public believes some myths about the press, and when the expectations that follow from these myths are not met in news stories, the public becomes disappointed and turns off the news. This chapter presents an analysis of two of these myths. The first myth is that news is what actually happened. The second myth is that journalists are objective.

■■ IJ NEWJ A REFLECTION OR A CONJTRUCTION?

If you were to ask someone how the news differs from entertainment programming, most people would say that entertainment is fiction and therefore made up by writers but news presents actual events that happened. We think of news as a reflection of the events of the day, that is, the media are merely holding a mirror up to reality.

But when we take a closer look at the news, it becomes clear that news does not *reflect* reality. Instead, it is a construction by journalists. News coverage is triggered, of course, by actual occurrences. But what we see presented as news by the media are not the events themselves. Instead, the media present us with stories *about* the events, and those stories are constructed by journalists who are influenced by processes and constraints much like fiction writers are.

Construction Process

The construction process essentially encompasses three tasks: (a) selecting what gets covered, (b) deciding what becomes the focus of the story, and (c) determining how the story gets told.

As for what gets covered, only a minute sliver of human activity is selected from all the possible stories that could be reported. Think of all the things you did last week. How many of those events were covered as news? Probably none. Why? Journalists don't think of you as a newsworthy person. Even though your week was filled with all sorts of things that interested and even excited you greatly, none of these things met journalists' particular definition of newsworthiness.

Deciding what becomes the focus of the story is known as looking for the hook. Journalists then write the lead (the first sentence) to set the hook. The hook is what pulls people into the story. Any event has many different elements that could be chosen as the hook of the story. For example, let's say a journalist covers a speech by a candidate running for office. The journalist could decide that the story should be: (a) the candidate gave a speech; or (b) the candidate looked tired giving the speech because of a hectic day of campaigning; or (c) the candidate is trying to make up ground in the polls where she now trails her opponent by only 5%; or (d) the candidate introduced a new position in her speech; or (e) the candidate's new position is at odds with the leaders of her party, and some controversy might be brewing. These are only five of many alternative ways a journalist could decide what the focus of the story should be. Each of these would result in a very different story about what happened. And each story would require a different hook to get people interested.

The journalist also decides how the story should be told. Following through with the example of the political candidate's speech, let's say that the journalist chose option (e) as the hook: the candidate's new position is at odds with the leaders of her party, and some controversy might be brewing. The TV journalist can decide to talk about the speech or to show the candidate laying out the controversial position. There could be reaction shots of audience members—either happy or shocked. The journalist could interview people in the audience, or party leaders, or the candidate's handlers, or the opposition candidate for a reaction. These are all choices the journalist must make. Then after these elements are selected, the journalist must decide how to sequence them in the story.

Thus, news is not something that happens; instead, news is what gets presented. We almost never see news events as they happen. Instead we are shown the media's manufactured construction of a very small set of selected events.

Influences and Constraints

What influences the construction process? There are many factors, such as commercialism, media routines, organizational forces, code of professionalism, resource constraints, advertisers, regulations, ideology, use of sources, deviance, and geographical focus.

Commercialism. Arguably the strongest influence on the construction of news is its commercial nature (Altheide, 1976). News organizations are businesses that compete with each other for audiences and advertisers. Success is often viewed in terms of which competitor appeals to the largest audience and thereby generates the greatest revenue from advertisers.

For most television stations, news is a moneymaker. Almost all broadcast television stations have newscasts, and most of these have grown in length over time. In 1950, the television networks presented 15 minutes of evening news, and local stations presented another 15 minutes. In early 1960, the networks increased to 30 minutes and so did local news. In the 1980s, many local stations went to an hour of evening news, realizing that it was a moneymaker for a station. Once a news department has a good crew, it doesn't cost the station any more to go from a 30-minute to a 60-minute newscast, and it gives the station the potential to double its revenues by selling twice as many minutes of advertising.

The shift to commercialism is seen most clearly in the way some news programs are themselves turning into ads. For example, Kaniss (1996) criticized news shows in the Philadelphia area by pointing out that during the November 1996 sweeps month the local CBS affiliate on its evening news show ran nine stories of the Titanic, a ship that sank 84 years ago but was the subject of a CBS miniseries. The local ABC affiliate frequently runs news stories about Mickey Mouse; the ABC network is owned by Disney. Local affiliates also frequently run news stories about stars on their network series, and they often run soft news stories on topics of made-for-TV movies appearing that night on the network.

Some advertisers pressure the media, and some are more successful than others. For example, compare the performance of two drug companies. In 1981, 124 people died from taking Oraflex, which was an anti-arthritis pill marketed by the Eli Lily drug company. The Food and Drug Administration had allowed the drug to go on sale in April 1981 despite an FDA investigator warning that Eli

Lily had withheld data on the dangerous side effects of the drug. But this received almost no coverage.

In October 1982, several people died from taking Tylenol capsules that were poisoned on store shelves, and this event received major continuing coverage. The Johnson & Johnson Company appeared to be less skilled at controlling stories about the poisoning of Tylenol capsules than was the Eli Lily Company at controlling the situation about Oraflex.

Lee and Solomon (1990) argue that there has been a major push to make news organizations more profitable. Conglomerates buy up news outlets and impose strong economic goals. This compromises editorial decisions. For example, the harmfulness of tobacco has been greatly under-reported because tobacco advertising is so important to the survival of many magazines and newspapers. Television has also been affected, even though no tobacco products have been advertised on television for three decades. The tobacco companies are large conglomerates with many products. A television news show that offends a tobacco company is in danger of losing advertising of other brands controlled by the large tobacco conglomerates.

Marketing Perspective. The pressures of commercialism set up a conflict between two perspectives on news. One of these is the professional responsibility perspective. This is where journalists regard themselves as having a responsibility to inform the public about the most important and significant events of the day so that people can use the information to make better decisions as citizens of that society. For example, journalists operating within this perspective would strive to provide in-depth information on candidates and issues during a campaign so that voters can make more-informed decisions. These journalists would also try to present clear explanations about economic conditions, implications of government policies, the patterns of changes in society, and other broadscale issues so the public is exposed to the context behind individual issues.

In contrast, there is the marketing perspective. This is where news workers pay careful attention to what kinds of stories and presentation formats generate the largest audience. For example, journalists operating under the marketing perspective are more likely to present stories that grab the attention of large audiences by highlighting the unusual so as to shock people.

Marketers must be careful not to alienate potential audience members. For this reason, newspapers have become less political, even to the point of rarely endorsing candidates. For example, in 1940 about 87% of the country's newspapers clearly endorsed one of the candidates for President; by 1992, the figure had dropped to 37%. Newspaper managers fear an endorsement would alienate many readers and would therefore cost the newspaper revenue. Also, radio and television stations almost never endorse candidates.

The influence of commercialism has moved the news away from the professional responsibility perspective and placed it squarely under the marketing perspective. As a result, there is a growing commitment to entertainment in order to attract large audiences. Postman and Powers (1992) illustrate this when they argue that what television news says it is presenting and what it actually presents are two different things. Journalists want us to believe that they are presenting the important happenings of the day that all citizens should know. But what they really present are superficial constructions designed to attract large audiences for advertisers. As a result, the news has attempted to become more entertaining. The stories are shorter. There is more focus on personalities than on leaders. There is more focus on celebrities than on people of substance. And there is more focus on gossip than on news.

This ambivalence between social responsibility and entertainment is in evidence in public opinion polls. For example, when Americans were asked whether television stations should broadcast live coverage of a hostage being held at gunpoint, only 22% said yes. But when those same people were asked whether they would watch such coverage, 59% said yes (Luntz, 2000). Most of us know that it is not responsible for certain events to be broadcast. However, we are attracted to such events and would watch if we could. The press knows what we want. If the press has accepted the business goal espoused in the marketing perspective, then it must give the public what it wants.

Story Formulas. Journalists are very busy people. Their days are filled with an incredible amount of detail that must be processed on short deadlines. A reporter at a daily newspaper may have to write several dozen stories every day. Do reporters spend hours thinking about the best way to communicate the essence of each story, then several more hours polishing up draft after draft? Rarely do they have this kind of time. Instead, they must assemble the facts of a story in a matter of minutes, then move on to the next story. How do they do this? They use formulas (Fishman, 1980).

Formulas are the procedures journalists soon learn as shortcuts to help them quickly select and write stories. The most popular information gathering formula is the series of questions: Who? What? Where? When? Why? Journalists confronted with a new story begin by asking these questions.

The most popular news writing formula is the inverted pyramid. This formula tells the journalist to put the most important information at the beginning of the story, then add in the next most important set of information. Journalists move down a list of information they have ranked according to importance until all the information is in the story. This formula was developed in the early days of the telegraph when journalists in the field sent their stories to their newspapers over telegraph lines. If the line went dead halfway through the story, the journalist would know that at least the most important information got through. We are way past the days of dependence on unreliable telegraph lines, but the formula still has value because editors will cut stories if they are too long. For example, a newspaper editor might want to use a reporter's 12-inch story but have room for only 8 inches, so the editor will typically cut off the last 4 inches.

Another popular formula is to use a narrative to tell a story in an entertainment format. Journalists who use this formula will begin the story with a heated conflict, a gruesome description, or an unusual quote—all designed to grab the reader's attention in an emotional manner. Then the writer moves through the plot, much like a fictional storyteller would.

Perhaps the most popular formula for telling stories in the news is what I call Simplified Extended Conflict (SEC). When covering a story, journalists look for some angle of conflict that appears very simple. They believe that a story that has no conflict will not grab the audience's attention, but if the conflict is complex, the story will not hold the audience's attention. Furthermore, if the story can be played out over several days—or longer—so much the better. A good example of SEC is in political elections. These always involve conflict between the candidates, and the race goes on for weeks or months. If the conflict is focused on the finer points of complex issues, the story will not appeal to the audience. Therefore journalists look for a simple form of conflict and that is best seen in the "horse race" metaphor. Political coverage is much more about who is winning and whether the challenger can close the gap and come from behind than it is about issues. Other examples of SEC are O.J. against the court system, the United States against Iraq, various crusaders against Congress, the little guy against city hall, the forces of pro-life against the forces of pro-choice. The press can present the conflict in these situations in a very simple manner and keep the conflict going for a long time. It does this by polarizing the people or issues in the conflict.

When the press has a big story that will consume news space for several weeks or months, it has an opportunity to develop the nuances of the parties in the conflict more fully. With political issues, the press could choose to tell the story of how competing interests have some common ground and how compromise is crafted. With criminal trials, the press could choose to tell the story of how humans can go astray and what justice means in each situation. Instead, the press rarely digs deeply into a story—illuminating its complexity and educating the public about the underlying nature of the problem. The press stays with the surface information—polishing it to a more glitzy finish to make it more attractive to passive viewers.

The use of these formulas is widespread across journalism, so that in a given locale, if a story is covered by one news vehicle, it is likely to be covered by them all. With minor variations, the information in (and structure of) a story in a small newspaper is the same as a story in a very large newspaper or on the television or radio news.

Resource Constraints. While the news gathering departments of the major broadcast networks and the major daily newspapers are very large and have considerable resources, there are limits. There are never enough resources to be able to cover all the events that happen in a given day. Choices must be made because of these constraints of time, space, talent, and place (Tuchman, 1978). As for time, organizations create deadlines and rhythms of work in order to be able to produce their product on time every day. All media vehicles have space limitations, either in the form of column inches in print vehicles or seconds in radio and television. Talent is also a constraint, with the varying abilities of journalists to ferret out information, organize it, and present it clearly. As for place, certain institutions are appropriate locations for news while others are not. Look at your local newspaper and notice that events happening in certain places—such as police stations, city hall, school boards, athletic fields, and so on—have a very good chance of being covered.

Organizational Forces. The two primary components of this constraint are organizational structure and ownership/control.

Organizational structures vary. Small companies are more flexible and entrepreneurial. They search out new needs and quickly adapt. In contrast, large companies are compartmentalized with each division having a special function and its own staff of technical people. Large bureaucracies are more resistant to change.

Ownership patterns can also influence the content. For example, the *New York Times* has remained in the hands of one family for more than 100 years. There is very high potential for the members of that family to have a strong influence on that newspaper. In contrast, other newspapers might be owned by a large media conglomerate with thousands of shareholders, each with a very low potential for influence.

While there are some examples of newspapers changing their editorial stance because of pressure from an owner, these are rare. What is more typical is a strong pressure from owners that the newspaper make a larger profit. This reinforces the marketing perspective.

Use of Sources. News is shaped by the sources of information used to construct the stories. The dominant news sources are public information officers in businesses and government units. Most companies and institutions have public relations departments whose sole job is to establish themselves as experts and feed information to journalists. Once a person is established as an expert source, he or she is called by journalists when they want an expert opinion on that particular issue.

How do journalists know who is an expert? Most journalists don't. They lack the experience or education to evaluate the credentials of many people who could serve as experts in news stories, so they chose people not on the basis of knowledge, but on their *appearance* of expertise and their willingness to tell a good story. This point is illustrated by Steele (1995), who examined how television news organization selected and used expert sources to interpret the news. She found that news organizations chose expert sources that reflected journalists' understanding of expertise. Experts were selected according to how well their specialized knowledge conformed with television's "operational bias," which places its emphasis on players, policies, and predictions of what will happen next. Steele concluded that these processes undermine the ideals of balance and objectivity as well as severely limit how news is framed.

Two journalists, Lee and Solomon, wrote a book titled *Unreliable Sources: A Guide to Detecting Bias in New Media* (1990) in which they expressed strong criticism of American journalistic practices. Lee and Solomon pointed out that all the major news organizations use the same sources, many of whom are unnamed, so the same types of stories always get covered. Over time the journalists become close friends of the sources, and the journalists stop looking for other points of view. A lot of the news comes sanitized from public relations firms, so the spin meisters influence how stories are covered as well as what is emphasized. Many experts who are quoted are employed by think tanks, which are really public relations shops funded by an organization with a particular point of view.

The military establishment has always had sophisticated public relations. In the 1960s, when the Soviet Union had 100 long-range missiles and the United States had 2,000, the Pentagon convinced the American people that the United States lagged far behind Russia in weapons, and the public ended up supporting greater defense budgets. During the Reagan administration, the Pentagon had an annual public relations budget of $100 million and employed 3,000 staff people. In the 1980s this public relations staff was used to stigmatize Muammar Qaddafi, then Saddam Hussein.

Lee and Solomon also argue that sources have an incestual relationship with journalists. They point out that many journalists go into government and serve as press secretaries or public information officers. Also, press secretaries go into journalism. Over time, the two professions converge, and this revolving door homogenizes the coverage.

Deviance. The media are interested in presenting things that deviate from the normal (Shoemaker, 1987; Shoemaker, Danielian, & Brendlinger, 1991). Deviance covers those things that are out of the ordinary, and the more they differ from reality, the more they are considered newsworthy.

With news coverage, there are two types of deviance (Shoemaker & Reese, 1996). One type is statistical deviance, which "causes things that are unusual (either good or bad) to be considered more newsworthy than commonplace events" (p. 47). For example, if a woman gives birth to four children over a decade, that is not news. But if a woman gives birth to quadruplets, that is unusual and therefore is newsworthy. The statistical probability of giving birth to four children at once is very low, so this gets covered.

The other type of deviance is normative, which refers to ideas or events that break norms or laws. For example, if a person goes to a bank and puts money into his account, that is normal and will not get covered. But if a person goes to a bank and withdraws money from other people's accounts at gunpoint, that breaks the law and gets covered. Thus the media like to focus on crime, because it happens outside the norm. Within crime news, there is a preference for violent action (Antunes & Hurley, 1977; Windhauser, Seiter, & Winfree, 1990) and crimes against people (Ammons, Dimmick, & Pilotta, 1982; Fedler & Jordan, 1982), which are rarer and more deviant than property crimes. Also, deaths due to violence are more likely to be reported than deaths due to disease (Combs & Slovic, 1979). This over-reporting of crime is also found in other countries, such as England (Roshier, 1981).

The irony is that we depend on the news to tell us what the norm is. In order to be well informed, we need to know how things typically work, what is likely to happen tomorrow, and what the relative risks of harm are. But the news media focus our attention on the deviant. Because we see so many portrayals of the deviant, we come to believe that the deviant is the norm.

Geographical Focus. Every day, important things are happening all over the world. But the American news media cover events in this country the most. There is also a fair amount of coverage of industrialized countries, but little coverage of Third World countries. For example, Larson (1983) examined international news coverage on television and found that events in the Third World were covered less than events in industrialized countries and that what coverage there was about the Third World was crises oriented (Larson, 1983). The same pattern was found by Potter (1987b) in newspapers. Kim and Barnett (1996) show clearly that news flow of information around the world is dominated by the Western industrialized countries at the center. This power is associated with the degree of economic development.

Even within this country, the news coverage is not balanced geographically. In the United States, events occurring in the Northeast and the Pacific Coast are covered the most, while events happening in the rest of the country are under-covered in the national news services (Graber, 1988).

News Perspective

All of the above influences shape how journalists select which events they'll cover and how they construct their stories. When we take all these influences and constraints together, we call this the "news perspective." This news perspective is not something that is consciously imposed by the owners of the media. Instead, it grows naturally out of the practices of the status quo and leads us to ask: How could the news be any other way?

People who are hired as journalists become socialized by this news perspective as they learn their jobs. The news perspective is so pervasive and common among journalists that it is taken for granted. It is also generally shared by journalists in all kinds of vehicles and all media, as evidenced in several research studies. One of these studies found that there is a considerable overlap in news stories at local television stations in the same market. Davie and Lee (1993) found that 56% of stories were the same, with network sources having more similarity. The non-overlapping stories were more likely to be from local sources. Also, Davie and Lee (1995) analyzed local television newscasts and found that there is a distinct preference for sensational stories that feature acts of sex and violence and are easy to explain. There was little differentiation among the stations, leading to the conclusion that the news sense of all local producers is almost the same.

Hudson (1992) also arrived at the same conclusion as a result of an experiment on more than 100 news directors and executive producers from all sizes of markets all over the country. He showed them a violent incident and asked them how much of the incident they would show in a newscast. Editors exhibited the same news judgment in all sizes of markets and across all kinds of stations.

Values. A set of values is at the base of the news perspective. Shoemaker and Reese (1996) argue that journalists exhibit eight mainstream American values. Notice how similar these are to your own values.

- individualism—people who do things their own way, even against powerful odds
- moderatism—fanaticism of any kind arouses skepticism
- social order—peace and order are valued; people who deviate from this are labeled wrongdoers
- leadership—there are high expectations of leaders; those who are found to be weak, dishonest, or immoral are investigated
- ethnocentrism—other countries are judged by American standards
- altruistic democracy—there is a democratic ideal of efficient government and participation by all citizens; deviations from this are news

- responsible capitalism—fair competition without unreasonable profits or exploitation of workers
- small town pastoralism—small towns and rural areas are the font of virtue

Advantage. The advantage of the news perspective is that it helps journalists simplify and organize the overwhelming amount of material they must sift through on a daily basis. The use of this perspective can be seen in "the routines of news detection, interpretation, investigation, and assembly" (Fishman, 1980, p. 18). Because this news perspective is shared among news workers of all levels (reporters and editors) as well as across different media, it acts as a kind of code of professionalism as it serves to legitimate the "intertwining of political and corporate activity" (Tuchman, 1978, p. 14).

Disadvantage. The disadvantage of the news perspective is that its limited vision results in a very narrow view of what is considered news. It also leads journalists to treat those selected stories superficially, thus distorting reality. Altheide (1976) argues that "the organizational, practical, and other mundane features of news work promote a way of looking at events which fundamentally distorts them. . . . In order to make events news, news reporting decontextualizes and thereby changes them" (pp. 24-25).

Changes. The news perspective has changed over time from social responsibility to marketing. The perspective of many editors used to be that they were charged with selecting what is important and presenting this information to their readers. They then used the criteria of significance, proximity, and timeliness. These are the classic journalism school criteria. The purpose behind this social responsibility perspective is to build an informed public, which is essential in a democracy.

With increasing competition among news vehicles over the past two decades, the news perspective has been changing to one of marketing. Now the primary job of editors is to attract and maintain as large an audience as possible. So editors are charged with guessing what readers would find most arousing and entertaining. The most important news criteria now are conflict, appeal to emotions, and visualization. Given these criteria, it is not surprising that the news has become much more sensational. To illustrate this, Slattery and Hakanen (1994) compared local television newscasts from 1976 and 1992. They found a dramatic decline in hard news coverage of the government, from 64% down to 19%, while coverage of human interest stories and sensationalism climbed from 10% to 41%. During the same time, there was a shrinkage in the news hole of the late evening newscasts from 13 minutes to 11.8 minutes, thus allowing more time for advertising. This is the classic pattern of the marketing perspective.

CAN JOURNALISTS BE OBJECTIVE? ▪▪

There is a strong ethic of objectivity in journalism (Parenti, 1986). But what does this mean? Editors may be objective in the sense that they don't want to publish a "slanted" story. However, they have no choice but to use their personal judgment in deciding which stories get assigned, which stories get written by the best reporters, which stories get edited down, and which stories get printed on the front page.

It is difficult to understand what journalists mean by objectivity. This can be illustrated by the following story. In the summer of 1995, Allan Little, a veteran foreign correspondent for the British Broadcasting Corp., was covering the war in Bosnia. One day, as Serbian soldiers approached a Muslim town, he wanted to tell the story of an impending massacre but his editor told him that such reporting would not be objective. Little was told to report just the facts of the day with no background and no interpretation, which he did. Although he knew that it was the practice of the Serbian forces to slaughter all the Muslims they could and that the town was unprotected and would soon fall into Serbian hands, he could not put that context into his news story. On July 11, the Serbian soldiers captured the town, rounded up the thousands of men and boys in the village, and killed them all. Little says, "I still to this day feel sullied and tainted that I pulled my punches on that one" (Randolph, 1997). The accurate or complete coverage would have been to report the event in the context of Serbian goals and past behaviors during the war. In that way viewers could see the true horror of the aggression and get a much better understanding of what was taking place. Instead, in order to preserve an editor's sense of "objectivity," Little was limited to reporting only the details of how far the Serbian army advanced each day. Which way of reporting would have been more meaningful to readers? In situations such as this one, a journalist and his editor are both trying to be what they think of as "objective," but they mean very different things.

As we have seen from the first section of this chapter, all journalists must make many decisions about news coverage, and while they use a news perspective to make these decisions, this perspective is not a formal list of steps to follow. Each journalist interprets the news perspective through his or her personal perspective. So the goal of objectivity is unattainable. If we hold the work of journalists up to the criterion of objectivity, we will always find serious fault. Therefore we need to shift to more reasonable and useful criteria—such as balance and context.

Balance

Many journalists prefer the criterion of balance, which is the recognition that when an event has more than one side to it, journalists should present more than one viewpoint. With some stories there are many sides. In stories of simple conflicts, there are usually two sharply differing sides. To be fair, journalists present both sides and try to do so with equal weight.

Are news stories balanced? Fico and Soffin (1995) looked at balance in newspaper coverage of controversial issues such as abortion, condoms in schools, and various government bills. Balance was assessed by examining whether both sides of an issue were illuminated in terms of sources interviewed for both sides, whether assertions for both sides were in the headline, first paragraph, and graphics. They found that 48% of stories analyzed were one-sided, that is, the other side was not covered at all. They counted the number of story elements that illuminated the different sides of each issue and found that on average one side received three more elements compared to the other side—therefore the average story was not balanced. Only 7% of stories were completely balanced. The authors concluded that professional capability and/or ethical self-consciousness are lacking in many journalists.

If journalists are unable to provide us with balance, then we must construct it for ourselves if we are to be media literate. This means we must seek out information from all sides of an issue. But how can we know how many sides there are? We can't. Instead we must develop a skepticism about all issues so as never to be confident we have all the information from all sides.

Bias in Ignoring Important Stories. There are problems about what gets covered. Jensen (1997) began Project Censored in 1976 to monitor news coverage in the mass media and determine whether there were major events/issues that were not being covered. He says,

> The essential issue raised by the Project is the failure of the mass media to provide people with all the information they need to make informed decisions concerning their own lives. Only an informed electorate can achieve a fair and just society. The public has a right to know about issues that affect it and the press has a responsibility to keep the public well-informed about those issues. (p. 10)

Why is there this self-censorship? Jensen (1997) says,

> The media are more concerned with their next quarterly profit than with the unique opportunity given them by the First Amendment. And most journalists are more concerned with keeping their jobs and increasing their income than with fighting for the public's right to know. (p. 12)

America's mainstream mass media basically serve three segments of society today—the wealthy, politicians, and the sports-minded. The news media have done an exceptional job providing full and, on the whole, reliable information to those who are involved in or follow the stock market and to those who are involved in or follow politics and to those who are involved in or follow sports. (p. 12)

Jensen (1997) says that there is no conscious conspiracy among journalists to censor the news:

News is too diverse, fast-breaking, and unpredictable to be controlled by some sinister conservative eastern establishment media cabal. However, there is a congruence of attitudes and interests on the part of the owners and managers of mass media organizations. That non-conspiracy conspiracy, when combined with a variety of other factors, leads to the systematic failure of the news media to inform the public. While it is not an overt form of censorship, such as the kind we observe in some other societies, it is nonetheless real and often equally as dangerous to the public's well being. (pp. 14-15)

Jensen says some of these other factors are story structure, simplicity, the age of the story, and whether other journalists—especially in the elite newspapers— cover it, and fear of libel suits.

In his 1997 book *Censored: The News That Didn't Make the News—and Why*, Jensen describes many seemingly important stories that did not receive much, if any, coverage by the news media. For example, in 1985, the National Institute for Occupational Safety and Health (NIOSH) found that over 240,000 people were in danger in 258 work sites around the country. It is the purpose of NIOSH to monitor safety in the workplace and to inform workers when they are in serious danger of contracting life threatening diseases from exposure to chemicals and other hazardous materials in the workplace. By 1995, NIOSH had informed less than 30% of the people whom it had found to be in daily danger a decade earlier. Thus NIOSH knew that 170,000 people were working in highly risky environments every day and let 10 years go by without telling them. The news media ignored this government negligence for more than a decade.

When a critic of the news is bothered that a certain story is not covered, an editor can always say: "We can't cover everything; I must draw the line somewhere." But sometimes this constraint excuse is used to cover up a decision that can be traced to the editor's news perspective—not to resource limitations. In this case, the critic is not arguing that every happening should be covered; instead, the criticism is a challenge to the editor's judgment in ranking the importance of particular stories.

This lack-of-resources argument becomes even more spurious when we see how much overlap there is in allocating these "limited" resources. For example, the Associated Press news service has more than 100 reporters in Washington, D.C., alone—and all of them are trying to develop the same contacts at the White House. In the presidential nominating conventions in 1996, there were more than 16,000 news people covering those non-events, that is, everyone knew who was going to be nominated well before the conventions.

The major news organizations all had budgets greatly expand over decades without providing an expansion in the amount of news. For example, the annual budget of the ABC network news department grew from about $1 million in the early 1960s to more than $300 million in the late 1980s, but with that enormous growth in resources, the amount and/or quality of news did not increase 300 times during that period.

Also, CNN and all-news radio shows have significant budgets and a very large newshole. But the number of stories they cover is very small compared to the space they have. Their news perspective has not allowed them to provide a greatly expanded breadth of stories. Instead, CNN maintains a narrow vision of what is important and continually presents a small set of stories over and over all day.

Bias Toward Particular Political Views. Those who follow the media closely often complain about a liberal or a conservative news bias, or they say that there is too much negativism. In an analysis of Gallup public opinion data, it was found that more than half of Americans felt that the media were influenced by advertisers, business corporations, Democrats, the federal government, liberals, the military, and Republicans (Becker, Kosicki, & Jones, 1992). The newspaper industry itself finds the same thing in its own surveys. For example, a survey by the American Society of Newspaper Editors found that a majority of people believe the media have political leanings (Jeffres, 1994).

What is interesting is that conservatives feel that the media have a generally liberal leaning, while liberals feel that the media are conservative. Conservatives complain that most news reporters are liberal in their own views, and these liberal journalists show their bias when they present their stories. In contrast, liberals feel that conservative commentators have too much power and have redefined the American agenda to stigmatize liberals.

In the early days of this country, most newspapers were founded by men who had a clear political viewpoint that they wanted to promote. Towns had multiple newspapers, each one appealing to a different niche of political thinking. Newspapers were biased politically, but the bias was clearly labeled. But by the late 1800s, newspapers had shifted from a political focus to a business focus with the goal of building the largest circulation. In order to do this, newspapers lost their political edge so as to avoid offending any potential readers. This model still underlies the mass media. Decisions are made to build audiences, not to espouse a political point of view. Sometimes arguing for a particular political point of view can be used as a tool to build an audience, but these instances are found within only those media with a niche orientation. Instead, the large national news organizations such as the television networks and the large newspapers try to present both sides of any political issue so as to appear objective and balanced.

It is important to be sensitive to whether particular news vehicles present a liberal or a conservative bias. But it is far more important to be sensitive to the broader bias underlying all news vehicles—that is, the bias of commercialism, entertainment, and superficiality. If all we do is debate the liberal-conservative issue when it comes to news bias, we are in danger of missing the larger picture: The news media are providing us with a worldview that not only determines what we think about (as in agenda setting), but also determines what we think, how we think, and who we are.

Context

The so-called new journalists take the perspective that the facts do not convey the importance of any story—readers need context. Without context the story has ambiguous meaning. For example, a story could report that Mr. Jones was arrested for murder this morning. That fact can convey very different meanings if we vary the context. Let's say that the journalist put in some historical context stating that Mr. Jones had murdered several people a decade ago, had been caught, convicted, served time in prison, but was recently let go because of a ruling of an inexperienced and liberal judge. In contrast, let's say that Mr. Jones, one of the candidates running for mayor, was arrested despite the fact that police had in custody another man who possessed the probable murder weapon and who had confessed. The fact of the arrest takes on a very different meaning within different contexts.

Although contextual material is very important, many stories present very little context (Parenti, 1986). For example, the many stories about crimes that we see reported every day are each limited to the facts of that one crime. Rarely is there any context about crime rates or how the particular crime reported in the story matches some kind of a pattern—historical, social, economic, and so on. Crime stories are like popcorn for the mind. Each story is small, simple, and relatively the same. They give our mind the sense that it is consuming information, but the stories have little nutritional value. After years of munching on this information, we have come to believe that most crime is violent street crime and that it is increasing all around us. But the real-world figures indicate that most crimes are white-collar crimes (embezzlement, fraud, forgery, etc.) and property crimes (larceny, shoplifting, etc.), rather than violent crime (murder, rape, armed robbery, etc.). Which type of crime do we see most often in our news stories?

The news media are often criticized for providing only superficial information. Thus the news media are not providing the public with enough guidance to make sound opinions about the important issues of the day. We can see evidence of this in public opinion polls that reveal that the public is missing key information. For example, in public opinion polls only 17% of people think crime is a big problem in their own community while 83% of Americans think crime is a big problem in society (Whitman & Loftus, 1996). That is, most people do not experience crime in their own lives and therefore do not think it is a big problem where they live. But they hold the opinion that the country is in bad shape.

Where do they get the idea that crime is a problem when they don't experience any in real life? From the media. The media constantly present stories about crime. Some of those stories are very high-profile events such as the O. J. Simpson arrest and trials; Lorena Bobbit's cutting off her husband's penis; or the Menendez brothers killing their parents. These high-profile crimes are repeatedly played out in the media, and their images stay with viewers. Also, the media, through the news, present a constant stream of crime news that reinforces the impression that there is a great deal of terrible crime.

What is the reality about crime? The crime rate has been falling, both in terms of crimes reported to the police as well as actual victimization rates. Also, home burglary rates have dropped 50% over the past two decades. Yet in a recent poll only 7% of Americans believed that violent crime had declined in the past 5 years (Whitman & Loftus, 1996). The news does not give us an accurate picture of crime in society; instead it continually tries to shock us with coverage of untypical events.

The media also do a poor job of informing us about the major issues of the day—such as the federal deficit. A recent poll found that most people do not understand what is happening with federal deficits. About 70% thought that the deficit was increasing over the past 5 years, 17% thought that it was the same, and only 12% knew that it was decreasing. The deficit decreased from 4.7% of gross domestic product in 1991 to 1.5% in 1996—the lowest level in 22 years (Dentzer, 1996). Apparently people are buying the political arguments that we have a serious problem with an increasing deficit. Or they do not understand the difference between deficit and national debt. Deficit is the difference between what the federal government takes in and what it spends in a given year. The debt is that which the federal government owes, which is now about $5.2 trillion and growing each year. Either way, the news media have failed to inform people adequately. This is additional evidence that the news industry is focused more on entertainment than on information.

Asking journalists to build more context into their stories presents two problems. First, journalists vary widely in talent, and it takes a very talented and experienced journalist to be able to dig out a great deal of relevant contextual information on deadline. Second, when journalists have the responsibility of constructing the context, they may be manifesting a lot of power to define the meaning of the event for the readers. Journalists can substantially change the meaning if they leave out (whether intentionally or through an oversight) an important contextual element.

Bagdikian (1992) argues that the most significant form of bias in journalism appears when a story is reported with a lack of context. The fear is that context is only the journalist's opinion, and opinion must be avoided in "objective reporting." "But there is a difference between partisanship and placing facts in a reasonably informed context of history and social circumstance. American journalism has not made a workable distinction between them" (p. 214). He says that "there are powerful commercial pressures to remove social significance from standard American news. Informed social-economic context has unavoidable political implications which may disturb some in the audience whose world view differs" (p. 214). So the media report undisputed facts about things, but ignore the meaning behind the facts and by so doing severely limit our ability to see that underlying meaning.

BECOMING LITERATE ABOUT NEWS ⊞

How can we protect ourselves from the illusion that we are being informed about the important events of the day when we faithfully expose ourselves to news messages in the media? The key is to develop higher media literacy with more elaborated knowledge structures and stronger higher-order skills.

Now that you have more information about news as a construction, the news perspective, the myth of objectivity, and the importance of balance, you have a stronger knowledge structure about media content. When you use this knowledge structure with advanced skills, you will be able to see much more in messages of news and information. Table 5.1 shows the cognitive, emotional, aesthetic, and moral skills you will need. It also provides some examples of knowledge across these four domains. These lists are not exhaustive. There are other examples of skills and knowledge that you could use to increase your media literacy during exposures to media messages.

Keep this template in mind when you watch the news. Think about how useful your knowledge structures are. Seek to elaborate your existing knowledge structures by using four strategies: (a) analyze the news perspective, (b) search for context, (c) develop alternative sources of information, and (d) be skeptical of public opinion.

TABLE 5.1

	SKILLS	KNOWLEDGE
COGNITIVE	Ability to analyze a news story in order to identify key points of information	Knowledge on the topic from many sources (media and real world)
	Ability to compare/contrast key points of information in the news story with facts in your knowledge structure	
	Ability to evaluate veracity of information in story	
	Ability to evaluate whether a news story presents a balanced presentation of the news event/issue	
EMOTIONAL	Ability to analyze the feelings of people in the news story	Recall from personal experiences how it would feel to be in the situation in the story
	Ability to put one's self into the position of different people in the story	
	Ability to extend empathy to other people contiguous to the news story	
AESTHETIC	Ability to analyze the craft and artistic elements in the story	Knowledge of writing, graphics, photography, etc., to TV news producers
	Ability to compare and contrast the artistry used to tell this story with that used to tell other stories	Knowledge of well told and poorly told stories and the elements that contributed to those qualities
MORAL	Ability to analyze the moral elements in a news story	Knowledge of criticism of news Knowledge of the meaning of bias, objectivity, balance, fairness
	Ability to compare/contrast this story with other stories	Knowledge of other stories on this topic and how those journalists achieved balance and fairness
	Ability to evaluate the ethical responsibilities of the journalists on this story	Highly developed moral code for journalism

Analyze the News Perspective

Remember, news is constructed by news workers. They make their selections and decisions based on their news perspective. So when we watch a news program on TV or read a newspaper, we are seeing as much (or more) about those news organizations than we are seeing about the events in the story—if we know what to look for. By keeping this in mind, we will be learning a great deal about news values while at the same time protecting ourselves from accepting the false belief that news is a complete, accurate, and balanced picture of our world. Getting a more accurate picture should be our goal. But to achieve that goal, we must seek out many sources and be actively critical of their information.

Search for Context

Often we hear the term *news and information* and read this as a single concept rather than two. But it is important to make a distinction between "news" and "information." News is that which is "new" in some sense. If it is something we already know, it is not news. Therefore news must be out of the ordinary, that is, deviant. It must make us think, "Gee whiz, I never knew that! Isn't that strange?" It must entertain or excite us in some way. In contrast, information tells us something of value about our world. It makes us think, "That is something I should know; that is something I can use."

Of course, this is not a neat, categorical distinction, that is, something can be both news and information. Sometimes the elements of news and information are clearly identifiable. For example, a news story might begin with the announcement that J. J. Jones was arrested for jumping out of a tree and mugging an old woman as she walked through the city park. This is highly unusual and deviant, so it would be covered as news. People watching this story would say, "Gee whiz. What is the world coming to?" If the story ends at this point, it is merely news. But if the story continues by putting the arrest in context, then it most likely also contains information, such as changes in the rate of crime in the park, reasons for the changes, the police department's success rate in solving those crimes, and the like. This context provides readers with something they can use—not just a fleeting emotional reaction. At higher levels of media literacy people can more clearly see this distinction between news and information—and demand more information.

Develop Alternative Sources of Information

In their book *How to Watch TV News*, Postman and Powers (1992) say that in order for people to prepare themselves to watch television news, they need to prepare their minds through extensive reading about the world. In short, if individual messages in the media do not provide much context, then you need to search that context out for yourself. With important social, political, and economic issues, this usually means reading books and magazines. But when you do this, make sure you read a variety of viewpoints. Context is more than getting exposure to one perspective on a problem—no matter how deep that perspective. A fully developed knowledge structure requires in-depth exposure to the issue from as many different points of view as possible. So if you find a detailed article on a topic in a conservative magazine, try to find the same topic treated in liberal, middle-of-the-road, and non-political magazines. Following this strategy will result in your knowledge structure on this topic being much more elaborate, and your resulting opinion will be much more sound.

Be Skeptical About Public Opinion

The problem with public opinion is not with measuring it accurately. There is good technology that can do this well, when opinions exist. The problem is that people often don't have an opinion about something, or they are not sure what their opinion is—they are ambivalent. To illustrate this, take your own informal opinion poll. Ask several of your friends for their opinions on the deficit, health care reform, campaign finance reform, capital punishment, and some local issues of concern to you. Notice that most respondents will feel that they should have an opinion, and they will give you one. Then ask them why they hold those opinions. Do they quote many facts in a logical, well-reasoned argument that provides a strong foundation for their opinions? Or do they act kind of embarrassed and defensive? Are those opinions deeply held and of strong value to them? Or are those opinions superficial and based on a few random facts? How do you feel about national policy being formulated on the basis of these kinds of opinions?

When we do these things, we will attain a higher level of media literacy about the news. This requires an interplay between our knowledge structures and our skills (see Table 5.1). Stronger skills translate into stronger knowledge structures.

▓ CONCLUSION

News is not a reflection of actual events; it is a construction by news workers who are subjected to many influences and constraints. Each day journalists must select from all of human activity those things that they feel should be reported. For each event selected, journalists must then decide what the focus of the story should be so that it will hook an audience. Finally, journalists must assemble the news elements into some structure in order to tell the story. In performing these tasks, news workers cannot be objective, so they try for the goal of being balanced. However, careful analyses of the news indicate that most stories are not balanced.

Formulas guide the construction process. The purpose of these formulas is to help news workers do their jobs efficiently. The formulas are part of the news perspective, which is shaped by many influences and constraints. The news perspective shifts the goal of news workers from informing the public to entertaining as many people as possible, thereby generating the maximum revenue possible. This has led to a focus on the trivial, the sensational, and the superficial. News now asks only for our eyeballs, not our gray matter.

Most of us feel we have a good understanding of current events, because we read newspapers and magazines and keep up with news on radio and television. But without a complete knowledge of the day's events themselves, we cannot tell if the news coverage is complete, balanced, or accurate. Instead, we must trust the media to give us the full picture. However, the media do not give us the full picture.

Being media literate requires us to search out a wide range of sources and to build stronger knowledge structures that provide us with the context that mainstream news programs do not provide. We need to be careful about analyzing the news perspective, search for context, develop alternative sources of information, and be skeptical. In short, we need to be more active and conscious in using higher order skills to process news messages.

FURTHER READING ■■

Altheide, D. L. (1976). *Creating reality: How TV news distorts events.* Beverly Hills, CA: Sage.

> This is an ethnography about how people in the newsroom create a community to get their news work done. The author's central thesis is that "events become news when transformed by the news perspective, and not because of their objective characteristics" (p. 173). He develops a construct he calls "news perspective" to explain how the staff select and treat the news. News perspective is a sort of bias that helps journalists simplify and organize the overwhelming amount of material they must sift through. This news bias is influenced by the constraints of commercialism, scheduling, technology, and competition. He argues that "the organizational, practical, and other mundane features of news work promote a way of looking at events which fundamentally distorts them" (p. 24). "In order to make events news, news reporting decontextualizes and thereby changes them" (p. 25). The biggest influences on the news scene are commercialism (ratings and the drive for profit), competition (from other media), and the community context (especially political ties).

Fishman, M. (1980). *Manufacturing the news*. Austin: University of Texas Press.

The author argues that journalists construct social reality for audiences. To do this, journalists develop routines so they do not have to invent new methods of reporting the world on every occasion they confront it. He makes a distinction between routine journalism and manipulated journalism. Routine journalism is the "good, plain, solid, honest, professional news reporting" that is produced through the "daily methods and standard practices of journalists" (p. 15). In contrast, manipulated journalism is the product of a political game where the news is produced to service certain interests. Even routine journalism displays an ideological hegemony that can be traced to "the routines of news detection, interpretation, investigation, and assembly" (p. 18).

Jensen, C. (1995). *Censored: The news that didn't make the news—and why*. New York: Four Walls Eight Windows. (332 pages with index)

Begun by the author in 1976, Project Censored invites journalists, scholars, librarians, and the general public to nominate stories they feel were not reported adequately during a given year. From the hundreds of submissions, the list is reduced to 25 based on "the amount of coverage the story received, the national or international importance of the issue, the reliability of the source, and the potential impact the story may have" (p. 15). A blue-ribbon panel of judges then selects the top 10 censored stories for the year.

Lee, M. A., & Solomon, N. (1990). *Unreliable sources: A guide to detecting bias in news media*. New York: Carol Publishing Group. (420 pages with index)

Written by two journalists, this book is a strong criticism of American journalistic practices. The central thesis is that economic norms govern the news much more than the quest to fulfill the public's right to know.

Postman, N., & Powers, S. (1992). *How to watch TV news*. New York: Penguin Books. (178 pages with index)

The authors argue that what television news says it is presenting and what it actually presents are two different things. They say that TV claims it presents the important happenings of the day that all citizens should know, but what it really presents are superficial constructions designed to create large audiences for advertisers. The authors say that in order for people to prepare themselves to watch television news, they need to prepare their minds through extensive reading about the world.

Shoemaker, P. J., & Reese, S. D. (1996). *Mediating the message: Theories of influences on mass media content* (2nd ed.). White Plains, NY: Longman.

In this book, the authors review research on media content and build toward a theory with assumptions, propositions, and hypotheses. The first two chapters lay the foundation for studying media content. Chapter 3 presents what is known about media content. The heart of the book is the next six chapters, which review all the different types of influences on media content. In Chapter 10 the authors lay out an organization that shows how effects and content can be studied together. Finally, in the last chapter, they present their theory, which is really a list of assumptions, propositions, and hypotheses in about 10 pages.

Tuchman, G. (1978). *Making news: A study in the construction of reality.* New York: Free Press. (244 pages)

The author hung out in news rooms over a 10-year period in order to find out how news workers construct reality. She found that news workers developed a code of professionalism that was based on the interests of the organizations they worked for, and that the central concept of this professionalism is the "news frame." The news frame is what news workers hold up to events to determine whether those events "fit" as news.

EXERCISE 5.1

Practicing Analyzing the News

1. Take a blank sheet of paper and draw the structure in Table 5.1 on it. That is, create two columns: Label one "Skills" and the other "Knowledge." Now create four rows and label them Cognitive, Emotional, Aesthetic, and Moral. Your figure should have eight blocks. Make a copy of this figure so that you have two.

2. Now watch a news story on television. Videotape the story so you can watch it more than once.

3. After a single viewing, write down the skills and knowledge you needed to achieve a basic minimal understanding of what the story says. Think in terms of your everyday viewing of news, where you just want to monitor the surface facts in order to keep up with the day's major events.

4. Now think about the skills and knowledge you would need to achieve a much more complete understanding of the meaning of the event in the news story. Think in terms of what it would take for you to be an expert on the event. This may require you to view the tape several times.

5. Look at what you have written in response to No. 4. Does it differ much from what you have written in response to No. 3? How much detail do you have in each of the eight blocks? With which blocks did you struggle the most? Why do you think you struggled with them?

6. Compare the results of your figures with those of a friend. Did your friend have more details in certain blocks compared to you? If so, did that additional detail extend your thinking? The more people's work you compare, the more you can see a range of differences.

EXERCISE 5.2

Inferring News Workers' Decisions

Gather together three or four newspapers for the same day—the more, the better.

1. Look at the composition of the first page across those newspapers, and think about the differences and similarities of their news perspectives.

    a. What are the major stories in terms of placement and size?

    b. What pictures and graphics are used? Are they used to present substance or are they used merely to make the page more appealing to the eye?

    c. How much of the front page is composed of non-news matter?

2. Read the major news stories.

    a. What criteria were used to select them?

    b. What kinds of elements are emphasized in the stories—are the facts primary or is the context primary?

    c. Is the story balanced or are there obvious viewpoints that are ignored?

3. Look at the sections of the newspapers.

    a. What sections are there? (such as sports, women, business, etc.)

    b. Look at how the space is allocated. How much space is given to ads? How much to hard news? How much to soft, entertainment-type news?

4. What happened within the past 24 hours that did not get covered?

5. In summary, which of these newspapers do you think is the best and why?

6. Later today listen to some news on the radio and watch some on television. How is the news different in these media compared to newspapers?

EXERCISE 5.3

Exercising Higher-Order Skills

1. Think of some current event of interest to you. Now pretend you are an editor of an newspaper. What elements would you want to have in the story?

    a. What sources would you want to interview?

    b. What facts and figures would you want to have?

    c. What historical contextual factors would you want?

    d. Would you want visuals—graphics or photographs?

CHAPTER
6

Key Idea: Media entertainment content follows clear formulas that are designed to attract and hold our attention. The elements in these formulas appear realistic but present patterns that are very different from the real world.

What Is Entertainment?

Most of us feel we have a good understanding of media content because we recognize the names and faces of movie stars. We know the words and melodies of popular songs. We can tell our friends about what happened in detail on our favorite television shows.

But how much do we know about the patterns of characters, actions, and themes across the media entertainment landscape? For example, do you know what the themes are that underlie most of media entertainment? What *types* of characters are most prevalent in entertainment? Do you understand why media entertainment follows certain conventions?

These questions are addressed in this chapter, where the focus is on television entertainment. Why television? Because television is the most pervasive medium for entertainment. Almost all of us get more of our entertainment from television compared to any other medium. What's more, we take this exposure for granted. So we are not conscious of the broad patterns of characterization and plot that we constantly see. But those patterns—even though they are fictional—can influence what we think about the real world.

ENTERTAINMENT FORMULAS ⊞

On the surface, it appears that the media present a wide variety of entertainment messages. But when we analyze those messages, we can see that they follow standard patterns. For example, a wide variety of songs has been presented as popular music in recordings, cassettes, CDs, and on the radio over many decades. Each of those songs follows certain formulas. None of those songs is a purely random sequence of notes. Musical formulas tell musicians which notes are played in sequence (melody progressions) and which notes are to be played together (chords). There are a small number of standard rhythms. All of the songs are creative variations of the standard formula.

There are also formulas for telling stories. All stories begin with a conflict or a problem. The conflict is heightened throughout the story, and the main characters try to solve the problem. Finally, during the climactic scene, the problem is solved and the conflict is eliminated. The entertainment stories in the mass media also have a fairly standard set of characters, and this set of character types does not change much across media or vehicles. For example, one study of characters appearing in shows across 32 channels on a typical cable system found the same patterns of gender, race, and age across all channels (Kubey, Shifflet, Weerakkody, & Ukeiley, 1996).

These formulas are used not only by the creators of media messages; they are also used by us—the audience—to help us easily recognize the good and bad characters and quickly find where we are in the story. Stories that follow the formulas the closest usually have the largest audiences, because they are the easiest to follow. With experience with media messages we learn the formula as we are being entertained. We are conditioned to expect certain plot points, certain pacing, certain types of characters, and certain themes.

The overall entertainment story formula is elaborated in different ways across different genres of entertainment. For example, when we view an action/adventure program, we expect different plot points, pacing, characters, and themes than when we watch a situation comedy or a romance. The action/adventure genre contains stories about spies, wars, space travel, police officers, and the like. We expect a fast pace, suspense, and violence. This violence is highly ritualized; that is, it follows a fairly consistent formula. The formula of violence tells us that it is okay for criminals to behave violently throughout a program as long as they are caught at the end of the show. This restores a sense of peace—at least until the commercials are over and the next show begins. As viewers we somehow feel comforted by all this violence. Also, we feel that it is permissible for police officers, private eyes, and good-guy vigilantes to break the law and use violence as long as it is used successfully against the bad guys. We do not have an absolute position that violence is good or that it is bad; instead, our position is situational. Violence is good if the people we like use it, and it is bad if other people use it.

Another genre is romance. This type of story begins with a young person experiencing either loneliness from lack of a relationship, or a relationship that is bad due to betrayal, jealousy, or fear. We identify with the main character and feel her pain. But she is full of hope for what seems like an unattainable goal. Through hard work and virtue, she gets closer and closer to her goal—even though she experiences frequent heart-rending setbacks—until the story climaxes with the fulfillment of the goal, which transmits intense emotions to the reader. Writers who have mastered this formula are very successful. For example, among all paperbacks sold in the United States, about half are in the romance novel genre. One romance novelist who has really understood the formula is Nora Roberts. She has published 127 romance novels, all following the same basic romance formula. In 1998 alone she had 11 titles on the *New York Times* Best Seller list. She has a total of 85 million books in print, and her work has been translated into 25 languages (Riggs, 1999). Has she produced a body of great literature that will be read for centuries? No, of course not. Has she recognized a market for a particular kind of story and manufactured many products to meet that need? There is no doubt of this.

The situation comedy formula is so well known by viewers that Nick has gone to 60-second sitcoms. They insert these between the old 30-minute sitcoms they program on Nick at Nite. One of these is *The Gaveltons*, which is about the adventures of America's most litigious family; another is *Spin & Cutter*, a buddy show about the stupid schemes of two lovable goofballs; yet another is *All's Well*, a Father-Knows-Best-style family comedy (Maurstad, 1998). We have no trouble recognizing the character types or following the highly truncated plots.

Even if the show is 60 minutes long instead of 60 seconds, the story must have a quick beginning where a problem is established, and conflict among attractive characters must be continually heightened to keep viewers interested. At the end of each episode, the conflicts must be cleanly resolved to the satisfaction of the audience—unless the show is a continuing drama, in which case viewers must be left with some major unresolved conflicts so they will want to tune in to the next episode. If the show is on television, all of this action must ebb and flow around breaks for commercials. In addition, each genre (situation comedy, action/adventure, soap opera, etc.) has its own special conventions.

There is a need for creativity, diversity, and departure from the commonplace—but only within the established formulas. This means making stereotypical characters appear fresh and giving the traditional plots new twists. It also means pushing the envelop of what is considered acceptable. Comstock (1989) pointed out that

> much of what is on television today [the late 1980s] would not have been considered acceptable by broadcasters or the public 20 or even 10 years ago. Public tastes and social standards have changed, and television has made some contribution to these changes by probing the borders of convention accompanying each season. . . . These conventions of popular entertainment provide television, as they do other media, with rules that minimize the possibility of public offense. (p. 182)

The public's tastes and social standards have continued to change.

Formulas are not static. They change over time, but do so at a slow rate so that audiences can get used to the changes. Television is very conservative, that is, TV programmers do not want to offend anyone and lose audience members.

Yet they continually take on controversial issues and push the envelop on violence, language, and sex. Many critics complain about television portrayals, especially in the early evening when children are viewing, yet each year producers keep presenting language that is a bit more outrageous along with sexually suggestive behaviors that leave less and less to the imagination.

A similar evolution of a formula has been occurring in popular music. The basic formula of popular songs is a story about love or sex. For example, in one content analysis of themes in popular music over the past 60 years, it was found that 70% of all songs have dealt with the topics of sex and love (Christianson & Roberts, 1998). What has changed in the formula is the way this theme is treated. Love used to be treated as an emotion, and lyrics were symbolic, that is, they suggested actions and left them up to the imagination of listeners. Now love is treated as a physical act, and lyrics are much more explicit in describing that act.

Why do formulas evolve? Public taste changes over time. People get bored with too much repetition and look for something slightly different. The media have become much more sensitive to these changes in taste and have shifted their focus from the product to the market. For example, in the book industry, editors used to search out those whom they thought were the best writers and published them. They would then try to convince the public that their writers were good so that the public would buy those books.

Now the media use a marketing orientation. This means they no longer begin with developing what they think are the best products, then try to develop a need in the audience for them. Instead, they begin with a focus on audiences and determine what a given audience wants. Then they develop products to fulfill those already existing needs. Book publishers now want to know that a large market exists for a particular book before publishing it. The same is true of television. Television programmers spend their time developing a finely tuned sense of what kinds of entertainment the public wants to see. When a certain kind of story does very well, programmers commission sequels, spin-offs, and clones of that story, thinking that these new shows will also do very well. When the work of a particular writer, producer, director, or actor does well, he or she becomes in high demand and the price for his or her services increases dramatically.

Television programmers are essentially conservative and fearful of offending viewers, so they present content that they believe reflects mainstream American values. They do this to avoid offending the people they want in their audiences. While television entertainment is substantially conservative, it continually tests the line of acceptability, especially in the areas of sex, violence, and language. Over time, that line changes as the public criticizes certain shows or as the public remains silent and indicates its consent.

The Fox television network is especially known for pushing the line of television programming. It aired shows such as *When Good Pets Go Bad* and

World's Scariest Police Shootouts. When these shows came under harsh criticism, Sandy Grushow, director of programming for Fox, made public apologies. In the late 1990s, Grushow spent a lot of time apologizing. Then in February 2000 Grushow decided to air *Who Wants to Marry a Multimillionaire?* The show was a sensation, drawing 23 million viewers, but again it was an embarrassment when it was revealed that the selected bride, Darva Conger, had not really intended to get married on the program but went through with it only to get an annulment several weeks later. Grushow apologized again, but this time offered an explanation for continuing to program these types of shows: "It's like someone who goes to their boss and says, 'We can make something at half the cost that will make twice as much money.' The boss would say, 'Go do it, but don't embarrass us.' This has turned into an embarrassing situation and now they have to fix it" (Bauder, 2000a, p. 3E).

CBS got on the extreme reality bandwagon with its show *Survivor.* CBS winnowed a set of 16 people from 6,000 applicants and deposited these 16 on a small island in the South China Sea. Each week the participants voted to eliminate 1 person until there were only 2 left. The 14 losing contestants then chose the winner of the survival game, and that winner got $1 million. CBS aired the 13 episodes in the summer of 2000. The CBS Survivor game was modeled after a Swedish version that aired in 1997. In that game, the losing contestant committed suicide one month after returning home. CBS officials assured critics that their contestants all went through 6 hours of psychological testing and that there would be no serious psychological problems for the losers of their game (Bauder, 2000b).

What makes a show popular? This is the key question for producers and programmers. In general, popularity is achieved with creativity within a formula. The media storytelling formula requires producers to distort social reality by making characters bigger than life; telescoping time so that events happen much faster than in real life; and making conflicts more dramatic, leading to a climax that neatly resolves the action.

REALISM

The media world may often appear like the real world, but it is very different. In the real world, most of life is fairly routine and uneventful. But in the media world—especially in films and on television—life is full of strong emotions, high drama, and fast-paced action. Television and film ignore things that are not visually interesting, such as thinking by ourselves, reading, walking, and other quiet activities that make up much of our lives. Activities such as housework, running errands, and small talk with neighbors are vastly under-represented. Instead of ennobling our ordinary experiences, television suggests that they are not of sufficient interest to document.

However, producers are under no obligation to present an accurate account of the mundane world. Their task is to build as large an audience as possible. To do this they must rely on all their creative powers to achieve a dramatic effect: They deliberately distort the world to surprise and startle us. Some creative people produce fantasy, which by definition is totally unlike real life—they do this to allow us to escape our lives and to see imaginative occurrences. Producers who try to capture real life do so in an intriguing manner. That is, they avoid presenting the mundane mainstream of real life and instead highlight the occurrences at the margins where there are particularly interesting people or events. This is not real life in the sense that it could happen or even did happen. For example, family dramas appear to be very realistic in their settings, characters, and types of problems encountered. But they are unrealistic in their pacing, with most problems solved in 60 minutes.

The danger, of course, is that if our exposure is exclusively to fantasy, we will see only the unusual. And if we take those entertainment messages at face value, without thinking deeper into the themes and lessons they portray, we will come to believe that the real world is like the fantasy world.

The way to deal with the unrealistic picture presented by television entertainment is *not* to pressure producers to make their world of fiction more realistic. That would be silly. Instead it is to educate viewers about the patterns they are seeing but not recognizing in the world of television entertainment.

Characters

The characters on television are very different from people in real life. This is not to say that there are not types of people in real life like almost every character on television. Instead, in the aggregate, the pattern in the population of TV characters is different from the pattern of people in the real world. These differences can be seen most clearly in two ways. First, when we look at patterns in the aggregate, we see that the demographic balance is very different in the television world compared to the real world. Second, we see that the characters are presented as stereotypes.

Demographics in the Aggregate. In this section we will examine the areas of gender balance, ethnicity, age, marital status, social class, and occupation.

As for gender, on television there are far more males than females. When all roles on television are considered, males outnumber females three to one. But this imbalance varies by type of program. In soap operas there is a balance among the genders. In situation comedies and family dramas there also is almost a balance, but in police/detective shows males outnumber females five to one.

As for ethnicity, 80% of all characters are white Americans. Until the late 1960s, only 2% of television characters were African American; then the figure climbed to about 10% and has stayed there ever since. Hispanics have not fared as well. Although Hispanics make up about 9% of the U.S. population, only 1.5% of all television characters are Hispanics.

As for age, three quarters of all television characters are between the ages of 20 and 50, while in the real world, only one third of the population is between these ages. Young children and the elderly are under-represented on television. Fictional characters under 19 years of age make up only 10% of the total television population even though they make up one third of the U.S. population. Also, characters over 50 years of age account for about 15% of all television characters. The most dramatic imbalance is in the over-65 age group. Barely more than 2% of television characters are at least 65 years old, but 11% of the real-life population is in this age bracket.

The marital status of women on television is known more often than that of men. The marital status of about 80% of the women is obvious compared to the marital status of about 45% of the men. Of those whose marital status you can tell, more than 50% of the females are married while less than one third of the males are married.

As for socio-economic status (SES), almost half the characters on television are wealthy or ultra-wealthy, and very few (less than 10%) are in a low SES bracket. As characters grows older, they are shown with a higher SES.

The higher prestige occupations are over-represented on fictional television. Nearly one third of the television labor force is professional and managerial, while in real life that figure is only 11%. Working-class people are greatly under-represented, except for a few television-world professions. For example, prostitutes outnumber machinists by 12 to 1; there are twice as many doctors as welfare workers; eight times more butlers than miners; and 12 times more private detectives than production line workers.

The world of TV work may be changing a bit. Vande Berg and Streckfuss (1992) analyzed occupations in prime-time television and found that there was a slight increase in the representation of women and in the variety of their occupational portrayals. Still, women remain under-represented and limited in their depictions in organizational settings. Males outnumbered females two to one in the workplace.

What can account for this dominance of males, whites, and youthful adults? Perhaps it is due to the demographics of the people who are television writers. Turow (1992) says that according to the Writers Guild of America, white males account for over three quarters of the writers employed in film and TV. Minorities accounted for 2% of all writers. During the fall 1999 television season, the four big television networks premiered 26 new series. In every one of those new shows, the lead characters and nearly all the cast regulars were white, even those on shows where the action takes place in urban high schools and New York City nightspots (Lowry, Jensen, & Braxton, 1999). Also during that season, there were 17 gay characters on the four major networks and about the same number of black, Asian, and Latino characters combined. A big reason for this is that there are many gays in Hollywood and not many minorities (Brownfield, 1999).

Stereotypical Portrayals. Characters in the television world are developed as stereotypes according to certain formulas, which make the characters easily and quickly recognizable to viewers.

There is a good deal of gender stereotyping for both males and females. The main character, who is typically a white, middle-class youthful male, is usually portrayed with positive personality characteristics such as competency, leadership, and bravery. Women and minorities suffer by comparison.

For females there are two primary stereotypes. If a woman is single, she is often portrayed as a sex object. There is a strong emphasis on the female body being attractive, desirable, and youthful. If a woman is a mother, she is usually portrayed as wise and nurturing. The profile of women on prime-time television has not changed much in 50 years (Elasmar, Hasegawa, & Brain, 1999).

Older characters, especially males, tend to be cast in comic roles. The elderly are likely to be treated with disrespect and are often shown as stubborn, eccentric, and foolish.

Also, government employees do not fare well in television stereotyping. An analysis of 1,234 prime-time series episodes from 1955 to 1998 reveals that government employees are often portrayed in negative roles. Of politicians, 51% were in negative roles—either as corrupt (such as Boss Hogg on the *Dukes of Hazzard*) or scatterbrained (such as New York Mayor Randall Winston on *Spin City*; Aversa, 1999).

Families. There have been some changes in the way families are portrayed on television. In domestic comedies, the adult members of families are now likely to interact more openly, and there is more expression of feelings in spousal relationships (Douglas & Olson, 1995). But the adults are also shown as having more conflicts with children. As a result, the relational environment has become more conflictual and less cohesive in modern TV families than in families from earlier decades. Also TV modern families are less able to manage day-to-day life and less able to socialize children effectively (Douglas & Olson, 1996).

Examples of stereotypes include

- the strong self-reliant police detective who uses unconventional methods to deal with the scum on the street; he is irritated by his authoritarian bosses but always gets the job done using his own unorthodox methods
- the nurturing mother who has kooky kids and an idiot husband
- the sexy young female actress/model/nurse/secretary who becomes the romantic interest of a male hero
- the young street punk who commits petty and violent crimes, usually for drugs; he is tough and sassy until police intimidate him into taking a plea bargain
- the doofus male adolescent who displays hilariously dysfunctional social skills; while he is very sensitive, he never learns from his social mistakes

There is a positive as well as a negative side to stereotypes. They are positive from the point of view that they make it easy for viewers to recognize character types and thus process stories quickly. But stereotypes can also have a negative effect, because they are often inadequate as well as biased, they often serve as obstacles to rational assessment, and they are resistant to social change.

We use stereotypes when dealing with real-world information, not just media portrayals. For example, when we meet a new person we try to "type" that person based on the characteristics we can immediately see, such as age, gender, appearance, how he or she talks, and so on. Once we have typed the person (chosen a person schema), we have a set of expectations for that person. For example, if we see a 5-year-old girl in a fancy dress playing with a doll on the steps of a church, we immediately call up a specific set of expectations. In contrast, if we see a middle-aged man with a beer-belly straining his dirty T-shirt, and he is chewing tobacco and cleaning a rifle, we call up a very different set of expectations. Stereotypes provide us with sets of expectations that we can access quickly as we encounter people and events. They are a necessary mode of processing information, especially when there are thousands of messages coming at us quickly every day and we need to create order out of "the great blooming, buzzing confusion of reality" (Lippmann, 1922, p. 96).

Plot Elements

Two of the most popular narrative elements are sex and violence. Why are these elements so popular? Because they serve the function of arousing the audience and getting viewers interested in following the action. They keep otherwise uncreative plots and uninteresting characters from appearing dull.

In the world of media entertainment, everything can be forgiven except dullness. In 1960, Newton Minow, then Chairperson of the FCC, said he sat down and watched television and saw "a vast wasteland . . . of blood and thunder, mayhem, violence, sadism, murder . . ." (Minow & LaMay, 1995). Years later when

TV was again being criticized for having so much violence, CBS president Howard Stringer was arguing against standards to clean up television by saying, "We don't want to turn the vast wasteland into a dull wasteland" (*USA Today*, 1993, p. 2A). And that is the key—TV and all the entertainment media must avoid being dull.

Sex. Sexual activity on television has been prevalent since the 1970s (Buerkel-Rothfuss, 1993; Cassata & Skill, 1983). If we limit our definition of sex to visual depictions of intercourse, the rate fluctuates around one (Greenberg et al., 1993) or two (Fernandez-Collado, Greenberg, Korzenny, & Atkin, 1978) acts per hour of prime time. In soap operas, the rate is even higher.

If we expand the definition to include all visual depictions of sexual activity, such as kissing, petting, homosexuality, prostitution, and rape, the hourly rates go up to about 3 acts on prime time and 3.7 acts per hour on soap operas (Greenberg et al., 1993). And when the definition is further expanded to include talk about sex as well as sexual imagery, the rate climbs to 16 instances per hour on prime time (Sapolsky & Tabarlet, 1990). Most of this talk about sex is on situation comedies in the early evening when it is presented in a humorous context.

A major study on this topic was conducted in the late 1990s when Dale Kunkel and his colleagues (1999) analyzed the content of 1,351 programs across 10 channels. They found that 54% of all shows contain talk about sex and 23% of all shows contain depictions of sexual behavior; 7% of all shows contain scenes in which sexual intercourse is either depicted or strongly implied. The overall rate is three scenes per hour. Two thirds (67%) of all network prime-time shows contain either talk about sex or sexual behavior, averaging more than five scenes per hour.

Perhaps more troubling than the high frequency of sexual portrayals is the way sex is portrayed. Most depictions of sexual behavior are not presented responsibly from a health point of view. Schrag (1990) reports that American children and teens view an average of more than 14,000 sexual references and innuendos on television each year. Of these, less than 150 refer to the use of birth control, so that the rate of unprotected sex on TV is very high, but there is a very low incidence of sexually transmitted diseases (STDs) or pregnancies.

The context of sexual portrayals was no more responsible at the end of the 1990s. Kunkel's study showed that rarely do writers who present sexual situations also show the consequences. Of all shows with sexual content, just 9% include any mention of the possible risks or responsibilities of sexual activity, or any reference to contraception, protection, or safer sex. Only 1% of all shows with sexual content had a primary emphasis throughout the show on issues concerning sexual risks or responsibilities. Half of all references to sexual risks or responsibility were minor or inconsequential. There were differences across genres, with talk shows having the highest (23%) and sitcoms having the lowest (3%) number of references to risk and responsibility (Kunkel et al., 1999).

Violence. Scholars have been monitoring the amount of violence on television ever since the early 1950s. Depending on the definition used, violence has been found on from 57% to 80% of all entertainment programs (Columbia Broadcasting System, 1980; Greenberg, Edison, Korzenny, Fernandez-Collado, & Atkin, 1980; Lichter & Lichter, 1983; "NCTV Says," 1983; Potter & Ware, 1987; Schramm, Lyle, & Parker, 1961; Signorielli, 1990; Smythe, 1954; Williams, Zabrack, & Joy, 1982).

The most consistent examination of television violence has been conducted by Gerbner and his associates (e.g., Gerbner, Gross, Morgan, & Signorielli, 1980). Since the late 1960s, they have documented the frequency of violent acts that fit the definition: the overt expression of physical force (with or without a weapon) against self or other, compelling action against one's will on pain of being hurt or killed, or actually hurting or killing. Signorielli (1990) reports that from 1967 to 1985, the hourly rate has fluctuated from about four to seven violent acts with peaks occurring about every 4 years.

The most comprehensive analysis of violence on television was conducted in the National Television Violence Study (1996), which analyzed the content of a total of 3,185 programs across 23 television channels for all dayparts from 6 a.m. until 11 p.m., 7 days a week, over the course of a television season. Those researchers report that 57% of all programs analyzed had some violence and that one third of programs presented nine or more violent interactions. This 3-year project also examined the context within which the violence was presented and found that rarely was the violence punished and rarely were victims shown as suffering any harmful consequences. Also, 37% of the perpetrators of violence were portrayed as being attractive, and 44% of the acts were shown as being justified. These patterns led the researchers to conclude that not only was violence prevalent throughout the entire television landscape, but that it was typically shown as sanitized and glamorized.

Verbal violence is even more prevalent on television than is physical violence. For example, Williams, Zabrack, and Joy (1982) report a rate of 9.5 acts of verbal violence as well as 9 acts of physical violence per hour on North American (U.S. and Canadian) television. Potter and Ware (1987) found about 8 acts of physical violence per hour and an additional 12 acts of verbal violence on U.S. television. Also, Greenberg and his colleagues (1980) report that an average prime-time hour of television contains 22 acts of verbal aggression and 12 acts of physical aggression.

Films contain a great deal of violence. The top grossing 50 films of 1998 contained a total of 2,300 acts of violence, according to the Center for Media and

Public Affairs, based in Washington, D.C. "Violence was not only a staple of popular entertainment, it was often portrayed as laudable, necessary or relatively harmless activity," said S. Robert Lichter, the center's president (Goldstein, 1999).

The level of violence in the media is far higher than the real-world levels of violence and crime. This was demonstrated by Oliver (1994), who analyzed the pseudo-reality-based police shows, such as *Cops*. She found that the FBI figures for murder, rape, robbery, and aggregated assault were 13.2% of all crimes, but in the television world these four violent crimes accounted for 87% of all crimes. Also, the FBI reports that 18.0% of crimes are cleared, but on television 61.5% are cleared—arrested, killed, or committed suicide. Again, television is focusing on the most arousing crimes rather than the dull ones.

Health

Almost all television characters are portrayed as being healthy and active. Only 6% to 7% of major characters are portrayed as having had injuries or illnesses that require treatment. Pain, suffering, or medical help rarely follows violent activity. In children's programs, despite greater mayhem, only 3% of characters are shown receiving medical treatment.

When medical problems and help are portrayed it is not in a preventative or therapeutic manner, but in a dramatic and social way. Physical illness and injury affect heroes and villains, males and females, and other groups alike.

Illness and health are the most important problems on soap operas. About one half of all characters are involved in some health-related occurrence. Hardly anyone dies a natural death on television, but death is dealt with openly and realistically on soap operas.

Prime-time characters are not only healthy, but they are also relatively safe from accidents, even though when they drive cars they rarely wear seat belts. And they are rarely portrayed as suffering from impairments of any kinds as a result of an accident.

Eating and drinking are frequent activities on entertainment programs. About 75% of all shows display this activity. But the eating portrayed is usually unhealthy. The traditional meals of breakfast, lunch, and dinner combined account for only about half of the eating; snacking accounts for the rest. Fruit is the snack in only 4% to 5% of the episodes.

Between 25% and 45% of the American population is overweight, but on television, only 6% of the males and 2% of the females are. Furthermore, characters do not gain weight from their high-calorie diets.

The use of alcohol, tobacco, and illegal drugs on television has dramatically declined over the years. Smoking was a frequent activity until the mid-1980s, but it has almost completely disappeared except in reruns of old movies.

Alcohol use has also substantially declined. When it is presented now, it is frequently shown with negative consequences. Until the mid-1980s, alcohol consumption was common on television. The drinking of alcohol was shown twice as often as the drinking of coffee and tea, 14 times that of soft drinks, and 15 times that of water. It was shown as sociable, happy, and problem free. Also, alcohol use was rarely portrayed as having any negative consequences. When negative consequences were shown, they were usually very slight, such as a temporary hangover. Despite high rates of consumption across many characters, only 1% of television drinkers are portrayed as having a drinking problem.

While television is showing more responsible portrayals of drug and alcohol use, the movies do not fare so well. An analysis of the 200 most popular movies of 1996 and 1997 reveals that characters frequently abuse drugs and alcohol. Moreover, these characters are not portrayed as worrying about the consequences (Hartman, 1999).

Prime-time characters are not shown with any kind of physical impairments. Rarely does a character even wear glasses; even in old age only one out of four characters wears them. Only 2% of characters on prime-time shows are physically handicapped. When they do appear, they tend to be older, less positively presented, and more likely to be victimized. Almost none appear on children's shows.

Estimates of the number of shows portraying a person who is mentally ill range from 11% to 17%. People portrayed as being mentally ill are shown as a negative stereotype. Almost half have no specified occupation and 75% have no family connections. They are shown to be active, confused, aggressive, dangerous, and unpredictable. In real life, mentally ill people are usually passive and withdrawn, frightened, and avoidant. On television they tend to be males, but in real life there is a balance between males and females.

As a group, the mentally ill on TV are more likely to commit violence and to be victimized. For every 10 normal male victims of violence, there are 17 mentally ill victims of violence. Mentally ill people are not treated sympathetically; they are shown as the bad guys, that is, crazed criminals who are very dangerous.

Doctors are greatly overrepresented on television compared to their numbers in real life. Health care professionals dominate the ranks of professionals, despite the paucity of sick characters on television. They are five times their numbers in real life, proportionally. Only criminals or law enforcers are more numerous. However, it is interesting to note that health care professionals are largely absent from children's programs.

Values

Examining the arts within a culture is a way to determine the values of that culture. For example, the ancient Greek and Roman cultures exhibited the values of perfection, harmony, and beauty. During the European Middle Ages, art reflected the dominance of the Catholic church with its focus on the life of Christ, especially His birth, miracles, crucifixion, and resurrection. Earthly existence was mundane and painful, while the afterlife was glorious. During the Renaissance, art reflected the values of a scientific approach to understanding the world. During the Romantic Era, the focus was shifted away from the logical and intellectual concerns that were dominant during the Renaissance and onto the emotions of humans. During the Modern era the arts were decoupled from the church and political institutions. Art glorified the individual and his or her unique way of looking at the world and constructing meaning (Metallinos, 1996).

Today we can examine across the broad span of messages from the mass media and ask the question: What do our stories tell us about our current culture? Some researchers and social critics have attempted to answer this question. Here are some of the themes they have found.

George Comstock (1989), a media researcher, says there are 10 major themes:

1. Material consumption is very satisfying. It is obvious that advertisements tell us that material possessions bring happiness and confer status. But the entertainment programs present the same theme. Comstock says, "It is not solely that so many stories revolve around the rich, but that in so many instances dwellings and their furnishings are beyond the means of those portrayed as occupying them" (p. 172). For example, the popular situation comedy *Friends* features Monica, a part-time cook, and Rachel, a waitress in a coffee house, who are shown supporting themselves in a well-furnished two-bedroom apartment in downtown Manhattan.

2. The world is a mean and risky place. There is a great deal of crime and violence throughout the television world.

3. The TV world has turned the social pyramid upside down by showing most characters as wealthy and powerful and very few of them as working class.

4. Males are more powerful than females in terms of income, job status, and decision making. This is slowly changing, but we are still far from a balance of power.

5. Occupational status is highly valued. Professional occupations are depicted as worthwhile, while manual work is uninteresting. People attain the status of a worthwhile profession through upward mobility from the middle class. This upward mobility is accomplished through self-confidence and toughness; goodness of character alone is not enough. The movement upward is usually quick and painless.

6. There are a few privileged professions where the people there are almost always shown as doing good and helping others. However, most business people are shady. Business people are frequently shown cheating, embezzling, and even murdering. Businesses are frequently portrayed as polluting, abusing their power, and taking advantage of the gullible public.

7. Law enforcers are overrepresented as being successful, strong, and justified. Private eyes are almost always shown as better than the police.

8. There is a belief in the occult, life on other planets, life after death, and hidden, malevolent purposes behind the inexplicable.

9. A person's self-interest is very important. People are motivated to get what they want regardless of the feelings of others. Examples include extramarital affairs, crime, hard-driving business people, and police who disregard the rights of others to achieve their goals.

10. There are often truly heroic acts portrayed where there are daring rescues, selflessness, loyalty to others, and the struggle against difficult odds to do the right thing.

Walsh (1994, p. 137), writing in *Selling Out America's Children*, argues that the media are teaching the following six lessons:

1. Happiness is found in having things.

2. Get all you can for yourself.

3. Get it all as quickly as you can.

4. Win at all cost.

5. Violence is entertaining.

6. Always seek pleasure and avoid boredom.

Walsh also argues that the values of the marketplace are: happiness equals wealth, instant gratification, and me first. In contrast, the values of a healthy society are: self-esteem comes from within, moderation, tolerance, understanding, and social responsibility.

In complaining about the direction of programming on TV aimed at young people, *U.S. News & World Report* columnist John Leo (1999) said,

> These shows are also carriers of heavy cultural messages, the most obvious being that parents are fools. In the teen soap operas, parents are absent, stupid, irrelevant, zanily adulterous, on the lam or in jail. The unmistakable message is that kids are on their own, with no need to listen to parents, who know little or nothing anyway. This helps the TV industry certify teenagers as an autonomous culture with its own set of ethics and consumption patterns. (p. 15)

Young people are a very important target for many Hollywood films, and a particular kind of film is believed to be the best draw for them. For example, in a profile of literary manager Warren Zide, *L.A. Times* reporter Claudia Eller examines the values operating in Hollywood. She says,

> When it came to getting the script for *American Pie* in shape to be sold, Zide said he and his colleagues advised (the writer) "to write the raunchiest script possible without worrying about the rating." Apparently it was good advice. The R-rated comedy about four high-school buddies who make a pact to lose their virginity before graduation piqued interest of several studios before it was sold to Universal Pictures for $650,000. (Eller, 1999, p. C5)

Eller also quotes Zide on his reaction to a script about teenagers on a spring break: "I hated when I was growing up and you go to see some R-rated movie and there's no nudity in it, and you're like, 'Oh, man, I was gypped.'" So now, as a literary agent, Zide asks, "Do we have enough T&A in it?" (p. C5).

■ BECOMING LITERATE ABOUT ENTERTAINMENT CONTENT

Now that you have more information about the patterns of characters, plots, and values of entertainment stories in the media, you have a stronger knowledge structure about media content. When you use this knowledge structure with advanced skills, you will be able to see much more in those messages. Table 6.1 shows the cognitive, emotional, aesthetic, and moral skills you will need. It also provides some examples of knowledge across these four domains. Do not restrict yourself to the specifics in Table 6.1; instead, use the information presented there to stimulate your thinking about other skills and knowledge. Then,

TABLE 6.1

	SKILLS	*KNOWLEDGE*
COGNITIVE	Ability to analyze entertainment content to identify key plot points, types of characters, and themes	Knowledge of elements in entertainment formula
	Ability to see entertainment formula	
	Ability to compare/contrast plot points, characters, and themes across vehicles and media	
EMOTIONAL	Ability to analyze the portrayed feelings of characters	Recall from personal experiences how it would feel to be in the situation in the story
	Ability to put one's self into the position of different characters in the story	
	Ability to control emotions elicited by the plot and themes	
AESTHETIC	Ability to analyze the craft and artistic elements in the story	Knowledge of writing, directing, acting, editing, sound mixing, etc.
	Ability to compare and contrast the artistry used to tell this story with that used to tell other stories	Knowledge of well told and poorly told stories and the elements that contributed to those qualities
MORAL	Ability to analyze the moral elements as evidenced by decisions made by characters, implications of those decisions revealed by the plot, and underlying theme	Knowledge of what moral systems say about different decisions as well as knowledge of the moral implications of your decisions
	Ability to compare/contrast ethical decisions presented in this story with those in other stories	Knowledge of other stories that have portrayed this topic both well and poorly
	Ability to evaluate the ethical responsibilities of the producers and programmers	Knowledge of values of people in the media industries

during your exposures to media entertainment, recall the knowledge you will need and consciously apply the skills in all four domains.

During exposure to the media, remember that entertainment messages follow a formula. The people who create this world must be creative within a rigid formula. Viewers want formulaic characters and plots so the entertainment is easy to follow. Look at how closely those stories follow the formula. Also, notice how stories deviate from the formula, and try to assess the magnitude of those deviations. How much can a story deviate before you become confused and lose sense of what is happening? Look at the stories that are most popular, that is, the highest-rated television programs and movies with the largest box office. How closely do they follow the formula? Examine the actors and actresses in those popular stories. What do they do that makes them so popular?

Keep in mind that the world presented in television entertainment differs from the real world in many ways. The television world contains fewer women, minorities, poor people, and blue-collar workers. The plots are often driven by sex and violence and have unrealistic messages about health in the background. The television world is based on certain themes that continually appear.

Keep asking questions about these stories. Be skeptical. Take nothing for granted. If you stay active during your exposures, you will be increasing your media literacy and thus gaining more control over how you construct your place in the real world.

■■ FURTHER READING

Cantor, M. G. (1980). *Prime-time television*. Beverly Hills, CA: Sage. (143 pages including index)

> Written by a sociologist who spent 10 years interviewing actors, writers, and producers, this book explains how decisions about content are made in the television industry. She develops a model to show that there are many forces that shape the development of any television program. The examples in the book are dated, but the principles still apply.

Greenberg, B. S. (1980). *Life on television*. Norwood, NJ: Ablex. (204 pages including index)

> This is a classic content analysis of American television drama in the mid-1970s. Each of the 13 chapters addresses a different content topic, such as the demography of fictional characters, sex role portrayals, anti-social and pro-social behaviors, family interaction patterns, sexual intimacy, and drug use.

Lichter, S. R., Lichter, L. S., & Rothman, S. (1994). *Prime time: How TV portrays American culture*. Washington, DC: Regnery. (478 pages)

> This is a look at what is on television written from a critical humanistic perspective. There are few statistics but lots of examples from programs to illus-

trate the authors' main point that the world of television is very different from the real world of families, work, sex, crime, and so on.

Medved, M. (1992). *Hollywood vs. America: Popular culture and the war on traditional values*. New York: HarperCollins.

This film critic argues that Hollywood has a value system that is very different from that of mainstream America. Hollywood glorifies the perverse, ridicules all forms of mainstream religion, tears down the image of the family, and glorifies ugliness with violence, bad language, and bashing America. Then the industry is puzzled why attendance is dropping and criticism is increasing.

Metallinos, Nikos. (1996). *Television aesthetics: Perceptual, cognitive, and compositional bases*. Mahwah, NJ: Lawrence Erlbaum. (305 pages with index)

This book lays out many principles of aesthetics, from both a social science and an artistic perspective. The author demonstrates that humans are bound by their perceptual capabilities and the functioning processes of their brains. However, people also create culture through their art. A person who is visually literate needs to have information in the areas of perception, cognition, and artistic composition.

National Television Violence Study. (1996). *Scientific report*. Thousand Oaks, CA: Sage. (568 pages with index)

The National Cable Television Association funded this $3.3-million project to examine the prevalence and context of violence on American television; the effects of warnings and advisories placed before violent programs; and the effect of public service announcements advocating the avoidance of violence. Some of the chapters are very technical and contain many statistics, but the overall report is the most comprehensive analysis of the issue of violence on television to date.

Postman, N. (1984). *Amusing ourselves to death: Public discourse in the age of show business*. New York: Penguin. (184 pages with index)

This is a strong, well-written argument about how the media, especially television, have conditioned us to expect entertainment. Because our perceptions of ideas are shaped by the form of their expression, we are now image oriented. We respond to pleasure, not thought and reflection.

EXERCISE 6.1

Watch a television program, then think about the following tasks.

1. *Analysis.* Break down the program by:
   a. Listing the main characters
   b. Listing the main plot points
   c. Were there violent elements? If so, list them.
   d. Were there sexual elements? If so, list them.
   e. Were there health-related elements? If so, list them.

2. *Compare/Contrast.* Select the two main characters
   a. How are they the same/different demographically?
   b. How are they the same/different by personality characteristics?
   c. How are they the same/different in the way they move the plot forward?

3. *Evaluation.* Think about all the characters and make the following judgments.
   a. In your judgment, which character was the most humorous? Why?
   b. In your judgment, which character was the most ethical in his or her behavior? Why?
   c. In your judgment, which actor/actress displayed the best acting skills? Why?
   d. In your judgment, which of the plot points were the strongest? Which were the weakest?
   e. In your judgment, what is the theme of this show?

4. *Abstraction.* Describe your show (characters and plot) in 50 words or less.

5. *Generalization.* Start with particular characters and particular happenings in your show, then infer general patterns about people and events in general.
   a. Think about the demographics of the characters in your show. Do the demographics in your show match the patterns of demographics in the real world?
   b. Think about the plot elements (sex, violence, health) in your show. Do these elements in your show match the patterns of these elements in the real world?

6. *Appreciation*
   a. Emotional: Was the show able to evoke emotions in you? If so, list those emotions and explain how the show triggered those particular emotions.
   b. Aesthetic: Is there something about the writing, directing, editing, lighting, set design, costuming, or music/sound effects that you found of particularly high quality? If so, explain what led you to appreciate that element so much.
   c. Moral: Did the show raise ethical considerations (either explicitly or implicitly)? If so, did you appreciate how the show dealt with those ethical considerations?

EXERCISE 6.2

Analyzing the Content of Television Entertainment

1. Write a definition of sexual behavior. This is not as easy as it might first seem. You must consider issues such as what the characters must do, the characters' intentions (a kiss or a hug is not always sexual), and what about talk (if a character talks about what he or she wants to do, does that count)?

2. Watch two different situation comedies and count how many acts occur that meet your definition of sexual behavior. Note the gender, age, and ethnic background of the characters.

3. Discuss your results with others in class who did their own content analyses of sex.

   a. What is the range in the numbers of acts found? Can this range be attributed to differences in definitions or differences in shows?

   b. Profile the types of characters who were most often involved in sexual activity.

   c. Are there any noticeable differences in character profiles across types of situation comedies?

4. Now try using your definition to analyze the content on soap operas, music videos, and action/adventure dramas.

   a. Do you see any big differences in the number of sexual acts across different types of shows?

   b. Do you see any big differences in the profiles of characters involved in sexual activity across shows?

5. Now think about how sex is portrayed in the television world.

   a. What types of activity are the most prevalent?

   b. How responsibly is sex portrayed in the television world—that is, are the physical and emotional risks often discussed or considered? Is sex portrayed as a normal part of a loving, stable relationship or is it portrayed more as a game of conquest or a source of silliness?

   c. Did you find anything in the patterns that surprised you?

6. What do you need to know about how sex is portrayed in the media and the role of sex in the real world in order for you to construct a strong knowledge structure on this subject?

CHAPTER 7

Key Idea: We live in a culture saturated with advertising messages. There are some popular criticisms of advertising that form the public discourse, but the issues of more important concern lie at a deeper level.

Commercial Advertising

Let's begin with the question: What are the products of advertising? Some of you might interpret this to mean what the clients of the ad agencies want to sell—laundry soaps, cars, soft drinks, hamburgers, and the like. Others of you might think that the products are the ads we see—after all, that is what the people in the industry create and show to us constantly. Both of these interpretations have some truth to them on the surface, but both miss the point of the real nature of advertising. The most important product of advertising is you.

Advertisers have trained you and all members of the public to give them your time, attention, and money. Advertisers have spent hundreds of billions of dollars over your lifetime to craft special messages that have put hundreds of thousands of images, jingles, ideas, and desires into your memory banks. They have done this with your permission and even your blessing. And they have even convinced you to pay them for conditioning you.

ADVERTIJING IJ PERVAJIVE

Our country is saturated with advertising. With about 6% of the world's population, the United States absorbs almost half of the world's advertising expenditure. Advertising expenditures account for 2.4% of our Gross National Product—that is a higher percentage than any other country on earth. To put this into perspective, the total money accounted for by organized crime (gambling, prostitution, drugs, etc.) is less than half of the money spent on advertising.

We are literally surrounded by ads constantly (see Table 7.1). A decade ago, it was estimated that the average American sees anywhere from 300 (McCarthy, 1991) to 1,600 (Clark, 1988) ad messages each day. Even if we take the low end of this range, that is about 110,000 messages each year or almost 20 ads for every waking hour. In 1971, the average American was targeted with at least 560 ads messages per day; in 20 years it had climbed to 3,000 per day (Koenenn,

TABLE 7.1   Pervasiveness of Advertising in America

Newspapers

60% of the typical newspaper is advertising. Newspapers are now primarily vehicles for ads more than
   for news. For example, the *New York Times* Sunday edition contains 350 pages of ads.

Despite the growth in the size of most newspapers, the space given to the news (the news hole) has remained the same. Newspapers have given about the same amount of space to news content since
   1910, however; the overall size of newspapers doubled during that time, but the percentage of the
   newspaper that contains news has shrunk by half.

Film

Movie theaters bombard viewers with ads. A series of ads is projected on the screen while the audience
   waits for the show to begin. Then, during the film itself, ads are embedded as various companies pay
   to have their products prominently displayed throughout the plot. Lays potato chips in *Poltergeist,*
   Wheaties in *Rocky III,* Bud in *Tootsie,* Milk Duds and Zagnut in *48 Hours.* There are 30 companies
   operating in Hollywood to place products within movies and TV shows. In *Santa Claus—The Movie,*
   McDonald's paid $1 million to the film makers to have a scene set in a specially constructed McDon-
   ald's restaurant. Some films have up to 46 different products prominently displayed and paid for by
   their sponsors (Fuller, 1997).

Radio

Some radio stations present 40 minutes of ads per hour.

Television

Most television stations present at least 40 ads per hour. In prime time, the Big 4 (ABC, CBS, Fox, and
   NBC) aired 14 minutes and 15 seconds of ads and promos on average during every hour, and in daytime the time is even higher with the average across all channels being almost 19 minutes per hour
   (Standard & Poor's, 1996, p. M38). Between 1965 and 1995 ads on network TV got shorter and more
   frequent—the average length shrank from 53.1 seconds to 25.4 seconds, and the number of ads per
   minute increased from 1.1 to 2.4 (Koenenn, 1997).

The average American household has the TV on more than 47 hours per week. Out of this time, about
   12 hours are ads. By the time a typical American leaves high school, he or she has seen over a quarter of a million TV commercials.

Ads are embedded in some TV shows. CBS's *The Price is Right* gets $1 million in payments from product
   producers each year; this is in addition to the prizes the manufacturers give away on the show.

Now advertisers are creating their own shows, often naming them after their products. For example,
   Nissan helped create a show to reach the target audience of its Pathfinder—a target of men and
   women with a median age of 40 and a median income of $75,000 (Matzer, 1996). Called *Pathfinder:
   Exotic Journeys,* it is a half-hour travel adventure show hosted by model Cheryl Tiegs. Subaru is developing a competing travel series named after its vehicle, Outback. Dodge has its action-adventure series called *Viper.* Dodge told producers it did not want sex or foul language so as to provide a "good,
   healthy family show that provides a showcase for our product" (p. D4). Dodge plans to develop Vi-
   per-related merchandise, much of it intended for children.

Computers

Internet advertising climbed to $544.8 million in 1997, an increase of 147% over the previous year, according to Media Advertising Solutions. Technology companies were the big advertisers, led by Microsoft. There is a discrepancy among reporting groups. One group (Internet Advertising Bureau) estimated the figure to be $906.5 million for the same time period (Maddox, 1998).

Internet Advertising Bureau says that in 1998 advertising on the Internet neared $2 billion. Almost half of this money came from computer and software advertisers (Maddox, 1999).

Non-Media

Ads are on the sides of buildings, taxis, busses, and even on the clothing of people walking the streets.

Third class mail (junk mail) in the 1980s grew 13 times faster than the population (Koenenn, 1997).

There are now talking billboards that are fitted with a low-power radio transmitter that tells motorists where to tune for more information on the product advertised on the billboard (Horowitz, 1996).

Ads have even moved into public toilets. Chicago's United Center sports area charges advertisers $1,000 a year for an 8-by-11 inch space on its bathroom walls (Horowitz, 1996).

Now ads will also appear on police cars in Oxnard, California, where the City Council approved a money-raising plan to sell advertising space on police cruisers ("Police Cars," 1995).

Pepsi-Cola has produced the first TV commercial in space by paying Russia to have their cosmonauts aboard their space station Mir deploying a can of Pepsi into space (Horowitz, 1996). PepsiCo, owners of Pizza Hut, has also sponsored the Russian space program in another way. In November 1999 the Russians launched a Proton rocket that had a 30-foot logo of Pizza Hut painted on it ("Pizza Pie in the Sky," 1999).

Sporting events are themselves vehicles for ads. Even the Olympics are advertising events. In 1984 the Olympic Games in Los Angeles became the first to be supported entirely by commercial sponsorship, and they made a big profit. VISA alone spent $25 million for exclusive advertising rights and on promotions. One by one all major sporting events are turning to sponsorships for funding.

Ads are in public schools. Whittle Communications gives to all participating public schools the equipment needed to receive satellite programming and provides them with a 12-minute news program daily. Inserted in those programs are 2 minutes of ads paid for by companies interested in getting their ad messages in front of youngsters. About 65% of the public in national polls objected to this, but Whittle went ahead in the schools that did not object (Turow, 1992).

Even the Pope has been commercialized. The Vatican acknowledges that the Pope's visits are costly, so it has agreed to sponsorship. The Pope's 4-day visit to Mexico in the winter of 1999 was sponsored by Frito-Lay and PepsiCo. Some Catholics criticized this practice, but the Church defends it. For example, Mexican Archbishop Norberto Rivera said that, "The church has the challenge to be present in all media." Apostolic Nuncio Justo Mullor said, "We live in an era of advertising and we are men of that era" (Sutter, 1999).

In Sweden they have tried interrupting personal phone calls with ads.

1997). Now that we are beyond the year 2000 all of these exposure figures are much higher, because the number of messages produced by the advertising industry substantially increases each year.

Each year, the amount of money spent on advertising grows dramatically. In 1900, about $500 million was spent on all forms of advertising in the United States. By 1940 it was $2 billion, so it took 40 years to multiply four times. In 1980 it was $60 billion or a increase of 30 times in those 40 years. Now in 2000 it will be over $220 billion. These numbers are so large, they are difficult to comprehend. Let's break the expenditures down by number of people in the population. In 1940 the industry spent $16 on each person in this country; by 1980 it spent $260 and now the amount is over $700.

An advertiser who wants to introduce a new product and break through the existing clutter to get consumers to realize that there is a new product on the market must spend about $50 million minimum for a national introduction of a new product in grocery or drug stores. Of course, the new advertisements add to the clutter making it even more expensive for the next product introduction. All of this behavior serves to increase the clutter exponentially. And we are still in a growth cycle.

Why can we expect continued growth? Because we—the public—do not mind all this advertising. Of course, we sometimes criticize certain ads we don't like, and sometimes we get upset when we watch television and have our shows repeatedly interrupted by commercial breaks. But our criticisms are minor compared to our unthinking support of advertising. By "unthinking" support, I mean that most of us do not realize how much advertising exposure we experience every day and how it has shaped our attitudes and behaviors.

Stop reading this chapter right now and do this quick exercise. Look around your room or out the window and see how many ad messages for products, events, services, and ideas you can spot. Look carefully. Try not to miss any. Do not overlook what is on your clothing. Are you wearing a hat, shirt, jacket, or shoes with a product name or logo clearly showing? If so, you are advertising that product for the manufacturer. How much is the manufacturer paying you to perform this service? Of course you are being paid nothing. Did you realize that you are paying the manufacturers a premium for these products for the privilege of advertising for them? Had you bought the same piece of clothing without the prized logo, it would have cost you less money. Therefore you have chosen to pay more for the privilege of wearing a particular brand. This is a good deal for those manufacturers who have you working for them *and* have *you* paying *them*!

■■ POPULAR SURFACE CRITICISMS

Over the years, there has been public criticism of advertising for all sorts of reasons. Five of these are illuminated below.

I call these "surface" criticisms, because we usually accept them at face value; that is, we rarely dig beneath the surface or analyze them. Instead, we accept someone else's opinion rather than really thinking about the criticism for ourselves. With a little thinking, we can see that each of these criticisms is a controversy—there are two legitimate sides. When you understand both sides, you can then build an informed opinion for yourself.

1. *Advertising is excessive.* The average person is exposed to several thousand advertising messages each day. Whether this is excessive or not is a matter of opinion. For example, when people are asked, "Do you think there is too much advertising on television?" about 70% say yes. But if they are asked, "Do you think that your being shown all this advertising is a fair price for you to pay to be able to see 'free' television?" again 70% will say yes (Miller, 1989).

But television is hardly free; it just seems free. Now, a large part of the cost of many products is advertising. For example, when you buy soap or toothpaste, about 35% of the cost is due to advertising. Also, most households now have cable television; these households pay for television and they also pay more when they buy advertised products.

Is advertising excessive? You must decide whether you are getting value for what you are paying for in terms of better entertainment, news, and products.

2. *Advertising manipulates us into buying things we don't need.* How do we define a need? If we stick to basic survival needs, then yes, advertisers ask us to buy many things beyond our absolute basic needs for survival. At base we really only need a set of clothes, a shelter, and some daily food.

The psychologist Abraham Maslow has pointed out that there are levels of needs beyond survival. Once humans have met the basic survival needs, they become concerned with other needs, such as safety needs, social needs, and self-actualization needs. We need to feel accepted by friends and colleagues. Dressing right helps with this. For social needs we need many different outfits of clothes. We need a certain type of car. We need to live in a certain kind of home. We need certain kinds of foods and beverages. We use all these products to define ourselves in social situations. Are these products luxuries or necessities?

3. *Advertising debases the language.* Some people complain that advertising slogans misspell words, use poor grammar, and glorify slang. Whether you are bothered by this or not depends on what your conception of language is. Some people feel there is a proper way to speak. They feel that when people do not speak properly, it is a sign of ignorance, and that is offensive to them.

Other people view language as something that is organic and growing to meet the changing needs of a culture. They feel that bending and breaking the rules of grammar, spelling, and expression are signs of creativity and should be valued. This is how new words get into the language.

4. Advertising is offensive or in bad taste. Who is to determine what bad taste is? This is a personal judgment. Some people are offended when they see ads for condoms or feminine hygiene products, but other people appreciate being exposed to that information.

5. Advertising perpetuates stereotypes. If advertisers are trying to sell to a wide audience, they must use stereotypes. A 15-second television commercial cannot develop a character in all the rich detail needed to make us feel that it is not a two-dimensional stereotype. Advertisers must present their messages very quickly. This requires simplifying everything, including characters.

When we analyze this criticism, we can see that the problem has less to do with stereotyping than it has to do with whether portrayals are negative or positive. If an entire class of people (such as all women or all African Americans) is portrayed as having negative characteristics, then you will argue that this is bad. If all young blonde women are portrayed as dumb, this is a negative stereotype and it is offensive to many people. However, if an entire class of people is portrayed as being attractive, smart, and successful, it is not likely that people would be offended by this, although this too is a stereotype.

❖ THINKING MORE DEEPLY

We need to look past the surface criticisms and analyze the nature of advertising more deeply. When we do this, we can see that there are several issues of foundational importance: social responsibility, children, deception, materialism, and subliminal advertising.

Social Responsibility

John Kenneth Galbraith, Harvard economist and advisor to presidents, views advertising as primarily a negative force on society. He argues that a good deal of the consumption in high-production economies such as ours is unnecessary. Manufacturers produce much more than Americans need to consume. If it weren't for advertising, consumers would buy much less. Because the management of companies is under a great deal of pressure to increase production (to increase profits and also beat last year's goals), they use advertising heavily. They must create and control demand. Second, Galbraith believes that the consumer is persuadable. The minimum needs of consumers are affected little by advertising (food, clothing, and shelter). But as a consumer's needs become psychological, advertising has a more powerful effect. Third, Galbraith believes this artificial demand—which is driven by advertising—leads to a misallocation of resources in society. We should be using the majority of our resources for the common good (such as public education, public parks, public transportation, etc.) rather than channeling those resources into private consumption (such as designer jeans, shampoos, etc.).

In contrast to Galbraith, historian David Potter regards advertising as a positive force on society. He sees advertising as a social institution comparable to the school and the church in its power to convey information and to teach values. An important value in America is the transforming of natural resources into abundance. Advertising supports this value and reinforces our inherent need to consume and enjoy doing so.

David Potter, however, does express some concern that advertising has no over-riding responsibility to society. Other institutions (such as the family, education, religion, etc.) are altruistic; they try to improve the individual and society. Advertising is very different. Advertising is selfish; its only responsibility is to serve the marketing objectives of the company that pays for it.

Some critics argue that advertisers should be more socially responsible. Advertisers depend on the goodwill of the public, so they should act socially responsible in order to maintain that goodwill. But often advertisers are so motivated by the marketing perspective that they completely ignore their social responsibility. For example, for 50 years liquor manufacturers have not used television to advertise their products because of a sense of social responsibility, in a voluntary attempt to protect children and teenagers from seeing liquor ads. But during the fall of 1996, Joseph E. Seagram & Sons began airing spots for two whisky brands on independent TV stations around the country. The company was motivated by the single desire to increase sales and felt it was bad business to continue avoiding the use of the powerful advertising medium of television. In defense of his company's move, Tod Ridriguez, general sales manager, said, "There are a lot worse things than alcohol ads on TV" (Gellene, 1996). Many people found this incident very upsetting and the Seagram Company's reasoning very self-serving. Incidents like this illustrate the shift away from social responsibility toward marketing.

Anheuser-Busch—the number one brewer—found beer sales flat in 1998. Its typical target audience is young men and they are typically reached in sporting shows. To increase their overall sales, Anheuser-Busch decided to increase beer drinking among women who accounted for only about 17% of their sales. So Anheuser-Busch decided to break their self-imposed barrier of not targeting women in the television audience and begin advertising on daytime TV. A consultant to the company said, "It should be done. For the beer people not to be selling full-bore ahead on one gender is absurd" (Arndorfer, 1998, p. 8).

Children

Children are regarded as an important market by advertisers. American kids (4 to 18) have a combined annual allowance of $70 billion, which is the total of Finland's gross domestic product ("Material Kids on the March," 1994). The younger children are targeted with ads on Saturday mornings where almost all the ads are for toys or food. Among the food ads, 90% are for junk food, such as sugary cereals, candy bars, potato chips, and fast food (Wharton, 1991).

Children's TV programs contain a high proportion of ads. Cable networks had the least amount (10:38 minutes per hour on average) compared to broadcast networks (12:09) and independents (13:29; Kunkel & Gantz, 1992). Also, less than 3% of the ads are for healthy foods, while 22% are for cereals and breakfast foods, 18% are for snacks and drinks, 6% for fast foods, and 34% for toys. Only about half of the ads in children's programs have a disclosure such as, "part of a balanced breakfast," "parts sold separately," or "ask your parents' permission."

In 1998, $2 billion was spent on advertising to children. This was 20 times more than in 1988. The average American child now sees more than 30,000 TV commercials per year ("Numbers," 1999, p. 21).

This leads parents and social critics to be concerned about children when it comes to advertising. Recall from Chapter 2 that young children have not developed to a point where they can understand certain elements about ads and therefore cannot protect themselves. Unfortunately, rarely do parents view ads with their children and discuss them; they become mediators only when children are disappointed with a product or when they are frustrated that their parents won't buy it (Adler et al., 1980).

Tobacco companies have been targeting young people (ages 14 to 24) for decades as a prime market. In 1991, the Joe Camel campaign was launched to appeal to teens by focusing a lot of ads around high schools and colleges. In 5 years the sale of Camels to teens went from $6 to $476 million (Holland, 1998). Teenagers are three times as likely as adults to respond to cigarette ads; 79% smoke brands depicted as fun, sexy, and popular ("Study Links Teen Smoking to Popular Ads," 1996)

Critics are upset about the new television program called *Teletubbies*, which is aimed at 1- and 2-year-olds. The show and the product spill-offs are training infants to want material goods.

The American Academy of Pediatrics suggests that doctors work with parents to evaluate how much TV kids watch and what they see, what video and computer games they play, what music they like, and what books they read. The academy recommends that children under the age of 2 not watch any TV ("Numbers," 1999, p. 76).

Deception

Perhaps the most damaging criticism of advertising is that it is generally deceptive. In everyday language, we think of deception as lying. Do ads lie? Very seldom is there an ad with a blatant falsehood. Advertisers know that if they present a claim they cannot support, they can be fined, so they avoid making explicit claims that can be checked for truth and are therefore regulated. Instead, advertisers make implicit claims that cannot be tested. Also, most advertisers know that their product differs from their competitors' in very minor ways, so the explicit claims they could make about their products are not very interesting or compelling.

How do advertisers make compelling claims about their products without lying? They use what is called "puffery," that is, they puff up their product with exaggerations that are expressions of opinion rather than claims of some objective quality or characteristic of the product. Puffery gives viewers the illusion that they are being given important information about the product, but this illusion evaporates when we look more closely at the ad. For example, have you ever seen an ad where any of the following claims were made: "the best of its kind," "the most beautiful," or "the finest"? These slogans at first seem to be telling us something, but upon closer examination, they are empty claims because they cannot be tested.

Also, some ads present implied superiority claims, such as "Nothing beats a great pair of L'eggs" (pantyhose), "The ones to beat" (Chrysler K cars), and "Nobody does it better" (Winston Lights cigarettes). On the surface, these slogans imply that their products are superior, but when we examine them more closely, we realize that they are not really making a clear comparison with another product.

Another element of puffery is when an ad tells the truth—but not the whole truth. For example, many brands that are labeled as a fruit juice drink contain only 10% fruit juice; the ad contains an element of truth, but it is misleading. Also, ads for many cereals show a brand as "part of this complete breakfast," which features several nutritious foods such as fruit, bread, and milk. This statement is literally truthful, but almost none of the nutrition in the claim comes from the cereal.

How do advertisers use puffery to suppress the truth? Jamieson and Campbell (1988) list the following tactics:

- Pseudo claims: An example of this is "X fights cavities," but we are not told how. Is it a chemical in the toothpaste, the movement of the brush on the teeth, or the habit of brushing?

- Comparison with an unidentified other: "X has better cleaning action." Better than what? Better than another brand? Better than not cleaning? There is an implied comparison that makes the product sound superior, but it really is a meaningless claim.

- Comparison of the product to its earlier form: "X is new and improved!" Again, on the surface this seems like a good thing—until we start thinking about it. What was wrong with the old version? And what is wrong with this current version that will end up being new and improved again next year?

- Irrelevant comparisons: "X is the best selling product of its kind." What kind? Maybe *kind* is defined so narrowly that there is only one brand of its kind. Also, maybe it is the best seller, because it is the cheapest or because it wears out so fast.

- Pseudo survey: "Four out of five dentists surveyed said they recommend X." Who are these four? Maybe they were paid to recommend it.

- Juxtaposition: A smiling person holds product so that viewers associate happiness with the product.

Thus advertising messages are designed to use puffery to trick us into believing there is more to the product than there really is. They give us the illusion of making a strong claim when in fact the claims are weak or non-existent.

This leaves us stuck between the truth and a lie. While most advertising is not technically false, it cannot be considered true (Preston, 1994). The ads cannot be regulated, because they are not technically false. But neither are they true. Apparently Americans regard this puffery as a form of deception, because in public opinion polls, 80% of people feel that television advertising offers primarily deceptive persuasion (Calfee, 1994). Also, only 17% regard TV advertising as a source of good information (Norris, 1983; Soley & Reid, 1983).

Materialism

Some critics claim that advertising makes us too materialistic. How much is *too* much? Some people believe we should conserve natural resources and live at a lower level of consumption. Other people believe that we should always strive for more of everything; if it looks like we might run short of resources, we will be able to figure out a way to solve the problem.

Though it has about 6% of the world's population, the United States consumes nearly 30% of the planet's resources. Americans can choose from more than 30,000 supermarket items, including 200 kinds of cereal. Do we really need all these material products?

Americans say they are dissatisfied with materialism despite all the abundance. In a recent survey, 82% of Americans agreed that most of us buy and consume far more than we need. And 67% agreed that Americans cause many of the world's environmental problems, because we consume more resources and produce more waste than anyone else in the world (Koenenn, 1997). Yet we continue to consume at a greater rate each year.

What drives the consumption? Advertisers do, and Americans have positive beliefs and attitudes about advertising. About 45% say they have a generally favorable attitude toward advertising, while only 15% have an unfavorable attitude.

Thus the public is schizophrenic about advertising. Despite the huge amount of advertising, which continues to grow each year, and despite the fact that most of us think advertising is deceptive, few of us hold a negative attitude about advertising. We believe we are too materialistic but keep asking for more products.

Subliminal Advertising

Is there such a thing as subliminal persuasion? That is, are there subliminal messages that have a powerful effect on us? In order to answer this question, we first need to be clear about what *subliminal* means. The popularized version of subliminal persuasion reflects a conscious effort on the part of the sender to deceive a viewer by adding something to a message that is not consciously perceivable by the audience—but the person's unconscious mind perceives that "extra message." For example, in the 1950s, James Vickery inserted messages of "Eat Popcorn" and "Drink Coke" into a theatrical film, and claimed that the theater audience bought much more popcorn and Coke, even though no one reported seeing the ads, because they were projected too quickly. Later it was found that Vickery's results were a hoax. But this story has entered our folklore, and many people believe that unscrupulous advertisers are exposing us to subliminal messages all the time.

The very idea of subliminal advertising having an effect on us is a hoax. The word *subliminal* means below our threshold to perceive. For example, the human eye cannot see an image if it is shown for less than about one sixteenth of a second—that is below our line of ability to perceive an image. This is why movies appear to show moving images when in actuality what is being projected is a series of still shots. If those shots are projected at about 12 per second, we would see a flicker in between shots, but we would still perceive motion. Once those individual images are projected at 16 per second, the flicker disappears, that is, it happens too fast to register an impression on us. The flicker between the individual images is still there, but we can no longer perceive it. Hollywood films are projected at 24 or more frames per second. At this speed there is no chance for any individual frame to register a unique impression on us. So even if an advertiser placed an ad in one frame every second, each of those exposures would be too brief to cross the threshold of our ability to perceive it. If we cannot perceive an image, then it can have no effect on us. I'll further clarify this point with an audio example. You can train a dog to come to you when you blow a dog whistle, which emits a very high-pitched sound that the dog can hear but you cannot. The pitch of the sound is outside of the hearing range of humans, that is, the sound does not cross the threshold into our perceptual ability to hear it. Can you train a person to come to you every time you blow a dog whistle? If people cannot hear the whistle, they cannot know when you are blowing it, and they cannot respond to a stimulus that they cannot perceive. Thus subliminal stimuli—because they are outside a human's ability to perceive them—can have no effect on humans.

When some people use the term "subliminal advertising effects" what they really mean is "unconscious effects of advertising." This unconscious influence *is* a powerful effect with which we should be concerned. Because we are exposed to thousands of messages each day, we cannot think about them all. Instead we consciously ignore them, but those sounds and images get into our ears and eyes, leaving traces on our subconscious. Bit by bit, those images build up and eventually exert influences on our attitudes and behaviors. For example, after an evening of watching television, we feel hungry and want to eat. Our stomach is not grumbling because we are not physically hungry. But our mind is telling us to eat something. Throughout the evening we have left the room during commercial breaks or zipped through the channels during these breaks. We were exposed to repeated images and jingles about tasty snacks, sizzling burgers, hearty soups, foamy beverages, and on and on. If someone called and asked us to recall which commercials we saw that evening, we would not be able to remember more than a small handful. Yet we are restless, and our minds tell us we are hungry.

Over years of evenings like this, we also learn many general lessons about consumption and how to solve problems. While each ad is trying to get you to buy a particular product, at a deeper level all ads are teaching you lessons about who you should be and how you can get there. To illustrate, let's consider an example of an ad for toothpaste, which on the surface is only an ad for a particular toothpaste. But it comes with several layers of deeper meaning embedded in the message. At a deeper level, the ad is a message about the importance of health. At an even deeper level, it conveys a message about consumerism, that is, you need to buy something to clean your teeth; you cannot simply use water to brush your teeth. Also at a deeper level is an implied endorsement for eating foods that will contribute to decay, because by using toothpaste you remove the risk—so a quick fix is possible, that is, you can have it both ways. You can see that a "simple" ad for a toothpaste carries with it several layers of meaning, some of which may be consciously processed (the surface claims made in the particular ad), and some of which are unconsciously processed (how to solve problems, the nature of health, etc.).

BECOMING MORE LITERATE ▪▪

In order to increase your media literacy about advertising, you need to have elaborate knowledge structures about advertising (see Table 7.2) and about your own needs. To build a stronger knowledge structure about ads, do Exercise 7.1, which is designed to strengthen your skills. Exercise 7.2 will help you become more aware of your needs.

Awareness of Ads

Ads are designed to present a single product claim. This is presented as the reason you should buy the advertised product, that is, the product will do something of value for you. That something of value might be in the form of a physical feature, a functional feature, or a characterizational feature. Physical features focus attention on the product itself and its ingredients (e.g., Buy our toothpaste because it contains XW7, which is the strongest decay fighting chemical ever!). Functional features focus attention on how the product is used (e.g., Buy our toothpaste because it comes in an easy-to-use pump!). Characterizational features focus attention on the psychological consequences of the consumption (e.g., Buy our toothpaste because it will make you feel safe from tooth decay—no matter what you eat!).

Ads usually present one simple claim and emphasize it over and over. If the claim focuses on a physical or functional feature, it is very easy to spot. Characterizational ads are more ambiguous. They are usually designed to make you feel something, then link that feeling to the product.

The other thing you need to be concerned about when you look at ads is to try to determine what the intended effect of the ad is. Most people think that an ad is designed to convince people to buy a product. Very little of the advertising we see has this intention. Many ads, especially those for new products, are only intended to establish an awareness that the product exists. Some ads are designed to create an emotion in us and to link that emotion to the product. Some ads are designed to inoculate us against the claims of competitors so that when we see an ad for one of their competitors we will not come under its influence. But the

TABLE 7.2

	SKILLS	KNOWLEDGE
COGNITIVE	Ability to analyze an advertisement in order to identify key elements of persuasion	Knowledge of topic from many sources (Media and real world)
	Ability to compare/contrast key elements of persuasion in the ad with facts in your real-world knowledge structure	
	Ability to evaluate veracity of claims in the ad	
EMOTIONAL	Ability to analyze the feelings of people in the ad	Recall from personal experiences how it feels to have a need for the advertised product
	Ability to put one's self into the position of different people in the ad	
AESTHETIC	Ability to analyze the craft and artistic elements in the ad	Knowledge of writing, graphics, photography, etc.
	Ability to compare and contrast the artistry used to craft this ad with that used to craft other types of ads	Knowledge of successful and unsuccessful ads and the elements that contributed to those qualities
MORAL	Ability to analyze the moral elements of an ad	Knowledge of criticism of advertising
	Ability to evaluate the ethical responsibilities of advertising	Knowledge of how ads can manipulate our attitudes and behaviors
		Highly developed moral code

most prevalent intention of ads is reinforcement. Most ads are aimed at target groups of people who already use the product. Thus the advertisement is designed to remind those customers that the product still exists and that it is a good one. People usually remember ads for products they already buy, so most of the effect of advertising is to reinforce existing attitudes and behaviors. Thus reinforcement is the most prevalent effect of advertising. Most ads are designed to make people feel good about the products they already have bought so that they will buy them again.

Awareness of Your Needs

The more you are aware of your needs, the more you can use advertising to control your life. If you are not aware of your needs, the more the constant flood of advertising messages will create and shape your needs—often without your knowing it. Stop reading this chapter now and go to Exercise 7.3.

How did you do on Part I? Were you able to come up with a long list of needs or could you think of only one or two? Was it easy or hard to rank order your needs? Then in Part II, were you surprised at how many products you have brought into your home? Were you surprised at how many were well-advertised brands?

Now ask yourself: How aware am I of my needs? Compare your rank ordered list from Part I with how you spend your money and time as indicated by the inventories in Part II. Is your primary need (from Part I) reflected in the inventories of your possessions and time (from Part II)? For example, let's say your number one ranked need was health. Did the inventory of your closet reveal more clothes for workouts than any other type of clothes? Did your inventory of your kitchen reveal an absence of highly advertised, high caloric, high fat, high sugar, high salt snacks? Did your inventory of your bathroom reveal more products for sore muscles or more for beauty? Is your toothpaste a decay preventer or a tooth whitener? Did the inventory of your time reveal that you are very active or mostly passive?

If your self-reported needs (from Part I) closely matched your inventories (from Part II), congratulations! You are aware of your needs and know how to spend your resources to satisfy them. But if there are discrepancies between your self-reported needs and where you spend your money and time, then you have a faulty sense of your needs. You might be telling yourself that your needs are A, B, and C while your real needs are X, Y, and Z. You are satisfying your real needs even though you are not aware of what they really are. More typically, discrepancies exist, because you are *not able* to satisfy your needs. That is, you are very aware of what your needs are, but when you go to the store you end up buying lots of things that really do not address those needs though you hope they will because you want to believe the puffery in the ads. But the will to believe is not enough. As time goes by you become frustrated that you cannot fulfill your major needs although it seems like you are doing what society (as channeled by advertisements) is telling you to do.

CONCLUSION ▪▪

Some people regard advertisers as unscrupulous manipulators who will do or say anything to get you to give them your money. They think advertising has changed the culture for the worse by making us too materialistic—creating a throw-away society of products, ideas, and people.

Other people regard advertisers as American heroes who are responsible for keeping the economy fired up by creatively encouraging more and more consumption. They argue that this has produced the richest society ever—one with the highest standard of living and the most variety in everything. They see advertising as a glamorous profession for creative people—a fast track to a rewarding career.

Who is right? Is advertising good or is it bad? What is the myth and what is the truth? You must decide for yourself. In making such a decision, it is risky to base it on a few intuitive impressions. Instead, it is much better to base your decision on a strong knowledge structure. Building such a knowledge structure requires you to be sensitive to the issues of how advertising influences businesses, the economy, critics, the public, language, and individuals—especially children. On almost all of these issues there is a range of opinion. When you understand that range and the philosophies underlying different positions, you are better able to construct a well-reasoned opinion for yourself.

EXERCISE 7.1

Becoming Sensitized to Advertising

1. How much advertising are you exposed to on a daily basis?

   For one day, carry around a sheet of paper in your pocket and write down every time you are exposed to an advertising message. Record the time, the product advertised, and the channel. Remember that channels can be media (newspapers, television, radio etc.) or they can be of other types such as posters (on walls, cars, kiosks, sidewalks, etc.), ads on clothing (sweatshirts, hats, footwear, etc.).

   How many ads were you exposed to in one day? How many different channels were used? How many of these exposures did you seek out?

2. Watch one hour of television and write down each ad. Remember that a promo for a station or a television show counts as an advertisement.

   How many did you record? Were you surprised at the number?

3. Go through your local newspaper page by page and count the ads.

   Are you surprised at how many ads there are? Does this amount bother you—if so, would you be willing to pay more for the newspaper if all ads were eliminated? About 80% of a newspaper's revenue comes from advertising. So if your newspaper currently costs 50 cents, that cost would increase to about $4.00 per copy if subscribers like you had to contribute all the revenue to your newspaper.

4. Get a piece of paper and make two lists. On one side, list all the breakfast cereals you can remember. Then turn the paper over and list all the shampoos you can remember.

   Go to a supermarket and count how many different cereals and shampoos are on the shelves. Were you able to name them all? What percentage were you able to name? Of those you did not have on your list, can you recall anything about their advertising campaigns? If so, why do you think you could not remember them when you made your list?

5. Next time you go to the drugstore or the supermarket to shop, try buying as many non-advertised products as you can in place of the advertised brands you usually buy.

   How much money did you save? Were the savings worth it or do you feel that you made a big mistake?

6. Run a taste test for your friends. Buy several brands of advertised cola and some obscure brands. Pour each of the different brands into separate cups. Ask your friends to taste each and tell you which cola is in which cup. Could your friends guess the right brands? Were they sure of their choices or were they making wild guesses?

EXERCISE 7.2

Look at several print ads from magazines and newspapers. Also, watch several ads on television. Use this set of ads in the following tasks.

1. Analysis:

   a. What is the main product claim (reason why you should use the product) of the ad?

   b. Is the claim presented explicitly or implicitly (do you have to infer it)?

   c. Do any of the ads use puffery?

   d. What is the intention of the ad? (Awareness, positive emotion, attitude change, inoculation, reinforcement, buy product)

   e. Look beyond the surface of the ads and the particular products, then list some values that the ads are teaching.

2. Compare/Contrast:

   a. How are product claims the same and different across the ads?

   b. Which product claims show up most often?

   c. How are intentions the same/different across ads?

   d. Which intention do you find most often?

3. Evaluation:

   a. In your judgment, which of the claims works best? Why?

   b. In your judgment, which of the claims does not work? Why?

4. Deduction: Can you see any patterns in these ads that exemplify any of the criticisms of advertising?

5. Appreciation:

   a. Emotional: Were any of the ads able to evoke strong emotions in you? If so, list those emotions and explain how the ad triggered the particular emotions.

   b. Aesthetic: Is there something about the writing, directing, editing, lighting, set design, costuming, or music/sound effects that you found of particularly high quality? If so, explain what led you to appreciate that element so much.

   c. Moral: Did any of the ads raise ethical considerations (either explicitly or implicitly)?

EXERCISE 7.3

Needs Inventory

Part I

On a sheet of paper write down your needs.

1. Begin by simply listing all your needs as they pop into your head.

2. Once you have a list, organize the elements into categories. Group all like needs together. For example, you might have several social needs (e.g., make more friends, become more popular, etc.), health needs (e.g., lose weight, exercise more, etc.), career needs, family needs, school needs, and so on.

3. Once your needs are in categories, rank order them. Which set of needs is the most important to you? Which is second, and so on.

   Put the paper in a drawer and go on to Part II.

Part II

1. Go through your clothes closet. How many changes of clothes (outfits) do you have? How many pairs of shoes?

   If you have one or two changes of clothes, you are operating at a functional level; that is, you are satisfied to protect your body from the elements and for the sake of modesty. If you have many sets of clothes, group them according to your needs; that is, which are your social clothes, your business clothes, your exercise clothes, and so on? Which set of clothes contains the greatest number of outfits? Why? Do you have the most clothes in an area that is the same as the one you designated as your highest-ranking need area in Part I?

2. Go through your kitchen cabinets and pantry.

   How many prepared foods (in boxes, cans, and bags) do you have compared to natural foods (milk, fresh fruit, fresh vegetables, etc.)? What proportion of the prepared foods are advertised brands and what proportion are unadvertised or generic?

3. Check your bathroom. How many "health and beauty" aids do you have?

   How many of those products are for basic health needs and how many are image enhancers? What proportion of the products are advertised brands and what proportion are unadvertised or generic?

4. Think about how you spend your time.

   How much time do you take getting washed, groomed, and dressed each day? How much time do you spend eating and snacking (how many times?)? What do you do with your leisure time—are you actively satisfying your needs or are you passively sitting in front of the TV set or listening to music while you are being told by others what your needs should be?

PART III

KNOWLEDGE STRUCTURES OF MEDIA INDUSTRIES

CHAPTER

8

Key Idea: The development of the media industries generally moves from the innovation stage to growth, peak, decline, then adaptation.

Development of the Mass Media Industries

I n this chapter, I'm asking you to think like a historian. This does not mean that I want you to memorize lots of names, facts, and dates. Instead, I want you to focus your attention on the broad patterns of how the media have developed over time and the factors that have shaped that development. In illustrating those patterns, I must present facts and dates, but those individual information bits are less important than the way they are arranged in patterns. Focus on those patterns and you will be able to organize a good knowledge structure about the development of the mass media industries. With such a knowledge structure, you will be able to continue your reading and thinking about the media industries much more efficiently.

PATTERNS OF DEVELOPMENT ▪▪

To organize our thinking about the development of the media industries and to show that all of these industries have changed in a similar manner, we can use a life cycle metaphor as a template. The life cycle metaphor provides a useful framework for examining the media industries because it focuses our attention on how the industries have gone through changes and why. The life cycle metaphor contains five stages: innovation (or birth), penetration (or growth), peak (or maturity), decline, and adaptation.

Each of the mass media industries began as an innovation. The innovation stage of a medium's development is characterized by a technological innovation that makes a channel of transmission possible or makes the transmission masslike in its capacity to disseminate information. All mass media industries are initially influenced by technological innovations that create and improve their capabilities. Without certain technological inventions and developments, the mass media would not exist.

The innovation stage also requires successful marketing or the medium will not be used by consumers and will not grow beyond this stage. A technological invention can create a channel of communication, but an entrepreneur with a vision must market that channel in order for it to be considered a mass medium. Entrepreneurs must have a mass-like orientation, that is, they must exploit the channel's potential to reach very large and broad audiences. For example, when individual newspapers shifted away from being political newsletters for small readerships toward a mass orientation of providing news to a general audience, this was a marketing innovation that transformed newspapers into a mass medium.

The penetration stage of a medium's development is characterized by the public's growing acceptance of that medium. As each medium grows, it is influenced by factors that shape its growth. These factors include the public's need and desire for the medium, additional innovations that change the appeal of other competing media, political and regulatory constraints, and the economic demands of the private enterprises that own and operate the mass media.

It is interesting to note that all innovations—whether they be media, a product, or an idea—penetrate society in about the same pattern. First, there is a small group of people (about 2.5%) who are the innovators. They are the risk takers, so they take a chance and try something new. If they like it, another group, called the early adopters, begins using it. This group, which is a little larger with about 13.5% of the population, is composed of opinion leaders. If they like it, they tell others and influence the adoption at a higher rate. Next comes the early majority, which is about one third of the population, followed by another one third of the population known as the late majority. Finally, the last group, called the laggards, is extremely traditional and does not like change. When this group finally adopts something, the innovation has fully penetrated society and is a great success.

The public's reaction to a new medium is based on the medium's ability to satisfy an existing need or to create a widespread need that it can then satisfy. Once an innovation has created a new mass media channel, that channel needs to appeal to a very large, heterogeneous population if it is to be effective as a mass medium. This is called penetration. Television, as compared with other media, was the fastest to penetrate the American public. Acceptance was rapid and widespread, as measured by the number of households buying a television set.

A medium can grow in three ways. First, it will grow if it can fulfill the needs of the public better than is currently being done by competing media. Television is so popular today because it fulfills public needs better than do the other media. It has replaced the radio as the general medium of entertainment, offering both a visual as well as an aural element in its messages. It is replacing the traditional distribution of films in theaters by giving the public the chance to see a wide range of current films (as well as older, classic films) in the comfort of the viewers' homes. It is trying to replace newspapers as the preferred medium for information on current events by offering more frequent on-the-spot coverage of news events.

A second method of growing is based on fulfilling an existing need more efficiently (in terms of time and money) than other media. People with relatively low needs for information will turn to television news, because since they already own a television, it saves them the cost of subscribing to newspapers and magazines. Further, the news presented on television is fairly easy to grasp in a short time. Newspapers and magazines, while presenting more detailed information, require far more work on the part of the receiver in terms of the time and effort required to process and comprehend the message. For people who watch a great deal of television, it is relatively easy to include news shows in their viewing schedules. Also, people with low reading skills favor television because of the time and effort they save by having someone read the news to them.

Third, a medium will grow if it can generate a new need or increase an existing need. Television is credited with increasing the American public's appetite for entertainment. The amount of viewing has steadily increased since television was first introduced, until now the average household has the set on for more than 42 hours a week, most of which is entertainment programming.

The peak stage is reached when the medium commands the most attention from the public and generates the most revenue compared to other media. This usually happens when the medium has achieved maximum penetration, that is, a very high percentage of households has accepted the medium and it cannot grow in penetration any more. Of course, it can continue to absorb a greater proportion of an audience member's time and money.

Eventually, the medium will be challenged by a newer one and go into a decline. In the decline stage, the medium is characterized by loss of audience acceptance and therefore by a loss in revenues. A decline in audience support results not from an atrophied need, but by the need being satisfied better by a competing medium.

A medium enters the adaptation stage of development when it accepts the challenge of redefining its position in the media marketplace. Repositioning is achieved by identifying a new set of needs that the medium can meet, since the old set of needs it used to fulfill is now met better by another medium.

COMPARIJONJ ACROJJ MEDIA INDUJTRIEJ ■

In this section, we'll look at the big picture across the media industries (see Figure 8.1). Later (in Chapter 11) you'll be presented with a lot more detail about each of these industries individually.

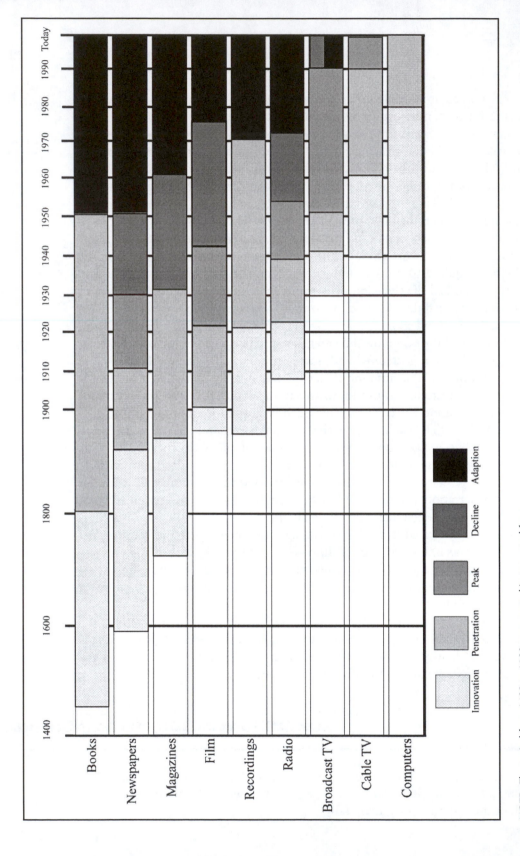

NOTE: The period from 1400 to 1900 represented in truncated form.

TABLE 8.1   Comparison Across Media Industries

Medium	Hours/Week	Total Revenue ($billion)	Per Person Expenditures/Year
Total	64.2	—	631.91
Broadcast television	15.5	30.1	—
Cable television	14.7	34.4	205.75
Radio	20.3	3.4	—
Recorded music	5.2	13.7	61.64
Daily newspapers	3.0	24.2	53.75
Consumer books	1.8	3.7	87.04
Consumer magazines	1.5	9.5	40.61
Movies in theaters	0.3	5.4	31.67
Home video	1.1	15.3	89.03
Online Internet	0.8	3.8	42.92

SOURCE: *Statistical Abstract of the United States: 1999* (2000). Washington, DC: Congressional Information Service. NOTE: The Hours/Week and Dollars/Year columns contain averages per person in this country. The Total Revenue column contains dollars in billions.

Indicators of Peak

We are at an interesting time in the development of the media industries. Broadcast television is in the later days of its peak, which lasted for almost 40 years. Now cable television is entering the peak stage. But keep an eye on computers and the Internet; as of today, this is a new industry still in the penetration stage, but it is growing rapidly and may reach a peak within the next decade.

The two major indicators of a medium occupying the peak are the time spent with it and the money spent on it. Look at Table 8.1 and notice that the time Americans spend with cable television (14.7 hours per week per person) is almost as high as the time the average person spends with broadcast television (15.5 hours per week). You might also notice that the average person spends even more time with radio (20.3 hours per week) and wonder why radio is not at the peak rather than broadcast or cable television. Look at the total revenue column. Both broadcast and cable television generate huge annual revenues compared to radio. When we identify which medium is the strongest (at the peak compared to other media), we need to look at both the time people spend with that medium as well as the revenue the medium generates. Notice that newspapers generate a very large amount of annual revenue, but people spend only a small amount of time reading newspapers relative to time spent with other media. When we look at both time and money indicators, it becomes clear that

TABLE 8.2   **Employment Patterns**

Medium	Establishments	Employees
Newspapers	8,644	403,000
Cable TV	10,950	128,963
Magazines	4,695	121,000
Radio	10,304	112,385
Broadcast TV	1,574	109,370
Books	2,503	85,000

NOTE: Figures are from the *Statistical Abstract of the United States: 1999,* 2000).

broadcast and cable television are dueling it out at the peak. But broadcast television is losing viewership to cable, and cable's revenues are growing faster than broadcast's. This means that cable is entering the peak and that broadcast television is in the later days of the peak. Broadcast television will soon enter the adaptation stage and have to make some major changes in its service in order to survive.

The newest and fastest growing medium is the Internet. Already it has surpassed movies in theaters. It has also surpassed magazines in per person expenditures. As of now only about one third of all people in this country have used the Internet, but this percentage is growing rapidly (*Statistical Abstract of the United States: 1999,* 2000). The Internet is in the penetration stage and within a decade or so may be in a position to challenge cable television for the peak.

General Employment Trends

Related to the growth and development of the media industries are the questions, "How large are the various mass media industries in terms of employees?" and "What are the characteristics of the people who work in the mass media?" You may be surprised to find that even though the media are so pervasive, less than 1% of the U.S. workforce is employed by a media company. Also, you should have some sense of the gender of the people who create the messages and control their distribution.

Overall Size of Workforce. The media are healthy and expanding in terms of employment. The total workforce across the media industries generally grows about 3% each year.

Newspapers are by far the largest employer; they also have the largest number of establishments of dailies and weeklies (see Table 8.2). There is a big drop to cable TV, where most of the employers are very small companies with only a handful of workers, mostly cable installers and maintenance people. The large MSOs (Multiple System Operators) also have sales and administrative staffs in addition to their maintenance people.

Radio and broadcast television stations are organized in a similar fashion, with departments of sales, production, engineering, and administration.

Demographic Patterns. When looking at the total labor force in this country, we can see a trend toward more and more women becoming employed outside the home. Now about 45% of the labor force is female. With the mass media industries, there has been a growth in the number of females employed, but there are many more males working in the mass media than there are females.

The media industries that have the highest percentage of females employed are magazines and books, where women make up more than 50% of the labor force. The greatest growth in terms of percentage of females has been in the newspaper industry. In 1960, only 20% of all people working on newspapers were female, but this percentage has been growing slightly each year. A major reason for this increase has been because newspapers have been moving away from the traditionally male-oriented press jobs and into more clerical and technologically oriented jobs. In broadcasting, 23% of all employees were female in 1960. This remained fairly static until 1972, when the federal government began monitoring hiring practices in businesses. Since that time there has been a gradual increase to the current figure of about 30%.

In motion pictures, about 40% of all employees are female, but this varies depending on the sector of the industry. In the large exhibition sector, about 45% of all employees are female. But in the production sector (actors, directors, producers, and writers), 95% are men.

A popular profession within the media industries is journalism. In this journalistic community there are about 67,000 reporters and correspondents, 23,000 writers and editors, and 67,000 radio and television announcers and newscasters. Most are male, white, and young. About one third of working journalists are women; this despite the fact that about two thirds of students in journalism schools over the past decade have been women. Only about 8% are minorities (3.7% are African American, 2.2% Hispanic, 1% Asian American, and 0.6% Native American). More than half of U.S. journalists are under 35; only 10% are 55 or older. Almost all have a college degree, either with a major in the skill of journalism or another content based area such as English, American Studies, Political Science, and the like. In this country there are over 300 universities with journalism/mass communication programs, and each year they grant about 20,000 bachelor degrees.

According to the American Association of Advertising Agencies, there are about 100,000 people currently employed in advertising agencies in this country: about 24% in creative, 15% in account management, 10% in media, 10% in financial, 8% in special support services, and the rest as secretaries and clerical help (i.e., about 33%). Employment in ad agencies grows at about 3% each year.

Women account for 34% of people in advertising but only 17% of top executives (those making over $200,000 per year). Characters such as Heather Locklear's Amanda on *Melrose Place* are very rare in the real advertising world ("Ad Agency Women," 1996).

Salaries by Gender. Men make higher salaries than do women. In newspapers, salary discrepancies exist even after the difference in education, experience, and newspaper size are controlled. In 1959, women earned about 64% of the salary of men; while that figure has increased (86%), there is still a discrepancy across the salaries of men and women.

Females who are employed in the media industries are usually in positions of lower status, earn less money, and have less education. For example, in newspapers, women hold about 120 managing editorships in this country's 1,700 newspapers. As for policy-making positions on newspapers, women hold about 361 (11%) while men hold 3,057 (89%). In book publishing, about 64% of editors, vice presidents, and professionals are men; however, there is better representation in the smaller publishing houses.

∷ CONCLUSION

This chapter is designed to help you start building a strong knowledge structure about the mass media industries. The framework of that knowledge structure should be that there are nine major mass media industries: book, newspaper, magazine, film, recording, radio, broadcast television, cable television, and computer. Each of these industries was born out of a combination of technological developments that made its channel of communication possible, and a mass marketing orientation that drove it, as an industry, to provide messages for as large and broad an audience as possible.

After an innovation stage, each industry entered a stage of penetration where it increased its appeal to more and more people. Acceptance of a medium is based on its ability to satisfy an existing need or to create a widespread need that it can then satisfy.

A peak stage is reached when the medium commands the most attention from the public and generates the most revenue compared to other media. This usually happens when the medium has achieved maximum penetration.

Eventually, the medium will be challenged by a newer one and go into a decline. In the decline stage, the medium is characterized by loss of audience acceptance and therefore by a loss in revenues. A decline in audience support results not from an atrophied need but because the needs are being satisfied better by a competing medium.

A medium enters the adaptation stage of development when it accepts the challenge of redefining its position in the media marketplace. Repositioning is achieved by identifying a new set of needs that the medium can meet, since the old set of needs it used to fulfill is now met better by another medium.

Most of the mass media are currently in the adaptation stage, where they share audiences and advertisers by serving a different function from the other competing media. There is reason to believe that they will continue refining their messages and services and thereby continue to survive in a healthy manner.

The media industries employ fewer workers than most people would guess, and those workers do not reflect the demographics of the population of the country. While the media have been trying to hire a larger proportion of women and minorities, those groups are still very much under-represented in the media workforce.

Take your media industries knowledge structure into the next two chapters to help you organize the information there. While reading those chapters, think about elaborating this knowledge structure by adding information about the economics and control of the media industries.

Key Idea: The businesses in the media industries are in strong competition with each other to acquire limited resources, play the high-risk game of appealing to audiences, and achieve a maximum profit.

Economic Perspective

A merican consumers spend over $200 billion per year on media products and services (Federman, 1996). How much of your money do you personally contribute to the media? Before you read on in this chapter, take a few minutes to complete Exercise 9.1.

If you are in an average household you spend about $570 annually—buying books, recordings, and movie admissions; subscriptions to magazines and newspapers; and purchasing hardware, such as TVs, VCRs, tape players, and other media products where your money goes directly to a media company.

How do the media spend the money you give them? It might seem to go to all those well-known entertainers with huge incomes. According to *Forbes* magazine (Kafka, 2000), George Lucas was the highest paid entertainer in 1999 with an income of $400 million. Oprah Winfrey was in second place with $150 million. David Kelly was the highest paid television producer, with $118 million income that year. Tom Hanks ($71.5 million), Bruce Willis ($54.5 million), and Julia Roberts ($50 million) were the highest paid actors. The highest earning writers were Tom Clancy ($66 million) and Stephen King ($65 million). As for singing groups, the Backstreet Boys ($60 million) and the Rolling Stones ($50 million) topped the list.

Clearly there is a great deal of money being exchanged for services in the mass media industries. To understand how the industry acquires and uses its resources, we need to learn to think like economists. This chapter is designed to introduce you to that way of thinking by first defining some fundamental terms and concepts. Then we examine how seven key economic characteristics account for the way the media do business.

BASIC TERMS AND CONCEPTS ▪

Economics is concerned with resources. Some of these resources are tangible, such as money, ink, paper, cameras, and microphones, to name a few. But many are intangible, such as acting talent, station loyalty, name recognition, and brand image. When we look at the media from an economic point of view, we are most concerned with how resources are used in the constant process of negotiation and exchange. People continually face decisions about which of their resources to give up in order to get other resources they want more.

Who are the key players in this ongoing negotiation process? The four major groups of players are (a) the people who control and own the media vehicles, (b) employees of the media companies, (c) advertisers, and (d) audiences. Each of these groups has a different set of resources and needs. The owners want to maximize profits by increasing their revenues and decreasing their costs. Employees want to increase their income and benefits for each hour worked. Advertisers want to rent time and space in the media vehicles so that they can get their messages to as many audience members as possible at the lowest cost to them. And audiences want to increase the value of their exposure by searching for more useful information and entertainment while avoiding boring messages and ads for products they don't want.

Notice that the goals of these four groups are at odds with each other so there is a situation of constant negotiation. A determining factor in these negotiations is the balance between supply and demand. For example, a newspaper wants to minimize its costs. Let's say you are an employee of the newspaper, and you want a raise in pay and benefits. If you are a receptionist or a secretary, the negotiating power is with the newspaper, because there is a very large supply of people with these skills relative to the demand. However, if you are an investigative reporter with extensive contacts in your city and a track record of writing shocking exposes that increase your newspaper's sales, you have a rare talent. There is a very high demand for this talent and a very small supply of it—therefore you will have the negotiating power.

Let's look at another, bit more complicated, example. A radio station wants to attract more advertisers, so it cuts the price of its ads by 20% in its highest rated show. Advertisers fight to buy those ad times (called "avails"), so demand for the avails at this station increases. The station, which used to air 9 minutes of ads during an hour, decides to air 20 minutes of ads, thus increasing its supply of avails to meet the increasing demand. The station likes this, because even though it has cut its income per ad by 20%, it is now selling more than twice as many avails; the station has almost doubled its total revenue. But the audience notices this change and becomes upset that there are so many ads and not nearly as much music. Most of the audience switches stations during the ads and never comes back. The station's ratings drop dramatically. Then advertisers become unhappy because it is no bargain to get a 20% discount on ads if the audience they expected is almost gone. Advertisers begin feeling they are wasting their money, so they stop buying those ads.

There are many possible examples to illustrate the point that these four groups are in constant negotiation to satisfy their conflicting needs and wants. Everything is linked in this complex economy.

There are three other characteristics that make this interrelationship even more complex. First, the situation is highly dynamic and interrelated. When a person at one media company makes a decision, it can often have an impact on other companies in the same industry and perhaps in other media industries. Returning to the radio station example above, when advertisers flocked to the station to get the discounted price for the avail, other radio stations (as well as television stations, newspapers, and local magazines) most likely lost advertising revenue. So when the revenues of one vehicle dramatically increase in the short term, the revenues of other competing vehicles are affected and usually go down. The same ripple effect can be seen with the expenses of media companies. For example, if several media companies started paying writers more money, the better writers would be attracted to those companies, and the other companies would either have to pay more or else make do with less-talented writers, which would lower the quality of their shows and result in losing audience size and hence in lower revenue. When something changes in a tightly linked industry, that change ripples outward and affects other players.

A second characteristic that contributes to the complexity is that sometimes decision makers are conflicted because they are experiencing cross-purposes, that is, a decision maker might be a member of more than one group—each with a different economic goal. Let's say you work at a small newspaper and also own half of the newspaper company. As an employee you might want a raise in salary, but this would increase expenses and therefore reduce profits, making your investment less valuable. On a different scale, let's say you work for a large newspaper and own stock in the company that owns the newspaper. A raise in your wages will benefit you a great deal more than a non-raise would benefit shareholders. So your needs as an employee greatly outweigh your needs as an owner.

Third, media vehicles compete in different markets. A market is a segment of the audience to which you offer your product or service. Markets differ in size, with the largest market in this country being the national one. Only a few vehicles, such as television network prime-time broadcast programs, *USA Today* newspaper, *TV Guide* magazine, and major Hollywood movies see themselves competing in a national market. More typically, vehicles carve out a special niche. One way of identifying a niche is geographically, as is the case with newspapers, radio stations, and broadcast television stations. Media vehicles in these industries have their own geographical locale, such as a city or a limited region. Another way of identifying a niche is by audience interest, which is common with magazines, books, and radio. For example, *Surfer* magazine appeals to a very different audience niche than does *Ladies' Home Journal*. College texts are marketed very differently from religious books. Country and Western formatted radio stations appeal to a very different audience than does a Rap station.

Clearly, the economics of the mass media industries are complex. The complexity is traceable to the fact that there are many different components, each with its own needs that are most often in conflict with the needs of other components. This requires a constant negotiation process, and as decisions are made, effects ripple out and influence the decisions of others. All parties are profoundly interlinked.

■ KEY ECONOMIC CHARACTERISTICS

When we sort through the economic complexity in the media industries, seven important industry-wide characteristics appear. These are: dependence on indirect as well as direct support from consumers, advertising as the engine, niche marketing, profit motive, first copy costs, the principle of relative constancy, and the competitive nature. An understanding of this set of principles will help you comprehend how the negotiation for resources takes place.

Dependence of Indirect as Well as Direct Support

The media industries generate well over $300 billion each year in revenue. When the media are taken together, this set is the ninth largest industry in terms of revenues (Albarran & Chan-Olmsted, 1998). It continues with healthy growth—growing about 20% faster than the GNP. Let's put this large number in perspective with other entertainment expenditures. For example, the gambling industry's revenues were $50.9 billion in 1997. That is more money than the country spends on all live events—concerts, plays, music, and spectator sports—combined. This is due to 37 states now having lotteries, 21 having casinos, and 45 having bingo (O'Brien, 1998). Also, the sex business in the United States is estimated to be $9 billion annually, including $4.1 billion in sales and rentals of adult videos (Davidson, 2000). This means that Americans spend five times as much on media as on gambling and sex!

How much do we spend on individual media? American consumers spend about $202.9 billion per year on media products, of which $26.5 billion was spent on newspapers and magazines, $23.2 billion on books, $6.3 billion is at the movie box office; $15.3 billion on videos, $13.7 billion on recorded music, and $23.1 billion on cable television. Americans also spent $89.7 billion on purchasing media hardware (televisions, radios, VCRs, computers, etc.) and another $5.1 billion on hardware maintenance and repair (*Statistical Abstract of the United States: 1999*, 2000).

If you've been adding up these numbers, you most likely have noticed a discrepancy. The annual total amount of money Americans spend to buy media products and services is much smaller than the total amount of money the media industries claim as revenue each year. How is this possible? The answer is that our direct support of the media is not the only revenue stream for those businesses. The media also receive revenue from us indirectly in the form of advertising. When you write a check to your cable television provider for your monthly bill, you are paying money directly to a media company. That is a direct cost. Other examples of direct payments are paying admission to a movie or buying a magazine, book, recording, or computer software. Also, when you buy hardware (TV set, VCR, computer, etc.) that is required to receive media messages, you are also contributing to a direct cost.

In contrast, you also support the media indirectly. Let's say you spend $5.00 for lunch at McDonald's. Some of that money (let's say $1.00) will find its way into McDonald's advertising budget and is sent on to a television network. That $1.00 of your lunch payment is an example of your indirect support of the media. It was a payment that originated with you but did not go directly from you to a media company. Had you not bought lunch at McDonald's, that $1.00 would not have gone to the television network, for example. Every time you buy an advertised product or service, you are indirectly supporting the media. Some advertisers spend a good deal on advertising, meaning that a high proportion of their selling price is a charge to you—the customer—for their advertising. For example, Procter & Gamble spends about $8.3 billion on marketing to generate sales of $33 billion, which means that about 25% of the cost of those products goes into marketing ("Procter & Gamble," 1996).

The media of books, films, recordings, and computers are supported almost entirely by direct costs to the consumer. There are a few examples of ads being stuck in books and recordings and displayed before films or in computer programs, but the revenue from these ads is minor compared to direct costs. With magazines, newspapers, and now cable TV, the costs are split between direct (subscription or newsstand selling price) and indirect (advertising). With broadcast television and radio, there is no direct cost for exposure to a program, but there is a high cost for purchasing the means to receive a program (radios and television sets), in addition to indirect costs in the guise of advertising.

The balance between direct and indirect support is shifting from direct to indirect payment. The reason for this is that the costs of some hardware such as

TVs, radios, CD players, VCRs, and computers is coming down each year, while the revenues generated through advertising increase each year.

Advertising as the Engine

Advertising is the engine that drives the growth of the media industries. The cost of doing business in this country has greatly increased as advertising continually becomes a stronger economic force. In 1900, about $500 million was spent on all forms of advertising. By 1940 it was $2 billion, so it took 40 years to multiply four times. In 1980 it was $60 billion or a growth of 30 times in those 40 years. Now it is over $200 billion. It is difficult to comprehend how much money this is, so let's compare it to the expenditures of the federal government (see Table 9.1)

Television (broadcast and cable) and newspapers account for well over half of all the revenue that goes to the media industries (see Table 9.2). With cable television becoming more aggressive in the advertising market, it is likely that its revenues will grow the fastest, thus keeping it in first place.

Why is advertising so important to our economy? There have been some dramatic changes in the economy of this and other Western countries over the past 100 years, and especially over the past 40, that have worked in combination with advertising to increase both the sale of goods and services as well as the importance of advertising. First, there has been a decline in the proportion of farmers and blue-collar workers, and an increase in the proportion of white-collar and professional workers. This means that people are not as self-sufficient and must buy their food and clothing. Second, there has been a high level of employment, which gives people the resources to buy goods and services. We have more discretionary income, which makes it possible for us to buy goods and services at a point well beyond the mere subsistence level. Over time, the standard of living has steadily increased as people's earning power increases and their expenditures for food, clothing, automobiles, housing, media, and luxuries have all increased.

Advertising has been the engine for this growth. Advertising makes it possible for new goods to enter markets and let us know immediately that they are available. With more product successes, more and more companies are willing to introduce an even wider range of new products. These companies fuel advertising agencies with money, which is passed through to the media. As the media grow, they offer more information and entertainment to us. More of us are spending more time with the media, thus generating many more audiences, which the media rent out to advertisers. The money cycles from us to products, to the manufacturers of those products, to those companies' advertising agencies, to

---

TABLE 9.1   Comparing Advertising Expenditures to Federal Spending in 1996

Education, job training, and social services	$60.1 billion
Transportation (highways, airports, trains)	$42.6 billion
Justice (federal courts, FBI, prisons)	$24.5 billion
Agriculture	$21.5 billion
Science, space, and technology	$18.5 billion
Foreign aid	$15.5 billion

These total "only" $182.7 billion, or considerably less than will be spent on all forms of advertising this year.

SOURCE: Table 1447 in *Statistical Abstract of the United States: 1999* (2000).

TABLE 9.2   Comparison of Profits Across Media Industries

Industry	Revenue*	ROR (%)	ROA (%)
Television broadcasting	28.8	22	18
Radio	10.2	20	—
Newspapers	44.2	17	26
Cable and pay television	41.5	15	9
Magazines	13.2	11	24
Films	32.5	11	9
Books	16.7	10	14
Audio recordings	11.0	7	14

NOTE: *In billions of dollars
SOURCE: Format adapted from Picard, 1989, p. 89; data from Standard & Poor's *Index to Surveys* (1996) and *Statistical Abstract of the United States: 1999* (2000).

---

the media. Advertising drives this cycle faster and faster each year. If we stopped buying advertised products, the cycle would slow down and eventually stop.

Building Audiences

Because advertising is the principal source of revenue for most of the commercial media throughout the world, media companies are in the business of constructing desirable audiences and renting them out to advertisers. A medium builds an audience by recognizing where there is a need for entertainment or information, then providing products and services to satisfy that need. This generally can be done in one of two ways. A media business can either (a) orient toward a *quantity* goal, that is, attract as large an audience as possible; or (b) orient toward a niche, that is, attract a special kind of audience.

The dominant mass media are always ruled by the law of large numbers. Therefore they must present whatever content they feel will attract the greatest number of consumers. For example, commercial television is the dominant mass medium today. In order for it to survive in its dominant position, it must present programming that appeals to as large an audience as possible. A small shrinkage in audience can mean a substantial reduction in revenue.

One type of desirable audience is the quantity audience. This is what the commercial television networks strive to construct, especially for their prime-time period (8 p.m. to 11 p.m. each night). A prime-time show that gets a rating of 11 will be regarded as a failure. This means that only 11% of all households—"only" 19 million people—watched it. Even though this is more than all the people who saw the Broadway smash hit *Chorus Line* in its extraordinarily long 10-year run, the television networks are not satisfied by such a small audience. A difference of one rating point for a show over the course of a single season could mean almost $100 million to the network, so networks are strongly motivated to increase the size of their audiences as much as possible.

In contrast, the radio and magazine industries are oriented toward crafting an appeal to particular types of audience. This audience may be relatively small compared to an audience for broadcast television, but small, highly targeted audiences have great value to many advertisers. Special groups of people have special needs. Businesses that market products for a special audience will pay a premium to the media vehicles that attract that special audience. For example, joggers as a group have a special need for information on running practices, equipment, and training techniques. They support several magazines that publish nothing but this type of information. Manufacturers of jogging equipment pay a premium to place ads in these magazines, knowing that the buying of advertising space in these magazines is a very efficient purchase, because the ads placed there will be reaching their most likely customers.

The niche audience is composed of a certain type of person that particular advertisers want to reach. For example, a company marketing sporting goods wants to reach adolescents and younger adults who like to participate in sports. Such a company would want to avoid the high cost of advertising on prime-time television, especially because many of the viewers of those shows are not sports fans. Instead, this company would prefer to concentrate its ads on ESPN, in magazines such as *Sports Illustrated,* and in the sports pages of local newspapers.

Advertising has also moved onto the World Wide Web. The Internet Advertising Bureau said that almost $1 billion was spent on Internet advertising in 1997 (Maddox, 1998) and nearly $2 billion in 1998. Almost half of this money came from computers and software advertisers (Maddox, 1999).

The new medium of the Internet is perfectly suited for marketing to niche audiences. Each Web site has a special service to provide and therefore attracts a special audience. One example of a desirable niche is college students. Marketers of books, travel, and computers are especially interested in this niche and are strongly targeting these people on the Internet (Sessa, 1999).

Profit-Making Motive

Almost all mass media are profit-oriented enterprises. As businesses, they are run to make as large a profit as possible. Profit is what a company has at the end of the year after paying all its expenses. So, profit is the difference between revenue, which is the total amount of income for the business, and expenses. To maximize profits, a business needs to keep expenses low while increasing revenue.

One of the largest expenses across all the media industries is personnel, which can be subdivided into two broad categories: talent and clerical. Talent is not so much artistic mastery as it is the ability to generate revenue. Some people have sales talent and can sell advertising space and time. Some people have writing talent and have large followings of readers who buy their books, magazines, and newspapers. Some have musical talent and continually produce recordings that go platinum. Some have acting talent and generate huge sales at theater box offices or high ratings for television programs. There is never enough talent to meet the demand, so media companies bid up the prices for the services of people who have this talent. The few talented people at the tops of their industries make large sums of money.

However, most of the positions in the media industries are fairly low-level jobs that entail routine assignments that can be done by many different people with little training. These are the secretaries, receptionists, ticket takers, and low-level craftspeople. A bit higher than these are the assistant producers, camera operators, disk jockeys, and the like. Some of these people have special talent and quickly move up to the top of their industry, but most of them do not.

The media pay the people with a lot of talent a lot of money, because these people are required in order for a company to generate large revenues. To counterbalance the large payments to talent, companies reduce expenses by paying clerical people as little as possible. Because the supply of potential workers for entry-level positions is so much larger than the demand, media companies can pay near minimum wage and get good workers.

Remember that profit is the payoff or reward for doing business. This reward can be conceptualized in several different ways. First, it can be regarded as the difference between a company's revenue (total income) and its expenses (total costs)—usually expressed as a percentage of revenues. For example, let's say you run a small magazine and at the end of the year you total up everything and find that your revenues (all income through subscriptions and advertiser's fees) came to $100,000. Your expenses (paying writers, editors, photographers, printers, distribution, taxes, office supplies, utilities, etc.) sum to $90,000. That means you have $10,000 left over after having paid all your expenses for the year. This is your reward. You get to keep 10% of all your revenues; that is, your ROR (return on revenues) is $10,000 divided by $100,000.

A second way of computing your reward is to compare your profit to your assets, which is the money you have invested in the business. Let's extend the same example above where you had a $10,000 profit at the end of the year. If you had $50,000 invested in the business (office furniture, computers, printers, fax, and other equipment), then your ROA (return on assets) would be 20%, which is very good.

Both ROR and ROA are very important indicators of the rewards of doing business, but they look at reward in different ways. For example, let's say you bought a radio station for $1 million and at the end of the year you had generated a profit of $10,000 on revenues of $100,000. That 10% ROR is pretty good, but the ROA is only 1%, which is terrible! You could have invested the $1 million in a passbook savings account at the bank and done much better. In another example, let's say you start a small weekly newspaper and your only assets are a computer and a few pieces of furniture totaling $4,000. Your newspaper generates revenue of $50,000, but your expenses are $49,000 so your profit is only $1,000. Your ROA is a very high at 25% ($1,000 profit divided by assets of $4,000), but your ROR is only 2% ($1,000 profit divided by revenues of $50,000).

Let's look at the ROR and ROA of the mass media industries (see Table 9.2). Newspapers appear to be the best of the mass media industries, because they have very high percentages on both ROR and ROA. Remember these are industry-wide averages; some newspapers do much better than these figures and others have been losing money.

On the weaker end is the audio recording industry with the lowest ROR. However, 7% is still better than the average for all industries in the United States. As for ROA, the cable television and film industries are the lowest, but both of these industries have huge asset bases, and this is what tends to make their ROA percentages appear smaller.

TABLE 9.3   Share of Total Advertising Expenditures by Medium in 1995

Share (%)	Medium
21.5	Newspapers
21.4	Television
18.6	Direct mail
6.6	Radio
5.9	Yellow pages
4.9	Magazines
0.8	Outdoor (billboards, posters, etc.)
20.3	Other (event sponsorships, in-store displays, etc.)

SOURCE: 1995 data from Standard & Poor's *Index to Surveys,* page M17.

First Copy Costs

This principle states that the cost of producing the first copy of something is much higher than the cost of the second or any subsequent copy. To illustrate, let's say you are a newspaper publisher and your daily cost of operation (cost of paying all your reporters, editors, salespeople, office staff, rent on building, depreciation of all your equipment, supplies, phones, other utilities, etc.) is $6,000. This is your fixed cost. If you print only one copy of the newspaper, you will have to sell it for $6,000 just to cover your fixed costs. If you print two copies, you would have to sell each for $3,000 to cover all your costs; your average fixed cost per copy is cut in half. If you print 60,000 copies, your average fixed cost per copy is only 10 cents. Thus, your average fixed costs keep going down as these costs are spread over more and more copies.

However, when you print more copies, the cost of paper, ink, and distribution increases; these are your variable costs, because they vary according to how many copies you print. The more copies you print, the more paper and ink you will need, and the price you pay for a roll of paper or a gallon of ink will go down, because you can buy these materials in bulk and get big discounts. While your total cost for ink and paper will go up when printing more copies, your *average* variable cost for these will go down. This is known as economies of scale. The bigger the scale of your business, the more likely your costs will go down either through your ability to demand greater discounts or because you are able to operate more efficiently beyond a certain point.

The more copies you print, the more your distribution costs will go up—both in total and on average. To illustrate this point, imagine that you publish only

1,000 copies of your newspaper. You could hire 10 youngsters, each to deliver 100 papers after school and pay them a nickel for each paper delivered. Thus your average distribution cost is 5 cents per newspaper. But let's say you wanted to publish 50,000 newspapers. You would need to hire 500 youngsters, and this would require you to develop a whole new layer of administration to recruit, train, and keep track of all these paper carriers. You would have to buy trucks and hire drivers to get the newspapers out to these 500 carriers quickly every afternoon. You would also have to hire bookkeepers to keep track of all the subscriptions and billing. So the average variable cost might increase from 5 cents to 15 cents per newspaper as you go from 1,000 to 50,000 in circulation.

The media companies, like any business, want to keep their expenses down, so they find the point at which the combination of their average fixed costs and their average variable costs is lowest. Beyond this point, distributing more copies only serves to increase unit costs and thus reduce profit. So newspapers, magazines, books, and recordings each seek the point where their average total costs (the sum of average fixed costs and average variable costs) are lowest.

On this principle of first copy costs, broadcast television and radio are different from the other media. They have no variable costs, only fixed costs. For example, with broadcast television, there is no cost to the station of adding an additional viewer to the audience. Viewers pay for their own television receivers, and they pay for the electricity to run them. The station has no distribution costs other than the electricity of the broadcast signal, and the power used to broadcast a station's signal is the same whether 100 or 100,000 sets are tuned in. It is fixed. With no variable costs and with a very high first copy fixed cost, broadcast television stations keep dropping their average total costs with each additional audience member added. For this reason, the broadcast media (both radio and television) are strongly motivated, more than any other medium, to increase the size of their audiences.

Principle of Relative Constancy

The consumer's proportion of economic support for the mass media is approximately constant in comparison to the general economy. This is the principle of relative constancy.

Mass media products have become staples of consumption in our society, much like food, clothing, and shelter. As staples, they receive a fixed constant share of the economic pie, a relatively fixed proportion of all expenditures. This was true in 1929 and still is more than seven decades later.

While the percentage of consumer spending on the mass media has remained constant at around 3% of GNP (Gross National Product) since 1929, that money breaks down differently year by year depending on the media available and the relative attractiveness of their messages. The percentage of media expenditure spent on newspapers and magazines peaked in 1933; movie admission peaked in 1945; books peaked in 1970. Expenditures for radios, television receivers, recordings, and computers is still growing.

Nature of Competition

Most mass media operate in a market of monopolistic competition. *Monopolistic,* because each firm is large relative to the size of the market for its products; also, there are very high barriers to entry in most media industries. *Competition,* because firms in an industry compete.

Unusually high profits in an industry typically attract new firms, which results in greater competition, expanded output, lower prices, reduced profits, and greater consumer benefits. But this trend is not apparent in most mass media industries (especially broadcasting), because the cost of entry is so high. Therefore the few existing firms in a market tend to monopolize their markets.

All media must compete in two markets simultaneously. In one market, a medium must act like a seller of services to the largest possible audience. In the other market, the medium must be a buyer of information and entertainment for the lowest possible price. There is a big overlap in each market within the media and between the media.

Another characteristic of the competition is that within a market all products are relatively indistinguishable, that is, the messages are not identical but are very similar. For example, the stories in *Newsweek, Time,* and *U.S. News & World Report* are very similar in terms of content, depth, and perspective. A situation comedy on ABC is very similar to one on CBS; the characters have different names, but the stereotypes, settings, and plot points are very similar. With computer software, all spreadsheet application programs are pretty much the same; also Web browsers are almost identical in features. The key to competition is making consumers believe that your product is different from the others. Media businesses do not really compete on product features as much as they compete on product images. This is why advertising is so important. Advertising gets people to look beyond the product features in order to consider product images as well as the psychological advantages of using the product.

BECOMING ECONOMICALLY LITERATE ■■

Perhaps the greatest degree of media illiteracy is in the economic area. People who are at low levels of media literacy usually do not understand the business nature of the media industries. Low literates do not have much context to understand the business motivations when their favorite television show is canceled, or when the rate of their cable subscription increases, or when a radio station changes its format. They feel anger that the media don't understand their needs and wants, but at the same time they lack an understanding of how decisions are made in the media industries.

People who are at higher levels of media literacy try to analyze changes to understand the degree of good that will come to them as consumers. They compare current changes to past changes in order to evaluate what the short-term and long-term implications will be. They consider who will benefit and who will be hurt by the shift in resources. From this information, they synthesize a reasoned opinion. The result of this thinking might be an emotional reaction of anger—much like the anger of the low-level media literate person. However, the people at higher levels of media literacy will have a clearly reasoned perspective on their anger. Such a perspective can be used to help them do something about it personally (such as changing their attitudes and behavior) or to do something about it in society (such as boycotting or putting pressure on the media organization). But in order to increase the effectiveness of your actions, you need to understand clearly what the problems are and the influences that led to those problems.

What separates the high and low media literate people in this area of economics? The difference is the degree of knowledge and the level of skills (see Table 9.4). Notice that media literacy requires an understanding of economics to be developed primarily in the cognitive area.

When you add the economic information from this chapter to your knowledge structure about the media, you develop a deeper understanding about how decisions are made. The most important concept in this chapter is profit. Remember that the media industries are composed of businesses that are run to make as large a profit as they can. They do this by attempting to maximize revenues and minimize expenses. Each of the media industries does this well, and each earns a profit much higher than the average of all industries in this country.

There are some key economic characteristics that you need to comprehend before you can understand how the media industries operate. First, almost all the media industries have several streams of revenue, both from direct costs to the consumer as well as indirect costs through advertising. Second, advertising is the engine that drives the profitability of the media industries as well as the health of the economy. Third, the media are primarily niche oriented in the building of audience. Fourth, there is a strong profit-making motive. The media achieve this by increasing their revenue each year and trying to drive down the cost of their expenses. Fifth, the cost of the first copy of their messages is usually much higher relative to subsequent copies, so there is a strong motivation to increase the size of their audiences. Sixth, the media seem consistently to account for about 3% of the GNP. However, expenditures shift around among the media

TABLE 9.4

	SKILLS	KNOWLEDGE
COGNITIVE	Ability to analyze reports on media industries and companies to determine revenue, expenses, and profits	Knowledge of revenue, expenses, and profits of media industries and specific companies
	Ability to compare/contrast across industries and companies on economic indicators	
	Ability to evaluate the economic health of media industries and companies	
	Ability to generalize from particular companies to industry trends	
	Ability to synthesize a prediction for future trends in the media industries and companies	
	Ability to analyze media industries and companies to recognize the operation of the seven economic characteristics	
EMOTIONAL	Ability to analyze your feelings in reaction to the economics of media	Knowledge of your experiences in buying and using media products
MORAL	Ability to analyze the moral implications of economic decisions	Knowledge of values in the media Knowledge of your ethical system
	Ability to compare/contrast the moral implications across different companies	
	Ability to evaluate the ethical responsibilities of the media to society	

depending on the relative attractiveness of the services and products the different industries provide. And seventh, most of the media industries compete in monopolistic markets. The barriers to entry are fairly high, and once a company gets into a market, it must compete for audiences, production talent, and advertisers with the other companies in that market. An interesting part of this challenge is that the products and services offered by the companies in a given market are fairly similar, so the companies must convince target audiences, prospective employees, and desired advertisers that they are somehow superior to the other competing companies.

■■ FURTHER READING

Alexander, A., Owers, J., & Carveth, R. (Eds.). (1993). *Media economics: Theory and practice* (pp. 245-266). Hillsdale, NJ: Lawrence Erlbaum. (391 pages with glossary, indexes, and appendices)

There are 15 chapters in this edited volume. It contains a good deal of technical economic information, but it is presented in a readable manner. Also, a 13-page glossary defines the key terms presented throughout the book.

Picard, R. G. (1989). *Media economics: Concepts and issues*. Newbury Park, CA: Sage.

This is a short introduction to the major economic principles that underlie the media industries.

EXERCISE 9.1

Estimating Your Personal Expenditures on the Media

1. Before you go any farther, stop and make a general estimate of how much money you spent on all forms of the media over the past year.

   Write your estimate here: $ _____

2. Now, let's itemize those expenditures. Think back one year from today and try to remember how much money you spent on each of the following over the past 12 months. If you want to do this accurately, get out your checkbook register and credit card receipts.

   $ _____ Cable subscription (multiply monthly bill by 12)

   $ _____ Magazine subscriptions

   $ _____ Buying individual issues of magazines

   $ _____ Newspaper subscriptions

   $ _____ Buying individual newspapers

   $ _____ Text books

   $ _____ Other books (pleasure reading, gifts, reference books, etc.)

   $ _____ Movie theater admissions

   $ _____ Rental of movies from video store

   $ _____ Buying videotapes (blank and pre-recorded)

   $ _____ Buying CDS, tapes, and other recordings

   $ _____ Buying blank audio tapes

   $ _____ Buying video (Nintendo, etc.) or computer games

   $ _____ Playing video games at arcades

   $ _____ Buying computer software and/or manuals

   $ _____ Subscription to computer services (America Online, Prodigy, etc.)

   $ _____ Buying hardware: radio, television, VCR, Walkman, computer, and so on.

   $ _____ Repairs on media equipment

   $ _____ TOTAL (sum all the figures down the column)

3. How close are your figures in No. 1 to the figures in No. 2?

4. Does the amount of money you spent surprise you? Why?

EXERCISE 9.2

Financial Analysis

1. Go to the library and get a list of media companies. Try *Hoover's Guide to Media Companies* or get your reference librarian to help you. Find two media companies that look interesting to you.

2. For each company, do a brief financial analysis by answering the following questions:

   a. How much revenue did the company have last year?

   b. What were the major sources of that income?

   c. Given the sources of income, would you say that the company is primarily concerned with media businesses, or are media businesses really a sideline to other more important businesses?

   d. What were the company's expenses for the year?

   e. What was the company's profit margin? (Can you get both ROR and ROA?)

   f. What did the company do with its profits? Did it disperse all or part to the shareholders who invested in the company? Or did the company keep all or most of the profits for investing in additional media properties or other businesses?

3. Given your two analyses of the companies, in which would you rather invest your money? Why?

CHAPTER 10

Key Idea: Ownership patterns show a strong movement toward concentration and away from localism.

Who Owns and Controls the Media?

Ownership and control are not always the same thing. If you own a computer, you can decide who you will allow to use it and when. You control it as well as own it. But if you own 10 shares of stock in a large media company, you are a part owner but in no real sense can you control it. Almost all of the powerful media corporations are owned by thousands of shareholders, but the control of each of those companies is in the hands of one person, the Chief Executive Officer (CEO). While the CEO is accountable to the shareholders, the amount of power he or she has in comparison to any one of the shareholders is enormous. Even if you were able to round up 100 of your closest millionaire friends and invest a total of $100 million in one of these powerful companies, your group as a whole would still own only a small percentage of the company.

When we think about control of the media companies, we should not think of the owners. Instead, we need to focus our attention on the decision makers or the CEOs. And the primary goal of CEOs is to maximize profits. This goal is accomplished most efficiently when a company is very large and is powerful enough to control all phases of the production of messages and their distribution in very large markets where it has very little or no competition. Thus, media businesses get more efficient and wealthy through the concentration of power.

But in American society there has been a strongly held value that power should be dispersed to as many people as possible. Thus the founding fathers created a democratic form of government rather than a more efficient totalitarian one. Over time, American society has retained the value of dispersion of power and has kept pressure on government regulators to prevent any one person or company from becoming too powerful. But the idea of "too powerful" is impossible to define objectively; instead it is a matter for debate. As you read through this chapter, you will be presented with lots of information about how the media industries are moving toward concentration. You will need to make up your own mind about whether this is a good or bad trend.

▪▪ COMPETING FORCEƧ

The essential tension between dispersion of power, called localism, and concentration of power can be seen clearly in the development of the media industries. Consumers favor localism; they want a marketplace with as many voices as possible so they have lots of choices about how to satisfy their various needs for information and entertainment. CEOs favor concentration; they focus on the capitalistic business environment where the goal is to maximize profits.

These key forces of localism and concentration operate in opposite directions. The localism force strains toward diversifying decisions by getting more people involved. The concentration force strains toward efficiency by consolidating resources and putting the power into the hands of a few people. In the section below, let's examine how these two forces have been competing.

Localism in American Culture

Localism is a populist perspective. It is based on the belief that control of important institutions should be in the hands of all of the people and that the best way to do this is to keep control decentralized, that is, at the local level where it is closest to individuals.

Localism is a part of the American tradition. This country was founded on the belief that the individual is more important than are institutions or governments. When government is necessary, it should be decentralized so as to be closer to the people's needs and more accountable to them.

Localism is not just an abstract philosophy. It has been put into practice, and it can be seen in the way people have organized schools, property taxes, land use, public health, business regulation, and many other political and social activities. Although the national government is very centralized and very pervasive in its powers, it does leave some powers to state and local governments, of which there are many. There are 18,000 municipalities and 17,000 townships. Within these, there are 500,000 local governmental units directly elected by local residents, and 170,000 of them have the power to impose taxes. Clearly, localism is a strong force in this country.

Concerning the mass media, there is also a strong feeling by many that the media voices should be kept local if they are to serve best the needs of individuals and society. The media started as innovations at the local level. When a government was called upon to regulate them, the governmental agencies usually favored this localism ethic in their policy making. A good example of this is how the federal government handled the development of the broadcasting industries.

In order to broadcast a radio or television signal, you must send the signal out on a frequency. If you and I want to use the same frequency to broadcast our different signals, then we will interfere with each other, and consumers will receive a garbled signal. There is a very limited number of frequencies on what is called the electromagnetic spectrum that are set aside for broadcasting. Someone has to decide who gets to use which frequencies, then enforce these decisions so that others don't come along and interfere. The federal government decided that it was the one to make the decisions, reasoning that the electromagnetic spectrum belonged to all Americans, much like a national park or any other resource that should be shared by all citizens.

In the early days of radio broadcasting, the federal government decided to require individuals to apply to the Federal Communications Commission (FCC) for a broadcast frequency. The FCC was immediately flooded with applications for AM radio frequencies. But the AM band on the electromagnetic spectrum allowed for only about 117 frequencies. The FCC could have chosen 117 applicants and awarded each of them their own frequency. This would have led to 117 AM radio stations, each using its frequency to broadcast its signal to the entire country. But that is not what the FCC did. Instead, the FCC divided the country into many local market areas and awarded some frequencies to each market. Also, each radio station was limited in the amount of power it could use to broadcast its signal so that the signals would not go beyond their local markets. This allowed the FCC to assign the same frequency to many different markets without having to worry about signals interfering with one another. The FCC chose this alternative, because it wanted to spread the limited resource of broadcast frequencies around to as many different people as possible.

By keeping ownership of radio licenses at the local level, the FCC believed it was setting up a system whereby the stations would be operated in the best interests of their local communities. Private businesses were allowed to broadcast on these frequencies provided they operate "in the public interest, convenience, and necessity." Therefore, the rationale for regulation in broadcasting is based on the following points: spectrum scarcity, localism, public interest, promotion of diversity of content, and prevention of monopolies.

Now the country has grown to about 215 broadcasting markets with 4,762 AM and 5,542 FM stations. When television came along in the 1940s, the FCC used the same procedure of allocating broadcasting licenses to local stations in the local markets. Now we have 1,574 regular broadcast television stations and another 1,400 low-power broadcast stations (*Statistical Abstract of the United States: 1999*, 2000).

For decades, the FCC prevented broadcasting monopolies from developing by limiting the number of stations any one company could own to seven AM, seven FM, and seven TV stations in total, with no two being in the same market. In the 1980s the rules were relaxed to 12 AM, 12 FM, and 12 TV stations. Then the Telecommunications Act of 1996 further relaxed the limits to a significant extent in the guise of opening up competition. Now companies can control TV stations serving up to 50% of the country; they can also own as many radio stations as they want as long as those stations do not cover more than 50% of the country's population. Also, the ban prohibiting a company from owning a TV and radio station in the same market was lifted.

Concentration as a Goal of American Business

Straining against this ethic of localism is a very strong trend toward concentration, consolidation, and centralization. Although almost every media company began as a small, local operation, they take on the characteristics of big business as they grow. Big businesses are complex organizations that market many different products and services but do so under a strong centralized system in order to achieve a more efficient operation. Big businesses grow by claiming a larger share of the markets in which they compete. They accomplish this by acquiring control of more resources, and this often leads to buying—or at least investing in—other companies.

A general industry-wide trend shows that fewer and fewer people own more and more of the media. This trend will probably continue as the cost of buying and operating a media voice keeps going up and as entry into the industry becomes more difficult. Today a person needs a great deal of money and expertise to attempt to buy a mass media voice. Because of this, only companies that already own media voices are successful in acquiring new voices. This is no longer a place for the amateurs who were so instrumental in the innovation stage.

As media companies grow larger and more centralized, there is a danger that they will narrow the range of voices that will get heard. For example, if you send a letter to the editor of a newspaper with a circulation of 1,000, there is a good chance that your letter will be published. But if you send the same letter to a newspaper with a circulation of one million, your chance of being published is much smaller. Thus, the larger and more powerful the media company is, the less access you have to make a contribution to its messages or to influence the way it makes decisions. Larger companies must filter out more requests, and in this filtering out process, there is a danger that some types of voices will not get heard at all.

With all the recent mergers and acquisitions in the media industries, ownership patterns have changed rapidly, but the one constant is the trend toward even greater concentration. For example, in 1983, Bagdikian (1992) conducted an analysis of media ownership patterns and found that the control of the media was essentially in the hands of 50 people—these were the CEOs of the largest media companies who in combination controlled more than half of the revenues and audiences in their media markets. Less than a decade later, Bagdikian found that the number had shrunk to 23 CEOs of corporations who control most of the business in the country's 25,000 media businesses. The number of companies controlling most of the daily newspaper circulation was 11. In magazine publishing, a majority of the total annual industry revenues went to two firms. Five firms controlled more than half of all book sales. Five media conglomerates shared 95% of the recordings market, with Warner and CBS alone controlling 65% of that market. Eight Hollywood studios accounted for 89% of U.S. feature film rentals. Three television networks earned over two thirds of the total U.S. television revenues (Bagdikian, 1992). And these figures within an industry *underestimated* the degree of concentration, because the powerful companies own properties in more than one media industry. For example, a newspaper corporation may own several radio and television stations and perhaps a magazine or two. You will see later in this chapter that additional mergers and acquisitions have made the media industries even more concentrated.

As the media become more concentrated, so too does the advertising industry. The large, national agencies are becoming larger in order to deal better with the larger media companies. As ad agencies grow bigger, they become much less interested in local retailers and local markets, instead favoring the much larger national market where they can make bigger deals and more money. Thus, most of today's advertising is for national brands. For example, when most people think of hamburgers, they think of McDonald's, Burger King, and Wendy's—not the local restaurant run as a family business. So the trend toward concentration is not just within the media industries; it is also true of retail stores and of advertising agencies. Through mergers and acquisitions, all of America's industries are becoming more concentrated.

CROSS OWNERSHIP AND CONTROL ■

Types of Concentration

There are three different trends toward concentration. First, there is the horizontal merger. This is when one media company buys another media company of the same type. An example is a newspaper chain buying another newspaper. This pattern was very popular during the 1980s when newspapers were being gobbled up by chains at the rate of 50 to 60 per year.

Second, there is the vertical merger. This is when one media company buys suppliers and/or distributors to create integration in the production and distribution of messages. An example is a book publisher buying a printing plant and some book stores.

Third, there is the conglomerate merger. This is when a media company buys a combination of other media companies and/or companies in a non-media business. An example is a film studio that buys a newspaper, several radio stations, a talent agency, and a string of restaurants. Paramount Communications owns Paramount studios, which is one of the leading producers of motion pictures, television shows, and cable programming. It also owns Simon & Schuster—the world's largest book publishing company. It is a major maker of entertainment video cassettes, and it controls 1,100 movie screens in the United States and 11 foreign countries (Bagdikian, 1992). Then in 1994, Viacom, which owns cable television services such as MTV, VH1, and Nickelodeon, took over Paramount Communications Inc. for $9.6 billion.

From the business point of view, cross-media ownership is very attractive. Not only is it very profitable, the arrangement allows for cross-promotion of products. For example, when Paramount released its movie *The Brady Bunch*, Viacom put on several weeks of *Brady Bunch* TV reruns on its Nickelodeon cable channel as a way of promoting the movie.

Mega Mergers

During the 1980s, there were 2,308 mergers and acquisitions involving media companies for a total of $214 billion (Ozanich & Wirth, 1993). This activity served to consolidate resources in fewer companies. Thus the CEOs of these newer, larger companies hold a greater concentration of power as they manage those resources. During the 1990s, mergers became more and more popular as media companies bought other media companies (see Table 10.1), and non-media companies also bought media properties (see Table 10.2) because they are so profitable. For example, Westinghouse Electric Corporation, which began as a manufacturer of air brakes in Pittsburgh in 1886, decided it wanted to change its line of business. By 1995, it had bought one of the major television networks —CBS—for $5.4 billion, then spent another $9 billion buying cable channels and radio stations over the next 2 years. In 1997 it moved its headquarters to New York City and took the name CBS ("CBS Headquarters," 1997).

Following the passage of the Telecommunications Act, the four largest corporate mergers in 1996 were all in the telecommunications industry: Bell Atlantic-Nynex, $21.3 billion; British Telecommunications-MCI, $21.3 billion; SBC Communications-Pacific Telesis, $16.5 billion; and WorldCom-MFS Communications, $13.6 billion (Jensen, 1997, p. 321). Also, in 1996 alone, there was $25 billion of merger activity in the broadcasting industry and another $23 billion in cable. The FCC used to watch the industry closely for problems with certain firms getting too powerful, that is, owning stations covering a large segment of the population. But since 1996, the FCC has been less concerned with preventing monopolies in this country and more concerned with allowing Ameri-

---

TABLE 10.1   Media Mega Mergers

- January 1986: Capital Cities Communications Inc. purchases American Broadcasting Company for $3.5 billion to create Capital Cities/ABC Inc.
- November 1989: Sony Corp. buys film and television producer Columbia Pictures Entertainment Inc. for $3.4 billion.
- January 1990: Warner Communications Inc. and Time Inc. complete $14.1 billion merger, creating world's biggest media conglomerate.
- September 1993: The New York Times Co. buys Affiliated Publications Inc., parent company of the Boston Globe, for $1.1 billion, the biggest takeover in U.S. newspaper history.
- July 1994: Viacom Inc. buys Paramount Communications Inc. for $10 billion after winning a bidding war against QVC Inc. to buy the movie, publishing, and sports company.
- August 1994: Viacom Inc. buys video rental chain Blockbuster Entertainment Corp. for $8 billion.
- 1995:
- August 1995: Walt Disney Co. acquires Capital Cities/ABC Inc. for $19 billion, making it the largest media company. ABC had been concerned about the fragmentation of television audiences due to cable, so it diversified and now owns ESPN and Lifetime cable channels as well as the Disney channel. This made Disney the first media company with four distribution systems: filmed entertainment, cable television, broadcasting, and telephone wires.
- October 1996: Time Warner and Turner Broadcasting System complete $7.6 billion merger. This becomes the world's biggest media company, with annual revenues of more than $20 billion.
- November 1996: Penguin Group, the international publisher, buys Putnum Berkley Group, a U.S. subsid- iary of MCA (owned by Seagram Co.) for $336 million. Penguin is strong with backlist books (Arthur Miller, Gabriel Garcia Marquez, Toni Morrison, E. L. Doctorow, Joyce Carol Oates) and Putnam has a strong front list (Stephen King, Terry McMillan, Tom Clancy, Patricia Cornwell).
- February 1997: A merger of two radio companies created Chancellor Media Corp., which took control of 103 radio stations that generate more than $700 million annually in revenue. The top ranked radio group is Infinity Broadcasting ($1.1 billion in revenue annually), which is owned by Westinghouse Electric Corp.
- January 1998: Compaq Computer Corp. buys Digital Equipment Corp. for $9.6 billion. This made Compaq one of the three largest computer companies in the world in terms of sales. This was the biggest buyout in the history of the computer industry to that point. Compaq is a Houston-based technology firm.
- May 1998: Conde Nast Publication Inc. buys *Wired*—the San Francisco-based cutting-edge bible of the cyberspace revolution. The deal was in excess of $75 million. The magazine was co-founded by a hus- band and wife team in 1993. At the time of the sale, *Wired's* circulation was 400,000 and it had $31.5 million in ad revenue. Conde Nast is a unit of Advance Publications (publishers of the *New Yorker, Vanity Fair,* and *Vogue*), which in turn is a division of the Newhouse newspaper publishing chain.
- December 1998: CBS Corp. raises $2.9 billion by selling a 17% stake in Infinity Broadcasting Corp., its ra- dio and outdoor advertising business. The initial public offering of stock is the largest ever in the media industry.
- April 1999: CBS Corp. announces agreement to buy King World Productions Inc., the leading syndicator of television programs, for $2.5 billion.

---

can companies to grow significantly stronger in order to compete and dominate in the world market (Albarran & Chan-Olmsted, 1998).

TABLE 10.1   Continued

- September 1999: Viacom Inc. announces deal to buy CBS Corp. for $34.5 billion. The merger combines film, television, radio, Internet sites, book publishing, and many other businesses. Viacom has the UPN Network, Blockbuster video rental stores, cable outlets (MTV, Nickelodeon, Showtime, Comedy Central), Paramount Pictures, Simon & Schuster, and Paramount theme parks. CBS includes the CBS television network, cable outlets (CMT & TNN country music channels), Infinity Broadcasting (over 160 radio stations), and Outdoor Systems (billboards). The FCC made the deal possible by abandoning its long-standing restriction against allowing one company to own two television stations in the same market. This merger allows Viacom to own two stations in each of six big markets: Philadelphia, Boston, Dallas, Detroit, Pittsburgh, and Miami. The new company is an example of vertical integration. It will be able to generate shows at Paramount Pictures, distribute them on CBS or UPN television networks and through Blockbuster stores, promote the sound-tracks on MTV and VH1, and do book tie-ins through Simon & Schuster. Critics say that this company will be too powerful; that is, a very few people will be making decisions affecting too much of the media industry's products and practices. FCC Chairman William Kennard says that he is merely recognizing the realities of globalization and new technologies.
- October 1999: Clear Channel Communications Inc. agrees to buy AMFM Inc. for $16.6 billion in stock, creating the nation's largest radio company.
- November 1999: Spelling Entertainment Group, Inc. sells Virgin Interactive Entertainment in order to concentrate its resources on its television and film operations (*Melrose Place; Beverly Hills, 90210*). Virgin produces video games (Nintendo) and computer games. Spelling is owned by Viacom, Inc.
- November 1999: American Media Inc., publisher of the *National Enquirer* and the *Star,* among other newspapers, acquired Globe Communications, Inc., publisher of *Globe and Sun,* for $105 million. David Pecker, chairman of American Media, said that the merger would create "one of the largest publishers of celebrity-driven content in the world." The new company is projected to generate about $400 million in annual revenue.
- January 2000: America Online Inc. agrees to buy Time Warner Inc. in $135 billion merger agreement, the largest ever combination in the media industry.
- January 2000: Time Warner, Inc. (Atlantic, Elektra, and Warner Brothers record labels) and Britain's EMI Group (Virgin, Priority, and Capitol record labels) agreed to merge their music businesses, thus creating the world's biggest music company with combined annual revenues of $8 billion. The new firm would represent 2,500 musicians.
- February 2000: Germany's Mannesmann AG merged with Britain's Vodafone AirTouch PLC for $180 billion, making it the largest merger in the history of the world. The combined company would have 42 million customers and be the leader in mobile phone service in 11 European countries.
- March 2000: The *Chicago Tribune* took over the Times Mirror Co., which publishes the *Los Angeles Times.* The $6.3 billion deal made the Tribune Company the country's third largest newspaper group with control of 3.6 million in daily circulation across 11 daily newspapers. The company also owns 22 TV stations (in Chicago, Los Angeles, and New York) and Internet sites. The new company reaches 75% of the country's households through its broadcast and cable TV services.

NOTE: Compiled from the following sources: Fabrikant, 1995; Greimel, 2000; Hofmeister, 1997a, 1997b; Holstein, 1999; Lorimer, 1994; Lyall, 1996; McDonald, 2000; Roberts, 1999; Silverman, 1998; Stanley, 2000; Sutel, 1999; *Timeline of Major Media Mergers,* 2000; White, 2000.

TABLE 10.2   Non-Media Companies Buy Media Companies

- June 1986: General Electric Co. buys RCA Corp., parent company of National Broadcasting Co. and NBC television network, for $6.4 billion. At the time, the deal was the largest non-oil acquisition in U.S. history. In the same year Capital Cities bought ABC.
- January 1991: Matsushita Electric Industrial Co. of Japan buys MCA Inc. for $6.9 billion.
- May 1993: US West, a telephone company, pays $2.5 billion for 25.5% of Time Warner. The new company plans to integrate the technologies that would provide a service where people could instantly order whatever programming they want (movies on demand), shop for products, and do their banking, listen to CDs, watch live sports and concerts, make travel plans, play video games, and so on.
- June 1995: Seagram Co. buys MCA Inc. from Matsushita for $5.7 billion and renames it Universal Studios.
- November 1995: Westinghouse Corp. buys CBS for $5.4 billion, giving the new company 15 TV stations and 39 radio stations that, combined, gives it direct access to one third of the nation's households.
- November 1996: Seagram Co. now owns about 80% of MCA, which owns Putnam publishing, films, records, and theme parks.
- December 1996: Westinghouse Electric Corp.'s CBS unit buys Infinity Broadcasting Co. for $4.7 billion, combining the nation's two biggest radio station operators.
- September 1997: Seagram Co. buys half of the USA Networks (reaches 70 million homes and includes the USA and Sci-fi channels) from Viacom for $1.7 billion in September 1997. Seagrams also owns Universal Studios, so it can produce and distribute programming.
- December 1997: Westinghouse Electric Corp. changes its name to CBS Inc. shortly after deciding to sell its traditional businesses, such as power-generation equipment and light bulbs.
- December 1998: Seagram Co. buys the PolyGram music company for $10.4 billion.
- February 1999: AT&T joins with Time Warner Inc. in a deal to offer local and long-distance telephone service, cable TV, and high speed Internet access over Time Warner's cable systems in 33 states. Because AT&T has already acquired Tele-Communications Inc., AT&T raises its access to 40% of U.S. households. This deal also lets AT&T back into providing local phone service, which it had been prevented from doing since its breakup in 1984.

NOTE   Compiled from the following sources: Bowen, 1993; CBS, 1997; Hofmeister, 1997a, 1997b; Lyall, 1996; Maney, 1995; *Timeline of Major Media Mergers,* 2000.

Phone companies keep looking for entertainment companies to buy. For example, GTE has 17-million phone lines and $20 billion in revenue annually. BellSouth is the biggest regional phone company, with 19-million phone lines that bring in a total of $16 billion per year. With all their cash, the phone companies are looking to invest in profitable businesses, especially those that would give them access to customers who want to buy information and entertainment.

International Perspective

Foreign companies have been buying American media properties, especially film studios, over the past decade. For example, Pathe, a French-Italian firm, bought MGM and United Artists. Sony, a Japanese electronics manufacturer, bought Columbia Pictures from Coca Cola. Also, about 13% of all American newspapers are owned by non-American companies (Albarran & Chan-Olmsted, 1998).

That foreign companies buy or invest in American media companies is not uncommon. In one year, companies from the United Kingdom made 188 deals totaling $23.6 billion to buy U.S. media companies; Japanese companies made 45 transactions for $11.9 billion; Canadian companies, 46 deals for $9.7 billion; France, 26 deals for $3.0 billion; and Germany, 27 transactions for $1.2 billion.

An example of how American companies attract foreign investors is Rupert Murdoch, who is from Australia where he owns newspapers in most of the major cities there along with Australia's only national daily, television stations, publishing houses, recording companies, and a major airline. He went to Great Britain and bought the *London Times*; two sex-and-scandal sheets with a combined circulation of over 8 million; a string of magazines; a string of provincial newspapers; and companies for manufacturing paper, printing, and distributing newsprint. He came to the United States and bought the *New York Post*, *New York Magazine*, the *Village Voice*, the *Chicago-Sun Times*, two other daily newspapers, and 17 suburban weeklies. He has also bought Metromedia's seven television stations in New York, Boston, and other major cities, giving him access to 21% of the total television audience. His empire earns more than $1 billion a year. Recently, Murdoch's Australian firm, News Corp., took over the American film giant, 20th Century Fox.

Globalization works both ways. American companies market their entertainment services worldwide. For example, by 1993, MTV was in cable systems in over 71 countries, reaching more than 500-million people (Barber, 1995, p. 104). By 1995, ESPN was offering programming to 150 countries in 18 languages (Mandese, 1995, p. 4).

■■ CONCENTRATION IN ADVERTISING

Manufacturers are buying each other up in an effort to get bigger and bigger. This gives them more power in the marketplace, helps their profits by diversifying, and gives them more power as advertisers. For example, Procter & Gamble has usually been the number one advertiser in the world since 1913. It sells its products in 140 countries and advertises heavily in all. It will spend more than $3 billion on advertising this year. On TV alone, it will buy over 28,000 ads; it would take you 10 days of solid viewing (24 hours per day, continuously) to watch them all. Therefore, Procter & Gamble exerts an enormous amount of power. Other examples include McDonald's, which has 17,000 franchise restaurants in 90 different countries: 760 are in Japan; their largest restaurant is in Beijing (Barber, 1995). Coca-Cola is in 160 countries (Barnet & Cavanagh, 1994), and two thirds of Coke's revenue comes from outside the United States (Barber, 1995).

Some very large companies have so many products that we as consumers do not realize that many of the products that appear very different are marketed by the same company. For example, PepsiCo, Inc., markets beverages (Pepsi, Slice, Mountain Dew, and root beer), but it also owns and controls the largest restaurant system in the world, which includes Kentucky Fried Chicken, Pizza Hut, and Taco Bell. In the fall of 1998, Coca-Cola bought Cadbury Schweppes beverage brands (Schweppes, Dr. Pepper, Crush, Canada Dry) outside the United States for $1.85 billion ("Coca-Cola Agrees," 1998). Also, Quaker Oats is only a cereal, right? Not exactly. It markets its cereal (in many forms) and also other cereals (Cap'n Crunch), Gatorade, Van Camp's Pork & Beans, Rice-A-Roni, Gaines dog food, Ken-L Ration dog food, Granola Bars, Rice Cakes, Aunt Jemima breakfast foods, and Fisher Price Toys. Quaker Oats is typically one of the top 30 companies in the world in terms of advertising budgets.

How about cigarettes? Are you trying to be socially responsible and not buy products that would support companies that market harmful products? You recognize the name of Philip Morris as a cigarette company—it manufactures and sells Marlboro, Merit, Virginia Slims, and Benson & Hedges. Did you know that Philip Morris Co. owns General Foods and Miller Brewing? General Foods includes Maxwell House coffee (Maxwell House, Sanka, International Coffees, Brim, and Yuban), Birds Eye Frozen Foods, Post cereals (Raisin Bran, Grape-Nuts, Honeycombs, Fruit & Fibre, 40% Bran Flakes, Crispy Critters, Pebbles, Super Golden Crisp, Alpha Bits), Tang, Country Time, Kool-aid, Minute Rice, Stove Top Stuffing, Dream Whip, Jell-O, Crystal Light, Ronzoni, Shake 'n Bake, Log Cabin Syrup, Oscar Meyer meats, Louis Rich, and many, many others. Miller of course makes Miller Hi-Life, Miller Lite, and Miller Genuine Draft, but it also makes Lowenbrau, Meister Brau, and Milwaukee's Best.

RJ Reynolds is another tobacco company. It manufactures and markets Salem, Vantage, Ritz, Doral, Magna, Camel, Now, More, and Winston. But it also owns Lifesavers, Care*Free gum, Del Monte Foods, and Nabisco. Notice that what we think of as two tobacco companies are responsible for many more products than just cigarettes.

Concentration in Advertising Agencies. Just as businesses that manufacture products are getting bigger and bigger, so are ad agencies. Half of all the advertising placed in this country was handled by one of the world's top 20 advertising agencies. This means there is an enormous amount of concentration, with many instances of an agency handling the accounts of direct competitors.

In 1986, three agencies—BBDO; Doyle Dane, Bernback; and Needham Harper—joined together to become the world's biggest. A month later, Britain's Saatchi & Saatchi took over the Ted Bates agency, creating a new number one ($7.5 billion worth of business). Agencies keep buying each other and consolidating so that every few months there is a new "largest advertising agency in the world." In May 2000, the London-based WPP Group PLC (which previously had bought the U.S. ad agencies of J. Walter Thompson and Ogilvy & Mather) bought the American agency Young & Rubicam. This consolidated firm now handles the business of the following huge advertisers: AT&T, Cadbury-Schweppes, Colgate-Palmolive, Ford Motor Co., Kraft Foods, and Sears (Wollenberg, 2000).

■■ ISSUES OF CONCERN

We have seen that the media industries have been moving steadily toward greater concentration both within each industry and especially across media industries. Critics fear that this trend has already put too much power into the hands of a very few people (see Tables 10.3 and 10.4). They feel that consumers are now worse off because of (a) less competition and (b) less access to the media. Let's take a closer look at each of these two criticisms.

First, critics argue that as competition decreases, the quality of media products declines. But has the quality of media products declined? There is no evidence that it has. A study done on newspaper content could find no change in content after a newspaper was bought by a chain (e.g., see Picard, Winter, McCombs, & Lacy, 1988). No evidence of change was found with the stories, the range of opinions on the editorial page, or the proportion of the newspaper displaying news.

Also, it does not appear that radio station content changes when a station is bought by a group. Lacy and Riffe (1994) looked at the news content of radio stations, comparing group ownership effects. They found group ownership had no impact on the financial commitment or the local and staff emphasis of news coverage.

But there are examples where the business side can spill over onto the editorial side at newspapers. This was clearly illustrated in the fall of 1999 when the *Los Angeles Times Magazine* was devoted to coverage of the Staples Center, a new sports arena. The publisher, Kathryn M. Downing, had entered into a partnership agreement on the issue with the Staples Center, agreeing to have the Staples Center promote the magazine in return for sharing profits. Downing did

TABLE 10.3 Most Powerful Media Companies in the United States

Below is an alphabetical listing of the 23 companies that control most of the media audience in the United States. Each of these companies is a conglomerate that owns businesses across several media industries. Next to each of these companies is a short, partial list of some of the main media properties for which that company is known.

1. A. G. Bertelsmann (Doubleday, Bantam Books, and other book publishers)
2. Capital Cities/ABC (newspapers, broadcasting)
3. Cox Communications (*Atlanta Journal* and 19 other newspapers; cable TV)
4. CBS (broadcasting)
5. Buena Vista Films (Disney motion pictures)
6. Dow Jones (*Wall Street Journal* and 22 other newspapers)
7. Gannett (*USA Today* and 87 other daily newspapers)
8. General Electric (owns RCA, which in turn owns the NBC television network)
9. Paramount Communications (book publishing, Paramount Motion Pictures)
10. Harcourt Brace Jovanovich (books)
11. Hearst (*San Francisco Examiner* and 13 other newspapers; magazines including *Good Housekeeping, Cosmopolitan*)
12. Ingersoll (37 newspapers)
13. International Thomson (120 daily newspapers; book publishing)
14. Knight Ridder (*Philadelphia Inquirer, Miami Herald,* and 27 other newspapers)
15. Media News group (*Dallas Times Herald* and 17 other newspapers)
16. Newhouse (26 newspapers, Conde Nast magazines, Random House books)
17. News Corporation, LTD. (*Boston Herald* and 2 other newspapers; magazines including *TV Guide, Seventeen, New York*; 20th-Century Fox motion pictures; Fox television)
18. New York Times (*New York Times* and 26 other newspapers)
19. Reader's Digest Association (books)
20. Scripps-Howard (23 newspapers)
21. Time Warner (magazines including *Time, People, Sports Illustrated, Fortune* books, Warner Brothers television and motion pictures)
22. Times Mirror (*Los Angeles Times* and 7 other newspapers)
23. Tribune Company (*Chicago Tribune, New York Daily News* and 7 other newspapers; magazines)

NOTE: This table was assembled with information from Bagdikian (1997) and *Hoover's Guide* (1996).

not tell her reporters or editors about the business partnership. When the journalists found out, they complained about not knowing the magazine had been turned into a public relations device for the Staples Center. Downing, whose background was as a business manager and not as a journalist, apologized, saying that she did not realize that her actions would damaged the journalistic integrity of the newspaper ("L.A. Times Publisher Errs, Apologizes," 1999).

The criticism that concentration of ownership reduces competition in a market seems valid on the surface, but it breaks down when analyzed. To illustrate, let's say a city has two newspapers. A chain buys one of those newspapers. The

TABLE 10.4   Detailed Profiles of Six Large Media Conglomerates

Sony Corporation had 1996 sales of $44.8 billion, making it the largest media company in the world. Headquartered in Tokyo, Japan, it employees 138,000 people. It manufactures televisions, VCRs, Walkman, Discman, and Apple Powerbook, among other electronic devices. It owns CBS Records and Columbia Pictures. It is in partnership with Microsoft to make SEGA video games. Its profit margin is about 12%.

Time Warner Inc. Is the second largest media company in the world with 1996 sales of $17.7 billion and 65,500 employees. It owns magazines (*Time, Money, Sports Illustrated, Life, Discover, Fortune, People, Entertainment Weekly, Martha Stewart Living, In Style*), book publishing houses (Time-Life Books; Little, Brown and Co.; Book of the Month Club; as well as large interests in publishing firms in Germany, France, Mexico, and Japan), comic books (*Batman, Superman, Bugs Bunny, Mad*), newspapers (Pioneer Press, which publishes suburban Chicago newspapers), television networks (WB, Courtroom Television, HBO), broadcast television stations, Warner Brothers movie studio (with its recently successful films of *Twister* and *Eraser,* along with TV shows *Friends* and *ER*), Looney Toons (which alone produces retail sales of $3.5 billion in cartoon merchandising), Time Warner Cable system (second largest cable operator in the country), recording companies (Atlantic, Warner Brothers), and Six Flags Entertainment. It also owns Turner Broadcasting, which includes the Cartoon Network, TNT, CNN, Turner Pictures, the MGM film library, Hanna-Barbera cartoon stars (Flintstones and Yogi Bear), and the movie studios of New Line Cinema and Castle Rock. It also owns a marketing data company, video games (Atari), Inland Container Corp., American Television and Communications Corp., and Temple Industries, which is one of the largest landowners in the country.

The Walt Disney Company has annual revenues of $12 billion and owns film studios (Disney, Touchstone, Miramax, Hollywood Pictures), ABC television network, theme parks, record companies, book publishing, and television production studios. It employs 71,000 people.

Viacom Inc. has revenues of $11.7 billion and employs 81,700 people. It owns movie theaters, radio and television stations, production studios (Paramount Pictures, Spelling Entertainment, Worldvision) Blockbuster Video, book publishers (Simon & Schuster, Macmillan, Prentice Hall, Scribner), cable networks (Comedy Central, MTV, VH1, Nickelodeon, Showtime, The Movie Channel, Sci-Fi Channel, USA Network, and All News Channel).

Cox Enterprises, Inc. owns the fifth largest cable system in the country, 19 newspapers, 17 radio stations (including 3 in Los Angeles), 6 television stations, companies in the industries of farming, timber, cattle, paper manufacturing, direct marketing, auto auctioning, and publishing. It has annual sales of $3.8 billion and employs 38,000 people.

Barnes & Noble, Inc. was begun by a 24-year-old who borrowed $5,000 to start a college bookstore. It has grown to annual sales of $2 billion and employs 21,400 people. It is in partnership with Bertelsmann, which is the world's largest publisher of English-language books, owning publishers such as Random House and Doubleday. It also owns one of the largest book clubs in the world, with 5.5 million members in the United States alone. Bertelsmann also publishes magazines such as *McCall's, Family Circle,* and *Parents,* which reach 50% of women in the United States.

NOTE: All information from *Hoover's Guide,* 1996.

chain-owned newspaper cuts subscription costs and ad rates. Readers and advertisers switch to the chain newspaper because it is less expensive. Eventually the other newspaper goes out of business. The degree of concentration in that market goes up. But this does not mean that the newspaper has no competition simply because it is the only newspaper in the market. The newspaper must compete for audiences and advertisers along with the radio, television, and cable stations in the market. Thus, if the newspaper degrades its news product, people will drop their subscriptions and turn to other sources of news. With lower circulation rates, the newspaper will need to drop the rate it charges advertisers, and this will produce less revenue. With less revenue, the newspaper will need to lay off reporters, and the news product will degrade further. This downward cycle continues until the newspaper is out of business. But this almost never happens, because chain-owned newspapers are driven by making large profits, and to do that, they must do everything they can to expand their circulations.

Newspapers, as well as all the other media, expand their revenues only by providing more and better services to consumers. How do they know what consumers want? They are constantly doing market research to test out new ideas. Also, they carefully monitor the public reactions, verbal as well as monetary, to their messages. When the public's tastes or wants change, the media know this, and they offer new types of products and messages.

Second, critics argue that as concentration increases, the individual's access to the media is reduced. "Access" here can mean two different things. One meaning is ownership, that is, how much access does an individual have to own a media property? Because most media companies are public corporations, any individual can buy a share of any company. But can a person own a media property fully? The answer still is yes. There are comparatively low barriers to entry in the magazine, book publishing, newspaper, and computer industries. With several thousand dollars, a desktop computer, and strong initiative, most people could begin a company in one of these media industries. Of course, he or she should be prepared to face very stiff competition to gain the attention of an audience and to gain the confidence of advertisers. But it is possible to create one's own media voice in those industries. In contrast, barriers to entry are much higher in the radio, television, cable, and film industries; and the conglomerate mergers over the past several decades have raised those barriers even higher, almost to the point of being prohibitive for any except the wealthiest individuals.

Access can also mean the ability to get your particular point of view heard through someone else's media property. This is still relatively easy to do at the local level, such as with newspapers and small-circulation magazines. Most still print letters to the editors, and most buy articles from people with little journalistic experience. And most markets have call-in radio programs where you can get your voice heard. In contrast, getting your voice heard in national media properties, such as *Newsweek* magazine or a TV or cable network, requires a great deal of skill and good connections because the competition to use those channels is so strong.

■■ CONCLUSION

Media critics are wary of the degree of concentration in the media industries. Their concern is focused on the central issue of which is more important: efficiency (brought about by industry integration and economics of scale) OR independence (diversity of content and easier entry into the market thus allowing alternative voices).

This is an issue about which you should have an opinion. But to synthesize a good opinion, you need to build it up from an analysis of the situation. This chapter provides such an analysis to begin your thinking. You should begin by considering which ethic you think should be dominant in the formulation of the media industries. Do you favor localism with its focus on the power of society —through citizen activism and government regulations—to make the media responsive to the different needs of the broad spectrum of people in the society? Or do you find more favor with concentration as a goal of businesses driven to operate more effectively and efficiently and thus generate as large a profit as possible for the owners?

Once you become interested in this issue and begin formulating your opinion, you need to monitor changes in this dynamic situation and continually update your knowledge structures. Over time, the government has been relaxing regulations and as a result businesses have been moving strongly toward concentration. But there is still a great deal of competition among the media industries as they try to claim more of our attention and a greater share of the advertiser's dollar.

■■ FURTHER READING

Bagdikian, B. (1999). *The media monopoly* (6th ed.). Boston: Beacon. (288 pages with index)

Bagdikian originally published this book in 1983 and has had to update it many times to keep up with the trend of consolidation in the media industries. He argues that the media are in the hands of too few corporations. This is an unhealthy condition, he says, because it focuses decisions too much on profit and not enough on quality or diversity of messages. Profits are maximized when corporations increase revenues, which means that program producers must not offend advertisers. He shows how advertising has pressured journalism to change the way it reports stories.

Maney, K. (1995). *Megamedia shakeout: The inside story of the leaders and the losers in the exploding communications industry.* New York: John Wiley. (358 pages including index)

This is a well-written description of the major players in the technologies landscape in the mid-1990s. There are lots of anecdotes and stories about what has been happening in the telephone, cable, computer, wireless, and entertainment industries. The book is full of facts and personal descriptions of the personalities involved. Things are happening so fast in these industries, however, with new roll-outs and buy-outs, that the book will soon be dated.

EXERCISE 10.1

What Is the Concentration of Media Ownership in Your Local Market?

This exercise asks you to be a detective in order to search out information in your local media market. See how creative you can be in coming up with strategies to get the answers to the following questions.

1. How many movie screens are there in your market?
   a. How many theaters control those screens?
   b. Are the theaters owned by chains? If so, how many chains control the total set of screens?

2. How many radio stations are there in your market?
   a. How many are group owned?
   b. How many of the stations are owned by companies that also own other media businesses in your market?

3. How many broadcast television stations are there in your market?
   a. How many are group owned?
   b. How many of the stations are owned by companies that also own other media businesses in your market?

4. Is your local newspaper owned by a chain? If so, does the chain own other media businesses in your market?

5. Are there any magazines published in your market and distributed only in your market? If so, does the controlling company also own other media businesses?

6. What is the name of the company that provides your market with cable TV service? Is that cable company an MSO (Multiple System Operator)?

7. In total, how many different media outlets (voices) are there in your market? How many individuals or companies control these voices?

8. If you wanted to express yourself through the media in your market, how hard do you think it would be to gain access to one of these outlets?
   a. For example, assume that you wanted to criticize some new government regulation or tax policy in your local area. Which outlet would be most likely to give you space or time to speak out?
   b. Which outlet(s) do you think would be the least likely or impossible?

9. Given your answers to the questions above, how concentrated do you think your market is—that is, do you think the outlets are in the control of too few individuals?

CHAPTER

11

Key Idea: Each of the mass media industries has its own unique history, economic characteristics, and ownership patterns.

Profiles of Media Industries

In this chapter, a brief profile is presented for each of the nine media industries. These profiles illuminate the issues raised in the three previous chapters. Each profile is organized to show the key characteristics in that industry's stages of development. Notice that some industries have not gone through all five stages. The profiles also present key economic indicators as well as information about the degree of concentration in each industry.

Before we get started on these profiles, I need to clarify the distinction between a vehicle and a company. For example, *Time* magazine is a vehicle. *Time* publishes 52 weekly issues each year, but the issues are not the same as the vehicle. Also, we need to make a distinction between the company that publishes the vehicle and the vehicle itself. Time Warner is the company that publishes *Time* magazine, but Time Warner also publishes many other magazine vehicles, such as *Money, Discover,* and *Fortune.* So when we talk about magazines, we must be clear about whether we are referring to the media channel (of all magazines), a vehicle (which is the title of a single magazine), an issue (which is the set of stapled pages on your coffee table), or the company (which usually owns and publishes several vehicles).

Now let's look at economic profiles of the media. Remember that the companies in these industries are businesses that are driven to maximize their profits. When you read the profiles below, think about how the five basic economic principles outlined in Chapter 9 are illustrated in the way they try to maximize revenue and minimize expenses. Unless otherwise indicated, the information in the profiles below is from the July 1996 Standard & Poor's *Index to Surveys*, and the profit figures are ROR.

■■ BOOK INDU/TRY

Innovation Stage

Book publishing was in the innovation stage in the mid-1400s when the printing press with moveable type was invented by Gutenberg. Book publishing was already well developed when this country was colonized. Until the 19th century, however, books were not a mass medium, because they were purchased and read only by the educated and the affluent.

Penetration Stage

During the late 1800s, there were several developments that transformed books into a mass medium. First, paperback books began to be published in the late 1800s, and this made books more affordable to the masses. Second, by 1900, public schools were widespread and literacy was commonplace. Third, large publishing houses were being established so many more books were being published and marketed.

Peak Stage

The book publishing industry has never reached a peak, that is, it has yet to achieve dominance among the mass media.

Adaptation Stage

The book industry competes well alongside the other mass media. It has adapted by becoming niche oriented; each niche offers a different kind of book to a different kind of audience. Each year, about one third of published titles are mass market type publications; 24% are trade books; 20% textbooks; 10% book club editions; and the rest are religious, professional, and specialty books.

Now when a publisher comes out with a new book, it is often published not only on paper but also in an electronic form called an E-book. These are hand-held, battery-powered devices where the words appear on a screen rather than a paper page. The books are the software that is plugged into this device that sells for $300 to $600. Introduced in 1998, fewer than 10,000 E-books were sold that first year, which is a drop in the bucket for a $23 billion a year industry (book sales in 1998). However, there are already 1,500 fiction and non-fiction titles available (Stroh, 1999).

Current Structure

There are about 3,000 book publishers. The industry produces about 68,000 new titles and sells about 2 billion books each year. The largest segment is the adult trade book, which includes general interest fiction and non-fiction, advice, and how-to books. These are the books typically found in the bookstores in malls.

Most of the books are sold through retail book stores. Most of the sales in this segment is the very large chains such as Waldenbooks or Barnes & Noble. But bookstores on the Internet are gaining market share.

Bookstores are going online on the Web. Amazon.com started in July 1995 and reached $15 million in sales the next year; however, their costs were $20 million that year. In 1996, Barnes & Noble had sales of $2.4 billion in its stores, then in May of the following year, it also offered sales online.

Revenue

Annual revenues did not break the $1-billion mark until about 1960, and as recently as 1980 revenues were only $4 billion a year. Now, the book industry has an annual revenue of about $23.5 billion (Book Industry Study Group, 1998). This is more than all ticket sales to movie theaters ($4.9 billion) and sales of pre-recorded music ($11 billion) combined.

This is an economically healthy industry that continues to grow each year in terms of both revenues and titles produced.

Expenses

There are many elements that make up the expenses of book publishing. Let's take a typical example of a hardbound trade book that lists for $19.95 in a retail bookstore. When this sells, the store keeps about 48% for its own expenses and profit, and sends the remaining $10.37 to the publisher. It costs the publisher about $2.00 to manufacture the physical copy of the book (composition, typesetting, jacket design, paper, ink, printing, binding, etc.). Another $3.00 is for overhead, which includes the expense of editors, office staff, marketing, and the like. The author gets about $2.00 in royalties. The remaining $3.37 is profit unless the stores return unsold copies—a common practice—and wipe out the potential profit.

Risk

Only one book in five is successful, meaning it makes money for the publisher after all the expenses and returns are subtracted from sales. The small number of successful books in essence subsidizes the industry and makes it possible for publishers to take chances on all sorts of "risky" books and new authors.

Because of the economic risks in the industry, publishers are continually searching for books they think the public wants, rather than searching for what they think are the best or most literary books. Publishers believe the public likes books on scandal and celebrities. This is why there have been so many books on O.J. Simpson in the past few years. Another example is Dick Morris, who was a political consultant in the White House and unknown to the public. No publisher was interested in a book deal with him until he was discovered to have frequented a $200-an-hour call girl, and the scandal made the front page in all the newspapers. His wife divorced him but publishers scrambled to sign him to a "kiss and tell" book about how he liked to suck on a prostitute's toes while telling her about his private conversations with the President. The negotiations ended with Morris signing a $2.5-million deal to write one book. Obviously the publisher thought that all the free publicity about Morris's disgrace would make the book high-profile and a best-seller.

If a bookstore doesn't think a book will sell, it won't even take a chance and stock it. The average bookstore carries about 20,000 titles at any given time. Remember that the industry publishes 68,000 new titles each year. Bookstores can handle only a small fraction of the new titles produced each year, especially when you consider that they need to keep in stock many "old" books, such as the Bible and other classics, reference books, last year's best-sellers, and so on.

Out of the 68,000 new book titles published each year, less than 1% make it onto any best-seller list; about half are new books and half from previous years (Gulbransen, 1998). In 1997, only 88 fiction titles made the lists; 85% of these books were written by authors who had been on the list before. The six major publishers (Random House, Simon & Schuster, Penguin Putnam, Bantam Doubleday and Dell, HarperCollins, Time Warner) accounted for 85% of the hardcover slots and 83% of the paperback slots. If you add in the titles of six other smaller houses, you account for 98% of all best-sellers.

Concentration

While there are 3,000 companies that publish books, only 1,500 of them publish five or more titles a year. Furthermore, the top five book publishers account for most of the revenue in this industry (Bagdikian, 1992). Book publishing is a segmented field with different sets of publishers specializing in certain sub-markets. But even within these sub-markets, there is a trend toward concentration. For example, in mass market paperback publishing, the top seven firms account for more than 80% of all sales.

Consolidation is taking place in book publishing with big companies merging and acquiring smaller companies. For example, The Penguin Group publishes primarily classics and reference books (Lyall, 1996). The Putnam Berkley Group is known for its successful best-sellers from such authors as Tom Clancy, Dick Francis, Patricia Cornwell, and Amy Tan. The Penguin Group recently acquired a U.S. subsidiary of MCA for $336 million. The merged company will account for about 12% of all book sales in the United States.

There is a strong trend toward concentration in the bookstore segment of the industry. In 1958, companies that owned more than one bookstore (chains) accounted for only 28% of all sales, and there were no chains with more than 50 stores. Now there are chains such as Barnes & Noble and Borders that own more than 1,000 bookstores. Chain-owned bookstores now generate over two thirds of all the revenue in the book industry.

NEWSPAPER INDUSTRY ■

Innovation Stage

The innovation stage of newspapers dates back to before the United States was founded. In the 1500s and 1600s in Europe there were printing presses and distribution processes that made newspapers a mass medium.

As far as this country's history is concerned, the innovation of newspapers was not a technological one but a marketing one. In the colonies, publishers made the decision to use the newspaper medium as a way to shape political opinion. These early newspapers were more like propaganda leaflets, and each had a very small circulation. By 1776 there were already 30 weekly newspapers in the colonies, and these newspapers went into a total of 40,000 homes. These newspapers were run by political parties, which dictated their content. The parties used their own newspapers to present their version of the news.

By the 1830s, a big shift in the purpose of newspapers was taking place. Publishers became much more interested in making money with their newspapers. To increase revenues, publishers needed to build large circulations. They were no longer interested in appealing to a small, select group of political partisans. Instead they needed to broaden their base. So publishers began hiring professional editors who could produce a product that responded to broader social needs and human interests rather than narrow political ideologies.

Penetration Stage

By the 1870s, newspapers had truly become a mass medium—the only one at the time. The telegraph was linking newspapers instantaneously to faraway locations where news was happening. New developments in printing presses made the printing of newspapers faster and cheaper. By 1900, improved transportation allowed distribution to a larger territory. Newspapers were being run in a more business-like fashion. They used economies of scale to lower their unit costs. And even though they were selling copies for a penny apiece, their profits were increasing dramatically because their volume was growing so fast. Between 1880 and 1900, the number of newspapers in America more than doubled, going from 850 to 1,967. In 1870, about 2.6 million copies were circulated daily to the 7.6 million households in America (1 out of every 3). By 1900, 93% of all households were subscribing.

With the decline of political partisanship, more and more readers found a broad range of newspapers interesting and useful. Advertisers also found the medium very useful.

Peak Stage

In 1919, newspapers reached a peak of penetration as the average household was receiving about 1.4 newspapers per day. The number of daily newspaper organizations was at a peak with almost 2,500 firms.

Decline Stage

Newspapers began to decline as the most important mass medium in the 1930s and 1940s as radio and then television took away the newspaper's functions of providing information and entertainment. Even more devastating was that the newer media eroded the base of advertising, especially among the national advertisers. The number of daily newspapers declined to about 1,750 in 1945 and has remained at about that level ever since.

Adaptation Stage

Since the 1950s, newspapers have redefined their role as a local medium for audiences and advertisers.

Although the newspaper industry has experienced overall growth, most of that growth has not been in big cities: The circulation of city newspapers has remained static. Most of the growth in circulation has been in the daily and weekly newspapers of smaller communities.

Revenue

Newspapers have two major streams of revenue. One is through subscriptions and newsstand sales, which generated $9.8 billion last year. However, the much bigger revenue stream is advertising, which brought in $34.4 billion. Over time, the advertising stream has grown much faster than the sales stream. In 1880 the average newspaper received 25% of its revenue from advertising; by 1910, advertising accounted for 50% of all revenue; and now the amount is almost 80%.

Historically, newspaper publishers have been reluctant to increase their prices to readers, so they have been asking advertisers to bear most of the increases in their expenses. But this has been changing recently. Throughout the 1980s and into the 1990s, there was a consistent shift of revenue burden to readers in the form of higher subscription rates and selling price of an issue at the news stand (Blankenburg, 1995).

Expenses

The biggest expense of newspapers is personnel costs, which account for about 60% of all expenditures. While this cost goes up each year, it has been doing so at a slow rate of about 3% to 4% a year.

Profit

The average profit margin for a newspaper company is about 17%, which is more than triple the median profit margin (4.8%) for Fortune 500 companies.

Chain-owned newspapers are even more profitable. The primary purpose of a chain-owned newspaper is to maximize the profits of the parent company. Therefore chain owned newspapers have a strong incentive to increase revenues (by eliminating competition) and reducing expenses (by using economies of scale). Of course, non-chain owned newspapers also have a similar profit motive, but chains have more economic power. Their (a) first copy expenses are amortized over larger circulations thus resulting in a lower per unit cost (first copy costs are fixed and these are very large in small circulation newspapers, that is, as high as 40% of total revenue, so the more papers sold, the lower the per unit cost); (b) reproduction costs decline as circulation goes up (additional pages do not cost as much as the first few pages), and (c) distribution process is more efficient with denser circulation patterns, and this works against multiple deliverers of multiple papers.

Concentration

Almost all of the 1,500 daily newspapers printed in this country have a local orientation, that is, they circulate to readers in their home city and the immediate, surrounding suburbs. There is only a small number of newspapers (such as *USA Today, Wall Street Journal, Christian Science Monitor*) that have national circulations. In this way, America is unique in newspaper localism compared to other industrialized countries of the world. In most foreign countries, newspaper circulation emanates from a few large cities and spreads out across the entire country. For example, Tokyo has 11% of Japan's population, but daily newspapers from Tokyo account for 70% of the total newspaper circulation in that country. London, with 14% of England's population, accounts for 70% of circulation. In America, New York City and Washington, D.C., combined have 7% of the population, but account for only 10% of the country's daily newspaper circulation. Clearly, in this country, newspaper publishing is done at the local level.

While publication takes place on the local level, ownership of newspapers is becoming more and more concentrated, that is, there are fewer people controlling more and more newspapers. The trend toward greater concentration is evidenced in two ways: reduction in competition among newspapers and an increase in ownership by chains.

Competition among newspapers has been greatly reduced. For example, the number of cities with competing daily newspapers is decreasing. In 1900, over 65% of all U.S. cities had competing newspapers, but now less than 1% do. Two reasons have been cited for the decline of newspaper competition. First, political parties no longer support newspapers as they once did, and there has been a decline in partisanship in the U.S. press. Second, advertisers are demanding large circulations without duplicate readership. As a result, the larger newspaper in a two-newspaper town gets the advertising and continues to grow. The smaller-circulation newspaper loses advertising and eventually goes out of business.

Chains have increased in size and number. In 1909, there were only 13 chains, and they owned only 2% of all newspapers. Chains grew slowly until 1970, when the majority of newspapers were still owned or controlled by small private groups—often a single family. By the 1990s, three quarters of all newspapers were chain owned (Picard, 1993).

As for control of circulation, the eight largest newspaper chains accounted for only 10% of daily circulation in 1900, but by the 1990s, chains controlled a total of 85% of the nation's newspaper circulation. However, no single newspaper or chain dominates the nation's news dissemination. For example, the two largest chains are Gannett Co., whose 82 newspapers have a combined circulation of about 6 million, and Thomson, whose 125 newspapers have a combined circulation of about 4 million. Together these two chains control more than 200 newspapers but less than 16% of the nation's circulation (Picard, 1993). In contrast, the three television networks have far greater control of the news flow than any combination of three newspaper chains.

With concentration of newspaper control, access by individuals becomes harder. In 1900, there was one newspaper for every 36,000 people in this country, but now there is only one newspaper for about every 170,000 people. While people have many newspapers to read, those newspapers are spreading themselves thinner and thinner. Access is much more difficult.

MAGAZINE INDUSTRY ■■

Innovation Stage

The magazine industry began in the United States in 1741, but until 1800, no American magazine lasted more than 14 months. Advertising support was hard to find, so magazines struggled to stay in business.

Circulations were very small, with the average circulation for a magazine being about 500 copies, and large circulation magazines selling between 2,000 and 3,000 copies.

New magazines kept springing up, and by the time of the Civil War there were about 700 magazines published in this country.

Penetration Stage

In the late 1800s, two things occurred that helped the penetration of the magazine industry. After the Civil War, education of children was made mandatory by most states, and the percentage of the population that could read grew dramatically. Also, in 1879 the U.S. Post Office made low-cost mailing available.

The magazine industry began a boom. By 1885 there were about 3,300 magazines, many with large circulations in the 100,000 range. In the 1890s magazines cut their prices to below production costs to increase circulation, and advertising revenue became very important.

By the end of the 19th century, magazines became a mass medium, that is, there were over 50 well-known national magazines, each with a circulation of more than 100,000.

Peak Stage

Magazines have never reached a "peak" in the sense that they became the mass medium that dominated all others. However, they did reach a peak of general popularity during the first several decades of the 20th century. Throughout this time, the magazine industry continued to grow because of three important factors. First, the incomes of people generally grew, so people had more money for discretionary spending. Second, people had more leisure time. And third, the spread of popular education greatly reduced the illiteracy rate and made people want to read more on a wider range of topics.

This peak was a different type of peak than that experienced by newspapers, because it was based on a unique set of characteristics that differentiate magazines from newspapers. Because magazines do not have to carry up-to-the-minute news, they can rely on more leisurely delivery systems. Also, they are capable of offering advertising to a national audience, because they are mailed out to subscribers all over the country. Newspapers have circulations limited to small geographic areas, such as their home cities.

Decline Stage

From 1930 to 1960, the magazine industry declined primarily because of heavy competition from radio and then television for advertising dollars.

National magazines had the hardest time surviving, not only because of the loss of advertising revenue but also because of steep rises in postal rates. In 1950 there were 40 magazines with circulations over one million; within 25 years, all but 10 had gone out of business.

Adaptation Stage

To survive, magazines became more specialized. They changed from trying to appeal to a mass audience and instead targeted narrow, specialized audiences. The roughly 10,000 magazines that exist today do not really compete with each other for readers or advertisers. For example, *Boy's Life* does not compete with

Forbes, and *Newsweek* does not compete with *Cosmopolitan*. Instead, each magazine tries to create a distinct audience base that it can rent to its own special set of advertisers. Magazines are niche oriented in that they aim less at *quantity* of circulation and more for a *quality* audience. Within a niche, there are usually a small number of magazines that do compete against one another. For example, *Newsweek* competes against *Time* and *U.S. News & World Report* for essentially the same readers and same national advertisers.

As an industry, magazines have adapted very well. Both the number of magazines and their circulation are up. The number of magazines and other periodicals has increased steadily from 5,500 in 1900 to 6,900 in 1950 to over 10,000 today. Now more than 50 magazines have circulations greater than one million. Still, the newspaper industry has a higher total circulation than the magazine industry. Monthly circulation of magazines is 350 million copies; newspapers, however, have a total circulation of 2 billion copies per month.

Current Structure

The magazine industry is subdivided into niches as follows: consumer magazines (such as *Reader's Digest, TV Guide*), news (*Time, Newsweek*), sports (*Sports Illustrated, Runner's World*), opinion (*National Review, New Republic*), intellectual (*Commentary, American Scholar*), men's interest (*Esquire, Gentleman's Quarterly*), women's interest (*Cosmopolitan, Better Homes and Gardens*), humor (*National Lampoon, Mad*), sex (*Playboy, Playgirl*), and business (*Forbes, Money*). Within each of these sub-markets, there is usually a small handful of magazines that account for most of the circulation there. Typically, these high-circulation magazines are published by the large companies, and these companies publish magazines in many of these sub-markets. For example, Time Warner publishes *Time, Sports Illustrated*, and *Money*.

Today, the magazine publishing business is highly competitive with easy entrance. An entrepreneur with a good editorial concept and a clear conception of an audience niche can be successful. However, most new magazines fail unless the owner can afford to stay with it for several years until the magazine finds its audience and begins to make money.

Revenue

The magazine industry generates about $9.5 billion in revenue per year (*Statistical Abstract of the United States: 1999*, 2000). Like newspapers, it has two primary streams of revenue. About 60% of the revenue comes from advertising. The other 40% comes from subscriptions and newsstand sales. There has been a generally steady growth in sales for over 50 years. The industry did not break the $1-billion mark in revenue until the mid 1950s, and now it is over $13 billion per year.

There is a growing trend toward more support from subscribers, especially through subscriptions. Single issue newsstand sales have been decreasing over time as the cost of magazines has been steadily increasing to the current level of an average of $3.10 for a copy. Subscriptions, which average $30.50 a year, are increasing in popularity because they are more convenient and more economical for consumers than buying individual issues at the store.

The top grossing magazine in 1997 was *TV Guide* at $1.1 billion, with a paid circulation of 13 million and ad revenue of $409 million. *People* was in second place with $1 billion in revenue, then there is a drop to *Sports Illustrated* at $820 million and *Time* at $805 million. *People*, *Sports Illustrated*, and *Time* are all owned by Time Warner ("Top 300 Magazines by Gross Revenue, " 1998).

Expenses

As for newspapers, the biggest expense of a magazine is personnel, but this has not been climbing very fast. In contrast, expenses for paper and mailing have been increasing rapidly over the past decade.

Concentration

The magazine industry is also a very concentrated mass medium. This can be seen in terms of both ownership patterns and sales.

As for ownership, most magazines are published independently. There are about 4,700 firms publishing the more than 10,000 magazine titles in this country. But most of the circulation and revenue are controlled by three firms.

While there are 10,000 magazines, 160 of them account for 85% of the industry's total revenues (Daly, Henry, & Ryder, 2000).

■ FILM INDUSTRY

Innovation Stage

The film camera and projector were invented in the 1880s by Thomas Edison, who owned the early patents and therefore had a monopoly. But by 1900 there were three companies marketing film equipment. These three companies also provided films and sold them outright to users as a way to encourage the sale of equipment.

Movie theaters began to be an alternative to the live entertainment of vaudeville shows.

Penetration Stage

In 1902, film exchanges were established so theaters could share films. Small producers consolidated their resources and formed studios for production and distribution. By 1905, there were over 100 film exchanges and the producer-wholesaler-retailer chain in the film industry became institutionalized. Five years later, there were 10,000 small theaters, each run by entrepreneurs who parlayed low investments into quick profits.

By 1912, producers were making full-length feature films. During this time, audiences began to regard movies less as a novelty and more as a habit.

The Hollywood star system was devised as a way to lure people to the movies by attaching identifiable names to an otherwise unknown film and by merchandising the star as an important part of the distribution process. The stars of those early films were chosen not on their acting skill, but on their contribution toward making a profitable picture.

Peak Stage

The peak of the film industry was reached in the 1920s and lasted into the late 1940s. Sound movies were introduced in 1927, and color was introduced in the late 1930s. In 1927, an average of 60 million people attended motion pictures *every week*. By 1929, this figure was over 110 million.

The number of theaters in the 1940s was about 20,000. The number of movie seats, including car spaces at drive-ins, reached a peak of 11.1 million in 1935.

Decline Stage

Starting in the late 1940s, the industry went into a decline.

The federal government regarded some of the very large film companies as monopolies and forced them to sell parts of their operations. For example, it became illegal for a single film company to produce, distribute, and exhibit films. So the large film studios sold off their theaters. After divestiture, film production companies lost some of their incentive, because they no longer owned their own theaters. Production dropped.

The number of commercial films released to theaters declined steadily from the 1941 peak of a record 497 films to a low of 203 films released in 1963. Costs skyrocketed. Massive advertising and marketing campaigns were necessary to build audience interest for each picture.

Adaptation Stage

Film studios adapted first by reducing their workforces and selling off their property. Not until 1970 did the production-distribution sector turn around financially.

Film studios now survive by producing films for television showings and by exporting films to foreign countries. Film companies began making films primarily for television showing in 1965, and have experienced steady growth since then. The United States is the world's largest film market and for more than 50 years has been the world's largest exporter of filmed entertainment.

The exhibition sector of the film industry did not turn around financially until the 1980s when it went to multiple ownership of theaters and to multi-screen theater complexes.

Current Structure

The film industry now has more establishments than newspaper and broadcast stations combined, due mostly to the large number of theaters. The number of motion picture theaters decreased from about 12,000 to 10,000 (a multi-screen complex is counted as one theater). The number of film production, distribution, and allied services companies increased from about 2,800 in the early 1960s to over 4,500 today.

Revenue

Motion pictures generate about $5.4 billion at the box office and another $15.4 billion from home video, plus $10.5 billion in TV program revenue.

The exhibition sector is composed of the theaters, with their total of about 26,000 screens (DeFleur & Dennis, 1996). This year, theaters will sell about 1 to 1.3 billion tickets. The revenues increase from year to year but not due to more people attending the movies; instead the increases come from higher ticket prices. About 70% of this revenue is sent to the film distributor. Movie theaters generate revenues through their two revenue streams: (a) the portion of the ticket sales they get to keep, and (b) high-margin concessions, such as popcorn, soda, and candy, which account for about 30% of their revenue.

Expenses

The most dramatic increase in the cost of making films can be traced to the rising fees of stars—even lesser-known stars. In 1929, the highest-paid silent film star was John Gilbert, who made $520,000 a year, or about $8 million in 1997 dollars. At his peak, the year he made *Gone With the Wind* and *Mutiny on the Bounty*, Clark Gable made $208,000. Jean Harlowe made $78,000 at her peak. When Garbo was the highest-paid actress, in the 1930s, she made $250,000 a picture, and in the 1940s Barbara Stanwyck was the highest paid at $225,000 a picture (LaSalle, 1996).

The current box office mega-stars are: Harrison Ford, Jim Carrey, Tom Cruise, Mel Gibson, Arnold Schwarzenegger, and Sylvester Stallone, who each get about $20 million per film. Second-tier people make about half that figure; for example, Demi Moore makes $12.5 million per film and Kurt Russell, $10 million. Third-tier actors such as Charlie Sheen get $5 million. Unknown actors can quickly increase their fees if their early movies are successful. For example, Sandra Bullock's fee climbed from $600,000 for *Speed* to $1.2 million for *While You Were Sleeping*, and she now gets over $10 million per film. Also, known actors can make a quick comeback with a successful film or two. John Travolta was down to $150,000 for *Pulp Fiction*, then bounced up to $10 million. Big-name directors also command high fees (usually about $3 million), but not as high as actors. Even bit players make a decent fee. Scale salary for the members of the Screen Actors Guild (SAG) is $522 *a day*, which is much better than the U.S. average for salaried workers at $500 *per week* (Dutka, 1995). However, a very small percentage of the 95,000 members of SAG are working on any given day.

With costs of films rising, studios have been appointing heads who are more adept at business than art. In the early 1990s executives and stars were showered with perks, and no expense was spared to make a film. Those days are gone as studios try to manage expenses more frugally (Eller & Bates, 1999).

Risks

The production sector is the most risky for several reasons.

First, a Hollywood feature film takes about 18 to 24 months from the inception of the idea to the actual theatrical release. In television the time is 3 months. Therefore there is a danger that a film might miss the changing tastes of audiences.

Second, the cost of making a feature film is very high, and it continues to escalate. The average cost of films, including their marketing, has doubled in the past 5 years. The average film now costs $35 million to make and another $15 million to market. This means that a film must gross more than $100 million at the box office to begin making money for the studio (remember that the studio shares the box office revenue with the theaters). However, the average movie makes only about $33 million. For example, in 1994, Hollywood released 332 feature length films. Only about 60 of these films generated revenue of even $20 million, and only about one third made any profit.

In order for a film to qualify as a hit, it needs to generate about $100 million at the box office. Typically only about a dozen films attain this status each year (Albarran & Chan-Olmsted, 1998).

Concentration

Each of the film industry's sectors (producers, distributors, and exhibitors) is very concentrated. While there are many small independent producers, distributors, and exhibitors, power is nevertheless concentrated in the hands of a few huge conglomerates that have holdings diversified beyond the film industry.

There are about 175 film distribution companies, but the film industry is dominated by the seven major film studios. These seven account for 75% of all distribution.

Typically the top 10 films each year account for one third to one half of the industry's total annual receipts. About one third of national admissions comes from nine major metropolitan areas. The 17 weeks of summer, Christmas, and Easter provide 40% to 50% of theater receipts (Guback & Varis, 1983).

While American firms produce only 10% of the films in the world each year, those films occupy half of the world's screen time.

The four largest film exhibition companies account for about 20% of all receipts among the nation's 26,000 movie screens. The largest exhibition chain, Carmike Cinema, controls 2,401 of these screens (Standard & Poor's, 1996, p. L18).

Because of the profitability of film exhibition, film distribution companies are getting back into exhibition. Until the early 1940s, the major Hollywood studios controlled production, distribution, and exhibition, when the federal government engaged in anti-trust proceedings and forced them to divest part of their holdings. The studios sold off their theaters. But now, with deregulation and with a more complex business environment, distributors are getting back into exhibition. For example, MCA Inc., which owns Universal Films, also owns 40% of Cineolex Odeon, a large chain of theaters. Viacom, which owns Paramount Pictures, also owns Cinamerica. In total, major movie studios now have ownership stakes in about 2,300 screens nationwide (Standard & Poor's, 1996, p. L19).

Current Trends

The film industry has always struggled to balance art and commerce, but recently the trend is much more toward business. For example, recent appointments of studio heads show that business people rather than people with creative credentials are being selected; Warner Bros. appointed Barry Meyer, a lawyer, as chairman; Universal Pictures appointed Brian Mulligan, a CPA, as co-chairman; MGM appointed Chris McGurk, a former financial analyst at PepsiCo. It is understandable that when films require huge budgets for production and promotion and when the risks of success are high that studios work to try to reduce costs. But they are ignoring the other task—improving the product. This has led industry insiders such as Joe Roth, chairman of Walt Disney Studios, to say, "In a business where there's always a tension between the creative and the financial establishment, we're at a historical low point where the financial imperatives seem to far outweigh the creative urges" (Eller & Bates, 1999).

THE RECORDING INDUJTRY ▪▪

Innovation Stage

Thomas Edison invented the original technology for the recording and playback of sound in the 1880s.

Penetration Stage

Several advances in technology helped to turn the recording industry into a mass medium. In 1925 Joseph Maxwell invented the juke box, which allowed recordings to compete with radio music. In 1947 the long-playing record was marketed.

Then in the early 1950s the sound quality of recordings was dramatically improved with high fidelity. In 1960, 34 million units were sold; this climbed to almost 59 million in 1970.

Peak Stage

Like book publishing, the recording industry never became a dominant mass medium.

Adaptation Stage

Technological advances keep changing the industry. Records were replaced by tapes (first eight track then cassette), then with CDs (compact disks). Advances in recording techniques (digital) and playback (boom boxes, car stereos, Walkmans, etc.) keep people buying new equipment. And the fast turnover in music styles and recording artists keep people buying new recordings.

The recording industry is still growing and competing well with the other mass media. There are now about 1,300 recording and tape production companies, 125 record processing plants, and 250 tape duplicating plants. Each year the industry ships about 500 million units—CDs and tapes.

Revenue

Revenue from pre-recorded music sales is now about $13.7 billion per year (*Statistical Abstract of the United States: 1999*, 2000). A high percentage (70%) of this total is due to the sales of compact disks (CDs). A recording that sells 10 million is a huge success; however, there are only one or two recordings per year that reach this milestone (Standard & Poor's, 1996, p. L38).

Retailers who can't sell all the tapes and CDs return them to the recording companies. The major recording companies each run their own record club; the returns are offered to club members at deep discounts. As a group, the clubs account for about 11% of all sales (DeFleur & Dennis, 1996).

Expenses

In the recording industry, the cost of manufacturing CDs is coming down while the cost of signing artists is going up. In the early 1980s it cost $3 to $4 to manufacture one CD, but now the cost has been reduced to under 75 cents, including the jewel box container. The big costs are for the artists and for promotion. It now costs about $500,000 to sign a name band to do one CD.

When the retail price is about $16.98, the cost to the manufacturer is about $7.54, which is itemized as follows: recording expense $0.65, manufacturing expense $1.25, packaging $1.30, advertising and promotion $2.00, artists' royalty $1.60, freight $0.09, and payment to musicians' trust fund $0.65. This leaves the manufacturer with a profit of $2.94. The distributor gets $1.50, and the retailer gets the remaining $5.00 (Dominick, 1999).

Producers must sell at least 300,000 to 500,000 copies of a CD before covering their costs. About 80% of all recordings lose money. In general, the revenue in the recording industry is divided as follows: 35% goes to the retail store, 27% to the record company, 16% to the artist, 13% to the manufacturer, and 9% to the distributor (Straus, 1995).

Concentration

The record and tape industry is very concentrated, with its powerful distributors on one end and the chains of retail music stores on the other end. Distribution is dominated by six major companies: Columbia, Warner Bros., Capital, MCA, Elektra, and Epic. These six control 80% of recording sales each year.

There are also thousands of independent record producers. These producers find talent, rent a recording studio to produce a recording, and get copies manufactured. Then they persuade one of the six major recording companies to distribute and market the recording. This is a high-risk endeavor; independent producers account for only about 20% of all hit recordings (DeFleur & Dennis, 1996).

Retailing of music is dominated by the major chains. With over 800 outlets, Musicland Stores Corp. is the largest (Standard & Poor's, 1996, p. L39).

RADIO ■■

Radio reached its peak of influence in the 1940s when it was the dominant national medium, relied on for entertainment and information. But then in the 1950s, television began taking away radio's audience and advertisers. Radio adapted by identifying new needs in the audience, and it has survived. In fact, it is prospering once again.

Innovation Stage

Radio broadcasting began in 1920 when it combined a new technology with old content forms from vaudeville and the dramatic stage.

In 1921 there were only five AM radio stations, and only about 1% of all the households in this country had a receiver.

Penetration Stage

Seemingly overnight, hundreds of radio stations sprang up. By 1923 there were over 500 stations, almost half of which were owned by manufacturers of radio receivers who created broadcasting stations as a way of stimulating sales of receivers to the general public. Then other kinds of organizations started radio stations. Newspapers and other publishers had about 70 stations, educational institutions owned about 70, and retail stores owned over 60.

Radio had evolved from a novelty into a business as it developed the concepts of station, sponsorship through commercial advertising, and network. Advertising was first introduced in 1922 as a way of supporting an increasingly expensive industry. Initially, advertising was of an institutional nature with price not mentioned and the hard sell avoided. More obtrusive types of advertising were not fully accepted until the late 1920s when advertising moved toward dominance. In 1927, 20% of radio network time was sponsored, and by 1940, over half was.

Peak Stage

Radio reached its peak in the 1930s and 1940s. In 1930, 50% of all households had at least one radio, and by 1947 this had increased to 93%. By 1936, there was an average of one receiver per household, and in 10 years, this had doubled. People were spending more time with radio than any other medium. Radio had a national orientation for both entertainment and advertising. The radio networks played a crucial role in creating and maintaining this national orientation.

Decline Stage

Radio ceased being a general national medium around 1950, when national advertisers began shifting their business to television.

Adaptation Stage

To survive, radio replaced its full-service, mass-oriented, family-type general entertainment format with specialized music formats designed to appeal to unique target audiences. By 1970, 300 radio stations were programmed principally toward African Americans; over 800 carried foreign language programs; and over 1,000 country and western music.

Radio stations replaced their national advertising revenue with local ad revenue.

Also to survive the competition with television, radio became more mobile. Car radios and portable radios let people listen to music and news anywhere—especially where they could not take a television set. Between 1950 and 1970, radio set production almost doubled, while the U.S. population increased by only one third.

Despite the dominance of television for the past five decades, the radio industry has adapted well and is very successful. The number of radio stations has grown dramatically from about 2,000 stations in 1948 to over 12,000 radio stations today (*Statistical Abstract of the United States: 1999*, 2000).

Revenue

When radio began broadcasting in the early 1920s, it received its income through the sale of home receivers. This continued to be a source of revenue to radio stations until the mid-1930s. During the 1920s, stations realized that the sale of receivers would not bring in enough revenue to support the growing industry, so stations began selling advertising.

Revenues increased each year until television began taking away advertisers in the late 1940s and early 1950s. Radio hit bottom in 1955 when revenues dropped to $554 million with only 2,669 stations broadcasting. But by the early 1960s more than 4,000 stations were broadcasting, and revenues were up to $700 million per year. By 1980, total revenues had climbed to $3.2 billion. Advertising revenues to the radio industry were about $18 billion in 1999 (*Statistical Abstract of the United States: 1999*, 2000).

The economic recovery of the radio industry can be traced to radio's shifting from a national medium to a local one. Now 80% of a station's revenue comes from local advertising. Thus radio stations compete primarily in local markets with newspapers for advertisers.

Concentration

In the 1920s, the federal government favored localism when it awarded radio licenses to local owners. The local stations were mandated to serve the needs of the communities in which they were broadcasting. But almost from the beginning, radio broadcasters began moving away from their mandate and instead have made decisions that have primarily helped their businesses to function more profitably. They have done this mainly through network affiliation and group ownership.

Instead of generating local programming, most broadcasters have chosen to affiliate with one of the large commercial networks. These affiliates get their programming from their networks, and this programming is national in content. Network affiliation began in 1927 when 6% of available radio stations became affiliated with one of the four radio networks: ABC, CBS, MBS, and NBC. The peak period of affiliation was reached in 1947 when 97% of the country's 1,062 radio stations were affiliated with one of the four national radio networks.

Now radio stations are not likely to affiliate with national networks, or if they do affiliate, they usually get only news and features from the network. However, this does not mean that radio stations now exhibit a wide variety of programming that reflects the local needs of their communities. Instead, radio stations are likely to affiliate with a certain type of programming such as Top 40, Golden Oldies, Album Oriented Rock, Country & Western, all news/talk, and so on. For example, most radio markets have a Top 40 station and these stations sound the same all over the country, regardless of the locale in which they broadcast. They all play the same songs on the same rotation, play the same lead-in and lead-out of the news, cover the same type of news stories with the same kind of formulas, and have the same kinds of contests and promotions.

Because of the profitability of well run radio stations and because of the limited number of stations available (about 12,000), large companies want to buy weaker stations and transform them into money makers. Each year about 1,000 radio stations change owners. The average sale is for about $1 million (Standard & Poor's, 1996, p. M36).

There has been a steady increase in group ownership of radio stations. In 1929, only about 3% of the country's 600 existing radio stations were group owned. By the late 1960s the figure had climbed to about one third of all stations, and that figure is even higher today. In 1992, the federal government loosened restrictions on ownership so that now someone (or a corporate entity) can own up to 20 FM and 20 AM stations. Then in 1996, the federal government loosened ownership regulations even more.

BROADCAST TELEVISION ■■

Innovation Stage

By the 1930s, the technology had been developed to make the transmission and reception of television signals possible. The first television stations went on the air in 1941. These were commercial stations on the VHF (Very High Frequency) band.

The first receivers were marketed in the New York City area where the first broadcast signals were. As stations began broadcasting in other metropolitan areas of the country, receivers were marketed in those additional areas.

By 1948, 2.5% of all households already owned a receiver.

Penetration Stage

By 1950, there were 107 television stations; all of these early stations were on the VHF (channels 2 through 13) band. By 1953 the first UHF (Ultra High Frequency; channels 14 through 83) stations went on the air. The number of stations grew to over 500 by 1960.

By 1953, 50% penetration was reached; that is, half of all the households in the country had a television set that could receive a signal. Television was catching on even though few homes had much of a choice in viewing alternatives. Only one third of television households could receive as many as four channels.

Peak Stage

By the early 1950s, television was reaching a peak. It quickly became *the* entertainment medium, thus reducing movie attendance and radio listenership. Over time it also became a primary source of information, thus reducing readership of newspapers and magazines. The public accepted this medium so quickly, because television was seen as fulfilling the audience needs for both entertainment and information better than any other medium.

Advertisers, especially national advertisers, realized this shifting media preference among audiences, and they too shifted their support to television. This resulted in severe reductions in national advertising support for magazines, newspapers, and radio. By 1960, commercial television accounted for a larger share of audience and advertising dollars than any other medium.

By 1960, the average household owned at least one set and could receive about seven channels. Almost every area within the entire country had local television stations. Television sets were turned on more than 5 hours per day in the average household. By 1980, 99.5% of all households had at least one television set; over 90% had color sets; over 50% had two or more sets. These household ownership rates are higher for television sets than for telephones or indoor plumbing.

To maintain its peak, TV had to attract the largest general audience and to generate the most revenue. Unless a prime-time program could generate an audience of at least 20 million viewers every week, it was canceled.

Because penetration is complete in this country and because the size of the population in this country is not growing very much, the television industry cannot substantially expand its audience anymore. In fact, it must now work very hard just to hold on to the audience it does have as competing media (especially cable television) offer alternatives to broadcast television. Competition is very strong, and it will get even stronger. To appeal to as wide an audience as possible, programmers are very careful to present material that will not incur rejection or restriction. Stations therefore attempt to show the least objectionable programming. To determine what is least objectionable, television relies upon proven formulas. This is why programming is becoming less diversified and more limited. When a particular program becomes very popular, programmers will try to develop similar shows in an effort to share in the popularity. Because a popular show generates a great deal more revenue than an unpopular one, programmers are unwilling to take a chance on new types of shows for fear of being held responsible for losing money for the station or the network.

Present Character

Broadcast television can still be considered to be at its peak. It has a higher reach than any other medium: On any given day, 88% of the American population is exposed to television; 71% to radio; 56% to newspapers; and 34% to magazines. There are now about 1,600 broadcast television stations, and they generate revenue of more than $21 billion each year.

But in some ways broadcast has started a decline, so its days of occupying the peak are numbered. The networks and stations are losing viewership. Until the late 1970s they got 95 share. By the 1990s, the combined viewing of the TV networks (ABC, CBS, and NBC) during prime time dropped to 61% in the 1991-1992 season ("Multichannel News," 1993) and is continuing to decline. People are finding alternatives to broadcast television. Cable television is expanding. Also, with VCR penetration at 74%, viewers are renting tapes or they are reprogramming the shows of broadcast television, and this reduces the power of station programmers who try to create the habit of viewing. There is also strong competition from pay channels and computer delivered services.

The survival of a program depends on reaching a large audience, especially one of women between 18 and 49, because they buy most of the commonly advertised products. A show does not usually survive unless it gets at least a 10 rating. A rating is a percentage of people in the U.S. population who watch a particular show. Thus a rating of 10 means that 10% or about 26-million people watched a show. A rating of 20 is very high, and a rating of 15 will put you in the top 10 most popular shows (Standard & Poor's, 1996).

Perhaps in the future, broadcast TV stations will not try to attain so broad an appeal and instead choose a particular target group for their programming and advertising. If this happens, programming will become more specialized and diversified.

Revenue

The television industry began strong and grew rapidly. By 1957, commercial television had gone over $1 billion per year, and now it generates about $32.4 billion a year. The revenue stream is from advertising, and over half of this is national (Standard & Poor's, 1996, p. M36). A drop in viewership means a drop in revenue. A television series that drops only one rating point over the course of a season could cost a network as much as $90 million.

The total number of television commercials more than doubled from 1967 to 1975, largely because of the reduction in the length of an average spot from 60 seconds to 30 seconds. Over the past decade the average spot has been reduced down to 15 seconds, and the number of television ads continues to grow each year.

Expenses

Television networks do not produce much of their own programming; instead, they license broadcast rights from the producer. The fee to broadcast a program is not large enough to cover the producer's costs. These deficits are usually between $50,000 and $300,000 per episode. Producers hope that a series will run long enough for them to make about 100 episodes and then sell it through syndication. A successful show like the *Cosby Show* was able to get $4 million per episode in licensing fees to television stations (Standard & Poor's, 1996, p. L30).

Network costs for proven shows are escalating dramatically. When *Seinfeld* retired, NBC feared losing *ER* so it agreed to pay $13 million per episode for *ER*, up from the previous $2 million an episode (Bauder, 1998). The producers of *ER* increased their season's income (22 episodes) from $44 million to $286 million.

Concentration

Television broadcasting has followed the same pattern as radio. The FCC attempted to reaffirm its perspective of localism as the guiding principle for licensing when it awarded television broadcasting licenses in the 1940s and 1950s. This decision required the establishment of hundreds of local stations, and the FCC had to find new spectrum space in order to provide these stations with their own broadcasting frequencies. As a result, the UHF band (channels 14 through 83) was set aside for television use in addition to the VHF band already in use (channels 2 through 13).

Commercial broadcast stations are licensed to provide service to local communities. But over the years, the FCC has done very little to ensure that the stations do in fact provide responsible service to their communities. Television stations have been permitted to affiliate with national networks and to buy syndicated services, both of which feature national programming. In 1954, network affiliates were already getting 50% of their total programming from their networks. Within two decades, local stations were producing only about 10% of their own programming. There are strong economic incentives for networking. Affiliates are able to share a program's production costs as well as its risks. If something is to be produced locally, it must be inexpensive and very popular compared to the alternative program from the network. Therefore, the affiliates air mostly network programming, which is aimed at a national, not local, audience.

Even though the average household can receive about 50 stations, most of the viewership is still going to the three big commercial networks (ABC, CBS, and NBC), although this concentration of viewership has been slipping. By 2000 the share of the television audience going to the broadcast networks during prime time had dropped to 47% (Lowry, 1998)—down from 92% in 1977. Cable stations increased to 32%, pay cable programs to about 6%, and independent stations to 12%. By 2000, over 97% of all U.S. households had the opportunity to subscribe to cable, and 68% of all households did. Also, 86% of all households had a VCR, which allowed them to watch movies instead of broadcast programming (Dizard, 2000)

Concentration in station ownership was initially limited by FCC regulations that restricted ownership to 7 television stations, but this limit was raised to 12 stations in the 1980s and now has been raised even higher. By 1995, 75% of all TV stations in the top 100 markets were licensed to multiple owners. About one quarter of these were owned by publishers of newspapers; but it is rare for a newspaper and TV station in the same market to be owned by the same company. In total there are 210 groups that own more than one TV station. Twelve of these groups own 10 or more stations each (Howard, 1995).

The advertising on commercial television is concentrated in the hands of a few very large advertisers who can afford to buy great amounts of time each year. For example, 20 companies account for more than half of all advertising on broadcast television.

CABLE TELEVISION ■■

Cable television has grown rapidly through the penetration stage and is entering the peak stage as it begins to eclipse broadcast television.

Innovation Stage

Cable television began in the 1940s as a means of delivering television signals to areas unable to receive broadcast signals because of distance or interference. Until the 1950s cable systems were quite small; each had a few hundred homes as subscribers and carried only three or four broadcast signals from the closest stations. They were generally confined to mountainous areas with little or no reception.

The owner of a cable system was typically a small local company, often in some related primary line of business, such as selling TV receivers. They were marginally successful as businesses. By 1952 there were only 70 systems, and they served a combined total of 14,000 subscribers, which represented less than 0.1% of all television households at the time. Growth was slow. Not until the late 1950s was more than 1% of television households reached by cable.

Penetration Stage

By 1960 there were 640 cable systems with a total of 650,000 subscribers, which was 1.4% of all households for an average of 1,016 subscribers per system.

By the mid-1960s, cable began expanding into areas that already received clear broadcasting signals, such as the urban areas of Los Angeles and New York

City. Also, cable systems began adding channels to make their service more attractive to potential subscribers. In 1970, 3% of the systems offered more than 12 channels, and by 1976, 26% of the systems did. By the late 1960s, some cable systems were even originating programming of their own.

In the early years of cable, broadcasters welcomed cable systems as a means of extending their broadcast viewership into areas their signal could not reach. But then cable systems began using microwave relays to bring in more distant signals, such as broadcast stations from far away markets and also signals from some superstations such as WTBS in Atlanta and WGN in Chicago. These new channels were in direct competition with local broadcasters. Broadcasters began complaining that cable was receiving payment from subscribers but not giving any of this money to broadcasters who originated and paid for the production of the programs. Cable systems were no longer viewed by broadcasters as expanders of audiences but as direct competition. So in 1962, the FCC began to regulate the selection of programming on cable systems. The FCC decided to allow cable systems to continue to use microwave relays to bring in distant signals. But if the cable system did this, it would also have to carry all the local signals, that is, it could not ignore a local broadcast affiliate and instead bring in a station in another market in its place. During the next decade, many other regulations were added until 1972 when a period of deregulation began.

By 1985 there were 6,600 systems serving a total of 32 million subscribers, which represented about 38% of all television households. The 50% penetration mark was reached in early 1988.

Peak Stage

It looks like cable television may be entering the peak stage. Within the past few years its total revenues have surpassed those of the broadcast television industry.

Now cable systems rival the networks in programming power. With more than 11,000 cable systems operating, there are about seven systems for every broadcast station in this country. But unlike the networks, there are no limitations on ownership. A cable company may buy one or many other cable systems. Such a conglomerate is called an MSO (Multiple System Operator). The number of MSOs is growing, and some of the larger ones rival the commercial television networks in terms of the size of the audience controlled through programming. And with about 130,000 employees, cable supports more people than broadcast.

The cable industry is taking steps to secure its position as the peak mass medium by heading off future challenges by computers. The cable TV industry has linked some computer technology with its existing services to offer what is called smart TV. Smart TV gives viewers much more control over their exposures. They can fast forward through the commercials (without having a VCR), pause live TV, download information from television shows, and even play along with game shows. Smart TV is a collection of three types of services. The first is Interactive TV, which allows viewers to interact with the shows they are watching. Second, there is Internet TV, which lets viewers use their sets to access the Internet. Third, there is Personalized TV, which acts like a VCR.

Revenue

Cable television has two sources of revenue: subscriptions and advertising. Most of their revenue is from subscriptions, but cable is now competing with broadcast TV for advertising dollars and is being very successful. In 1990, cable generated $2.4 billion in advertising revenue, and predictions are that this will increase dramatically (Koplovitz, 1990).

By 1992, cable had surpassed broadcast TV for the first time with total revenues of over $21 billion from a combination of subscriber fees and advertising. Now subscription revenues are now about $25 billion per year, and ad revenues bring in another $4 billion (Standard & Poor's, 1996).

Concentration

Cable systems are treated as natural monopolies—like utilities such as electricity and water companies. They are extremely concentrated, because there is almost never cable competition within their area of coverage. They are franchised on the local level and must therefore meet the requirements that the local community writes into its contract, such as time requirements for wiring the community, control of rates, and percentage of profits. Entry is controlled by economic cost, which requires capital-intensive construction and franchise requirements. However, once entry is achieved, the system typically has sole rights to the market for 10 to 15 years, and during that time it is a monopoly.

There are no ownership limits on multiple system operator (MSO) size. The top four firms in 1965 accounted for only about 20% of all cable subscribers. But in the past 30 years, the major MSOs have continued to consolidate and to build efficient clusters. The top four MSOs (TCI, Time Warner, Continental Cablevision, and Comcast) now have a combined share of 50% of all cable subscribers (up from 38% share just since 1993), and the top eight MSOs now have a combined 64% share (Chan-Olmsted, 1996).

The MSOs will continue to grow by buying up smaller cable systems or by trying to put some out of business in those rare markets that are overbuilt and where there is competition. Barrett (1996) examined the business practices of MSOs in two overbuilt cable markets and found that they used a variety of tactics to deter entry by rivals—especially price cutting and litigation.

▪▪ COMPUTER*∫*

Innovation Stage

The computer as we know it was invented in the 1940s. ENIAC (Electronic Numerical Integrator and Calculator) weighed 30 tons and was several hundreds of times less powerful than the typical desktop computer of today.

At first computers were very large, slow, expensive, and were energy hogs. Only the government and large businesses could afford to buy and use them until the 1980s when relatively low-cost desktop personal computers began to be marketed.

The computer is a fundamentally different type of medium from everything that came before. All media up to this point were channels to deliver uniform, intact messages from senders. Now, with a computer, each of us can customize messages by cutting and pasting from a wide range of sources and media, then send them out for display to a particular friend, to a great number of people simultaneously through email, or simply make them available on the World Wide Web where millions of people can come and view your messages and even download them to their own computers where they can undertake further manipulation. The real innovation was the digitization of information, that is, all bits of information were reduced to a binary code. This digitization allowed for fast computations and it also led to seamless sharing of information of all forms (data, words, sound, pictures, video, etc.) across all media.

Other key innovations responsible for the computer becoming a mass medium are the affordable personal computer, easy-to-use software, and the Internet.

The Internet is a network of computer networks designed to move information around among users. It has no centralized controlling body or mechanism. It was originally set up by the Pentagon in 1969 in such a decentralized structure so as to make it resistant to breakdown by attack. A bit of information sent across the country has many alternative paths it can take, so if one path is blocked (or down), the information can take one of the other many alternatives and arrive just as quickly. The Pentagon originated the system by linking up government computers with those at universities across the country. Since that time, many other networks from all over the world have attached themselves to the Internet. Since 1975, its cost has been supported by the National Science Foundation, but that responsibility is now being turned over to businesses that want to use the Internet to advertise their products and services. Anyone with a PC (personal computer), a modem, and some accessing software can get onto the Internet. Once on the Internet, people can cruise around the different parts, send email to specific people, post messages on bulletin boards, enter chat rooms where interactive conversations take place on a particular topic, play games, and download information, images, or software that others have made available. These services have become very popular and are attracting new audience members constantly.

Penetration

There are now 40 million personal computers in homes; as of 1995, half of all home computers had a compact disk (CD) player; Maney, 1995).

Over 97% of the country's schools have computers—one for every 11 students, which is up from one computer for every 63 students just 10 years ago (Intelligence Infocorp, 1996).

Every minute, 40 novices log on to the Internet for the first time. Every year the number of users doubles. By the mid-1990s it was already up to 40 million worldwide. Also, every 10 minutes a new corporate or academic network is added; now up to 100,000 networks are linked. Data traffic has increased over more than 300% in the past few years (Simons, 1996).

By the mid-1990s, about 26% of adults in the United States (or 51 million people) had access to the Internet (Bimber, 1996). A popular part of the Internet is the World Wide Web, which is like a notebook. Any user can create his or her own Web page, which is usually a billboard with graphics. Many businesses have created Web pages to display their services. Users who visit a Web page can usually click on one of the displayed icons and get more information about that person, service, or product.

Computers are now in the later days of the penetration stage and are entering the peak stage. This industry has been growing rapidly at 30% per year (*Hoover's Guide,* 1996).

Current Trends

Clearly the computer medium is doing very well in the penetration stage. Many companies are successfully selling hardware and software services.

Whether computers grow to a peak and replace television as the dominant medium remains to be seen.

By the year 2000, 49% of America's households had a computer and 89% of those computer households had a modem. Overall 32% of America's households were considered frequent Internet users (Dizard, 2000). The primary reasons for going online are to get news and/or information as well as to use email.

The computer has been taking people away from other media. A 1998 survey reports that only 38% of young people had read the newspaper the day before while 69% of seniors had. The under-30-year-old group are the heaviest users of Internet news sources (Pew Research Center, 1998). Newspapers have been losing readership, so they have been adapting to the Internet. An early adapter was the *San Jose Mercury News*, which began providing news summaries on America Online in 1994. It then created its own Web site and provided the full-text copy of its editions there, first free then for a fee (Dizard, 2000). Satisfaction with TV is declining among children. When asked which one medium they would prefer to have if they could have only one, only 13% said TV; 33% picked computers (Rideout, Foehr, Roberts, & Brodie, 1999).

The World Wide Web is huge, with about 800 million pages as of the summer of 1999. It is a great resource, but the bad news is that it is difficult for a person to get to most of it. The most comprehensive search engine today is aware of no more than 16% of the Web; most search engines are able to access less than 10%; even if you used all the search engines, you could get to only about 42% because that is all that has been indexed (Dunn, 1999).

There is a convergence of media driven by computers and digitization. With the newer technologies, especially digitalization, companies are becoming more defined by their content products rather than channels of distribution (Albarran & Chan-Olmsted, 1998). For example, television networks are defining themselves much less in terms of television and more in terms of entertainment and news.

Some bookstores are creating a strong presence on the Internet to capture a slice of the $3-billion annual market in college textbooks. Some sites advertise discounts of up to 40%. However, those who conduct systematic comparisons conclude that college bookstores offer prices just as low if not lower, on average, than the prices offered by e-bookstores (Leovy, 1999).

Revenue

There are three components in the computer media industry. Each has its own stream of revenue. First, there is the hardware component of PCs and peripherals. This accounts for about $100 billion per year. Second, there is software, which had sales of $86 billion in 1995. Then there are online services, which now account for about $1 billion per year and are growing at an annual rate of 27% (Standard & Poor's, 1996, p. C102). Profit margins run about 20% to 25% annually on software and about 10% to 15% on hardware (Standard & Poor's, 1996, p. C127).

By 2000, the Internet accounted for $13 billion in revenue, with about two thirds paid by consumers and the other one third by advertisers (Dizard, 2000).

By 1997, Knight Ridder had 32 Web sites but was losing money. The cost of the Web sites was $27 million while the revenue from them was only $11 million. However, they see this as an investment that will pay off in the long run when more consumers log on to their sites to get their news (Dizard, 2000).

In 1999, the computer hardware sector of the industry accounted for $229.2 billion in revenue and the software sector accounted for an additional $199.3 billion (*Statistical Abstract of the United States: 1999*, 2000).

This new industry hopes to take customers and revenues away from other industries such as catalog houses and book clubs, which do $350 billion in revenues; video stores that rent 3.6 billion videos a year; and video games that sell at 73 million units per year (Kantrowitz, 1993).

Expenses

Lots of money must be spent to provide the infrastructure to make this new medium financially successful. Expanding the conduit of information into American households is the fiber-optic cable. In 1991, 5.6 million miles had been wired, and 40 million homes were connected by the year 2000. Local phone companies are spending about $100 billion to build networks to connect all homes and buildings with fiber-optic cable—a job that is expected to be completed by 2010 (Maney, 1995). Fiber-optic cable is able to carry a tremendous amount of information. Old phone lines can transmit a few pages of text per second, but a single hair-thin fiber-optic line can transmit about 5,000 pages per second.

In total, computer industry spending is increasing at about 20% per year from about $6 billion in 1994 to $14 billion in 1999 (*Hoover's Guide*, 1996).

Personnel costs are relatively high and growing. For example, the average wage of the 1.4 million people working in software services design in 1997 was $58,688; the average wage of the 1.6 million people working in hardware design, manufacture, and maintenance was $53,044. Compare these to the U.S. average wage of $22,984 across all industries (*Statistical Abstract of the United States: 1999*, 2000)

Concentration

The computer industry is very new, and there is great flux in the way companies grow quickly, get bought by larger firms, or go out of business. However, there are some trends that reveal evidence of concentration.

The top six hard drive manufacturers account for 90% of the total market of 60 million units per year.

Within the software component, Microsoft is the largest company, with sales larger than the next two companies combined (Standard & Poor's, 1996, p. C107). Microsoft is the creator of the MS-DOS and Windows operating systems, which run 80% of all PCs. The company has annual revenues of about $20 billion ("Microsoft '99 Revs Up 29%," 1999).

CHAPTER

12

Key Idea: We are members of many different niche audiences as defined by where we live, as well as our demographic and psychological characteristics.

What Is An Audience?

What is an audience? At first, this question may seem very simple and may seem to have an obvious answer. Up until several decades ago, most people treated it like a simple question. We were all believed to be part of a mass audience. Hence we had terms such as *mass media* and *mass communication*. The term mass communication came into use about 100 years ago when early social philosophers posited that newspapers, magazines, and books communicated their ideas to all audience members in roughly the same way. Once a writer perfected his or her message, it would affect everyone the same way.

The term *mass* did not refer to a *large* audience as much as it referred to a certain *type* of audience. Early sociologists focused on the way people felt about themselves and others in social networks in industrialized societies. They believed that people in the modern mass society were becoming both isolated and alienated from other members of society, because increasing technology was turning people into machines.

THE IDEA OF A "MASS AUDIENCE"

In order to be a "mass," an audience needs four characteristics. First, the audience composition is heterogeneous. This means that the audience is composed of people of all kinds, and no one is excluded. Second, the audience members are anonymous. The message designers don't know the names of anyone in the audience nor do they care to, because the designers regard everyone to be the same and interchangeable. Third, there is no interaction among the members of the audience. People don't talk to each other about the media messages, so the messages do not get modified in conversations. Instead, those messages have a direct effect on each person in a uniform manner. And fourth, there is no leadership. The mass is very loosely organized and is not able to act with the unity that marks a crowd (Blumer, 1946). Blumer also pointed out that a mass has "no social organization, no body of custom and tradition, no established set of rules or rituals, no organized group of sentiments, and no structure or status roles."

Support for the Idea of a "Mass Audience"

Starting with the industrial revolution in the mid-1800s, the United States and the Western European countries were regarded as having mass societies. Because the countries were heavily industrialized, it was believed that this technological progress had shaped the lives of people. Less industrialized countries did not have mass societies, because people there were tightly integrated into social networks in which they interacted continually with others on a daily basis. So the United States was regarded as having a mass society and India was not, even though the population of India was much larger than that of the United States.

Because it was believed that communication did take place in a mass-like fashion, it was assumed that a message reached everyone in the same way and was processed by everyone in the same manner. It was also believed that the processing itself was very simple, that is, people were vulnerable, they had no psychological defenses against messages because they did not discuss messages with other people.

As evidence for this position, social critics pointed to the way Adolph Hitler used the mass medium of radio in the 1930s to mobilize the German population to support him. Kate Smith's radio telethons for war bonds in which she raised millions of dollars were also offered as evidence that people were highly susceptible to media messages. Another often-cited example of the public's seeming lack of defense against media messages is provided by the widespread reaction to Orson Wells's 1939 Mercury Theater presentation of *War of the Worlds*. Some listeners actually believed that the Earth was being invaded by Martians.

Sociologists of the 1930s and 1940s were very vocal in their warnings about the dangers of mass communication. A more careful analysis of the three examples mentioned, however, reveals that most people were not affected by those messages (Cantril, 1947). Further, it was later shown that the people who were affected were not all affected in the same manner nor did they all react in the same way.

You may be thinking: That idea of mass audience is silly. How could anyone really believe that an audience was like that? That conception of audience does sound rather silly now as we look back on it from the 21st century. But at the time, this was the accepted way of thinking about audiences. However, our thinking about audiences has changed dramatically. Use this insight to alert yourself to the fact that there are likely to be current beliefs that will be found to be silly when we look back on 2001 in several decades. How can we protect ourselves from the current faulty beliefs? We need to develop strong knowledge structures and carefully analyze our existing opinions and our experiences. In short, we need to be highly media literate.

Rejection of the Idea of "Mass Audience"

By the 1950s, it became apparent to many scholars that the assumption of the audience as a "mass" was incorrect. Friedson (1953) was the first to criticize this view of the audience. He felt that people attend movies, listen to radio, and watch television within an interpersonal context. Discussions of media material frequently take place before, during, and after exposure. There is a well-developed web of organized social relationships that exists among audience members. This social environment influences what audience members will expose themselves to and how messages will affect them. Media behavior is merely a part of their more general social behavior. Friedson warned that "the concept of mass is not accurately applicable to the audience" (Friedson, 1953, p. 316). Since Friedson made this point, many other researchers have supported this position (Bauer & Bauer, 1960; Brouwer, 1964; Williams, 1974).

Today we look back on such thinking and find it rather naive. Was it that earlier days were more simple? Was life more innocent and easy? No. That is not the reason. The reason is that sociologists used too simple an explanation to describe the media and its audience at the turn of the century. This is not a criticism of sociologists. In social science, simple explanations are usually better than complex ones that no one can understand. However, the explanation must also be useful, and this idea of a mass audience was found not to be useful, because when scholars carefully observed how people behaved, they realized that some of the elements of the definition of mass did not fit. For example, people did interact with each other and talked about media messages. Also, there was a leadership structure where certain people were regarded as opinion leaders and influenced the attitudes of other people.

Today, the term *mass communication* is still used, but rarely is there a time when everyone is exposed to the same message. Even with events like the Superbowl, only about 60% of people watch. And more important, those people who do watch the Superbowl do not all experience the same thing. Some viewers are elated as their team is winning; others are depressed as their team is losing; some are happy there is a reason to party and have no idea who is playing; and many are bored as the game becomes one-sided. There is no common experience. Also, during the viewing, people talk to each other and help each other interpret events.

There is no "mass" communication, because there is no "mass" audience. Instead, there are many audiences, some with structures and leadership and others without these characteristics. Some audiences last for only a few hours (Superbowl viewers) while others last for a whole season (diehard football fans). Some audiences are based on a need for immediate information (viewers of CNN), some on in-depth information (readers of news magazines), some on a need for a religious experience, some on a need for political stimulation, musical entertainment, romantic fantasy, and on and on.

Marketers know that there is no mass audience. Therefore, they almost never attempt to sell a product, service, or media message to everyone. Instead, they try to determine how the total population can be divided into meaningful segments. Then marketers identify an audience segment or two where the people might want or need their product. Advertisers then target these audiences for their messages and ignore other people.

Each person is a member of multiple audiences. You are a member of a local community that the local newspaper and cable TV franchise targets. You are a member of virtual communities when you get on the Internet—communities that quickly form and may last for only one evening. You are a member of certain hobby groups that are targeted by certain magazines, although other members of your audience are spread out all over the world and will never met you in person.

■■ CONCEPTION/ OF /EGMENTED AUDIENCE/

All media produce content to attract a certain type of audience. Some of those media (newspapers, magazines, radio, and television) rent their audiences out to advertisers who want to get their messages in front of certain types of people. For example, a classical music radio station will play only a certain type of music as well as present interviews and news about certain artists in order to attract an upscale, highly educated, older audience. The station then rents this audience out to advertisers such as luxury car dealers, jewelers, and travel agencies.

Identifying audience segments is an important task for media organizations and advertisers. Over the years, audience segmentation schemes have become more complex in an effort to generate more precise groupings. This is illustrated by showing the development of thinking over five types of segmentation methods: geographics, demographics, social class, geodemographics, and psychographics.

Geographic Segmentation

This type of segmentation scheme is most important to newspapers, radio, and local television where there are geographical boundaries to the coverage areas. But it has also been useful to other media when thinking about getting their messages out to certain regions of the country.

This is the oldest form of segmentation, and it worked well when regions of the country were culturally diverse. A company would begin a business in a certain locale and produce products that the people in that locale wanted. Because of limits on distribution, that company would do business in only that one area and advertise in only that one area. If that company wanted to expand, it would move out from its home locale to other places in the region where the product met a need. If there was a nationwide need, then the company could expand into national distribution and advertising—but then there would be no need to do geographic segmentation. As many businesses took their products into the national market, regional differences eroded.

Geographic segmentation is becoming less useful as the country becomes more geographically homogenized. We are a mobile society. Each year, about 20% of the population moves to a new home. Therefore, regions are not as insulated as they once were, nor are regions as different from one another as they once were. Over time there has been an increased sharing of foods, music, clothing, and other cultural elements across regions.

Demographic Segmentation

Demographics focus on the relatively enduring characteristics about each person—such as gender, ethnic background, age, income, and education. These are fairly stable characteristics and have been quite useful in classifying us into meaningful audience segments. While some of these can be changed (such as education and income), that change requires a great deal of effort.

The usefulness of demographics as an audience segmentation device has been diminishing. Decades ago when adult women stayed home and raised children, it made sense to market household and child care products to women only. Also, radio and television presented female-type programs during the daytime hours when women were home. But now that the percentage of women in the labor force is the same as that of men, gender is less useful as a segmenter.

Ethnicity also used to be a stronger demographic segmenter than it is today as the range of income, education, political views, and cultural needs is much greater within any ethnic group than it is across ethnic groups. With the tremendous growth of credit, household income has not been as useful a segmenter, either. Also, some demographic groups, such as teenagers, have really increased their spending. American teenagers spent $109 billion in 1995. Males spent an average of $67 per week and females $65 ("Teen Spending Up Again," 1996).

Educational level is also less useful. Fifty years ago, having a college degree put you in an elite—the top 5% of the population. But now 20% of American adults have at least one college degree, and another 20% have earned some college credit.

Social Class

We could think of social class solely in terms of household income level, but then social class would mean the same thing as the demographic of income. Why would we need both types of segmentation schemes if they put the same people into the same groups? Instead, social class is a mix of characteristics. One of those characteristics is income, but psychological characteristics are also part of the mix. For example, being in the lower class, of course, means a low income. But you as a college student have a very low income. Do you consider yourself lower class? No, obviously there is more to the definition. Being in the lower class means taking the psychological perspective that what happens in life is not under your control. You feel that you were born into a situation with not much opportunity and that you must struggle to maintain your existence. Because fate has put you in this situation, all you can do is try to make the best of it that you can. Therefore when you get a windfall of money, you feel you should have as much fun as you can before someone takes it away from you. There is no point in saving for a tomorrow that will never come.

Being middle class means holding the belief that it is good to put off immediate pleasures for more important longer-term goals. Thus middle-class people have a strong work ethic, believing that work is good for them and for society in general. The fact that you are in college is a good indication that you hold a middle-class perspective. You believe that it is a good idea to make economic, time, and lifestyle sacrifices for 4 years now, so that later you will receive much larger rewards for your efforts. You believe that your current actions influence your future. You believe that you control your fate—not the other way around.

Being upper class does not simply mean having more money; it means being able to control more resources—yours and those of others. It means the ability to raise large sums and wield lots of power.

Geodemographics

A recent innovation in consumer segmentation is geodemographics, which is a blend of geographic and demographic segmentation. It is based on the assumption that we choose to live in neighborhoods where other people are like us. Neighborhoods therefore tend to be homogeneous on important characteristics, and these characteristics change across neighborhoods.

One example of geodemographic segmentation is the PRIZM scheme, which was developed by Claritas Corporation in 1974. PRIZM is based on a complex analysis of U.S. census data. It began with the 35,000 zip code neighborhoods, and concluded that there were 40 different kinds of neighborhoods in this country. It gave the clusters memorable (and trademarked) nicknames such as "Sun Belt singles" (which are southern suburban areas populated by young professionals), "Norma Rae-ville" (named after the movie of a working-class woman who unionized factory employees), "Marlboro country" (evoking a western rural area with rugged men on horses), "Furs and station wagons" (typified by new money living in expensive new neighborhoods), and "Hard scrabble" (which represents areas in the Ozark mountains, Dakota badlands, and south Texas border).

Psychographics

Psychographics is the current cutting edge of segmentation schemes. It is not limited to one or two characteristics of people but uses a wide variety of variables to create its segments. Typically a psychographic segmentation scheme will use demographics, lifestyle, and product usage variables in segmenting consumers. There are many examples of psychographic segmentation. Two stand out as being very influential.

Twelve American Lifestyles. William Wells, director of advertising research at Needham, Harper & Steers in Chicago, developed the 12 American lifestyles that include Joe the factory worker and his wife Judy; Phyllis the career woman and her liberated husband Dale; Thelma the contented homemaker; and Harry the cigar chomping, middle-aged salesman. Each of these creations represents a different lifestyle. For example, Joe is a 30s lower-middle-class male who makes an hourly wage doing semi-skilled work. He watches a lot of television, especially sports and action/adventure programs; he rarely reads. He drives a pickup truck and knows a lot about automotive parts and accessories. In contrast, Phyllis is a 30s career woman with a graduate degree. She reads a lot, and when she watches television, it is usually news or a good movie. She likes fine food, dining out, and travel.

VALS Typology. VALS (Values and American Life Styles) was developed at SRI (Stanford Research Institute) at Menlo Park, California. After monitoring social, economic, and political trends during the 1960s and 1970s, Arnold Mitchell constructed an 85-page measurement instrument that asked questions ranging from people's sexual habits to what brands of margarine they ate. He had 1,635 people fill out the questionnaire, and the answers became the database for his book *Nine American Lifestyles*, published in 1980. In the book, Mitchell argued that people's values strongly influence their spending patterns and media behaviors. So if we know which value group a person identifies with, we can predict a great deal about the products and services that person will want. For example, one of the groups is called Experientials. The people in this value grouping enjoy trying new and different things. They like to travel. They are early users of new types of products. They are constantly looking for something different.

The VALS typology has made SRI very successful, with income over $200 million per year. By the mid-1980s, SRI had 130 VALS clients, including the major TV networks; major ad agencies; major publishers such as Time; major corporations such as AT&T, Avon, Coca-Cola, General Motors, P&G, RJ Reynolds, and Tupperware. For example, Timex, a giant corporation best known for its watches, wanted to move into the home health care market with a selection of new products including digital thermometers and blood pressure monitors. It decided to focus on two VALS segments: Societally conscious and the Achievers. Everything about the packaging and the advertisements were chosen with these two groups in mind. Models were upscale, mature, in comfortable surroundings with plants and books. The tag line was, "Technology where it does the most good." Within months all Timex products were the leaders in this new and fast-growing industry.

❚❚ MEDIA EXPOSURE

The amount of time people spend with the media continues to grow. According to the *Statistical Abstract of the United States,* Americans now spend an average of 3,297 hours with the media per year—this is more than 42 hours per week. About half of it is watching the TV screen, which includes broadcast, cable, pay, and movie rentals.

We each have our own pattern of exposure to the media. Seldom is there an overlap in patterns across all individuals, and this is one reason why there is no mass audience. Each of us constructs our own pattern to satisfy our personal needs. Although we have a wide variety of media and messages available to us, we usually select a small sub-set of them that tend to serve our needs best. We each have our preferred media and our preferred vehicles, and we use these preferences to develop our habits of media exposure. For example, most of us watch television, but we do not watch all of television. Only when the number of channel choices is low (around three or four) will we expose ourselves to a high proportion of those available channels. But when there is a large number of channels available (such as the 50 or more on most cable services), we will tend to select only one or two types of programming (from the genres of news, drama, comedy, education/information, talk, soap operas, music, game shows, etc.) and limit our viewing to the channels with this type of programming (Youn, 1994). Thus each of us has our own channel repertoire of between about three and six channels; rarely do we check out the options outside our repertoire. Having a VCR or remote control does not increase our channel repertoire. In cable households, the repertoire is a bit larger (between five and eight channels) although the number of channels available to viewers is much higher (Ferguson, 1992).

Television viewing is inertial. The best predictor for a program's rating is the rating of the lead-in program and the lead-out program (Cooper, 1993). For this reason, television programmers will put similar type programs together (like four situation comedies back to back) to hold onto their audience. If they interrupted the block of situation comedies with a game show, they would lose all the viewers who did not have that type of program in their viewing repertoire.

While we form media habits in terms of our repertoires and inertial flow through a block of time, the habits do not hold day after day. This was revealed through research that shows that repeat viewing of any particular program is low (Barwise & Ehrenberg, 1989). For programs shown every day, only 50% of the people who watched one day would watch the next. There is the same drop off for viewing of weekly shows. The drop off is lower with news and soap operas, because viewers of these types of programs exhibit a stronger daily habit. The loss of audience is not due to choosing a new show but to not watching TV at all. If people are watching TV the next day, they probably will watch the same show. Therefore the decision to watch TV is different from the decision about what to watch.

Awareness of Exposure

Do we really know how much TV we watch? Probably not. For example, parents often over-estimate how much TV their children watch—reporting time when the children say they are playing with their toys (Alexander, Wartella, & Brown, 1981). Also, large discrepancies were found by Anderson, Field, Collins, Lorch, Pugzles, and Nathan (1985).

The amount of attention given to the television screen varies with age. At age 1 there is 10% attention; age 3, 50%; age 13, 80%; and with adults it averages 60% (Anderson, 1985). Children may appear to be exposed to the set in the judgment of parents or other observers, but their attention is usually very low—even to the point where they do not consider the activity viewing.

Adults also might have the television set on and be in the same room, but not pay much attention to it. Attention to the show varies by genre with movies, children's programs, and suspense shows having the highest concentration (attention 76% of the time). Commercials, sports, news, and daytime soap operas have the lowest (attention only 55% to 60% of time; Comstock, 1989).

Blurring of Media Channels

To most people, messages are much more important than channels; many people don't even know the difference between channels. For example, most people who are watching television do not know if what they are watching is on a broadcast station (network affiliate or independent) or a cable channel. Some won't know whether they're watching a pay movie on a premium channel, a Hollywood rental movie, or a made-for-TV movie on a network. As consumers, we care more about selecting a particular kind of message than about choosing a channel. So we do not often make distinctions among channels.

Differences across media are also blurring over time. Newspapers are becoming more like magazines, with an editorial outlook that features more soft news and human interest pieces that are not time sensitive and that appeal more as entertainment than as information. Trade books are becoming shorter and less literary. Computers, with their games, encyclopedias, and Web pages, are becoming more like films, books, magazines, and newspapers. Given the focus on messages and the convergence of channels, the content is becoming much more of a concern than the delivery system.

Some futurists argue that we are moving toward a convergence where all the media will be one—"a single, high capacity, digital network of networks that will bridge what we now know as the separate domains of computing, telephony, broadcasting, motion pictures, and publishing" (Neuman, 1991, p. x). Just as the cotton gin and assembly line symbolized the onset of industrialization and mass society, the personal computer may come to symbolize the onset of deindustrialization and the decentralization of information processing (p. 1).

This is an exciting time to be in our culture. There are so many messages being made available. And the new technology of computers will allow us to access them all and arrange them in any manner that suits us. This opportunity requires that we become more media literate in order to make the most of the media's positive aspects and avoid its potential harm to us.

■■ CONCLUSION

Think of audiences as strata in a pyramid. At the top of the pyramid we are all the same—certain messages (like the Gulf War coverage) bring us all together. At the bottom of the pyramid, we are all unique individuals. At each layer of the pyramid there are audience segments. Media marketers continually search for the right segment to which to pitch their message. The marketers who are successful at this build meaningful audiences by giving people what they want and need in the form of particular kinds of entertainment and information. Once the marketers have constructed their niche audiences, they rent them out to advertisers.

Over time, thinking has moved away from trying to group us all together into one general mass audience and instead moved toward a mid-level model of putting us into meaningful segments in terms of our media message preferences. Accompanying this is a change in thinking away from channels and more toward types of messages. Thus, companies who own television stations have diversified by buying magazine companies, book publishing houses, and cable systems, so as to avoid being bound by the limitations of any one channel in the new media environment. They no longer think in terms of being the most powerful newspaper chain, for example, but the most powerful media conglomerate. The goal is no longer to create the one message that will attract the greatest number of total people. Instead, the game is to construct a constellation of audience segments by crafting special messages to each segment; thus, when all exposures across all segmented audiences are totaled, the conglomerate controls exposure to a huge number of people.

We join an audience every time we expose ourselves to a media message. Because we all have a great deal of exposure to the media, we are constantly joining audiences.

There are profound differences in exposure patterns across people. Each of us has preferences for certain kinds of messages, so we actively seek those. Our active seeking results in regular patterns of exposure to certain media and certain vehicles, because we can depend on them to satisfy our needs best. This is our media exposure repertoire. However, we are also being constantly bombarded by all sorts of messages from outside our repertoire. Because we have not sought out those messages, we tend not to perceive them; we think they don't exist. Being media literate means being more aware of the messages that are being aimed at you as a target by some marketer. For some of those messages, we should be very thankful and increase our appreciation. For other messages, we should be skeptical and increase our analysis of them. These tasks are accomplished better when we understand something about how marketers assemble us into audiences.

FURTHER READING ■■

Neuman, W. R. (1991). *The future of the mass audience.* New York: Cambridge University Press.

Neuman begins with a balanced discussion of the difficult idea of postindustrialism and with the conflict between fragmentation and homogenization. He argues that education contributes to fragmentation, with people now able to peruse their specialized interests. Family is changing as women enter the workforce in large numbers. He also shows that media use is fragmenting.

He says the central question is whether or not the proliferation of new communications channels will lead to fragmentation of the mass audience. He argues that this is not a new issue but is a continuing and central problem of political communications. The key issue is that of balance: balance between the center and the periphery, between different interest factions, between competing elites, between an efficient and effective central authority and the conflicting demands of the broader electorate. This is the conflict between community and pluralism.

EXERCISE 12.1

Segmentation Exercise

1. Think about the students at your college or university. Are they all identical? Or are there segments—several different groups of students that are clearly identifiable by how they dress, act, and talk.

   a. Segment the student body. Try to identify about four to seven segments.

   b. For each segment, come up with a catchy name. Then describe the students in each segment demographically and psychologically.

2. Think about the different media and vehicles that would appeal to each group. For example, which groups would prefer film over books, and so on?

   a. What would be the favorite television show(s) of each group?

   b. Which radio format would each group prefer?

   c. Which magazines would each read?

   d. Which CDs would each buy?

   e. Can you think of other media differences?

3. Let's say you are interested in starting a campus newspaper. Pick one of these groups as your primary target.

   a. What kind of news and entertainment would you want to feature in your newspaper in order to build a strong appeal among your target audience?

   b. What advertisers would be most interested in getting their messages in front of your target audience?

PART IV

KNOWLEDGE STRUCTURES OF MEDIA EFFECTS

CHAPTER

13

Key Idea   The media exert a wide range of effects—immediate and long term, positive as well as negative—across five levels.

Broadening Our Perspective on Media Effects

Suzanne is baby-sitting her two younger brothers, ages 4 and 6. She is reading a magazine while they are watching the Power Rangers on television. She sees an ad for a new shampoo and tears out the coupon in the magazine ad, making a mental note to buy some of this brand when she is out shopping later today. Her brothers are starting to shout at the television screen, so she puts on her headphones and turns on the radio. She really likes the song she is hearing and wonders, "Who is singing this? I've never heard it before."

She begins to daydream about her date tonight. "I hope Tim takes me to another horror flick. It's so much fun to scream my lungs out and attack him during the bad parts."

When the song on the radio is over, the DJ goes right into an ad, not telling her the title or artist. She is frustrated, so she tries to remember the melody by humming it so she can ask one of her friends later.

Suddenly her thoughts are interrupted when her brothers begin screaming at each other, then wrestling around on the floor. Suzanne runs into the TV room and breaks up the fight. "You guys better behave yourselves or I won't let you watch *Power Rangers* anymore! Get back in your own chairs now."

Peace restored, Suzanne picks up a newspaper and notices a story about a drive-by shooting where a gang of youths imitated some action in a recent movie. She thinks, "The media have such a bad effect on young kids. My brothers are going to end up in jail if they keep watching those shows. Thank goodness the media don't have any effect on me!"

Many of us have a narrow view of media effects. We look for high-profile tragedies as evidence of a media effect and use those isolated incidents to conclude that all media effects are like that.

We look for startling changes in our behaviors or attitudes and when we don't find this type of thing, we conclude that the media don't really affect us. But they do. To illustrate this, let's use the weather as a metaphor.

Media effects are like the weather in many ways. Weather is always there, but it can take many forms. Sometimes it makes you shiver, sometimes it makes you wet, and sometimes it gives you a painful sunburn—but it is all weather. Also, it is very difficult to predict the weather with any precision, because the factors that determine the weather are large in number, and their interaction is very complex. Supercomputers are used to try to handle all those factors in highly complex models. They help increase the predictive accuracy on the broad level, that is, they can tell us how much rainfall and how many sunny days a particular locale will have this year. But they cannot tell us with accuracy who will get wet on which days. While the Weather Bureau cannot control the weather, we as individuals can control the weather's effect on us. We can carry an umbrella, use sunscreen, or close ourselves off from elements we don't like. And we can run out to embrace a beautiful day.

Like the weather, the media are pervasive and always around us. Also, like the weather, media influences are difficult to predict, because the factors that explain such effects are large in number, and their interaction is very complex. We use powerful computers to examine large sets of variables in trying to make such predictions, and we have learned much about media effects. We know in general that certain types of messages will lead to certain kinds of opinions and behaviors, but we cannot predict with precision whose opinion or behavior will be changed. And as individuals, we do not have much power to control the media, but we have a great deal of power (if we will use it) to control the media's effects on us. In order to know how to use this power, we must be sufficiently literate about media effects.

There is an important difference between the weather and the influence the media have on us. With the weather, we all recognize its different forms and know when they are happening. It is fairly easy to tell the difference between rain, fog, and snow, because there is much tangible evidence whenever these occur. But with media influence, the effects are very difficult to perceive until someone points them out. Then they become easier to spot.

What is the effect? Or rather, what are all the effects? An understanding of the full range of media effects is an essential ingredient in media literacy. Knowing what to look for helps us monitor the effects the media have on us. The purpose of this chapter is to make you sensitive to the wide range of probable media effects so that you will know what to look for in your everyday lives.

FOUR-DIMENJIONAL PERJPECTIVE ■
ON MEDIA EFFECTJ

Literacy requires a broad perspective on media effects. Effects need not be limited to things we can observe in a person during exposure; effects can also take a long time to occur. Thus timing is important. Effects need not be limited to behaviors; they can also show up as attitudes, emotions, acquisition of facts, and changes in body functions. Thus the type of effect is important. Effects need not be limited to negative ones; they are often positive. Thus direction of effect is important to consider. Finally, effects need not be only those that we intend to happen; many effects happen to us without our intending them to happen. Thus intentionality is important to consider. In order to broaden our knowledge about what a media effect is, we need to take a four-dimensional perspective—timing, type, direction, and intentionality.

Timing of Effects

Media effects can either be immediate or long term. This distinction focuses on *when the effect occurs*, not on *how long it lasts*.

An immediate effect is one that happens during exposure to the media message. If it does not happen during the exposure, the opportunity is lost. If the effect does happen, it might last for only a short period of time (such as becoming afraid during a movie) or it might last forever (such as learning the outcome of a Presidential election), but it is still an immediate effect because it changed something in you during the exposure. For example, when you watch a news program, you learn about the events of the day. Or while reading a newspaper, you learn that your favorite sports team won an important game. If you watch an action/adventure film and you begin jumping around in your seat and wrestling with your friends, this is clearly an immediate effect, because it is triggered by the film and your reaction happens during the film.

Long-term effects show up only after many exposures. Neither a single exposure nor single message is responsible for the effect. Instead, it is the pattern of repeated exposure that sets up the conditions for a long-term effect. For example, after watching years of crime programs and news reports, you might come to believe that your neighborhood is a high-crime environment. No single exposure or event "causes" this belief; the belief is slowly and gradually constructed over years of exposures until one day it occurs to you that you better buy another set of locks for your doors.

Type of Effects

Most of the concern about the media focuses on behavioral effects. For example, there is a belief that watching violence will lead people to behave aggressively; that watching portrayals of sexual activity will make people engage in illicit sex acts; and that watching crime will make people go out and commit those crimes.

However, there are five levels (four levels in addition to behavior) in which media have demonstrated effects. They are: cognitive, attitudinal, emotional, physiological, and, of course, behavioral.

1. *Cognitive Effects.* Media can immediately plant ideas and information into our minds. Learning is the acquisition of facts so that they can be recalled later.

Some of this learning is factual and some is social. Factual information is usually acquired through formal learning. This is what you focus on in your schooling. You learn names, dates, definitions, happenings, and so on. College courses are oriented toward getting you to build knowledge structures of factual information. But you learn much more than factual information during your college years. Outside of class you learn how to make friends, how to get along with others in your dorm or apartment, how to get invited to the right parties, how to join sororities or fraternities, and more. This is social information. You acquire this social information by observing how others behave and watching *what happens* to them when they behave in certain ways.

As children we learn a great deal about our world by observing role models—parents, older siblings, friends, others. Observation of social models accounts for almost all of the information communicated to children up until the time they begin school. And media provide an enormous number of models and actions from which children might learn. Given the large amount of time children spend with the media, pictorially mediated models (especially TV) exert a strong influence on children's learning about social situations.

Even as adults we continue to pay careful attention to social models. When we do not have the social models we need in our real lives, we can usually find them in the media. Some of us want most to learn from social models who are powerful, extremely witty, physically attractive, or very successful in a particular career. We develop a vicarious relationship with a professional athlete, famous actor, powerful politician, or wealthy role model. By observing these role models in the media, we gather lots of social information about what it takes to be successful and happy.

2. *Attitudinal Effects.* The media can create and shape our opinions, beliefs, and values. Attitudes can also be learned immediately. We could watch a political candidate give a speech and decide that we like him. If we had no attitude

about that candidate prior to the viewing of the speech, then this immediate effect is one of opinion creation. It is also possible that the immediate effect converted us to this candidate and away from liking his opponent. The media can also create and change attitudes immediately (McGuire, 1973).

The media also exert long-term attitudinal effects. For example, the media reinforce already held opinions and beliefs (Berelson & Steiner, 1964; Klapper, 1960). We might not see any change during any given media exposure, but this does not mean that an effect is not occurring. The reinforcement effect serves to give the existing opinion greater weight, thus making it harder and harder to change as it is reinforced continually over time.

The media influence what we believe about the world in general. Over time, we come to believe the world is a mean and violent place after years of exposure to crime (Gerbner, Gross, Morgan, & Signorielli, 1994). And, over a long period of time of exposure to advertising messages, we can have our attitudes shaped about drugs (Adler et al., 1980), nutrition (Atkin, 1982), and beauty (Tan, 1981).

3. Emotional Effects. The media can make us feel things. They can trigger strong emotions such as fear, rage, and lust. They can also evoke weaker emotions such as sadness, peevishness, and boredom. Emotional reactions are related to physiological changes. In fact, some psychological theoreticians posit that emotions are nothing more that physiological arousal (Schachter & Singer, 1962; Zillmann, 1991). If we feel a very high level of arousal and don't like it, we might label it hate. But if we like it, we might label it love.

4. Physiological Effects. Media can influence our automatic bodily systems. These are usually beyond our conscious control, such as the contraction of the pupil of the eye when we look at a bright object. We cannot control the degree to which the pupil contracts, but we can look away from the object and thus prevent the iris from contracting.

With the media, there are many physiological effects that usually serve to arouse us (Zillmann, 1991). A suspenseful mystery serves to elevate our blood pressure and heart rate. A horror film triggers rapid breathing and sweaty palms. Hearing a patriotic song might raise goose bumps on our skin. Viewing erotic pictures can lead to vaginal lubrication, penile tumescence, and increased heart rate (Malamuth & Check, 1980). A farce might make us laugh and not be able to stop even when laughing becomes painful. Or listening to music can calm and relax us by reducing our heart beat and bringing our rate of breathing down to a regular, slow rate.

5. Behavioral Effects. Media can trigger actions. For example, after seeing an ad for a product, we might leave our house and go buy the product. Or we might read about something in a magazine and call a friend to talk about it. Or we watch a violent movie and as we file out of the theater afterward, we act aggressively by elbowing people out of the way so we can get out the door first.

Direction of Effect

The effect can be in a constructive or destructive direction. These terms are value laden. Who is to decide what is constructive or destructive? The answer can be approached in two ways: the individual and society. From the individual perspective, a constructive direction is one where the effects lead you toward some valued goal. If your goal is to get some information in order to satisfy your curiosity, then finding facts in a book, newspaper, or on television can be very satisfying. This can move you toward your goal of having more information and achieving a higher level of knowledge.

We can also look at it from a broad societal point of view. If the media teach people how to commit crimes and trigger that behavior, then the media are exerting a destructive influence.

Intentionality

Oftentimes we intend for an effect to happen, so we consciously seek out particular messages in the media in order to get that effect. For example, we may be bored and want to feel high excitement. To satisfy this conscious need, we go to a movie that presents a great deal of action and/or horror. During the movie, our blood pressure and heart rate go way up and we are on the edge of our seat with fear. We have satisfied our need.

Also, when we seek out factual knowledge in the media, we are consciously trying to achieve a positive cognitive effect. For example, you read the morning paper to learn about which sports teams won their games yesterday, you watch a cooking show to copy down a new recipe, you listen to your car radio driving to work to learn how to get tickets for a concert. The information does not need to be extremely important, and it need not be remembered for more than a few minutes in order for an effect to have occurred. Every day there are hundreds of examples of your using the media to pick up a fact that you can use.

There are many times when we expose ourselves to the media for a particular reason, but other effects that we were not seeking also occur. For example, most of our viewing of prime-time television is purely for purposes of entertainment. We look for funny portrayals so we can laugh or we watch our usual dramatic programs to see what happens to our favorite characters. During these exposures we usually have our intended effects occur, that is, we will laugh and we will get some information about the travails of our favorite characters. But other effects are also occurring—effects we did not seek out, and perhaps effects that we are not even aware of until someone later points them out. For example, our program may be interrupted by a series of advertisements and some of those jingles or sayings stay with us. Or perhaps we get hungry from seeing so many food products advertised. While watching our shows, we might learn some lessons about the fragility of relationships or that the world is a mean and violent place.

Unintentional learning occurs all the time. For example, you might watch a movie merely to be entertained, and during the movie you learn facts about the country in which the movie takes place. Thus, we can learn without consciously seeking out information. We listen to CDs primarily to be entertained, but we also unconsciously pick up the attitudes of the rappers.

Unintentional effects are not limited to immediate learning. They can be long term as well, and they can be attitudinal, emotional, physiological, and behavioral. For example, after years of watching exciting movies you develop a belief that the real world should be much more exciting. Also, your emotional and physiological reactions may have become desensitized, that is, it may take more excitement to make you happy. You did not intend for this to happen, but it happened anyway.

Even when you are receiving an intentional effect, you may be experiencing unintended effects at the same time. For example, you watch a violent movie solely for the excitement, and the movie does deliver the excitement you wanted. However, the movie may also deliver other effects with the excitement. You may experience an emotional desensitization effect. Also, you have the elements forming to generalize to a belief that the world is a mean and dangerous place, which is a long-term cognitive effect.

In order for unintentional effects to occur, the person must be passive, not active. And this makes the unintentional effects dangerous in the eyes of many television critics. When a viewer is passive, her defenses are down. She is not aware that any learning is taking place and hence she is not actively evaluating and processing the information. But even when you are trying to be an active viewer, unintended effects can occur. For example, let's say you watch a news program like *Crossfire* or *Meet the Press*. You understand that the people on that program are spinning the story in a way to reach their own particular goals. They are not there to inform you about the complexity of the situation; they do not want to reach a compromise or a synthesis of a higher realization on the issue. Instead, they dumb down the issue and present their polarized position so the general public does not get lost, and they make their position look as attractive as possible so that most of the public will agree with them. Now, if you are actively watching this and processing this information, you can protect yourself from the influence of either message by acting media literate and trying to synthesize the two positions and construct a more common ground on the issue. This is much better than simply accepting one of the polarized positions. You feel good. You feel that you have avoided being swept away by superficial argument. However, there is a residue left behind. There is a distrust of political figures. There is a belief that politics is argumentation rather than compromise and resolution. There is a feeling that government is about process and not resolution of problems.

The highest form of media literacy is the ability to move beyond the active controlling of an exposure and also conduct a self-reflexive examination of the residue. This is impossible to do until you recognize all the effects that are possible from the exposure. Because what the residue really is, is the transparent dust that gradually builds up into an effect much later. It is hard to see in the present; and it is hard to understand how something so insubstantial as a bit of residue from a particular exposure could amount to an important effect.

■■ CONCLUSION

A key step in increasing your media literacy is to expand your perspective about what a media effect is. Don't think that the media affect only others, such as young children who don't know any better or the criminal types who claim they copy what they see in the media.

We live in a media saturated environment, and the effects are constantly happening to us as they shape our knowledge patterns, attitudes, emotions, and behaviors. They even trigger physiological reactions, such as change in our heart rate, blood pressure, and other bodily functions. And we don't even need to experience a change in order to see that the media have had an effect on us, because the most prevalent effect is reinforcement—that is, solidifying our existing beliefs and behaviors.

In our everyday lives, the immediate and long-term processes work together. The immediate process gives us a new fact that either extends our learning (extensive) or adds weight to our already existing structure (intensive). In the long term, we look for patterns across these facts and infer conclusions about how the world operates. These generalized conclusions then form our knowledge structures, which then guide our search for facts in subsequent exposures to media messages.

Being media literate requires that we understand the full range of media effects. We need to recognize when those effects are having a negative influence on us so we can protect ourselves. And we need to recognize when the effects are having a positive influence on us so we can appreciate and enhance their power.

Mander, J. (1978). *Four arguments for the elimination of television.* New York: William Morrow. (371 pages)

> Mander has written a strong criticism of television. His arguments are more anecdotal and casual than scientific or compelling. His arguments are: (a) TV mediates experience and this removes viewers from experiencing real life; (b) TV colonizes experience, that is, a few people control the content and their perspective is imposed on all viewers; (c) TV makes us sick physically (ingesting artificial light) and mentally (dims the mind, hypnotizes, suppresses imagination); and (d) it has inherent biases against subtlety (away from the sensory, toward the extraordinary).

Potter, W. J. (1999). *On media violence.* Thousand Oaks, CA: Sage. (304 pages with index)

> In this book, I examine one form of media content—violence. I review the research on violent content and how it affects us.

CHAPTER

14

Key Idea: The media can exert an immediate effect on us as individuals.

Immediate Effects of Media on Individuals

R ecall from the previous chapter that the distinction between immediate and long-term effects is not how long the effect lasts, but rather when the effect occurs. In this chapter we will examine effects that occur immediately—during exposure to a media message or immediately after. Immediate effects can occur across all five effect types: cognitive, attitudinal, emotional, physiological, and behavioral. Let's take a look at 12 immediate effects.

COGNITIVE ⠿

Short-Term Learning

We use the media to learn about the particular events of the day. Much of this information stays with us for several hours and then we forget it. Also, certain advertising messages (such as jingles, sale prices, key selling appeal, store hours, etc.) stay with us for a short period of time to allow us to act on that information, then we forget it.

Frequent exposure to the media leads many people to believe that they are staying informed. While the media do provide information to people, that information is quickly forgotten unless people transfer the information from their short-term memory into their long-term memory. Think about the last time a friend told you his or her phone number. If you did not call your friend, that number was never moved from your short-term memory into your long-term memory, so it was forgotten. But if you used the number and kept using the number, it is in your long-term memory and you can recall that number right now even though you originally learned it many months ago.

The same is the case with all kinds of information we learn from the media. Like all information, the information from the media first enters our short-term memory. We are continually clearing out the facts and images in our short-term memory in order to make room for the new facts and images that are constantly coming in. When we clear out our short-term memory, we select information that is important and encode it into our long-term memory; if the information is not important, we delete it. During our media exposures, very little is deemed important enough to transfer it into long-term memory, thus almost all of what we are exposed to in the media is deleted.

Americans regard television as their main source of news (Robinson & Levy, 1986), but research shows that people do not remember much from television news stories (Gunter, 1987). American children who watch a lot of television are less informed about the world than their counterparts who watch little television (Lee & Solomon, 1990). Also, Meisler (1994) reports that in a recent poll of eight countries Americans knew less about current events than did citizens in the other seven nations.

This problem can be traced to three factors: (a) most news stories on television or radio do not contain much information, (b) people who rely primarily on television news do not also get news from other sources, and (c) most stories are presented with little context to help viewers make sense out of the story and place it into their existing knowledge structures.

Intensive Learning

When we encode information into our long-term memories, that learning can be intensive or extensive. These are immediate effects of the media, because the encoding is done either during the exposure or shortly after.

Intensive learning adds information to a person's existing knowledge structure, that is, people acquire another example of the same information they already have. To illustrate, imagine that a person is following a political campaign and has built a knowledge structure about the candidates as well as their positions. The person tunes in the evening news on television and hears that one of the candidates has changed her position on an important issue. The person adds this information to his or her existing knowledge structure. This is intensive learning.

Extensive Learning

In contrast, extensive learning refers to the acquisition of information on a new topic. For example, a person opens the newspaper and finds out that there is going to be an election on a proposition to institute a curfew on all students on campus. The person never heard of this issue before but now has some important information on a new topic. If this information is related to an existing knowledge structure, the person can "add on" to the existing knowledge structure thus making that structure broader than before. If this new information is not related to any existing knowledge structure but is still important, the person will create a new knowledge structure.

ATTITUDINAL ▦

Opinion Creation

The media provide information and images that can trigger the formation of a new opinion or attitude in you. This is most likely to happen the first time you see a new television program or movie. You immediately develop an attitude about whether it is good or bad. You also immediately develop attitudes when you see a new actor or actress, read a new author, hear about a political candidate, or are exposed to a controversial issue.

Advertisers try to create positive attitudes about their product by using a process referred to as *canalization*. Advertisers know it is too difficult to create a brand new need in you, so they find out what needs you already have and build a "canal" in your mind between your existing needs and their product. For example, let's say you feel a high need to be popular. You see an ad where a character looking and acting like you is surrounded by the kinds of people you want to be your friends. The character is respected and admired because of drinking a certain cola or wearing a certain brand of jeans. The designer of this ad has built a psychological canal between your existing need to be popular and a particular product.

Mass media are effective in creating opinions among people who were not previously inclined one way or another on an issue in question. If an issue is really new, people have less pre-disposition to moderate the influence of the advertising message.

Opinion Change

Media can change a person's attitudes and feelings about something. For example, after watching a teenager insult her parents and be rewarded for this by the admiration of other characters, a child could change his or her attitude that it is okay (and even desirable) to insult one's parents. Or people who watch a political debate might not just acquire new information on an issue but might also change their opinion of one of the debaters.

Conversion of opinion can, but rarely does, occur as an effect of an advertising message. When conversion does occur, the conditions that ordinarily prevent conversion are either less active, are non-existent, or actually encourage change themselves. Groups and group norms are usually weak or non-existent if conversion occurs. Persons under cross-pressures are particularly susceptible to conversion, because their opinions are unstable.

The influence of interpersonal sources is more powerful than the influence of the mass media. However, interpersonal sources are not necessary to conversion, and if they are not present or a person has low influence, then the mass media are effective. Mass media are most effective in reaching opinion leaders, who in turn influence other persons.

Inoculation

Medical doctors inoculate people against disease by exposing them to a mild form of the disease so that their bodies can build up an immunity. Later, when those people are exposed to that disease, they are not susceptible and do not get sick. This effect is sought by designers of media messages who want to make their audience's attitudes resistant to change. For example, advertisers will try to inoculate their target audiences against an upcoming claim about to be made by their competitors. In this case, advertisers will design a message to belittle the upcoming claim, so that the target audience will think the claim to be false or silly. Later, when people are exposed to the competitor's claim, they will not be affected by it.

Reinforcement

This effect is often overlooked, because we have been conditioned to think of effects in terms of change. But the very powerful effect of reinforcement is evidenced by non-change. The media can reinforce already existing attitudes and thus make them more resistant to change.

This is an especially desired effect for advertisers. It has been estimated that up to 80% of all advertising is designed not to change the attitudes or behaviors of consumers, but to reinforce already existing opinions and brand loyalties.

A media message that exerts a reinforcement effect adds weight to an already existing opinion. Because the opinion does not change from negative to positive, this effect is difficult to measure. But there is a change, that is, the opinion becomes weightier or more fixed. The more reinforced an opinion is, the harder it is to change.

EMOTIONAL ■■

Temporary Reaction

Storytellers know they must evoke our emotions in order to attract and hold our attention. Writers who want to tell an adventure story need to make us feel suspense, mystery, and fear. Writers of drama need to make us feel jealousy, anger, sadness, love, and happiness. Writers of comedies need to make us feel silly. The better the story, the more strongly our emotions are evoked.

Usually the emotions aroused by the media dissipate shortly after the story is over. For example, think of the relatively strong emotion of fear generated by a horror movie. This fear, while intense at the time, is short lived, even in children, who are more susceptible to the emotional effects of the media (Cantor, 1994). After watching a horror movie, children may look under their beds and in their closets to make sure their environment is safe, then lie awake in bed hoping they will not be attacked (Wilson & Cantor, 1985). Although the fear can last up to several weeks with some children (Cantor, 1994), it is typically gone by the next day.

PHYSIOLOGICAL ■■

Certain content (especially violence and erotica) can temporarily arouse people physiologically. But this type of arousal usually dissipates within an hour after exposure.

Temporary Fight-or-Flight Arousal

We have certain physiological reactions hardwired into our brains. One of these is our fight-flight reaction when we are presented with danger. If we see a predator coming after us, our survival instinct is triggered. We must fight off the predator or run away. Our bodies get us ready for this by releasing adrenaline into our blood stream, which increases our heart rate and blood pressure.

The media frequently present us with situations where we identify with a character who is then put into danger. Vicariously we experience the need for survival. Our bodies automatically release adrenaline into our blood streams. If we stop and think about what is happening, we know that the danger is not happening to us. But still our bodies are primed for fight or flight.

Temporary Sexual Arousal

Sexual arousal is also hardwired into our brains. When we see someone who is physically attractive to us, we become sexually aroused. This arousal ensures the propagation of the human race. The person who arouses us need not be a real person. The attraction may be to a character on a television screen or an image in a magazine—but still there are enough visual cues in these depictions to trigger a physiological response in us.

■■ BEHAVIORAL

Imitation

Children as young as 2 have been found to imitate behaviors they see in the media (Comstock, Chaffee, Katzman, McCombs, & Roberts, 1978; Tan, 1981). In a survey of young children, 60% said they frequently copied behaviors they had seen on television (Liebert, Neale, & Davidson, 1973).

The copying need not be identical to the action seen on the screen—it can be generalized to similar actions. For example, children may watch Superman jump off a building and fly across town to rescue someone. Children will imitate this by jumping up and down with their arms outstretched as they run across the backyard. If they watch two kickboxers beat each other to death, they will imitate this by spin-jumping around, kicking, chopping their arms at each other, shouting, and grunting. Seldom will they actually hit each other. By fantasizing, the "hitting" is in their minds as they imagine they are inside the kickboxing world that they saw on television.

Usually this play is harmless. But because so much of it is triggered by violent messages, the potential for actual physical harm is there. Once in a while, when a real weapon is available, the resulting physical harm can be very great.

Activation

The media can exert a triggering effect on our behavior. For example, when watching an ad, we might jump out of our chair and rush to the store to buy the product.

Activation is different from imitation. With imitation, viewers take it upon themselves to emulate a specific behavior seen in the media. In contrast, with activation viewers are reacting to a suggestion to do something, such as go to the store to buy an advertised product. Viewers do not see the literal behavior portrayed, so there is no pattern to imitate.

Advertising does, of course, have an activating effect on our purchasing behaviors. After all, this is the ultimate goal of all advertising campaigns. Those campaigns try to lead you to this effect in steps. For example, first a company lets you know it is in business. Then it builds a positive attitude about its products. Eventually it tries to trigger your behavior to try a product.

■■ CONCLUSION

A key step in increasing your media literacy is to understand what the immediate effects of media exposure are. Some of these effects are obvious, such as temporary learning, sexual arousal, and imitation. Other effects, such as attitude reinforcement, are not so obvious. It is important to monitor the occurrence of these immediate effects so you can control them. Try to increase the obviously positive ones, such as intensive and extensive learning. Also, be aware of the possible negative consequences when others try to create or change your attitudes, set off physiological responses, and trigger your behaviors.

EXERCISE 14.1

Recognizing Immediate Effects

Think about the differences between cognitive, attitudinal, emotional, behavioral, and physiological effects. Then think about what has happened to you in your life after particular media exposures.

Take a blank sheet of paper and divide the page into five rows and label them Cognitive, Attitudinal, Emotional, Behavioral, and Physiological effects.

For each row, see if you can list at least two effects that have happened to you immediately after being exposed to the media. Name the immediate effect, then describe a specific example of how the media have affected you or someone you know.

Use the list below to guide your thinking.

1. *Cognitive:* Media can immediately plant ideas and information.
2. *Attitudinal:* Media can create, change, and reinforce opinions.
3. *Emotional:* Media can trigger an immediate emotional reaction, such as fear, attraction, sadness, laughter, and so on.
4. *Behavioral:* Media can make you do something.
5. *Physiological:* Media can arouse you or calm you.

CHAPTER

15

Key Idea: The media exert many effects that take a long time to manifest themselves.

Long-Term Media Effects on Individuals

One night when I was out jogging, I saw my neighbor walking her new dog—a Doberman with a nasty face.

"That's a pretty big dog, Rene," I said as I slowed down—being careful not to get too close to the muscular dog straining at the leash.

"Yes, this is Spike," she replied.

"Hi, Spike. Good boy, Spike." I weakly smiled, wondering whether I should hold out my hand to pet his jet-black head. His glowing eyes stared at my hand as if it were his next snack.

"I got him for protection."

"Protection from what?"

"Protection from muggers," she said to me as if she were a kindergarten teacher and I was a 5-year-old.

I looked around. In our peaceful upscale suburban neighborhood, the only people stirring were a few homeowners walking their very large dogs. "Rene, there are no muggers in this neighborhood. And in the five years I've lived here, there has never been a mugging."

"See. It pays to have a big dog."

I was puzzled by this logic, but decided to probe. "Rene, if you're really that concerned about crime, have you also put extra locks on your doors or bought a home alarm system?"

"Don't be silly. Criminals rarely break into houses. The danger is from the muggers."

I felt like telling her that if she were familiar with real-life crime statistics, she would know that there is a much higher likelihood that her house would be burglarized than that she would be mugged—even if she walked around all night without her dog. Also, it was very unlikely that her house would be burglarized, especially in this neighborhood, and that the risk of burglary had been going down over the past decade as property crime rates have been dropping.

"Don't you watch the news?" she said. "There is so much crime, and every day some poor soul gets knifed or killed!"

Then it became clear to me. She was getting her information about risks in her neighborhood not from her neighborhood, but from the media. Newspapers and television shows were telling her that crime was taking place every day. The media were scaring her to get her attention. And they certainly had her attention. They also had shaped her beliefs about crime, stimulated her to spend money on a guard dog, and altered the way she spends her evening taking care of the none-too-affectionate Spike.

When I suggested that she was being influenced by the media, she laughed and told me I was naive not to realize the risk I was taking. I felt the same way about her.

Long-term effects are more difficult to recognize than are immediate effects. They often take months or even many years to exhibit evidence of their existence; by then it is difficult to convince people that the effect they observe today was brought about not by the message they just saw but by thousands of messages building up over a very long time.

If we know what to look for, we can be sensitive enough to spot some of these long-term effects before their manifestations are so obvious. In this chapter, we will examine 15 of these long-term effects spread out across all five effect types: cognitive, attitudinal, emotional, physiological, and behavioral.

■ COGNITIVE EFFECTS

Learning Agendas

By choosing certain images and themes, the media focus our attention on particular things while telling us to ignore other things. Called agenda setting, this effect was first observed in the political arena where the media were found to be very influential in telling us what to think *about* (Shaw & McCombs, 1977). For example, the media, through a continual stream of stories about social welfare programs, are effective at telling people that this is something worth thinking about; but the media are not effective at convincing people that they should support or reject social welfare programs. The agenda-setting function of the mass media is quite powerful, especially when there is an overlap in coverage among the various media.

This agenda-setting effect is not limited to telling us what to think about politics and current events. It is much broader. It tells us what kind of music we should listen to; what kinds of people we should regard as beautiful, smart, or successful; and what kinds of events are important. By bringing certain kinds of people to our attention, the media create celebrities. The media confer status on certain people, and we continue to hear what these people have to say even when they don't have anything important to say. The non-celebrities have not been given status, so we do not hear what they have to say, even if it is something potentially important. This is the agenda-setting effect.

The longer something is kept off the agenda, the harder it is to get onto the agenda. When the media ignore an issue, people stop talking and thinking about it. Noelle-Newman (1984) refers to this as the spiral of silence.

Hypermnesia

Hypermnesia appears to be the opposite of forgetting. Instead of a person being *less* able to recall information from a message as time goes by, there are situations when people become *more* able to recall that information (Wicks, 1992). For example, a man reads a story in a magazine about forest fires but is not able to recall many of the facts after the reading. During the next few weeks, however, the television presents stories about several big forest fires in his area, and he begins to recall more of the facts from the magazine story. This is hypermnesia. It seems very strange that a person could know less immediately after reading something compared to much later. We are more used to thinking that the opposite occurs, that is, that our learning is highest right after an exposure and then our memory of those facts gradually erodes.

How is hypermnesia possible? The key to understanding hypermnesia is to recognize that when we are exposed to information, the facts are recorded somewhere in our brains. On topics where we already have a good deal of knowledge, the recording of new facts is done in a highly organized manner by cataloging them quickly and accurately in the knowledge structure that we have previously developed on that topic. When we are asked about that information, we have no trouble retrieving it.

But with a topic that is new to us, we don't have a knowledge structure on that topic. The new facts may be stored haphazardly inside other knowledge structures, and this makes those facts very difficult to retrieve. As we begin to learn more about the new topic, we construct a new knowledge structure on that topic and sort through our older knowledge structures to bring all the facts on that topic together in one place. During periods of rest (such as sleep) our minds sort out the facts and move them around to where they can be more efficiently catalogued. Once all the facts on the new topic are assembled into a new knowledge structure, they are easier to recall.

Generalization

Generalization is the process of observing a few occurrences of something, perceiving a pattern that ties those occurrences together, then inferring that the pattern reflects something more general than those occurrences. That "something more general" can be a claim about how all people behave or how things work. For example, a person watches a local news program and hears a story about a house that was vandalized in an area near his apartment. Then he hears a story on radio that a local bank was robbed. Next he reads the newspaper and sees that there was an assault in his town last night. He has learned three facts—one from each message. But later that night he might generalize from these three facts and draw the conclusion that crime has become a real problem in his town. This conclusion was not given to him in the media, but the media provided him with some facts that could set up his jumping to this conclusion.

Let's consider another example. A person watches a situation comedy where several teenagers are very witty and joke their way out of trouble. She then watches a stand-up comedian who wins the admiration of his audience. Then she watches a romantic comedy where the characters are attracted to each other because of their shared sense of humor. She has learned facts about how these televised characters behave and the consequences of their behaviors, then generalizes to a conclusion that humor is a very useful tool that can get her whatever she wants.

Often this generalization process results in faulty ideas. To illustrate, in a typical public opinion poll, 83% of Americans will think crime is a big problem in society (Whitman & Loftus, 1996). However, most of these people will never have experienced a crime in their real lives. Furthermore, almost no one knows what the real rates of crime are. So where do so many people get the idea that crime is a major problem? They generalize from watching the coverage of specific crimes in the news and from the depiction of crimes in fictional programs. The media present a constant stream of crime news that reinforces the impression that there is a great deal of terrible crime.

What is the reality about crime? The crime rate has been falling, both in terms of crimes reported to the police as well as actual victimization rates. Also, home burglary rates have dropped 50% over the past two decades. Yet in a recent poll only 7% of Americans believed that violent crime had declined (Whitman & Loftus, 1996).

Exposing Secrets

For many people, the media, especially television, serve to expose secrets about how the world works. The media do this by restructuring social arenas, according to Joshua Meyrowitz in a fascinating book titled *No Sense of Place* (1985). Meyrowitz argues that the media affect us not through their content per se, but by changing the "situational geography" of social life. Meyrowitz says that we all change the way we act depending on whether we are in public or private. When we are in public, we perform on stage in front of others, such as colleagues at work. In contrast, we have "backstage" or private behaviors that we reserve for intimates, such as very good friends or spouses.

The media expose important social secrets by taking viewers backstage, and this often results in a negative effect. For example, Meyrowitz (1985) points out that adults used to be able to retreat to their private backstage area, which was hidden from children. While in the backstage, adults could talk about adult things (child-rearing practices, anxieties, sex, death, etc.) with each other without children being exposed. Parents could keep their shortcomings and anxieties backstage and thus hidden from their children. Then, once parents had discussed how to handle their children, they could come onstage and take on the role of confident authority figures.

The media, especially television, expose these adult secrets to children. When children watch situation comedies on television and see parents as buffoons, and when they watch talk shows and see all the problems that some adults have, children lose their belief that adults have superior wisdom and experience. It is much harder, then, for parents to establish authority over their children. Thus Meyrowitz argues, "Children may love television because it extends their horizons of experience, because it expands their awareness of adult behavior and adult roles, and because it keeps them abreast of the latest adult attempts to control them" (p. 45).

Another example is in the political arena where much of the President's life used to be kept backstage. Now all of the backstage information about a President's sexual indiscretions, overeating problems, draft avoidance, previous banking practices, and so on, are brought into the foreground, and it is much harder for that person to appear Presidential—that is, like a person possessing the superior qualities necessary to make all the decisions a President must make.

The electronic media are especially powerful at being able to destroy the place of backstage, because electronic media such as television present "expressive" information that was once accessible only in intimate face-to-face encounters. Through TV, viewers have access to the personal expressions (how people talk and act) of people from all over the world, that is, information that was once available to only a few people. Television undermines the behavioral distinctions between foreground and background, because it provides all kinds of information to all kinds of people. It leaves no secrets.

■ ATTITUDINAL EFFECTS

Sleeper Effect

This is an effect that takes a relatively long time to occur. During exposure to a message, a person discounts the message because of a dislike of the source. But over time, the person forgets the source, and the negative feeling about the information goes away, then is replaced by a positive feeling.

To illustrate, let's say you listen to a political pundit deliver an analysis of the problem of illegal immigration, about which he expresses a certain opinion. You do not like or respect the political commentator, so you do not agree with his opinion while you are viewing the show. Several weeks later, you are in an argument about illegal immigration, and you start citing many of the facts that you learned from the commentator. You also express the same opinion as the commentator did. But you have now forgotten about the commentator who made you feel bad. All you remember is the opinion and the supporting facts, which make you feel good.

Reinforcement

Much of the information presented by the media are things we already know, and many of the people and places portrayed there are things we have already seen. Our exposure to these familiar things serves to reinforce the attitudes and beliefs that we already hold. The more the media reinforce a particular belief, the weightier it becomes and the harder it is to change.

Most advertising—estimates of up to 80%—is not designed to create or change our opinions; instead it is designed to reinforce already existing opinions. Advertisers target their consumers and present them with millions of dollars worth of messages to keep them from changing their minds about a product.

Socialization

This is a life-long process whereby people acquire certain attitudes and beliefs by taking from the media certain lessons and themes about society. Throughout this long-term exposure to all kinds of messages (news, ads, movies, cartoons, talk shows, etc.), we infer patterns across the individual facts, events, and character portrayals. These inferences become our beliefs about how the world is constructed. This effect is similar to the cognitive effect of generalization. Both of these reflect the process of inference where people are exposed to a few instances of something and infer general patterns from these few instances. With generalization, the inferences are about factual patterns in our society, such as the rate of crime, the proportion of women who work, the proportion of people who are on welfare, and so on. In contrast, socialization reflects on inferences about how people should interact with one another and with their social world.

There are many examples of how the media gradually socialize us into believing certain things. Because this effect is so important and so subtle, I'll present several examples in detail below.

Materialism. One of the themes in advertising is that material goods are what count most. Happiness is defined in terms of wealth. We are taught that problems can be solved only by buying something. Furthermore, once we buy something our problem will be gone in a matter of seconds. Everything is commodified, and we define ourselves in terms of what we buy. We are not taught that problems are complex, that they require effort from us, and that they often take days, weeks, or even years to solve.

Commercials sell products on the surface, but their more important and longer-term effect is to sell an entire way of life—a way of experiencing social reality that is compatible with the needs of a mass-production, mass-consumption, capitalist society (Parenti, 1986). In a recent poll, two thirds of parents said their children define their self-worth by their possessions. More than half the parents of kids ages 2 to 17 admitted they've bought something for their child that they disapproved of. And one in three parents is working longer hours to pay for things their children feel they need. Now $2 billion are spent annually on marketing and advertising aimed at kids (Wride, 1999).

An advertisement does much more than provide information about its product. It also tells us what the product means. It does this by linking the product to our culture by using symbols. It also tells us what it means for us to be part of our culture. It tells us that if we don't accept the message of materialism, then we are alienated from our culture. In order to be happy, we must own things and avail ourselves of commercial services. These things improve our lives. Over time we become obsessed with acquiring material goods and overlook the things in life that do not cost money (inner peace, harmony, strong relationships, family, respect for others, etc.).

A corollary to this is the belief that new is better and that old things wear out, lose their usefulness, or both. New is better, because new is improved. So your old friends are not as good as potential new ones. Your spouse is not as good as a potential new romantic attachment. Thus we lose a sense of security, because we are socialized not to believe in permanence.

Nutrition. Attitudes about nutrition are influenced by the mass media, especially by TV. People who say that TV is a major source of information on health and nutrition are significantly more complacent about health, are non-exercisers, and are poorly informed about health matters. Preteens who watch more TV have lower levels of nutritional knowledge. Moreover, the nutritional value of children's diets varies inversely with their amount of TV viewing. This is understandable, given the world of television where there are seldom ads for grains, fruits, or vegetables. Instead, food ads are for processed, packaged foods that are usually high in fat, salt, and sugar. Characters in the entertainment portions between the ads are more likely to be shown snacking instead of eating a nutritious meal. And although they rarely exercise, they are rarely overweight or out of shape.

Americans are getting fatter. Stacey Schultz (1999), writing in *U.S. News & World Report,* says "the United States is now secure in its position as the fattest nation in the developed world" (p. 82). When we look at people 25 years old and older, we find that 63% of men and 55% of women are overweight. Furthermore, 18% of American adults are classified as obese, and this figure is up from 12% in 1991. Obesity is computed using a body mass index that adjusts for a person's height. For example, a woman who is 5 feet 5 inches tall is considered overweight if she weighs 162 pounds and is considered obese if she weighs 186 pounds or more (Schultz, 1999).

Beauty. Exposure to ads for beauty products causes adolescent girls to place more importance on beauty-related characteristics in their real-life personal roles. Also, women who watch ads of thin models can have their perceptions of their own bodies altered (Myers & Biocca, 1992).

Syndicated columnist Ellen Goodman (1997) writes that advertising has given girls many new body parts to worry about:

> A glance at any teen magazine is a new anatomy lesson. Eyes are now subdivided into half a dozen distinct areas from brow to lash, each of which need to be thinned or thickened, shaved or shaded. Teeth demand brightening as well as straightening. Thighs have grown cellulite. Lips require "plumping." Arms bulge for biceps, and every unmentionable inch of the body seems to need perfume of some kind or another.

She likens this "evolutionary speedup" to the trend in medicine where practitioners are getting more specialized with their attention on only one part of the body. However, there is a difference between medical and beauty developments. "Medicine changed to make their patients feel better. The beauty industry changed to make their customers feel worse" (Goodman, 1997, p. A9).

Drugs. Children's exposure to non-prescription drug advertising has no influence on their attitudes toward non-prescription medicines, their actual use of OTC (over the counter) drugs, or the use of illicit drugs. Also, there is no relationship between exposure to televised medicine advertising and use of illicit drugs.

However, the findings are different for cigarette advertising. Pollay and his colleagues (1996) conducted a study that tracked 20 years of cigarette ads and found that teenagers are three times more likely than adults to respond to cigarette ads. He also found that certain ad campaigns were particularly effective with children and adolescents; 79% of teen smokers use the brands depicted by the Marlboro Man, Joe Camel, and the fun couples of Newport.

Lack of Responsibility. The major effects of the media manifest in how we see our world. For example, we are more materialistic, and we tend to absolve from responsibility those with whom we identify most—those like ourselves. A good example of this hit me when I was reading the business section of a newspaper recently. There was a major story headlined, "Economy to start ninth year of expansion" (Skidmore, 1999). The story presented facts showing that manufacturing activity continued to climb, construction spending was up, and personal incomes were up. On the same page there was a two-paragraph news brief titled, "Record number file for bankruptcy." This news brief said that "more Americans filed for bankruptcy in 1998 than ever before" when 1.44 million filed bankruptcy petitions, up 2.7% from the year before. Of course there are always going to be people who need to file for bankruptcy no matter how good the economy is. But what is startling is that the filings for bankruptcy increase year after year at the same time that the economy gets better year after year. Even though more people are employed and their wages are increasing and the cost of goods remains steady (no inflation), more and more people are filing for bankruptcy. If these two trends co-occurred only this year, we could argue that it might be an anomaly. But the trends have been co-occurring for almost a decade.

One explanation is that people in general have more resources, but that for a growing number of people these resources are not enough to meet their expectations. More and more people are living beyond their means. Furthermore, when these people get in trouble, they do not scale back their consumption so as to get their expenditures more in line with their incomes; instead, they bail out on their creditors. People who file for bankruptcy are admitting they made many mistakes. But by filing for bankruptcy, they are saying that they cannot pay for those mistakes and so are asking someone else (their creditors, who pass the costs along to the general consumer) to pay. They are also saying, "Please do not hold me responsible for all my irresponsible spending."

Instant Gratification. Our instant access to news and entertainment provided by the media has trained us to expect instant gratification in everything. Ritzer (1993) calls this the McDonaldization of America. McDonald's hamburger stores provide everyone with food immediately for little money. Other chains include: Burger King, Wendy's, Hardee's, Arby's, Big Boy, Dairy Queen, TCBY, Denny's, Sizzler, Kentucky Fried Chicken, Popeye's, Taco Bell, Chi Chi's, Pizza Hut, Domino's, Long John Silver, Baskin-Robbins, and Dunkin' Donuts. The list goes on and on.

Other, non-restaurant, businesses are trying to emulate McDonald's. The vice-chairman of Toys 'R Us said, "We want to be thought of as the McDonald's of toys" (Ritzer, 1993, p. 3). Other chains with these ambitions include companies in car care (Jiffy Lube, AAMCO Transmissions, Midas Muffler & Brake Shops), tax preparation (H&R Block), child care (Kinder Care), health care (Pearle Vision Centers, Nutri/System), and retailing (Walmart). All of these companies are in business to provide us with instant gratification. And it is clear that we appreciate their services, because we keep increasing their revenues each year.

Other examples of our desire for instant gratifications are ATM machines that provide us with cash 24 hours every day; FedEx that we can use to send anything overnight; Home Shopping Network where it is easy to order products without having to leave one's house; and now the e-stores on the Internet where we can buy anything and have instant shipment to our homes.

Even sex has been McDonaldized. We can experience explicit sexual situations by buying magazines and videos and calling dial-a-porn phone numbers. Instantly we can engage in sex, albeit vicarious, without having to go through the trouble of meeting another human being.

The effect of having all these goods and services constantly and instantly available is to reinforce our desire for instant gratification. This reinforcement socializes us to make quick decisions, to think it is silly to do without, and to deal with machines rather than people.

There is so much available and it is so easy to get that we cease to think about things in much depth. For example, if there were no fast food restaurants, you would have to plan out a week's meals, go to the grocery store and select all the elements of those meals, unpack those elements at home and put them in some storage system, then assemble the elements into your meals. But today, we don't have to give much thought to meals. We can drive home from work and, on impulse, stop in at a fast food restaurant and get a fully assembled dinner in a bag.

The media foster in us a need for immediate gratification. The media themselves are so varied and available they offer us the possibility of immediate gratification for anything we could possibly want. Also, with cable offerings of all kinds and RCDs (remote control devices), we can immediately increase our gratification. Have you ever been watching a sporting event in real life and find yourself trying to fast forward through the slow parts to get to the action? Or have you ever listened to one of your friends tell a story and wished you could push a button to speed through the boring parts to get to the "good stuff"? If so, you have been conditioned to believe that you can make time move faster.

In relationships, do you wish you could meet that "special someone" right away? Do you feel that there is something wrong with you if you haven't been swept away by love in the past several months? When you do get excited by someone, do you wish things would progress more quickly? Then, after you have developed a relationship with that "special person," have you ever quickly become bored, wishing that someone better (or just newer) would come along to sweep you away again?

In careers, we expect very high rewards very quickly without much work. It comes as a surprise how difficult it can be to get even a mediocre job—then how much work is required to hold it. In the media, the velocity of success is very fast.

Belief in Alienation. For almost 30 years, social scientists have been documenting a big decline in social connectiveness. Television has consumed more and more of people's time, leaving less time for real-world activities. Now with computers and the Internet this trend is accelerating. People who spend more time on the Internet are often found to be more lonely and depressed. Kids who spend the most time with the media (more than 10.5 hours per day) are not as content as those who spend less time (Rideout, Foehr, Roberts, & Brodie, 1999).

Critics of this effect say that the Internet gives lonely people a chance to connect with others through chat rooms, bulletin boards, support groups, and email. Also, most people who are heavy users of the Internet say that they watch much less television (Perry, 2000).

EMOTIONAL EFFECTS ■■

Stunting Emotional Development

Some critics have made the argument that watching a great deal of television stunts a child's emotional development. They point out that by the time children reach the age of 5, they have been exposed to about 6,000 hours of television. The high levels of exposure to television, coupled with the extreme level of stimulation presented by television, leaves viewers with no time for reflection. On television there is a new shot every 3.5 seconds on average. There are sound effects, music, laugh tracks, and constant interruptions. The pace is extremely fast, with new images replacing old, new shows replacing old. This short-circuits the natural, emotional development people need to become healthy human beings; it strangles the development of children's own voices, and denies them their imaginative powers. According to some neuro-anatomists, excessive TV viewing—more than 4 or 5 hours a day, 7 days a week—will take a serious cognitive toll. They believe that the brain's limbic system, the mysterious, sub-cortical part that researchers call the image-making center, will develop more slowly in young people who spend half of their waking hours in front of the TV set. Their emotional growth is stunted.

Television viewing makes people think they are experiencing emotions, but these are not real because they are not two-way, that is, there is no interaction. Viewers cannot influence the behavior of TV characters, so there is no emotional exchange. Emotions require physicality, that is, people touching each other; TV does not provide this. Without adequate emotional development, people do not develop a sense of guilt or a conscience.

Also, TV gives so many images to viewers that viewers do not have to generate their own images; they do not practice what-if situations or think things through. They can't even fully process much of what they do experience on TV—there is too much. Also, viewing weakens their will. TV takes over and gives them all their excitement; people don't have to generate their own entertainment any longer.

Desensitization

Some things in the media are presented so often we can no longer treat them with wonder or awe. Our tolerance has been increased so that things that used to entertain us or impress us no longer do.

This is especially important with the issue of violence. Viewing TV violence leads to lowered sensitivity to aggression and violence. Even watching a single violent film can make children temporarily less aware of and less concerned about aggressive acts in others. There is a relationship between the amount of exposure to TV violence and the willingness to use violence, to suggest violence as a solution to conflict, and to perceive violence as effective (Liebert, Neale, & Davidson, 1973; Tan, 1981). This effect has also been found in adults who have been exposed to strong violence against women (Linz, Donnerstein, & Penrod, 1984, 1988) or even relatively mild forms of violence (Thomas, 1982).

Another form of media desensitization is a result of the superficial treatment media give to certain issues. This superficial treatment by the media cloaks the apathy of the audience by allowing us to feel that by knowing about a problem, we are doing something about it.

This desensitization can have positive effects in a therapeutic setting. People who fear something (such as dogs, heights, flying in airplanes) can be gradually desensitized (Dorr, 1981; Foa & Kozak, 1986; Goranson, 1970; Rushton, 1979).

PHYJIOLOGICAL EFFECTJ ■■

Increasing Tolerance

Your body builds up a resistance to certain experiences. For example, the first time you see a horror film, your body responds with a fight-or-flight reaction by substantially increasing your heart rate and blood pressure. As you continue to view horror films over the years, your body's reaction to this stimulus is not as strong. Your heart rate and blood pressure still increase but not as much. You are building up a higher physiological tolerance for this type of message. In an extreme case, with massive exposure to this type of message, you might even extinguish all physiological reactions to horror.

Shifting Brain Activity

Critics—such as Marie Winn in her book *The Plug-In Drug* (1984)—caution that television hooks children into entertainment, keeps their brains functioning at a low level, and makes them passive acceptors of the media messages as presented. Also, Marcuse (1964) argues that the mass media in America hammer the population into having a one-dimensional mind, that is, people's minds become paralyzed so that they are incapable of independent thought; they cannot criticize or oppose the messages in which they become immersed.

Healy (1990), in her book *Endangered Minds,* argues that children's minds are changing because of exposure to the visual media, especially computer games. Recent studies suggest that intensive game playing actually redraws the brain's neural maps. And children who play a lot have cognitive strategies that are parallel—not sequential. This could make it more difficult for children to learn sequential tasks such as reading or mathematical reasoning—both of which are very linear and analytical.

Healy says that children who enter elementary school are smarter each year in some ways but that they are less able to handle school and its requirements. Children are less able to pay attention and to listen. This is because many children have information overload from the constant bombardment of media messages, so they shut down when they get to school, or they have become accustomed to a level of stimulation much higher than a teacher can provide, so they become bored. Healy says that the visual media (especially television and video games) are responsible for this condition of over-stimulation, because those media strongly stimulate the right side of the brain while ignoring the left side. Because the left side of the brain is used less it develops more slowly, leading children to have trouble with reading, arithmetic, and other traditional academic subjects.

Instead, the right side is stimulated by the fast-changing scenes on TV as well as video games with lots of novelty and movement. The visual media are very spatially oriented. This is especially the case with computers, which require a different form of skill. By playing computer games, children

acquire new ways of learning. They're honing special graphics and motor skills. They can process huge amounts of visual information in parallel. On a daily basis, they scope out new games, grasp the operating rules, navigate bewildering 3-D geographies, and jump through abstract mental hoops with concentration usually reserved for competitive test taking. (Gross, 1996, p. 64)

■■ BEHAVIORAL EFFECTS

Learned Helplessness

Some argue that television causes a decrease in persistence, because viewers are learning to be helpless. This learned helplessness comes not from watching any one particular show or type of programming; it comes from the act of watching television itself. They believe that television, regardless of its content, sets up a context in which the viewer's feedback, stimulation, and rewards do not depend on what the viewer does beyond turning the television set on or off or changing channels. Because of the lack of connection between action and experience, they believe that television viewing makes an environment in which learned helplessness patterns can emerge. They further believe that educational programs are especially harmful, because they make learning look so easy and don't require anything from the viewer.

Displacement

The media have changed the way we spend our time. The media consume us by consuming our time. The *Statistical Abstract of the United States: 1999* (2000) says that the average person spends 3,297 hours with the media a year—that's about nine hours each day. Almost half of this time is spent watching television.

Only a small portion of our media exposure is exclusive of other activities. For example, while we are watching television, we might also be talking on the telephone, or doing the dishes, or reading a magazine. If we were to add up all the time we spend engaging in different activities during a day, it would total more than 24 hours. Thus, the media exposure figures can be misleading if we think of that time as displacing other activities.

Acknowledging this overlapping of exposure is important, because it reveals something about the nature of our exposure—much of our exposure to the media does not command our full attention. The media are often only a background to other activities. Thus the exposure shapes our mood subconsciously.

There is also a concern that exposure to the media—especially with escapist fare—will prevent people from using their time more productively. This is especially an issue with children and their schoolwork. Also, there is a concern that for very young children who have a television viewing habit—playtime is pre-empted (Singer, 1982). When TV structures a child's life, the child spends less time creatively making up his or her own games and situations.

Narcoticizing

The media can be like a powerful drug. The first exposure to a new magazine, CD, TV show, or the like, can bring a rush of excitement. So we go back to it in order to get the same feelings again. It is habit forming. For example, people can get hooked on the media, especially on computers. As early as 1995, when only 6% of households were online, there were already people showing signs of Internet addiction. These online junkies revealed a compulsion to check email 20 to 30 times a day, to make the computer a higher priority than anything else, or to spend time away from important real-life activities such as talking to spouses or kids. Internet Addiction Disorder is a term coined in the mid 1990s by a psychiatrist who was seeing more and more patients who were unable to control their use of the Internet. These people typically forgo sleeping, eating, and other activities to spend time on the Internet. This includes obsessions with chat rooms, games, pornography, gambling, and shopping. Some married people have extra-marital affairs online; day traders get hooked on the stock market.

Estimates are that about 6% of Web users could be addicted—that is 6 million people (Yang, 2000). Therapists have already developed 12-step plans to help these people (Vranizan, 1995).

When we build up a tolerance to an effect, we want more. Each time we go back, we require more from the media to get the same rush. With entertainment, we want a more outrageous story line, more attractive characters, more visual effects. But if the media can give us only the same kinds of messages, we do not feel the rush. Over time our expectations become very high and we find ourselves flipping through 50 channels and saying, "There's nothing on!" What we mean by this, of course, is that "TV is no longer able to exceed my expectations and to significantly arouse me in a surprising way." But we keep exposing ourselves to the TV anyway, because, for many of us, it is better than not watching.

This narcoticizing effect also works with news content. At first we are excited about finding out what is happening. But then, over time, we don't want to hear the same old news. We want stories that will surprise us, so we look for more bizarre happenings, more dramatic confrontations, and more arousing debates. Our tolerance for these increases and our expectations grow beyond what news stories can provide. We continue to watch—fearing that we will miss something important or something truly arousing.

Disinhibition

This is the process of gradually wearing down inhibitions that prevent you from behaving in certain ways. You may not like to dance in front of others, but after several months of watching dance programs, your resistance wears down and you find yourself dancing in a club. Also, most of us have been raised to solve our problems in non-aggressive and non-violent ways. However, after years of exposure to violent portrayals in the movies and on television, where attractive characters use violence successfully to get what they want, our aversion to using violence gradually wears down. One day when someone steals the parking place we want, we find ourselves screaming and pounding on the offender's car; the inhibitions that prevent us from behaving violently have been worn down and no longer can prevent us from behaving violently.

■ CONCLUSION

We live in a media-saturated environment, and media effects are constantly happening to us as they shape our knowledge patterns, attitudes, emotions, and behaviors. Long-term effects are more difficult to trace to the media than are immediate effects. This difficulty is responsible for many people not realizing many of the effects the media have on them over the long term. The long-term effects are powerful, because they take a long time to develop and therefore have the weight of many years and thousands of exposures.

Being media literate requires that we become sensitive to these many long-term effects. We need to recognize when these effects are having a negative influence on us so we can protect ourselves. And we need to recognize when the effects are having a positive influence on us so we can appreciate and enhance their power.

EXERCISE 15.1

Recognizing Long-Term Effects

Think about how the media may have exercised a subtle effect on you over the long term. On a blank sheet of paper, divide the page into five rows, labeling them cognitive, attitudinal, emotional, behavioral, and physiological effects.

For each row, see if you can list two long-term effects that illustrate how the media have affected you.

Use the list below to guide your thinking.

Long-term effects: Slow accumulation of information, attitudes, and images leads to effects that take months or years to manifest themselves.

a. *Cognitive:* Acquisition of information and knowledge structures.

b. *Attitudinal:* Erosion or building up of certain attitudes.

c. *Emotional:* Increasing or decreasing emotional reactions over time.

d. *Behavioral:* New behaviors can be learned in the short term but not performed until much later.

e. *Physiological:* Increased tolerance for certain content; physiological dependency on the medium or certain content.

EXERCISE 15.2

What Have You Internalized From the Media Culture?

1. When you are driving and listening to your car radio, do you switch the station, looking for something else even when you are satisfied with the song you are currently hearing—thinking maybe a better song is on another station? Do you flip through the channels on the television set looking for something better?

2. In romantic relationships, which is more important to you: commitment or perfection?

    When you are in a romantic relationship, are you happy when you make a lasting, strong commitment to the other person? Or do you worry that this person may not be the absolute best one for you and perhaps there is someone a little better out there?

3. In college, do you value learning or efficiency more?

    Do you make a commitment to each course and attend every session and try to get all you can from them? Do you take a wide range of courses (some you know nothing about) in order to expand your experience?

    Or do you look for ways to spend your time better during class time, such as going on a job interview, finishing a term paper for another course, catching up on sleep, and so on? Do you look for courses on the basis of which ones require the least amount of work for the highest grades?

4. In your career, which will be more important to you: loyalty or success?

    Will you find a job and build your entire career there to pay back your employer for your first big opportunity? Or will you take the first job as a stepping stone to something better and leave as soon as you have learned all you can in that job?

5. When you have a major problem, are you upset when you cannot solve it in a short period of time?

CHAPTER

16

Key Idea: There are many factors about you and media messages that in combination increase the probability that the media will have an effect on you.

How Do the Effect Processes Work?

wo boys go to the movies and watch *The Deer Hunter*, a film in which American prisoners during the Vietnam War are forced by their captors to play Russian roulette. Russian roulette is a game where one chamber in a revolver contains a bullet while the other chambers are empty. Each player in the game takes a turn pointing the gun at his own head and pulling the trigger. If he is lucky and the chamber is empty, the gun does not fire and the player lives. If he is unlucky, the chamber contains the bullet, which is fired into his brain killing him instantly.

Several days after watching this movie, the boys are playing in their parents' bedroom and find a revolver under the bed. They decide to play Russian roulette. Eventually the gun fires, killing one of the boys.

Should the media portrayal be blamed for this death? This is a very important question. Some people would argue that the boy caused his own death. Some would argue it is the fault of the parents for having a loaded gun available. Some would blame the producers of *The Deer Hunter*. And still others would generalize this example into an argument about how irresponsible all media are. Sorting through all this attribution of blame is at the heart of the issue of media effects. This chapter presents some insights that you should use when trying to understand the complex issue of media effects.

THE INFLUENCE PROCE**ſ**S

When most people think of media effects, they want to identify a particular message from the media as a clear cause of a particular action. Thus in the above example, critics blame the adolescents' viewing of a particular portrayal in a particular movie, *The Deer Hunter*, as the trigger for playing the game of Russian roulette. The desire to simplify the world into direct cause-effect relationships reflects our human need to understand our world. While simplification might help in making things seem clear, it rarely captures the essence of the processes that are occurring all around us. With the media, we are constantly subjected to processes of influence. Yes, the media do influence us in all sorts of ways. But the process of that influence is rarely a simple direct cause-effect relationship. If we are serious about trying to understand the processes by which the media affect us, we need to examine the issues of causation, thresholds, non-linear relationships, contingent conditions, necessary versus sufficient conditions, and direct versus indirect influence. Is this a complex topic? Yes, of course it is. But if you wonder why certain people are affected by the media while others are not, you need to understand more about the process of influence. If you have wondered why you do not seem to be influenced by the media, you need to take a closer look at these processes to determine if your perceptions about your "lack of being influenced" are accurate.

Cause and Effect

When we think of attributing effects to the media, we raise the issue of causation. After all, if the media do not cause the effect, how can we say that the media have had an influence? But there are several ways of thinking about causation. One way is to think of the media as *determining* the effect. Another way is to think of the media as *influencing the probability* of an effect.

Deterministic Causation. The word *causation* has a special meaning for social scientists. In order for an argument for a causal relationship to be convincing, it must demonstrate three conditions. First, there must be a relationship between the hypothesized cause and the observed effect. Second, the cause must always precede the effect in time. And third, all alternative causes for the effect must be eliminated.

The problem with making a strong case for the media causing certain effects lies with the second and third conditions. To illustrate, let's consider the hypothesis that television violence causes aggressive behavior among viewers. Because a great deal of research has been conducted to test this hypothesis, researchers are generally able to meet the first condition by showing that there is a relationship between exposure to violence and a person being more likely to exhibit aggressive attitudes and even behaviors. However, researchers have a great deal of difficulty meeting the remaining two conditions. Except for short-term experiments, it is very difficult to argue convincingly that the viewing of TV violence really preceded a person's aggression. Aggressive behavior (which is the presumed effect) often precedes the TV viewing (which is the presumed cause). It is often the case that aggressive people seek out violent content. Viewing the content reinforces their aggressiveness, which leads them to watch more violence. At best, the relationship is reciprocal, where each of the two factors is (to a certain extent) the cause of the other.

The requirement of ruling out alternative explanations is also a problem for social scientists. Returning to our example of the Russian roulette game, perhaps the boys were raised in a household that strongly valued competition and the ridiculing of people who were afraid of challenges. Perhaps one of the boys was severely depressed and saw this game as a way to commit suicide. Or perhaps the boys had played with the gun many times before, thinking that it was not loaded. Each of these conditions could be responsible for the death. Unless we can rule out all these (and all other) alternative explanations, we cannot conclude that the media exposure determined the shooting.

Probabilistic Causation. There is another way of thinking about causation—probabilistically. As we have seen above, deterministic causation seeks to explain influences in a simple manner, that is, the argument is that one thing (the media) caused the effect (the shooting). At times, many of these influences may all act in unison to push us in a particular direction. When this happens, none of these individual influences can be regarded as causing or determining the outcome by itself. Instead, each of the factors contributes its own special push; that is, each increases the probability of there being an effect.

Media effects are almost always probabilistic, not deterministic. There are many factors about the audiences, the messages, and the environment that rachet up the probability that an effect will occur.

Thresholds

There are some effects that do not show up until media exposure exceeds a certain point. For example, viewing television generally does not have a negative influence on children's academic performance until it reaches a point of about 30 hours per week, when it really begins cutting into study time (Potter, 1987a). So if Jane increases her television viewing time from 10 hours to 20 hours per week, she is not likely to show a decrease in academic performance. But if Bob increases his viewing from 30 to 35 hours per week, he will show a drop in grades. Unless you understand thresholds, the pattern in this example might not seem possible. It does not seem fair that Jane can increase her TV viewing by 10 hours and experience no negative effect on her grades, but Bob increases his TV viewing time by only half as much and his grades go down. This pattern does not make sense unless we understand what it means to cross a threshold.

Perhaps the boys who ended up playing Russian roulette were already close to a dangerous threshold before seeing the *Deer Hunter*. Perhaps they were depressed and bored; perhaps they had no respect for guns; perhaps they lost the ability to distinguish fantasy from reality after years of playing video games; perhaps their parents did not care about them and had no household rules about their behavior. All of these factors in combination could push a boy close to the threshold where one exposure to the *Deer Hunter* could take him over. Should the exposure to the movie be blamed? Yes, it did move the boy over the threshold. But we must also blame all the other factors that put the boy so close to the threshold to begin with.

Non-Linear Relationships

The effect process is rarely linear. A linear process is in evidence when one unit of input is associated with one unit of output. For example, Figure 16.1 is an illustration of a linear relationship, because one unit of reading a book is associated with one unit of learning. In contrast, Figure 16.2 shows a non-linear relationship where the amount of reading needs to be considerable before the reader achieves the first unit of learning. However, readers who keep working at the task of learning will eventually get to a point where the learning will increase relative to the work. And when they reach a point on the right side of the Figure 16.2, they are receiving *more than one* unit of learning for each hour of reading. This particular non-linear relationship has been referred to as the "learning curve." It is a graphic representation of the principle that the more one knows about a given topic, the more efficiently one will be able to learn more about that topic.

There are many other non-linear relationships possible, and several have already been discovered in media effects research. Figure 16.3 presents the J-curve, which expresses the relationship between the use of the mass media and the importance of an event. Figure 16.4 presents the S-curve, which expresses the rate of diffusion of innovations in a society over time. Other examples are the bell curve (Figure 16.5), the advertising exposure plateau curve (3 to 10 exposures optimal; Figure 16.6), and the sine curve (Figure 16.7).

All of these figures have smooth lines. Another form of non-linear pattern is the catastrophic event. In Figure 16.8, a person increases his or her television exposure with no change in aggressive behavior, then suddenly something happens and the person's aggressive behavior increases enormously. The catastrophic event could be something in the exposure, but it could also be something in the viewer's life, such as a severe injustice, a chemical imbalance in the brain, or the loss through violence of a loved one.

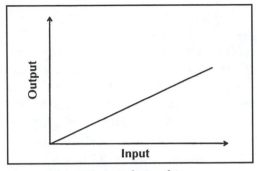

Figure 16.1. Linear Relationship

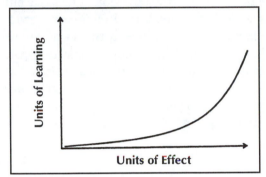

Figure 16.2. Learning Curve

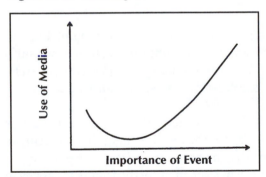

Figure 16.3. J Curve

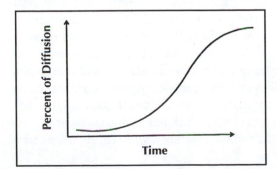

Figure 16.4. S Curve

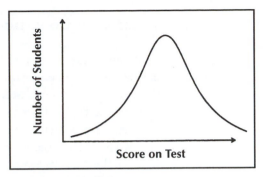

Figure 16.5. Bell Curve

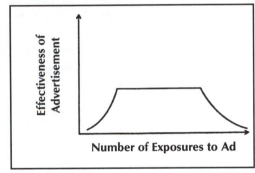

Figure 16.6. Plateau

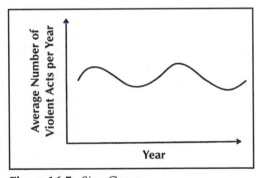

Figure 16.7. Sine Curve

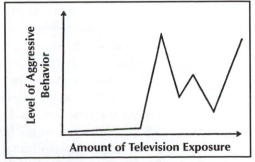

Figure 16.8. Catastrophic Change

Contingent Conditions

When we expose ourselves to the media, we bring into play our own motives, expectations, and emotions. Each of these can contribute to or take away from the effect. Also, as we interpret the meaning of messages, our skills come into play. For example, if Greg watches a violent fight on television and sees that the perpetrator was attractive and rewarded, he is likely to begin behaving aggressively. Here, the violent message leads to aggressiveness. If Cindy has poor attention skills as she watches the same violence, she might not understand the meaning of the violence and become confused, not aggressive. The violence in this case leads to confusion. And Marcia watches the same violent message but laughs at it, because she thinks it is farcical and unrealistic. In this case the violence leads to laughter. From these three examples, can we say that violent messages lead to aggressive behavior? In general, there is not a consistent pattern—it depends on the message and the person. When we use an approach that takes all these simultaneous factors into consideration, we discover that, *under certain conditions*, a violent message can cause aggressive behavior. In short, the effect is contingent on certain conditions—it cannot be generalized to all people and all conditions.

Necessary Versus Sufficient Conditions

To illustrate this distinction, I will use the example of starting a fire. In order to start a fire, you need fuel, oxygen, and heat. Having only oxygen is not sufficient to create a fire; you must have all three. To start a fire, none of the three elements alone is sufficient, but each is necessary; that is, you cannot have a fire if any one is missing.

With the media, there are no sufficient conditions, that is, no single factor is sufficient to guarantee an effect. An effect is the result of many factors acting in concert. Among those factors, some may be necessary, that is, the effect could not occur if one of these were missing. However, many of the factors are not even necessary; factors can be substitutable. For example, let's return to the Russian roulette example. Among the many factors that led to the death of that teenage boy were the revolver, exposure to the *Deer Hunter* movie, and peer pressure among the group of friends. None of these factors can be regarded as sufficient, and only the revolver can be regarded as a necessary condition; without it there would have been no game of Russian roulette. Exposure to the movie was an influence, but something else could have given them the idea (a book, an interpersonal conversation, etc.). Peer pressure was an influence, but we could substitute depression—if the boy were alone and severely depressed, he might have played the game by himself.

Direct and Indirect Influences

The media effect process is not always direct. The effect *can* be direct—we read something and we learn it. Or we see an ad on TV and it changes our existing attitude. But the effect can be indirect through others. A friend watches the news and tells us about an event. Or a friend tries to change our attitudes using persuasive techniques gained through watching television.

The effect can be indirect through institutions. The media have changed the way families are structured, so we are raised in a different manner than we might have been. The media have changed the way politics are conducted, so we live under the decisions of a different type of leader.

Countervailing Influences

There are constantly many competing factors in the process of influence. Some of these come from the media, while others come from institutions, interpersonal interactions, and within ourselves. At times, many of these influences may be acting in different directions—thus having the overall effect of seeming to cancel out each other's influence. One example of this is in the issue of children's creativity and daydreaming. Some people argue that TV *stimulates* daydreaming, because TV is so stimulating that viewers will want to relive some episodes. Other people argue that TV *reduces* daydreaming and imagination, because television has such rapid pacing that it leaves children no time to stop to reflect or daydream. TV's ready-made images don't engage the imagination like a book does. Also, TV presents so many fantasies that the viewer can access with very little effort, why bother to expend the creative effort needed to daydream?

Does television exert these two countervailing influences on children's imaginations? Valkenburg and Van der Voort (1995), in a Dutch study of elementary school age children, examined the effect of television viewing on daydreaming. They found that there was an important interaction between type of daydreaming and type of TV program. There is more than one type of daydreaming: positive-intense (characterized by vivid, pleasant, and child-like daydreams), aggressive-heroic (action characters acting violently), and dysphoric (escapist). A positive-intense daydreaming style was found to be stimulated by watching non-violent children's programs and to be inhibited by watching violent dramatic programs. An aggressive-heroic daydreaming style was stimulated by watching violent dramatic programs and inhibited by watching non-violent programs.

Another example of a countervailing effect is with exposure to television violence. Some theorists say that exposure to high amounts of explicit violence is bad, because it can trigger a learning effect. But other theorists say that exposure to high amounts of explicit violence might be good, because it can sensitize people to the brutal nature of violence and therefore make people more sympathetic to its victims and less likely to perpetrate it themselves. The two effects of disinhibition and sensitization may be happening simultaneously, thus canceling each other out so that on the surface it appears that there is no effect.

▓▓ CONTRIBUTING FACTORS

As we have seen in the above section, the process of influence is a complex one that involves many factors that increase (or decrease) the probability of an effect occurring. What are these factors? The major ones are listed below in two categories: factors in the media messages and factors in you.

Factors in Media Messages

Content of the Messages. It matters what you expose yourself to, because messages are very different across media and vehicles. People who expose themselves to news are likely to learn about current events, while people who expose themselves to soap operas will learn what the characters have done that day. Both types of content result in learning, but the type of learning is different.

Content differences also influence long-term effects. If you watch a lot of television in general, you will likely to come to believe that the world is a mean and violent place because there is so much crime and violence across the television landscape (Gerbner, Gross, Signorielli, Morgan, & Jackson-Beeck, 1979). This is especially true if you watch mostly crime and action/adventure programs (Potter, 1991). But if you watch only pro-social programming, such as *Mister Rogers' Neighborhood, Sesame Street,* and similar programs, you will likely internalize a very different attitude about the world.

When the media present a relatively constant picture of a social world, their effect is more powerful, because all the content is pointing to the same type of effect. When the media present messages that are the same as those presented by other institutions, such as family, education, religion, and the legal system, then all those messages reinforce one another. But when there are differences across messages, the media messages are often regarded as the most important. This is especially true for people who spend more time with the media than other institutions and for people who like, trust, or are aroused more by media messages than messages from other sources.

Context of Portrayals. People learn social lessons by watching what happens to characters on television. If a character's behavior is portrayed as being successful and rewarded, the viewer will learn that that behavior was good and useful. If the behavior is punished, the viewer will learn that the behavior was bad and should not be tried (Bandura, 1994). Also influential are characters who are attractive and who perform actions that appear justified.

Observation of social models accounts for much of the information communicated to children, and the media provide an enormous number of models and actions from which children might learn. Given the large amount of time children spend with the media, those mediated models exert strong influence on children's learning about social situation.

Factors in You

Developmental Level. A person's developmental level is a very important factor in the media effects process (Dervin & Greenberg, 1972; Hawkins & Pingree, 1982; Murray, 1980; Roberts, 1973; Singer & Singer, 1981). *Developmental level* refers to the level of ability a person has for cognitive functioning—making sense of the world. Recall from Chapter 2 that Piaget has shown that infants operate at a very low level of cognitive functioning. But as infants grow older, their minds mature, and they move up one level at a time until by age 12 their minds have developed to a point where they can function like adults. For example, pre-schoolers have difficulty comprehending and making use of the order of isolated events in a plot. They lose track of the order in which things happen and relationships among separate events in a plot. They have difficulty in making inferences about the causes and meanings of actions, and they have difficulty understanding characters' motives and the consequences of their actions. When they watch television, they focus their attention on the micro elements of particular sound effects, voices, bits of music, and small segments of motion or color. As they age, they are able to organize these individual elements into meaningful chunks. This conceptual chunking allows them to begin to understand plot and character development (Roberts & Bachen, 1981).

Because of differences in cognitive development, children learn different things from the media at different ages. Younger children are not able to follow the narratives in news stories or dramatic plots, so they construct less meaning from them. Thus they cannot engage in much generalization, and this protects them from constructing false images of the world or internalizing many of the themes in the culture. But they are more susceptible to the claims of advertisers, because they are not skeptical of that information. Also, young children are more likely to be frightened by monsters and scary sound effects. As they age, children develop the ability to protect themselves from certain kinds of messages, but they become vulnerable to the negative effects of others (Roberts, 1973).

Motivations. When people have a conscious need for a particular kind of information, they will actively seek out this type of information in the media, and the chance of them learning from this experience is high. When people are passive, learning can still occur, but it is not as likely.

People who have more education and higher intelligence are more motivated to seek out information from the media (Roberts, 1973). These people select the information that has the greatest utility to them.

Personal Information. People with the largest amount of knowledge learn the most from media (Comstock, Chaffee, Katzman, McCombs, & Roberts, 1978; Rice & Wartella, 1981). When people have a great deal of knowledge on a particular topic, they have a strong, well-developed knowledge framework. They are usually motivated to acquire more information on various topics and thus seek out media that will provide them with this information. When they see a new message on the topic, they are able to integrate that new information quickly and efficiently into their existing knowledge structure.

If a person's knowledge structure is composed primarily of information only from the media, then this structure may be dominated by media-stimulated generalizations and internalizations from the media world. In many topics, we have no choice but to rely primarily on media information. This is what makes the media such a powerful socializing influence—we cannot check out the media's information by comparing it to information from other sources, such as real life. For example, almost no one knows what it feels like to be a professional athlete. We are given some insights about what the life of a professional athlete might be like, but almost no one has an opportunity to check those insights out for themselves. This is true of almost all news content. The same is true of much fictional programming. Viewers do not know what it feels like to be a professional athlete or a multimillionaire, or a detective, or many other portrayals on TV. Because viewers do not have an opportunity to check it out in real life, it is impossible to prove the messages false or inaccurate. When people are asked if TV entertainment is credible and a reasonable representation of the way people live, most people say yes. As you increase your amount of viewing, your perception of the reality of TV entertainment programs increases. This is especially true among children and those who have the least amount of variety of real-world experiences.

Degree of identification is also a key factor in the effects process, because people will pay more attention to characters with which they identify. We become involved in the media-depicted events through a psychological relationship with the characters in a two-step process. First, we make a judgment about how much we are attracted to the character and how much the character is like us—or how we would like to be. Second, we engage in an "as if" experience in which we imagine ourselves in the role of the character.

Viewers identify with characters similar to themselves, but who also have qualities that they would like to possess but do not. Generally, we have a greater liking (positive affect and emotion) for characters who are more similar to us in age, gender, ethnicity, or interests (Himmelweit, 1982; Weiss, 1971). While most people tend to select same-gender characters, girls often choose male characters as role models; boys rarely choose female characters. Girls look for physical attractiveness in their selections for role models; boys look for physical aggressiveness. Identification is usually with a positive object, but it can also be induced through negative sentiment.

Viewers form strong attachments to certain characters, depending on what those characters do and say (Hoffner & Cantor, 1991). The stronger the attachment, the stronger the probability of an effect (Bandura, 1986, 1994).

Arousal. When viewers are aroused, their attention is more concentrated and the experience is more vivid for them. They will remember the portrayals better and will be more likely to act while aroused (Comstock et al., 1978; Zillmann, 1991).

Certain production techniques tend to arouse viewers. These techniques include fast cuts, quick motion within a frame, loud music, and sound effects. Also, certain narrative conventions (such as suspense, fear, life-threatening violence, and erotica) can lead to arousal.

Sociological Factors. The effects of the mass media are influenced by messages from society and its institutions. If you hear a fact that is counter to your political or religious beliefs, you are likely to discount the fact and forget it or to remember it as an example of a falsehood. Thus the degree to which you are socialized influences the degree to which the media can have an effect (Comstock, 1980; Murray, 1980).

With children, parental involvement in media exposure serves to influence learning. Children increase their understanding and recall of both central and incidental program content when adults provide comments to guide their children's attention and understanding during viewing. However, most parents do not usually provide critical insights during TV viewing with their children (McLeod, Fitzpatrick, Glynn, & Fallis, 1982; Roberts, 1973).

People with strong interpersonal ties will use them to filter media messages (Comstock, 1980; Liebert & Schwarzberg, 1977). The more a person identifies with a peer group, and the more cohesive the group is, the more the person will be influenced by the group and the less effect the media will have by itself.

The degree of prior socialization is also related to the amount of influence the media will have. Parental support for aggression as a means of problem solving has been found to have a greater influence on attitudes favorable to the use of aggression than the viewing of TV violence (Comstock, 1980; Hawkins & Pingree, 1982; McLeod et al., 1982).

Existing Value Structure. If a person's set of values, especially a child's, is well developed, the values will be used as a standard to judge media messages and the person will not be so influenced by those messages (Himmelweit, 1966). Your existing values serve as an anchor. When you see something that goes against your values, you are offended and you resist the message. But when messages continually challenge your values, you will slowly drift to a new attitude over time.

Lifestyle. People who have active lifestyles where they interact with many people and institutions are less affected by the media. People who have fewer real-life experiences because of lack of money, education, or vitality are more likely to have much greater exposure to media that is not counterbalanced by other experiences. This is why the poor, those with low SES, ethnic minorities, and the elderly are particularly susceptible to the influence of the media, especially television, because they expose themselves to a great deal of TV due to their sociological and psychological isolation. TV becomes their window on the world and their primary source of information.

■■ MEDIA LITERACY AND BLAME

Let's return once again to the Russian roulette situation at the beginning of this chapter and re-address the question: Should the media be blamed for the death of the boy who shot himself? This question is continually asked when we hear about a killing that is modeled after a portrayal in a movie or a video game. Although a death resulting from someone imitating something they saw in the media is cause for public attention, the public discourse about this problem is very weak. People will typically blame either the media, or the gun, or the parents of the killed boy. There is little understanding that these three and many other factors are all contributing influences. If we are to blame one, we should blame them all.

We need to understand that in our complex society, seldom does a single element cause an effect. Influences work in combination. This is not hard for us to understand when it comes to what causes a fire, for example. A fire requires fuel, oxygen, and heat. All three must be present in order to have a fire. With media effects, there are many factors about the media portrayal, factors in the life of the people involved, and factors about the real-world situation that all contribute to a probability that an effect will occur. No one of these factors will increase the probability from zero to 100%.

Who is to blame? It depends on how you ask the question. If the question is: Should the gun manufacturers be held solely responsible for crimes committed using their guns? the answer is no, of course not, because there are other influences involved. If the question instead is: Are the gun manufacturers blameless? the answer again is no, because their guns were essential ingredients in certain violent crimes. The key here is to recognize multiple influences and not allow any one of the influences to be absolved simply because it was not the *only* influence.

But our public debate is so poverty stricken that critics or the public fixate on only one factor and blame that. A good example of this is the problem of violence in society. Let's look at instances of armed robbery and killings with firearms. There are people who blame only gun manufacturers and the gun dealers who make these weapons so available in this country. Alex Penelas, Mayor of Miami, Florida, filed a lawsuit against 26 gun makers to hold them liable for crimes committed using their guns. Also, a jury in Brooklyn, New York, recently found that 15 gun manufactures were negligent and 9 liable in three shooting incidents (Hiaasen, 1999). In reaction to this blame, certain groups, such as the National Rifle Association (NRA), vehemently deny that guns are to blame at all. The NRA has enlisted the help of some state legislators to stem these lawsuits. In Florida, Representative George Albright (R-Ocala) introduced a bill to make it a felony for local governments to sue firearm manufacturers.

The press contributes to the problem by dealing with it as a typical, simplified conflict situation. The controversy makes a better story when opinions are polarized and very superficial. This makes it easy for the press to avoid having to clarify the nuances of the opinions held by people in the debate. The press can keep the focus on the conflict between people rather than focus attention on progress toward a synthesis where the debate is resolved.

The best way to protect yourself from the poverty of this—and many other—debates about the media is to build a strong knowledge structure about how media effects occur. A key idea in that knowledge structure is that effects come about from a process of influence where many factors alter the probability of the effect occurring. We must also consider thresholds; non-linear relationships; contingencies; necessary and sufficient conditions; indirect influences as well as direct ones; and countervailing influences.

Media-literate people avoid the trap of looking for a simple deterministic causal influence. Instead, there are many factors in the influence, and each of these factors increases the probability of an effect occurring.

The effects process is complex. That is why it requires a person of relatively high media literacy to appreciate the situation. People who are at low levels of media literacy will either believe there is no effect because they do not know what to look for, or they will focus on artifacts that might not be attributable to the media. Either way, low-level media literacy misleads people by giving them a false sense of awareness.

Despite the complexity of determining what a media effect is, we do know there is a wide range of effects from minor to serious effects. Knowing the factors that increase the probability of an effect occurring is the first step in the process of controlling their influence on you.

EXERCISE 16.1

Profiling the Probability of an Effect

1. Analyze a particular media effect along with its pattern of factors that would influence the probability of the effect actually occurring. For example, choose the viewing of a violent movie and its potential effect on your behaving aggressively immediately after viewing the film.

   a. Look at the 10 contributing factors in this chapter and use them to write a profile of the characteristics that would need to be present in the film and in you that would increase the probability of your behaving aggressively. For example, under context of portrayals, what contextual characteristics would need to be in the film in order to increase the probability of an aggressive effect.

   b. Now using the same 10 contributing factors as a guide, write a profile that would keep the probability of an aggressive effect as low as possible.

   c. Look at the two profiles. Which one is closer to what you experience in your life? Are there factors about you personally that put you at risk for this type of effect? Are there characteristics about the films you typically see that increase your risk?

2. Do the same exercise above with another effect. Refer to Chapters 14 and 15 for choices.

3. Think about the possible effects of the media in your life and try to apply the following ideas:

   a. *Thresholds:* Have you noticed no effect in some area until you passed a certain level of exposure? What was the effect and the level of threshold exposure?

   b. *Non-Linear Relationships:* Can you think of a non-linear relationship in your life between media exposure and some effect? Can you draw a diagram of the shape of that non-linear relationship?

   c. *Contingent Conditions:* Can you think of something that had an effect on you but not on your friends or family? What was the contingent condition that put you at risk but not the other people?

   d. *Necessary Versus Sufficient Conditions:* Think of a particular media effect, such as newspaper political advertising changing viewers' voting opinions. Are there any sufficient conditions? Are there any necessary conditions?

   e. *Direct and Indirect:* Can you think of any indirect effects the media have had on you? For example, have your friends formed an opinion from media messages then gotten you to adopt that opinion without your ever being exposed to the original media messages?

CHAPTER

17

Key Idea: The media, especially television, have fundamentally changed many of our institutions.

Media Influence on Institutions

The effect of the media is not limited to individuals. The media also profoundly influence our institutions. Some institutions, such as politics, have changed fundamentally due to the direct influence of the media, especially television. Some—such as the family, society, and religion—have changed because of many different social pressures, while the media have served to heighten these pressures. And media have brought about the emergence of other institutions, such as sports.

In this chapter, we examine how the media have influenced these five institutions. The more you know about the present character of these institutions, the more you can appreciate the power of the media. This chapter also illustrates how the media can have an indirect effect on you through these institutions. The more you understand about these dynamics, the more media literate you will be.

FAMILY ▪▪

Decline of the Traditional Family

In the span of just one generation, the makeup of the American family has changed radically. The number of traditional two-parent families has shrunk, eclipsed by childless couples, single parents, and people living alone (Perkins, 1996). From the early 1970s to 1998, the percentage of American households made up of married couples with children dropped from 45% to 26%. Marriage has also dropped from 75% of all adults in 1972 being married, to 56% in 1998. Also, the percentage of children living with single parents went from 4.7% in 1972 to 18.2% in 1998 (Irvine, 1999).

One argument for the cause in the decline of the traditional family is that the rates of divorce are very high in this country, and they have been climbing since television first penetrated our culture. In 1960, 16% of first marriages ended in divorce; by 1996 the figure had climbed to 40% (Whitman, 1996).

The steep rise in the divorce rate took place during the same time period that television went from an innovation to the dominant mass medium. But this is only a pattern of covariation. Just because the two went up together does not mean that one caused the other. Recall from the previous chapter that demonstrating causation—especially deterministic causation—calls for a stronger argument. Such an argument requires two elements beyond covariation: (a) the cause preceding the presumed effect in time and (b) the ability to rule out all other explanations for the effect, leaving only the media as the explanation. With this situation, we cannot present a convincing argument for either of these two elements.

But remember that there is also probabilistic causation, which allows for many contributing causes of an effect. Using this perspective on media effects, the important question becomes: Are the media, especially television, one of the contributing factors to the fundamental changes in the American family? The answer to this question appears to be yes for the following reasons.

Television Content About Families

Critics point out that television too frequently portrays divorce, single-parent households, and alternative lifestyles. These portrayals presented over many different kinds of shows and over many years tend to be internalized by viewers. Over time, people become dissatisfied with their own marriages and seek adventure with other partners.

Television Exposure

Television affects the family as a group in terms of how family members spend their time and how they interact with one another. For example, much of television viewing in families is done by individuals viewing by themselves. More than two thirds of all households have more than one TV set, so individual viewing is possible in most homes. Also, with 65% of households having cable, and the average cable service providing more than 50 channels, individual viewing is desirable so family members do not have to compete for the television. Each family member can watch what he or she wants by viewing a separate TV in a separate room.

Families differ in the centrality of television in their homes (Medrich, Roizen, Rubin, & Buckley, 1982). This is a continuum where at one end the television is the center of life and at the other end it is rarely on or is muted. Centrality is related to exposure. Children raised in a house where TV is central will watch more, because the TV is so important to all family members.

Also, the layout of the house influences television viewing patterns. Families who live in traditional homes with a closed floor plan (lots of walls and doors dividing the living space into private rooms) are more likely to view TV individually. Families in community-oriented homes (lots of open space and few doors) prefer communal viewing (Pardun & Krugman, 1994).

Even when family members view television together, there is less interaction than if the television were off and the family members had to entertain one another. For example, over one third of families have TV on during meals and this reduces conversation among family members.

Television viewing also slightly reduces the amount of time parents devote to child care, because it serves as a baby-sitter and substitutes for reading bedtime stories (Comstock, 1989). Parents and children tend to talk less to one another when viewing television, but they are often in close proximity—so there is more touching, hugging, and so on.

Parental Control

Most parents exercise little overt control over the amount or kind of television their children watch. Instead, viewing conventions develop based on power structures in the household. For example, when the members of most families view together, the power is with those who have status—usually the father, followed by the mother, then the older children. Also, viewing control patterns have been found to differ significantly across different types of families. McLeod and Chaffee have identified four kinds of families:

Laissez faire: Parents leave children and each other alone; everyone decides what they do for themselves. Television viewing is usually done individually with each person deciding what to watch and for how long.

Protective: Parents set up lots of rules and impose them on the family. Rules are constructed for "everyone's good." There are strict rules for media use.

Pluralistic: There are lots of discussions and debate; uniqueness of individuals is preserved. Each person seeks out media messages unhampered by others.

Consensual: There are lots of discussions and debate; strong motivation to agree and conform. In these households there are rules for media use, but these rules are developed by the family as a unit.

Even more important than rules is the example set by parents in their own media exposure habits. Television habits are formed early. The amount of television viewed is quite stable from age 3 onward, probably because it depends on family patterns that do not change much over time. Parental example is the strongest influence on children's television uses and abuses.

Also important is how parents interact with their children during exposures. Parents who watch television with their children and help them understand and critique the messages are extremely valuable in helping their children develop higher levels of media literacy. Unfortunately, parents today spend 40% less time with their children than parents did in the 1950s (Pipher, 1996).

When it comes to the media, parents have found their roles changing dramatically. For example, Pipher (1996) points out, "Good parents used to introduce their children into the broader culture; now they try to protect their children from the broader culture. Good parents used to instill the values of the broader culture; now they try to teach their children values very different from the ones the world at large teaches" (p. 11). She argues, "Rapidly our technology is creating a new kind of human being, one who is plugged into machines instead of relationships, one who lives in a virtual reality rather than a family" (p. 92). "When people communicate by email and fax, the nature of human interaction changes" (p. 88). The conveniences of technology serve to cut us off from others. We depend less and less on others (at least face to face). People are things or services, not human beings. She says that 72% of Americans don't know their neighbors, and the number of people who say they have never spent time with the people next door has doubled in the past 20 years. Children are losing social skills as they grow up in a consumer-driven electronic community.

Other Contributing Factors

Even if we accept the argument that television has influenced the trend toward the breakdown of the traditional family, we must realize that there are also other influences, such as economic ones. For example, it takes more money to support a family. The median household income is now just over $30,000. Both adults are likely to work, and this makes it harder for them to have children and raise them at home. The percentage of females in the labor force has been steadily climbing; now about 60% of all females 16 years old and older work (*Statistical Abstract of the United States: 1999*, 2000).

Another reason is that careers have become more important to many people than their families. Wage earners work longer hours, and this takes them away from the home for a higher proportion of their waking hours. There are strong stressors of time, money, and lifestyle that make people regard the home as a place to recover from the workplace, not a place where they have high energy. No longer is family of paramount importance in most people's lives (Pipher, 1996).

Clearly, family structures and interaction patterns have been changing over the past four decades. There are many reasons for this. Television is a key element—but not the only one—in this change. The additional elements of economic demands, rise in the importance of careers, and changes in lifestyle preferences have all contributed to the probability of change in the institution of family.

POLITICS ■■

The mass media have always had an influence on shaping the way politics have been conducted. Since the founding of this country, candidates for political office have relied on coverage of their campaigns in newspapers and magazines, and they have bought ads in these media in order to get their messages out to the electorate and to create an image for themselves. When William Henry Harrison ran for President in 1840, he wanted to change his image so he would appeal more to the voters, who were mostly common people who distrusted the rich. He was afraid of being perceived as an aristocrat, because he was the wealthy son of a governor and the owner of a palatial Georgian mansion on a 2,000-acre estate worked by tenant farmers. Instead, he wanted to be perceived as a farmer and backwoodsman in order to increase his appeal to the electorate. In his newspaper ads, he was shown wearing a coonskin cap and drinking cider by a log cabin. This image was everywhere during the campaign.

At about the same time, Daniel Webster created the first political pseudo-event for the press. He camped out with Green Mountain boys in the woods and challenged to a fist fight anyone who called him an aristocrat.

Harrison won his election, but Webster lost his. Using the media does not guarantee victory. But not using the media can guarantee defeat. Candidates for public office from city council to President of the United States must establish name recognition among the electorate; and along with a recognized name, they must instill a positive image. The media are the channels that make it possible for candidates to achieve these goals quickly and across many people.

When radio came along, politicians used it to reach more of the electorate. In the 1930s, Thomas Dewey, a crusading New York City district attorney, ran for governor. On the final day of the campaign, he was on radio from 6 a.m. until midnight, inviting people to phone in and ask him questions. Most of the calls were from one of his assistants who spent the day in a phone booth with a pile of coins.

When television came along in the 1950s, politics began to change dramatically. Since that time, there has been a gradual and continual erosion of the amount of influence the political parties are able to exert. No longer do people have to be a member of a political party and go to its functions in order to feel informed and involved. Now primary elections are much more important, and the party's nominating conventions are much less important. But the biggest change is in the cost of campaigning, because it is essential to use television, and television is very expensive.

Primaries

Television has increased the importance of primary elections for Presidential candidates. The nomination of Presidential candidates used to be decided in party caucuses and conventions. In 1940, primary elections were held in only 13 states. By 1976, 30 states had primaries. Now almost every state has either a primary election or a caucus.

Now someone who wants to run for President must do well in the early primaries to get press coverage. Candidates who do not do well are not put on the press's agenda, and the public rarely hears about them. Those candidates who do well get a great deal of coverage, and this is free publicity for their campaigns.

Nominating Conventions

The media have changed the Presidential nominating conventions of political parties by focusing so much of the public's attention on them. The historical purpose of these conventions was for the loyal party members to gather at a national meeting to cut deals and weald power. The result of all this negotiation was to select a candidate to represent the party in the Presidential election. Now, the candidates are known well in advance of the "nominating" conventions, so those meetings have been transformed into advertising platforms for the parties. Thus the delegates are instructed to give a favorable impression of the party to the public. This means showing harmony and togetherness rather than debating important issues.

Campaign Spending

Television's increasing importance in political campaigns has resulted in great increases in campaign spending. In the early days of television, expenditures on the media for political advertising increased 600% (adjusted for inflation) between 1952 and 1974 (Comstock, 1980). By 1972 spending was greatly increased in the Presidential election, with McGovern spending $30 million and Nixon $60 million. The reason for the increase was a major shift in the way the campaigns allocated their money. For example, in 1956, 85% of Presidential campaign expenditures was for setting up rallies for in-person speeches by the candidates. Three elections later, with total expenditures four times greater, more than half the money was spent on television ads (Comstock, 1989). And the television budget continued to increase dramatically, resulting in smaller budgets for field operations, such as setting up rallies, local campaign offices, buttons, bumper stickers, and more.

Shortly after the 1972 Presidential election, where the candidates spent $90 million, Congress passed some campaign reform legislation that placed strict limits and regulations on spending. In the 1976 election, each candidate spent about $9 million.

Despite the limits imposed by Congress, the money required to run for President is increasing dramatically again, and a good deal of it is being spent very early in the campaigns. Candidates must spend huge amounts of money early to get name recognition. For example, in 1984, the Democratic front runner, Walter Mondale, spent more than $30 million to win a single primary. His two challengers (Jackson and Hart) spent a total of more than $21 million in a losing effort—that is more than $55 million spent by Democratic candidates in a single state! The Republican was Ronald Reagan, an incumbent President at the time and running unopposed in the primaries, spent $18 million. When the primary campaigns were over, Mondale was nominated as the Democratic candidate and Reagan as the Republican candidate. During the general election that fall, the two Presidential candidates were each allowed to spent $40 million, which was the limit imposed by Congress. But Political Action Committees (PACs), which were not regulated, were allowed to raise as much as they could and spend it any way they wanted. The wealthy right-wing National Conservative Political Action Committee spent $14 million to campaign for Reagan.

Politics has become a very big money game. In the 1996 Presidential election, over $152 million of federally approved funds were spent—this is the money raised and spent by the Presidential candidates according to limits and procedures imposed by the Federal Election Commission. Also, over $477 million of federally approved funds were spent on Congressional races. In addition to federally approved spending, Political Action Groups can raise their own money and spend it in their own public relations campaigns to support a candidate or to run negative ads against their candidate's opponents. In 1996, PACs spent $430 million for these campaigns. Thus more than $1 billion was spent in one year's election campaigns for President and Congress (*Statistical Abstract of the United States: 1999*, 2000).

When people say that "too much" is spent on political advertising it is not clear what they think the "correct" amount ought to be. This is the point made by columnist George Will (1996), who says that the annual sum spent on political campaigning is less than that spent on yogurt. Also when you take a 2-year period and include all the money spent by all candidates campaigning for state and federal offices, it equals the same amount as that spent by the nation's two largest commercial advertisers—Procter & Gamble and Philip Morris. This $700 million works out to be a combined total across all elections of $1.75 per eligible voter per year.

Content of Advertising

Critics also complain that much political advertising is either negative or fluff (non-informational). Roger Ailes, the media consultant who produced the new Nixon in 1968, agrees, saying that television is only good for covering three things: visuals, attacks, and mistakes. As a result of this reasoning, there have been high proportions of negative ads in Presidential campaigns. For example, in the 1988 Presidential election, 70% of ads were negative. In the 1996 campaign, about half of all the money spent by PACs was on ads *against* a particular candidate (*Statistical Abstract of the United State: 1999*, 2000).

Campaigns that are played out in the media are typically dominated by sound bites—the short story with a catchy phrase. Sound bites are so short that they do not give the candidate an opportunity to convey his or her position with any sophistication or depth. The sound bite appears to have gotten so short that it cannot shrink anymore. The sound bites stopped shrinking at about 9 seconds in length after a steady decline from 43 seconds in 1968.

Campaign Staffs

The increase in television involvement in political campaigns has altered the makeup of campaign staffs. The most important person in a campaign used to be the campaign manager, who had extensive contacts among party workers and could pull in favors and get lots of members active in setting up rallies, passing out bumper stickers, and going door to door to hand out party literature. Now the most valued people in the campaign are the public opinion polling expert and the media consultant.

The polling expert finds out what the public wants in a "leader"—that is, how the candidate should look, how the candidate should act, and the stand the candidate should take on important issues. The media consultant then crafts ads and pseudo-events for the media to make the candidate appear like that ideal image.

U.S. media experts are being hired to influence elections in other countries. Both major political parties in Israeli hired expensive American consultants to run their 1999 election campaigns for prime minister (Makovsky, 1999).

News Coverage

The press usually presents campaigns as horse races. In an analysis of over 1,300 election stories carried by ABC, CBS, and NBC during the 1988 primaries, it was found that more than 500 dealt with who appeared to be winning and another 300 dealt with campaign strategies, for a total of more than 60% of the coverage. This clearly exhibits the horse race mentality. In contrast, only about one story in six covered the issues ("Campaign '88," 1988).

The front runner is the candidate who wins the very first primary. The press then creates expectations for candidates and the campaign outcome. Throughout the campaign, the press reports polls to set up these benchmarks about who is winning and by how much. When something different than the expected occurs, it is deemed newsworthy.

Media coverage fluctuates with the performance of the candidate in the preceding contest. The most attention generally goes to the candidate who was the winner or who has emerged surprisingly as the challenger. Candidates who falter become progressively less able to compete, because they begin slipping off the media agenda (Patterson, 1980).

There is a trend toward using new sources of information on politics—such as on MTV and talk shows (e.g., *Larry King Live*). Hollander (1995) found that attention to MTV and late night shows is not related to gains in political knowledge, but instead to attention to talk shows.

Agenda Setting

Media can directly affect how people process information about political events, and this priming effect influences behavior (Iyengar & Kinder, 1987). By focusing on some issues and ignoring others, the media set the agenda for the campaign. The agenda alters the public's priorities. The high-priority issues, then, are what the public focuses on when examining the stance of candidates. Thus if a candidate is strong on many issues and weak on one, and the press gives that one issue high priority, then the public will think that issue is very important and therefore rate that candidate low.

In summary, television has made it possible for candidates to quickly build name recognition and plant a favorable image in the minds of the voters. But this comes at a high price. Television advertising is very expensive and thus requires candidates to raise large sums of money continually. There is also a price to the institution of politics, which has been forever changed.

There are some key benefits to this change. As voters, we are given a lot more information about candidates, and media attention to the campaigns begins earlier. Also, with this additional information and the opportunity to vote in primaries, we are given more power to select the candidates who will run in the general elections. But there is also a downside—the information we are given about the candidates is usually very superficial and often negative. And the mainstream media also set the agenda, thus channeling our interest to a few selected topics and away from all others. We can counteract this downside by being careful to analyze the information we do get and to seek out more extensive and intensive information to build stronger knowledge structures about the political process and its players.

■■ RELIGION

Commitment to religious institutions has been dropping in this country, especially among younger people such as the 76.5 million people in the generation known as the baby boomers, who were those born between 1946 and 1964. About two thirds of these baby boomers dropped out of organized religion during the past several decades, although some of them are starting to return (Woodward, 1990). Even so, about 80% of Americans consider themselves religious and believe in life after death. But only 57% (43 million people) attend a church or synagogue on a regular basis.

The Bible is still the all-time best-selling book. Sales continue to grow—up 50% during the past few years; 91% of all Americans own an average of three versions. However, fewer people are spending time reading it, with the result that there is Bible illiteracy. More than half of Americans can't name even five of the Ten Commandments, and two thirds don't know the names of the four gospels. Religious organizations are trying to jazz up the old book, and now there are more than 3,000 different editions designed to appeal to different readers. It is being promoted by celebrities such as Hammer, the rap artist, and Sinbad, the comedian. Newer versions of the Bible include: the TouchPoint Bible, which is organized by topics such as anger and self-control; the Positive Thinking Bible, by Norman Vincent Peale; the Devotional Bible for Dads, which is folksy and chatty; and the Complete Idiot's Guide to the Bible.

Some newer versions of the Bible display a high degree of political correctness. For example, some versions have changed "Son of Man" to "Human One" and the Lord's Prayer reads: Our Father-Mother who art in heaven (Watanabe, 1999).

Religion on Television

Religious programs have been on television ever since its earliest days in the 1950s, but it was not until the 1970s that this type of programming became very visible. There is a controversy over how large the viewing audience is for religious television. The televangelists claim that the audience is very large. In contrast, Fore (1987) says that the audience for the electronic church is far smaller than claimed. In surveys, about 71 million people say they have watched one of these programs each week. But Nielsen diaries put the figure at about 24.7 million a week, and this is a duplicated audience; the unduplicated figure is about 13.3 million who watch at least 15 minutes a week. The number who watch for an hour or more is less than 4 million. Only the top religious programs draw an audience of more than 2 million viewers (Horsfield, 1984). The demographics of the audience are more female, older, lower educated, lower income, and more blue-collar (Hoover, 1988; Horsfield, 1984).

The best predictor of religious program viewership is whether a person is affiliated with a church. It is the churchgoers who watch religious TV. Thus, religious programs are preaching to the converted and do not serve many nonchurchgoers (Horsfield, 1984). Fore (1987) says that about 77% of the heavy viewers are church members who attend services fairly regularly. About 14% said they watch religious television instead of going to church. The viewing of religious television seems to be associated with church attendance, giving, and private religious behaviors like prayer and Bible reading (Hoover, 1988). Therefore, the effect of these shows is possible reactivation of inactive members or channeling members from one church to another.

Religious programming on television is shaped by the same forces that shape television content in general (Horsfield, 1984). The three major forces are:

1. Sensationalism: There is a strong emphasis on producing material that will quickly capture and hold viewers' attention.

2. Instant gratification: Programmers strive to provide immediate answers to easily defined problems.

3. Oversimplification: Programming avoids in-depth, demanding analyses of issues, events, and human relationships and instead relies heavily on stereotyped characters, plots, and relationships.

Money

A big theme on all religious programs is the appeal for money. In 1983, Abelman (cited in Fore, 1987) conducted a content analysis of the 40 leading religious shows and found that in an average hour, the viewer was asked to donate $328; a person who watches 2 hours a week is subject to direct appeals for about $31,500 a year. Most of these appeals are to allow the televangelist to stay on the air, not to fund missions to help clothe or feed people.

Figures for yearly contributions in the late 1970s were: $60 million to Oral Roberts, $46 million to Christian Broadcasting Network, and $20 million to Jimmy Swaggart (Horsfield, 1984). By 1983, Pat Robertson's CBN brought in $101 million, of which $89 million came in as donations. In 1985, Jim Bakker's PTL Club had an income of $72.1 million, with $42 million in direct contributions and the rest earned from a new $30-million Victorian style hotel and biblical theme park, the 2,500-acre Heritage USA. PTL's expenses that year were $89.7 million. Jimmy Swaggart generated about $45 million annually in the 1980s, 80% of which was spent to keep his show on the air (Fore, 1987).

Television's Influence on Individuals' Religious Experiences

What do viewers get from watching religious television programs? Hoover (1988) argues that the electronic church has had a revitalizing effect by recognizing individuals' experiences of dissonance, frustration, and cultural crises. By depicting the culture as out of control, religious programs present themselves as offering stability and a clear purpose. They have done this by developing a total, universal explanation of life that proposes to resolve the dissonances felt in contemporary life.

What is the appeal of the electronic church? Fore (1987) explains that the electronic church appears authoritative at a time when authority appears to be in disarray. It highlights competition between God and the devil. It places emphasis on individuals as the foundational societal unit and charges them to act. And it is generally affirming of the social values most people hold, and it reinforces this belief system with attractive personalities.

Television's Influence on the Institution of Religion

Some social critics, such as Hoover (1988), argue that the main effect of the electronic church has not been the changing of people's beliefs. Instead the main effect of the electronic church has been the changing of the institution of religion in America. How has religious television done this? It has broken down denominational boundaries, thus bringing evangelicals and fundamentalists into the mainstream. And it has changed the way we see politics and religion—the electronic church has taken on a political prominence.

Television as Religion

Some scholars think of television as becoming a dominant institution that has taken over some of the functions of religion (Gerbner & Gross, 1976). They say that television implicitly communicates values and interpretations of the world by presenting lessons about success, power, and dominance. By conveying status to certain people, television identifies those people much like priests who guide our thinking.

Television is seen by some as the new American religion:

> Television is the new "cultural storyteller," an agent of norms and values as much as of news and information. Television fulfills this function very much in the way traditional storytellers did—by a process of dialectic, not didactic—where the stories evolve with the culture, retaining most, but not all, of their formal integrity by changing to suit its audiences and new contexts of expression. (Hoover, 1988, p. 241)

Fore (1987) says that television is

> beginning to replace the institution that historically has performed the functions we have understood as religious. Television, rather than churches, is becoming the place where people find a worldview which reflects what to them is the ultimate value, and which justified their behavior and way of life. Television today, whether the viewer knows it or not, and whether the television industry itself knows it or not, is competing not merely for attention and dollars, but for our very souls. (p. 24)

> Television is itself becoming a kind of religion, expressing the assumptions, values, and belief patterns of many people in our nation, and providing an alternative worldview to the old reality, and to the old religious view based on that reality. (pp. 24, 25)

These writers are very critical of the idea that television is becoming the dominant religion in this society. "The values, assumptions, and worldview of television's 'religion' are in almost every way diametrically opposed to the values, assumptions, and worldview of Christianity and the historic Judeo-Christian tradition in which the vast majority of American profess to believe" (Fore, 1987, p. 25). Also, Hoover (1988) cautions that contemporary religion is at odds with many of TV's messages—the messages of materialism rather than of sharing and asceticism; force and violence dominate the value systems instead of love and cooperation; classes of people are objectified and manipulated, not encouraged and cared for. Many evangelists see TV as secular humanism that is competing with the values they espouse; therefore, TV is the enemy.

Critics fear that the technological worldview poses three threats to religion (Fore, 1987). First, it is diverting a major portion of the world's interests, motivations, satisfactions, and energies away from a religious center. Second, it is robbing genuine religious vocabularies of their power as people know more about TV characters than religious symbols and figures. Third, the new technological environment encourages the growth of religious concern that rejects or ignores organized religion. People spend more time with electronic devices than they do with people. With increasing channels and content options, people can pick only those things that reinforce already held beliefs. This puts the development of beliefs into the hands of individuals rather than the institution of religion. Thus, communication is treated more as a commodity to serve an individual's immediate needs, rather than as a broad cultural phenomenon that brings us together into a large community where the needs of the community are more important than the needs of any individual.

Fore (1987) contrasts the central myths of television with the central values of religion. He says television presents five myths: (a) The fittest survive (social Darwinism); (b) Power and decision making start at the center and move out (Washington, D.C., is the center of political power; New York the center of financial power; Hollywood the center of entertainment power); (c) Happiness consists of limitless material acquisition (corollaries include that consumption is inherently good and that people are less important than property, wealth, and power); (d) Progress is an inherent good (it is good to keep moving but it is less important to have a goal); and (e) There exists a free flow of information (this is a myth, because there is almost no chance for non-establishment information to get a wide hearing).

Television is forcing churches to adapt. Comstock (1989) says, "In the case of cultures in which traditional religious observances have a visible and important place, television is one of the central components of modernization that channels public energies toward secular pursuits" (p. 246). As people become more secular, religion has to adapt either by fighting against the trend of secularization and thus becoming less relevant to people's everyday lives, or it must change its values. For example, in Israel, television took time away from participation in celebrations and activities associated with Jewish religious practice, so television broadcasting was outlawed on the Sabbath. But the public demanded that the prohibition be lifted, and it was (Katz & Gurevitch, 1976).

In summary, the key benefit of religious programs in the media is that they provide more experiences to worship for those people who are already religious. But critics are concerned that television itself has become a religion, as evidenced by many people's ritualized viewing. This has critics worried, because the values presented on television are very different from the values presented by organized religion.

SPORTS ■

Focus on Money

Sports have changed dramatically over the past four decades. The reason is big money. Not only have the revenues been skyrocketing; now the focus of sports is almost exclusively on money.

To illustrate this trend, in 1959 Red Sox star Ted Williams returned his contract unsigned to management; that is, he rejected the $125,000 offer. Coming off a year in which he hit "only" .259, he felt he was not worth all that money so he asked for a pay cut of 25%, which was the maximum pay cut possible.

Those days are gone. Over the past 30 years, salaries for baseball players have been increasing rapidly. In 1995, the average salary was $1,110,766 per baseball player. In total, baseball clubs spent $924 million for players. The range is pretty wide across clubs, with the New York Yankees at the top with their average player making $2,000,271. Montreal had the lowest average salary at $411,142 ("Average Baseball Salaries," 1995).

Football salaries are also high. In the 1995 NFL season, the salary cap was $37.1 million per club, and 26 of the 30 teams in the league went over that maximum. Dallas spent the most at $62.2 million; Jerry Jones—the owner of the Dallas Cowboys—spent almost $40.5 million in signing bonuses, including $13 million to Deion Sanders. Seattle had the lowest payroll at $33.3 million ("NFL Teams," 1996). Four years later, in the 1999 season, salaries were even higher. Dallas paid its players $55 million in salaries and bonuses, but the Cowboys' spending was matched by the Arizona Cardinals and were outspent by the Tennessee Titans ($56 million), New England Patriots ($57 million), and the Tampa Bay Buccaneers ($58 million). Even the most frugal team (the Oakland Raiders) spent $40 million. The median earnings of the 2,000 NFL players in the 1999 season was $430,000. Five players (Troy Aikman, Drew Bledsoe, Brett Favre, Deion Sanders, and Warren Sapp) were each paid more than $6.2 million for that one season. Another 50 players were paid more than $3 million, and an additional 400 players made more than $1 million each ("National Football League 1999 Salaries," 2000).

Michael Jordan earned $4 million for the 1995-1996 season when he led the Chicago Bulls to their fourth professional basketball championship in 6 years. He was named the most valuable player of the year, and many regard him as the best basketball player of all time. Yet his salary ranked him the 27th highest paid player in the league at the time. After becoming a free agent, he was signed for $18 million per year, making him the highest paid player in the league—temporarily. How high can salaries go? Several years ago the NBA instituted a salary cap per team. The 1996-1997 salary cap for the Bulls was $24.3 million. But the Bulls were able to pay Jordan whatever they wanted because the salary cap does not apply to the resigning of a team's existing players (Rhodes & Reibstein, 1996).

The owner of the Chicago Bulls, Jerry Reinsdorf, could afford it, because the value of his franchise climbed from $17.5 million in 1985—Jordan's rookie year—to $178 million in 1996. The owner had a huge yearly income from broadcast rights, merchandising, and ticket sales. The Bulls play at the United Center where there are 216 suites, each selling for $175,000. All games were sold out, and there was a waiting list of over 17,000 fans for season tickets.

Players have been demanding higher salaries and getting them. Owners have been cultivating additional revenue streams, such as luxury skyboxes at stadiums, apparel merchandising, and very lucrative television contracts. When players ask for more money, the owners must pay them. The owners then raise the prices of tickets, concessions, parking, apparel, and other souvenirs. For example, Superbowl tickets sell for between $200 and $350 a seat—that's the list price.

Sports and Television

The biggest increase in sports revenue is from television. Without a television contract, no sports league could survive. The American Football League got started in the early 1960s with a TV deal for $1.7 million. In 1965, CBS got the National Football League (NFL) rights for $14.1 million. Now 30 years later the NFL sells a year's broadcasting rights for $500 million per season. This sum is so large that it is shared by five networks: ABC, NBC, ESPN, Fox, and TNT.

Television broadcasters pay these huge fees to sports organizations, because broadcasters know that large numbers of us will watch. Broadcasters then rent us out to advertisers willing to pay huge sums for the opportunity to get their commercial messages in front of us. In its broadcast of the 2000 Superbowl, ABC generated revenues of $130 million. Their three dozen advertisers paid an average of $2.2 million per 30-second spot—up 38% from the 1999 Superbowl.

The increase was driven by higher demand from 17 Internet site advertisers ("Superbowl Ad Costs," 1999).

The list of most popular sports on television is headed by the NFL with an average rating of 16; major league baseball is second with an 11.1. The cost of a 30-second ad in football is about $130,000, and about $80,000 in baseball. Golf and tennis are the least popular sports with average ratings of about 4.5 and 3.8, respectively. But these sports deliver a high-quality audience, one that is very affluent and hence very attractive to companies who advertise luxury products.

With television and advertisers putting so much money into these sports, they demand that the sports be exciting. So they have forced some changes to the games themselves. For example, basketball now has a shot clock that requires players to shoot the ball much more often. Basketball now has the 3-point play, which is much riskier and hence more exciting. Football has the 2-minute warning (new in the mid 1960s) and television time outs. Uniforms are more colorful. All of this is to increase viewer interest and thereby provide advertisers with a better audience.

Advertisers also want the coverage to be more entertaining. For example, the coverage of a football game takes more than 3 hours, although the game itself takes 60 minutes and there is less than 10 minutes of action on the field during the 60 minutes that the clock is running. So the announcers must provide lots of anecdotes, statistics, and color commentary. The director must provide lots of replays, slow motions, shots of the crowd and cheerleaders, and so on.

The NFL has gotten extremely greedy. This is illustrated in the way Los Angeles was treated in 1999. At that time, the NFL wanted Los Angeles, which is the second largest media market in the country, to have an NFL franchise. A Los Angeles billionaire put together an ownership group. The city put in $150 million in state revenue bonds to build parking structures around an existing facility—the Los Angeles Coliseum. But the NFL Commissioner, Paul Tagliabue, objected to the deal, saying that the municipality was not putting in enough taxpayer money and because of this the team would not be profitable for its owners—projecting an annual profit of only $25 to $28 million per year. The city of Houston offered $200 million in public money for a new stadium, plus private investment in an adjacent football museum. When the city of Los Angeles would not put more taxpayer money into its offer, the NFL awarded the franchise to Houston (Flanigan, 1999).

Sports Marketing

Companies are willing to grant huge fees to athletes who endorse their products, because such endorsements work to increase sales. For example, in 1985 when Boris Becker signed a multi-million dollar deal to promote Puma tennis shoes and rackets, the company's sales increased 25%. John McEnroe's endorsement of Bic disposable razors increased the company's market share from 12% to 23% of total razor sales.

Sports marketing has really grown by focusing on product endorsements by athletes. In 1983, $25 million was spent on endorsements; by 1988 that had doubled to $50 million. By the time he retired as a basketball player in 1999, Michael Jordan was making more than $40 million per year in product endorsements.

Event Sponsorship

Businesses are happy to contribute large sums of money to sports—as long as those businesses get high visibility for themselves in return. For example, Frito-Lay gave $15 million to the Fiesta Bowl and in return received 3 years of sponsorship rights to that college football game. This means that the name of the game was changed to the Tostitos Fiesta Bowl and that this name had to appear on all the signage and be mentioned by all announcers referring to the game.

By 1986, more than 2,100 companies were sponsoring sporting events and spending a total of more than $1 billion a year on all kinds of sports. This money bought some companies the leverage to change the names of some sporting events. The Boston Marathon was renamed the John Hancock Boston Marathon, and the Sugar Bowl football game was renamed the USF&G Sugar Bowl. This advertising money gives sponsors a stronger presence at particular sporting events, and sometimes their ads can overwhelm the sporting event itself. For example, Budweiser sponsored the Marvin Hagler-Sugar Ray Leonard middleweight fight in 1987. For $750,000 it got the right to cover the ring mat and the ring posts with its logo.

The Olympic Games

Even the Olympic Games have become a huge revenue generator. In 1964, NBC paid $1.5 million to the International Olympic Committee for the rights to broadcast the Tokyo Summer Olympics. By 1980, the cost had skyrocketed to $85 million when NBC acquired rights to the Moscow Summer Olympics, despite the fact that the Soviets wanted $210 million plus $50 million in production equipment to be left behind. The broadcast was never made, though, due to the boycott of the 1980 games by the American government. ABC paid $225 million for the Los Angeles Summer Games in 1984, and $91 million for the Winter Games in Sarajevo. Despite losing money on the Winter Games, ABC came back with an even higher bid of $309 million for the 1988 Winter Games in Calgary. NBC acquired the rights to broadcast the 1988 Summer Games in Seoul, Korea, for $300 million. NBC paid $456 million for the 1996 Atlanta games, while CBS bid $375 million to broadcast the 1998 Nagano Games in the Winter Olympics. NBC broke its record by bidding $705 million for exclusive U.S. rights to broadcast the 2000 Summer Games in Sydney, Australia, and another $545 million for the 2002 Winter Games in Salt Lake City. The total NBC package is worth about $1.3 billion—none of the other U.S. networks entered a bid (Nelson, 1995). NBC recently bid $2.3 billion for the rights to the Summer Olympic games in 2004 and 2008 and the Winter Games in 2006 even before the sites were decided ("NBC Gambles on the Future," 1996).

Where does this money go? It is paid to the International Olympic Committee (IOC), which also sells rights to broadcast the games to media in other countries. When ABC paid $309 million for the 1988 Winter Games, the EBU (European Broadcast Union, which represents 32 countries and a population of several hundred million) paid $5.7 million, and the Soviet Union along with its Eastern European allies, North Korea, and Cuba, paid a combined total of $1.2 million. Thus it is clear that the United States (or rather advertisers on U.S. television) really support the games—without them, the Olympics would be very different.

The Olympics have become a major venue for advertising. The modern Olympics have always accepted advertising. In 1896 there were ads for Kodak. Coke began its association with the games in 1928. But as the games got more expensive, planners needed more advertising revenue. The 1976 games in Montreal experienced a $1-billion deficit. By 1984, the Los Angeles games showed a $215-million profit (Manning, 1987). Now, almost all athletes have corporate logos on their clothing. Sponsorships are sold for each event and for the games in general. Companies use the event as an opportunity for global marketing.

In 1984 the Olympic Games in Los Angeles became the first to be supported entirely by commercial sponsorship, and they made a big profit. VISA alone spent $25 million on the rights to be the only credit card allowed to advertise at the Olympic Games and on promotions. An additional 146 corporations were official sponsors of various events. By the 1996 games in Atlanta, the IOC had signed 180 companies and brands to contracts allowing them to promote themselves at that Olympics (Grimm, 1996). The top 10 of these official sponsors (such as Coke and IBM) paid a total of $2.1 billion (Jensen & Ross, 1996). This more than offset the total cost of $1.7 billion for holding the 1996 Atlanta games (Boswell, 1996). The Olympics are very profitable for the IOC.

The Olympics are less profitable for the television network that outbids its competitors and is awarded the rights to broadcast the games. This huge expense for the broadcast rights is only the beginning. Production is another big expense. In the 1984 Los Angeles Summer Olympics, the United States sent

500 athletes to compete; ABC sent 3,500 people (1,400 engineers, 1,800 support personnel, 300 network production and management people). To produce 188 hours of coverage, they used 205 cameras, 660 miles of camera cables, four helicopters, three houseboats, 26 mobile units, 35 office trailers, and 404 hardwired commentary positions. There were microphones on basketball backboards, underwater in the diving pool, in boxing ringposts, and in equestrian saddles. The cost of covering the games was $100 million. This is why the television networks must sell a great deal of advertising. For the 1996 games in Atlanta, NBC sold a total of $675 million of ad time to 50 advertisers. More airtime was devoted to commercials than to the actual sports action (Farhi & Shapiro, 1996).

In summary, sports have become more exciting and entertaining to the general viewer over the past several decades. The public is showing increased interest in sporting events and personalities of all kinds. But the price for this continues to climb. As a viewer, you pay the price in the form of higher cost of admission to games as well as more frequent interruptions of televised games for advertising messages.

■■ SOCIETY

The same forces that are fragmenting politics, religion, and the family are also fragmenting society. But there is some irony in this situation, because on the surface, the media appear to be a unifying force. The mass media give us the illusion that we are all experiencing the same messages. When we see a show on TV or hear a song, we often assume that everyone else has also seen it or heard it. Or when we read about a national figure in the newspaper or magazine, we assume every one else in our society also knows who that person is. People get the feeling everyone else is tied into the same things that they are. But this is an illusion.

Instead, the media are serving to fragment us, that is, we are becoming more and more different from one another as we share smaller and smaller sets of shared experiences over time. How? Although we all have *access* to the same messages, we cannot possibly *expose* ourselves to them all. For example, you probably have access to 50 different television stations, but you can watch only one at a time. You must make choices. It's our choices that fragment us. Because each of us has a different set of interests, we are all screening out a different set of messages. While our *access* to the media may be the same, everyone is paying attention to a different set of messages. Over time our knowledge structures develop very differently; we have very few shared experiences.

These knowledge structures are what we use for context when we interpret new messages. Because our contexts are so different from one another, our interpretations differ. These differences remind us of how little we have in common. This trend toward difference continues as more messages are made available and we screen in only a very small sub-set of them.

When we look at this fragmentation phenomenon from the media point of view, we find irony. The mass media are driven to appeal to as many of us as possible. For example, programmers at ABC, CBS, Fox, and NBC, as well as Hollywood producers and publishers of general magazines and best-selling books, want to construct messages that appeal to as wide an audience as possible. So they strip away as much context as possible so the messages don't require much in the way of interpretation from their audiences. For example, when you watch a situation comedy on prime-time television, you don't need much contextual information. You are not required to know anything about the history of situation comedies, or their economic nature, or the political environment of getting one on the air. You don't even have to know what the characters did on the last episode in order to follow this episode. Very little is asked of you as a viewer, compared to what is asked of you when you watch a documentary on Egyptian hieroglyphics or a Shakespearean play. With situation comedies, you don't need to bring much context to the viewing. And the viewing of situation comedies does not contribute much to the contexts you already have, so this common viewing along with millions of other people does not really build a common context.

Donnelly (1986) describes this fragmentation of society when he says that we are currently living in an Autonomy Generation that will soon change to a Confetti Generation. In the Autonomy Generation, people believe that each individual is the center of all relevant values:

> We are responsible only to ourselves, and we alone can decide which activities and ways of behaving have meaning for us and which do not. We live subjectively according to our own feelings with little need for outside reference. . . . We interpret life in terms of what's in it for us, seek authenticity by transcending society and external value systems, and insist on being ruled only by the laws of our character. . . . We live in the present, responding to momentary perceptions, relationships, and encounters. To us, what is most important is how outside events are perceived and understood by the individual. (p. 178)

He says we experience what Durkheim called *anomie,* the peculiar pain derived from individuals' inability to identify and experience their community.

Donnelly says that the new electronic media have five characteristics that will affect society: quantity (in terms of availability and use), speed (delivery and satisfaction), weightlessness of images (no context), remoteness (bring faraway information close), and choice (explosion of alternatives). Because the present generation does not possess the cultural tools to absorb such an explosion of information, we will become the Confetti Generation. A Confetti person is inundated by experience but ungrounded in any cultural discipline for arriving at any reality but the self: "We will witness an aggregated version of today when all ideas are equal, when all religions, life-styles, and perceptions are equally valid, and equally indifferent, and equally undifferentiated in every way until given a value by the choice of a specific individual" (pp. 181-182).

Whether Donnelly is overstating the problem remains to be seen. He may be right if the literacy of the people in society does not keep up with the changes in our world.

■■ CONCLUSION

The media have changed institutions, especially television and especially over the last three decades. These institutions affect us, therefore the media exert an indirect effect on us through these institutions.

The family has changed from the traditional two parents with one working outside the home and the other staying home taking care of the children. Television has been blamed for making people more materialistic, so more people have to work longer hours to get the means to buy all the new products that have become necessities: multiple cars, multiple TV sets, stereos, computers, cellular phones, and on and on. Thus people spend more time in the workplace and less time with family members. When the family is together, its members are likely to watch TV in separate rooms. Parents are less likely to watch with their children and to talk about the shows with them. With little adult supervision over television viewing, video game playing, and computer usage, children experience worlds apart from the family. The shared experience is disappearing.

Politics has changed from a process of interpersonal persuasion, speech making, and backroom power deals to one of opinion polling, broadscale negative television ads, and images that look good on television. The power of the primaries (especially the earliest ones) has greatly increased, while the purpose of nominating conventions has evaporated. Now more than ever the campaigning process is driven by big money that allows candidates to produce slick ads and to saturate television audiences with them. Spending lots of money will not guarantee a victory, but spending little money will guarantee a loss.

Religion has moved onto television to provide messages to the already religious. Without advertising, these religious programs depend on the donations of viewers. And they are able to raise a great deal of money each year. For many people in this society, television is becoming a religion, as they structure their time around television viewing in a ritualistic manner, seek to learn the fundamental lessons about life from television, and take great comfort in hearing the news and watching the entertainment.

Sports have made changes to become more entertaining and thus appeal to more viewers. With more viewers, television stations charge advertisers more. Stations pay higher sums of money to owners for the right to cover their sports. The owners become more wealthy. The players demand higher salaries and get them. This upwardly moving spiral of ticket prices, revenues, and salaries accelerates each year. Television coverage makes this spiral possible.

Society is fragmenting. Television has the ability to bring everyone in society together by giving us all common, shared experiences every day. In the early days of television broadcasting this was perhaps the case. But now, with most households able to access 50 or more channels, no two people's viewing habits are the same. We each have an incredible variety of messages at our fingertips. In the pursuit of this variety, we lose the sense of shared community.

The media, especially television, have influenced these changes. But we must be careful not to think that they are the only influence. We live in a complex society where family, sports, religion, politics, society, and many other forces are constantly working, often at cross purposes. The media are important players in all this, because they transmit information about change so quickly and broadly. The pace of life is accelerating. Those who are media literate can have an influence on the direction of that pace—at least for themselves.

FURTHER READING ▪▪

Bianculli, D. (1992). *Teleliteracy: Taking television seriously.* New York: Continuum. (315 pages, including index)

> David Bianculli was a TV critic/columnist for 15 years before writing this book, which is a defense of television. Admitting that 90% of TV content is "crap," he feels that there is nevertheless a great deal of value. He presents a manifesto of 10 points intended to gain more respect for TV. The most interesting part of the book is the first section, where he presents a 150-question literacy quiz (75 questions about TV and 75 about classic literature and music). The TV questions are very easy to answer while the other questions are very difficult. His point is that the population is very TV literate. He also presents a fascinating history of criticism of various forms of literature and music dating back to Plato; this clearly shows that there are people who think every new piece of art is bad and that every new medium is dangerous.

Donnelly, W. J. (1986). *The confetti generation: How the new communications technology is fragmenting America*. New York: Henry Holt. (239 pages, including index)

Donnelly is a former ad-man who retired from Y&R to write this book. His main point is that people (especially Toffler and other futurists) who make predictions about new media focus on the technologies and ignore the audience. Because of this, their projections of media use in the future are way off (e.g., 200-channel cable by 1990).

EXERCISE 17.1

Becoming Sensitive to Changes in Institutions

I. Interview your parents, asking them the following questions. Ask them to think back to when they were your age or younger for their answers.

A. Family

1. What was the most important medium in the household?
2. How many televisions were in the house and who controlled them?
3. Were there viewing rules? Restrictions for kids?
4. Did family members ever read books or magazines to one another?
5. Did family members listen to radio or music together?

B. Politics

1. Where did people get most of their information about political campaigns? Conversations or media? If media, which ones?
2. Did they go to political events, such as rallies, speeches, meetings?
3. Can they remember any political ads? If so, what sticks out in their minds about those ads? Images? Negativity?
4. Do they have any strong memories about news coverage of nominating conventions, the campaign, or election returns?

C. Religion

1. Did they used to listen to religious programs on the radio or watch them on television?
2. What was their opinion of religious leaders at the time?
3. Do they feel that religion has changed in the past several decades? If so, do they think the media had any influence?

D. Sports

1. Did they used to attend sporting events in person?
2. Did they follow sports through the media? If so, which sports and which media?
3. Are they aware of any changes in their favorite sports over the past few decades? If so what is their reaction to those changes?
4. What is their reaction to the salaries paid to athletes today?
5. What is their reaction to the amount of advertising at the games and during media coverage?

II. Next, interview your grandparents and ask them the same questions.

III. Ask yourself the same questions.

IV. Compare the pattern of answers across three generations. Do you see any changes in attitudes, perceptions, or the way people live their lives? If so, can you attribute any of these changes to the media?

PART V

PUTTING IT
ALL TOGETHER

CHAPTER 18

Key Idea: The more primary knowledge we have about our world, the stronger the context we have for evaluating the accuracy and the usefulness of information from the media.

The Importance of Real-World Information

Children recite jingles instead of poetry and they know brand names instead of the names of Presidents. More students can identify Mr. Peanut and Joe Camel than can identify Abe Lincoln or Eleanor Roosevelt. They can identify twenty kinds of cold cereal but not the trees and birds in their neighborhoods.

Pipher, 1996, p. 94

Back in 1922, before the mass media became so dominant in our culture, journalist Walter Lippmann wrote a book called *Public Opinion* in which he said,

"Each of us lives and works on a small part of the earth's surface, moves in a small circle, and of these acquaintances knows only a few intimately. Of any public event that has wide effects, we see at best only a phase and an aspect. . . . Inevitably our opinions cover a bigger space, a longer reach in time, a greater number of things, than we can directly observe. (p. 79)

Our world is far more complex today, which makes his comments even more significant. Are our opinions and beliefs keeping pace with our world? Are we willing to search out more information from a wider variety of sources so that we can use the complexity to arrive at more reasoned opinions? Or do we uncritically accept partial sets of facts and infer simple conclusions? It is a far greater challenge to be media literate today than it was 75 years ago.

IMPORTANCE OF INFORMATION ▪▪

We are immersed in a flood of information. Today, the English language contains about 500,000 words—five times more than 400 years ago during the time that

Shakespeare wrote (Wurman, 1989). The world's great libraries are doubling in size every 14 years, a rate of 14,000% every century. In the early 1300s, the Sorbonne Library in Paris contained only 1,338 books and yet was thought to be the largest library in Europe. Today, there are many libraries with more than 8 million books. Internationally, about 1,000 books are published every day. The total of all printed information doubles every 8 years. More information was produced in the past 30 years than in the previous 5,000.

With this constant flood of messages, we must face the fact that we live in an information society. We cannot avoid being bombarded by information every day. But all this information does not necessarily make us more knowledgeable. There is a difference between information and knowledge. Information is facts, data, and impressions. Knowledge is the construction of information into meaningful structures. In order to construct useful knowledge structures, we must scan for useful information, screen out faulty information, and knit together the elements of good information into a useful pattern. Unless we have good knowledge structures, the flood of information is nothing more than noise; that is, we have little ability to tell what stands out as useful.

In order to be media literate, you need to develop strong knowledge structures on a wide range of topics—about the media and about the real world. This requires that you have a plan that identifies important topics. Then you must actively seek out information on these topics so you can build knowledge structures. Don't passively wait for the media to give you all the information you need.

What is a good plan for identifying real-world topics? This book cannot decide that for you, but it can give you some things to think about, and it can stimulate you to think about developing a plan for yourself.

This chapter is not a catalog of all the knowledge that a media-literate person should have. Such a list would be impossible to provide in the space of one chapter. Several authors have made strong arguments for the importance of such a list (Bloom, 1987; D'Souza, 1991), and a few scholars have attempted to build such a list (Hirsch, 1987; Hirsch, Kett, & Trefil, 1993).

While there is a core of information that, arguably, everyone should have, there are substantial differences across people in what information they will need to become media literate. People operate in different cultures, and they have different interests and different sets of experiences, so their needs for information differ. This chapter therefore presents an argument for the importance of a broad base of knowledge.

Good knowledge structures are essential in protecting media-literate individuals from unwanted effects from the media. The broader and more accurate your knowledge structures are, the more you will be able to orient yourselves toward positive effects and avoid the influence of negative effects. Knowledge structures serve two functions in this process: an orienting function and a confirming function. When we are not very media literate, the media control these functions. Being highly media literate means that we have shifted control of these functions over to ourselves.

Orienting Function

Seldom are messages complete enough for us to understand them without having to draw from some contextual information outside the message. For example, if we read in a story that the United Nations has sent troops into Bosnia, at minimum we need to know what the United Nations and Bosnia are. It would also help to know what the intention of the United Nations is and why it would want to send troops into Bosnia.

It is helpful to think about any media message as a core cluster of facts that sits at the center of a set of progressively larger concentric circles. Each circle contains facts that help us to make meaning of the media story at the center. The more developed our knowledge structure, the wider our context of understanding. Therefore we must be able to access a good deal of general information in order to be able to make meaning from any media story that we might encounter.

Where do people get this orienting knowledge? They need a liberal education. *Liberal* in this sense means broad. People who have a very narrow education—no matter how much deep it is—will have difficulty making meaning out of the many media messages that fall outside of their areas of expertise.

Confirming Function

Typically, in our everyday exposure to the media, we acquire partial sets of facts on topics. The messages often leave out important elements, either because of time or space limitations or because producers assume we would not be interested in more detail. When we have only a partial set of information, we are in danger of inferring wrong patterns about the world. An example of this happens when we view the evening news and see a very partial set of the day's events. Because there is so much crime and harmful action left unbalanced by constructive events, we infer that the world is a mean and violent place. Unless we are given a useful context (such as actual crime rates), we are likely to infer wrong patterns.

Thus when we are exposed to a statement, we need to compare it to a standard in order to be able to judge its merit. If we do not make such a comparison, we simply accept it without evaluating it, so all statements are accepted.

What can serve as a standard to judge new statements? There is no single place to go to get an objective standard. Rather we must develop a skepticism that keeps us continually searching for confirming information. There are two ways to do this.

First, we could go to credible sources of information. Typically, primary sources are more credible than secondary sources. For example, an article we read about a candidate's position is a secondary source—the primary source is the candidate. The secondary source may have presented a complete and accurate account of the candidate's position, but maybe the reporter mis-stated something or left something out. Thus the possibility of distortion is part of the risk of using secondary sources.

Second, we could search out multiple sources and compare the resulting accounts. Following through on the example of the candidate, above, we could search out other magazine, newspaper, and broadcast reports of the candidate's position. We could also ask the candidate's opponent and other people active in politics. From this set of resulting information, we could get a much more accurate fix on what the candidate believes. None of these sources by itself presents the full picture. Even the most primary source—the candidate herself—might be flawed, because she might not point out inconsistencies in her voting record or how her position has changed over time.

These strategies are especially important when dealing with facts illustrated through numbers and percentages. A percentage is the comparison of two numbers; that is, comparing one figure to a base number. Sources might faithfully report a percentage using accurate numbers, but had they made the comparison to a different base number, the entire meaning of the situation would change. For example, after the Health and Human Services department of the federal government released the results of a 16-year tracking study of drug use among the nation's adolescents (12- to 17-year-olds), the lead sentence in a story by the Associated Press was, "A 105 percent jump in teen-agers' drug use since 1992 instantly became a campaign issue" ("Teen Drug Use," 1996). In the ninth paragraph, the story explained that in 1992, 5.3% of adolescents said they had used an illegal drug in the last 30 days and in 1995 the figure was 10.9%. Thus, if we compare 5.3% to 10.9% we get an increase of 5.6%. But if we compare the increase of 5.6% to the 1992 base of 5.3%, the increase is 105%. Which percentage is accurate? They both are—but the two convey really different pictures of drug use.

Another example is the reporting of a survey about women and abortions (Leo, 1996). The Guttmacher Institute, which is strongly in favor of abortion rights, released a report that said that Catholic women have an abortion rate 29% higher than Protestant women. This makes it sound like Catholic women are the heaviest users of abortion. But this is not the case. A closer look at the data indicate that Catholic women have an abortion rate right at the national average. Protestant women have an abortion rate much lower than the national average. So when you compare Catholic women to Protestant women, the rate of abortion is higher with Catholics. But if you compare Catholic women with non-religious women, you find that the rate of abortion among Catholics is only one quarter the rate among non-religious women. Again, which set of facts is accurate? They both are, but the interpretations are very different.

Even if we are highly media literate, we will, of course, still rely on media messages as sources of information. But we will also seek out information from other secondary sources as well as primary sources. By assessing the relative credibility of the sources, we can then weight the relative value of information from each source. And by looking for patterns of consistency in the information across the sources, we can arrive at a more solid understanding of the topic.

TYPE/ OF INFORMATION ■■

There are two types of information: factual and social. We use both the media and real-world institutions as sources of these types of information.

Factual knowledge refers to parameters about the world that are usually not in dispute (not open to individual interpretation). Examples include the size of the population of this country, names of political leaders, final scores of a sporting contests, the distance between cities, and so forth.

Social knowledge relates to shared understandings about human interactions. Examples include the way people should behave in certain roles (such as parent, professor, partier, stranger, colleague, etc.), and the moral themes within a culture or institution.

Need for Factual Information

Social critics have a lot of ammunition when they target the educational system of the United States. For example, the National Assessment of Educational Progress monitors the learning of our nation's youth in public schools. The results of its recent testing were that the majority of America's high school seniors did not know basic facts about U.S. history, and they could not use what they did know to back up their opinions. Among 12th graders, only 43% attained at least the basic level, 11% were proficient, and 1% were advanced. Scores on math and science have been improving, but scores on reading and writing have been going down (Buzbee, 1995).

However, children don't seem to have trouble identifying the celebrities who get the most media coverage. When children ages 9 to 12 were asked to identify names of people, Michael Jordan and Michael Jackson topped the recognition list at 96% of respondents. Hillary Rodham Clinton was recognized by 82%. Boris Yeltsin got 21% and Nelson Mandela was low at 20% ("Names & Faces," 1995).

Thus, it seems that the media, especially television, are the dominant teachers of the nation's youth. But television is largely focused on entertainment and popular culture. It does not teach literature, languages, history, mathematics, or other academic subjects that form the basis of a strong knowledge infrastructure. It does not teach useful skills (such as writing, critical reading, analysis, and problem solving) that are the essential tools of an educated person. The media could teach this type of knowledge and skills, but they prefer instead to focus on entertainment. They are, of course, only responding to what the public wants.

This would not be a problem if the public school system were providing a strong education of core knowledge and skills to all students, and television were used as a minor diversion a few hours a week. However, this is not the case. The public's base of knowledge is very narrow, according to E. D. Hirsch, who wrote a book titled *Cultural Literacy* (1987). He believes that there is a set of core information that the educational system needs to instill in every individual. Without this broad base of general information, individuals cannot be regarded as being educated, that is, they are not literate about the culture within which they live. He argues that the educational system is not fulfilling this function.

The public's level of higher-order skills is also not very strong. For example, in a poll of 400 chief executives conducted by *Fortune* magazine, 77% rated the American public education system as fair or poor—the lowest ratings possible. These business leaders said that they needed an educated workforce that could think, write, analyze, and solve problems in order to function in the information age. They felt that the American educational system was failing in this task.

Social critics present a bleak picture, but what they fail to acknowledge is the enormous amount of learning that does take place every day. All of us have some very good knowledge structures. All of us have mastered the rudimentary skills of literacy, and many of us operate at high levels of proficiency on the advanced skills. Of course, the general population's skill level could be better, and the social critics perform a useful function in reminding us of this. But bringing this issue down to the personal level, it is important for you to realize that there is a range of knowledge and abilities in society. You must decide for yourself where you want to be in that range. To help you think through this issue, look at Exercise 18.1.

Need for Social Information

Social information is perhaps even more important than factual information. The media, especially in their entertainment messages, show how people behave, how they achieve success, how they form relationships, what they do when they are unhappy, and so on.

Real life offers a wide latitude on these social lessons. This latitude includes many if not almost all of the media portrayals. However, those media portrayals do not cover the gamut of human experience; they tend to emphasize the unusual and the dramatic. Therefore it is not that media portrayals are not possible or that they are unrealistic. Instead, the problem is on the aggregate level where people come to think that life should be more unusual and dramatic. To put their perspectives back into a real-life balance, people need to have real-life experiences in order to see a greater range of social lessons.

EXAMPLES OF FAULTY BELIEFS ■■

A *Newsweek* poll (Marin, 1996) found that 48% of Americans believe UFOs are real and 29% think we've made contact with aliens. Another 48% think there's a government plot to cover up the whole thing. What makes the results of this poll especially interesting is that almost none of these people claimed to have had direct contact with UFOs or aliens. However, almost half the population believes there are UFOs and that there is a government plot to cover up the fact that aliens have landed on Earth. Where do people get these beliefs? Apparently they have seen something in the media that has led them to this belief. Instead of checking it out with real-world information and finding that none exists, they have decided on pure faith to believe that real-life evidence does exist, even if they have not seen it—thus the need for the companion belief that the government is covering it up. Almost half the American population—at least on this one issue—is satisfied to hold a rather strange belief and base it on absolutely no evidence.

There are many examples of people holding faulty beliefs. Examples of eight topics are presented below. On each of these you can see that public opinion might have been different if people had been provided with a more complete set of information.

Crime

Most people over-estimate the rate of crime, especially violent crime. A Gallup Poll commissioned for the White House Office of National Drug Control

Policy found crime and violence to be the top national concern among adults (Ostrow, 1996). Most people have not been involved in a crime. Where do they get the idea that crime is the most important problem facing our country? The media continually show us criminal portrayals, both in the news and in entertainment programming. With all this vicarious exposure to crime, most of us generalize to a pattern that there is a great deal of crime in this country and that it continues to increase.

But is this opinion an accurate generalization? Despite the public thinking that crime is a top concern, it has been decreasing steadily for more than a decade. From 1986 to 1996, the total number of crimes committed per year dropped 7.3%: Murder was down 14.0%; rape down 4.7%; robbery down 10.1%; and burglary down 29.9% (*Statistical Abstract of the United States: 1999*, 2000). In 1996 alone, the murder rate fell by 8%, violent crimes dropped 4%, and there was also a drop of 2% in serious crimes. In each of the past few years, fewer than 24,000 people were murdered—this is only about 40% of those killed in traf- fic accidents. Cities with the largest populations showed the largest drop in crime.

The media continually focus on the high-profile violent crimes, which gives us the impression that crime is very prevalent and even growing. Once in a while there will be a story about overall crime rates or an analysis of the trends, but these are rare compared to the message that crime is everywhere.

In his book *Crime and Punishment in America*, Elliott Currie (1998) argues that most Americans believe that our legal system is soft on crime, that is, that the criminal justice system is much too lenient with criminals. But most people have no idea what the arrest, conviction, and incarceration rates are.

Critics say that there are 10 million violent crimes a year but only about 100,000 criminals go to prison each year. Let's analyze this claim. The first problem is that most violent crimes (60%) are not reported to the police. Many of these are schoolyard fights or barroom altercations; however, there are also many serious violent crimes that are not reported to police. Only two thirds of robberies, one half of aggravated assaults, and one third of rapes are reported, according to victim surveys.

The next problem is that only a small percentage of crimes are cleared by an arrest. Out of the 10 million violent crimes, only about 640,000 (6%) have an arrest and thus enter the criminal justice system.

Once in the system, only 165,000 arrests end in a conviction. The rest are dropped for lack of evidence, or the defendant is acquitted. About 90% of those who are convicted go to prison, and prison sentences are tough. For murder, the average time served is more than 10 years (and this does not include those who get life sentences or are condemned to death); sentences for rape average more than 7 years; robbery sentences average more than 4 years. American sentences are much stiffer than those in other industrialized countries.

In Los Angeles County there are about 1,000 homicides each year. About half are solved, that is, result in an arrest and prosecution. Of the total homicides, only 32% result in a conviction, and only 16% of those convicted were sentenced to serve 15 years or more. About 0.5% were sentenced to death (Hadly, 1997).

Clearly, America is not soft on crime once a person is convicted. Incarceration rates are high and continue to grow. As of 1994, there were 919,143 adult prisoners in 1,291 state prisons and another 93,708 in 70 federal prisons (Bureau of Justice Statistics, 1994).

Currie (1998) points out that from 1971 to 1996 the number of people in state and federal prisons in this country increased six times, from 200,000 inmates to 1.2 million. There are also another 500,000 inmates in local jails. This 1.7 million is the size of the city of Houston and twice the population of San Francisco (pp. 12-13). From World War II to the early 1970s, there were about 100 inmates for every 100,000 people in the U.S. population. By the mid-1990s that had climbed to 427 per 100,000.

Texas leads the country in incarceration. From 1991 to 1996, Texas *increased* its prison population by 80,000—that is more than the total prison population in all of Germany, a country of 80 million people. Texas has a total population of 18 million people.

Legal System

America has become a highly litigious society. The courts are clogged; the number of cases filed in state courts in 1990 was over 100 million. In federal courts, filings have increased 69% since 1980. The number of lawyers more than doubled from 1970 to 1992 (from 355,000 to 805,000), which meant that in 1992 America had 70% of the world's lawyers (Will, 1991). By 1998, the number of lawyers in the United States had increased to 912,000; at the same time there were only 740,000 physicians in all specialties (*Statistical Abstract of the United States: 1999*, 2000). This means that Americans are supporting far more people to help them with their legal health than with their physical health.

Why so many lawyers? Samuelson (1992) argues that the dramatic increase in the number of lawyers and law suits has some legitimate reasons, such as increases in crime, divorce, regulations, and government. But there is something else. Glendon (1991) points out that until the 1950s the focus of constitutional law was on the structure of our political regime—the allocation of powers among the federal government's branches and between the federal and state governments. But over time the focus has changed to the individual and his or her rights. This change coincides with the rise of TV and its theme of satisfying the individual. Thus we have been conditioned to look out for our personal rights and to sue when we feel we have been wronged, just as characters frequently do on television.

Government

Politicians have been running for President on a platform of reducing the size of the federal government ever since 1980. They promise to cut inefficiency and waste and to lower taxes. Have they done so?

Quinn (1996) says that it is a myth that the federal government has gotten smaller overall. However, some aspects have gotten smaller. Helped by the demise of the USSR in 1989, defense spending has been cut in half since 1970, when figured as a percentage of Gross Domestic Product (GDP). The federal payroll peaked in 1990 and has been decreasing since. And there are caps on discretionary spending.

But the overall size of the federal government has remained at about 22% of GDP. The growth has been in the areas of debt servicing, Medicare, and social security. In contrast, state and local governments are growing—up 23% since 1980. Most Americans are paying less (about 2% less compared to 1985) in federal income tax. But this is more than offset by increases in state and local taxes.

Another myth about the federal government is that it spends huge amounts of money on foreign aid. In 1998, the federal government spent about $13.8 billion in foreign aid—that is three quarters of 1% of the federal budget (*Statistical Abstract of the United States: 1999*, 2000). Most people think the amount is much higher. Also, most people think that this money is simply sent to other countries. Not so. The Business Alliance for International Economic Development said that 80% of the foreign aid budget is spent in the United States, explaining, "The livelihoods of hundreds of thousands of Americans—farmers, truckers, assembly line workers, software developers—depend on U.S. foreign assistance" (Rothberg, 1996).

American Products

Some people argue that allowing foreign-made products into our market will take jobs away from Americans. This argument sounds reasonable on the surface, but let's look at it in greater depth, using the automobile market as an example.

What is an American-made automobile? Did you know that Jaguar cars are made by a wholly owned subsidiary of Ford Motor Company? Lamborghini, the Italian sports car maker, is wholly owned by Chrysler Corp. The Lotus is a General Motors (GM) product. The Mazda Navajo four-wheel drive vehicle is made in the Ford Explorer plant in Kentucky; and 50% of Saab is owned by GM. Also,

Ford Motor Company purchased Land Rover, a previously British company, from Germany's BMW. Ford now markets Jaguar, Volvo, Aston Martin, and Land Rover in its line of luxury cars (Holstein, 2000).

Also, some purportedly American-made cars are not made by Americans. For example, the Ford Festiva is made by Kia of Korea. The Plymouth Laser is a Mitsubishi Eclipse, and vice versa. The Ford Probe is really a Mazda MX-6 made by Mazda in Flat Rock, Michigan. And the Geo Prizm, which seems to be a model of Chevrolet, is really a Toyota Corolla made in Fremont, California ("It's Pretty Hard to Tell," 1993).

In addition, many American companies are part owners of foreign car companies and visa versa. In 1998, the European car maker Daimler-Benz bought Chrysler, and the next year DaimlerChrysler AG purchased a controlling interest in Japan's Mitsubishi Motors Corp. General Motors has paired with Fiat. Ford Motor Company has paired with both Mazda and Volvo. This merging and buying is motivated by a desire by car companies to achieve efficiencies in sharing parts (Hyde, 2000).

The global economy is very interdependent, with overlapping ownerships. The idea of a purely American-made car is passé. Even if the automobile were assembled in an American plant, many of the parts would come from all over the world. Also, a foreign-made automobile sold in the U.S. benefits this economy, because the dealership supports Americans. The servicing and replacement of parts by local mechanics, as well as gasoline and oil are all purchased in this country. The taxes (sales, gasoline, licensing, and tolls) all benefit local governments.

The idea that buying a seemingly foreign-made product does not benefit workers in this country is superficial reasoning. Economists tell us that foreign trade does not lessen or add to jobs; instead it shifts them from lower unskilled positions to higher-paid, skilled jobs (Quinn, 1996).

In the June 21, 1999, issue of *USA Today*, General Motors had a full page ad (p. 5A) in which they said in bold headlines, "The men and women of GM proudly salute the General Motors 'Suppliers of the Year.'" Underneath this headline, they listed 185 companies "whose efforts have helped raise the quality standards of GM products." Of these companies, 114 were in foreign countries—spread across 26 foreign nations. This raises the question: What does it mean when we say a car is American?

Employment and Wages

The media continually present stories of corporate downsizing and layoffs—3-million corporate layoffs were announced between 1989 and 1995

(Brenner, 1996). This leads people to feel insecure in their jobs. One third of American workers fear that someone in their household will lose a job this year.

Also, people think the unemployment rate is high. But the unemployment rate has been going down and now is at 4.4%, which is a very low figure (*Statistical Abstract of the United States: 1999*, 2000). The problem in this generally good picture is with people who do not have a high school degree–their unemployment rate is almost twice as high. The opportunities for workers with only a high school education or less are becoming fewer: "The typical work-bound high school graduate can find entry level employment only in service-oriented jobs, offering poverty-level wages. . . . This marks a dramatic change from the time when the country's manufacturing industries offered satisfying careers and high wages for workers without college degrees" (Educational Testing Service, 1990, p. 3).

While a very high percentage of the population is working, the earning power of families has not increased much since 1970. The median family income was $37,005 in 1997, up from $33,942 (adjusted for inflation) in 1970 (*Statistical Abstract of the United States: 1999*, 2000), despite the fact that during that time there was a 56% increase in the number of families with two working parents (Brenner, 1996).

Births and Deaths

We continually hear about increasing numbers of children on welfare and increasing numbers of children born out of wedlock to very young mothers. However, the birthrate for American teenagers dropped 2% in 1993. For every 1,000 women ages 15 to 19, about 60 gave birth.

As for death, the reporting of high-profile crimes makes us believe that most of us will eventually meet a violent death. But we are 10 times as likely to die a natural death (such as from heart disease, cancer, or even pneumonia) as a violent one. In the violent death category, we are more likely to die in an accident than to be murdered. We are even more likely to commit suicide than to be murdered (*Statistical Abstract of the United States: 1999*, 2000).

Risks

When we rely exclusively on the media for information, we come to believe we are at risk of being injured by the high-profile catastrophes that are frequently covered in the news. Those things that are not covered make us believe that there is much less risk than there really is. For example, when we compare causes of death per 100,000 people, smoking accounts for 21,900; motor vehicle accidents, 1,600; diagnostic X rays, 75; lightning, 3; and asbestos in school buildings, 2. However, among the things on this list, the public is most concerned about asbestos in school buildings, and when the media focused on this story in the late 1980s, the asbestos removal industry grew from almost nothing to a $4.2-billion enterprise (Matthews, 1992). And there are people who will feel uncomfortable about a dentist x-raying their teeth, but who feel much less uncomfortable smoking, which is 293 times riskier.

Another way to compare risk is to look at how many days, on average, a behavior will cut from your otherwise normal life span. On average, smoking cigarettes cuts 2,500 days from a male's life and 800 days from a female's life; being overweight by 30% cuts 1,300 days; working as a coal miner, 1,100 days; being poor, 700 days; nuclear reactor accidents, .02 days (Allman, 1985).

Some people are terrified of flying but feel no risk when riding in a car. Wurman (1989) says the number of passenger deaths per 10 million miles is about 22 in an automobile compared to 2 in an airplane. Also, most people travel much more often in an automobile so their risk is far higher in an auto than in an airplane.

We all feel an uncomfortable sense of risk at times, perhaps when we drive through a "bad" neighborhood, or walking alone at night, or flying in an airplane. Where do we get these feelings of risk? For most of us it is the memory of a story we saw in the media of a mugging or a plane crash. Those gruesome images, although very small in number, stay with us and lead us to unrealistic assessments of risk. The media are silent about many risky behaviors. If we depend exclusively on mainstream media messages for our information, we will generalize to a very unrealistic world in which our sense of danger will be very much misplaced.

CONCLUSION ■

The media can greatly expand our knowledge by giving us information on topics that we cannot experience for ourselves. They can take us deep under the sea, into outer space, back in history, and into the Oval Office. But the pictures they give us of these places, events, and people is partial and often without much context. If we accept this information as is and do not check it, analyze it, or expand it, we get only a limited picture and may be inferring patterns and themes that are faulty.

How do we know how our government works and who has the real power? How do we know about historical figures? Most of our information comes to us through the media. We depend on this media information, because it is impossible for us to have first-hand exposure to historical events or even to current events. So we are dependent on the media for information. Some of this information is good and some of it is not so good. We must develop the skills to know the difference. It is not always clear what is fact and what is faulty.

Being media literate means consciously processing the information in all messages, as well as recognizing useless information and screening it out while keeping useful information and building a strong knowledge structure. This requires searching out multiple sources of information and determining the relative credibility of the different sources then evaluating the variety of claims. It requires analyses of the relevant positions, then synthesizing the worthwhile elements into a reasoned opinion that has been consciously derived and can be defended. It is important that you develop a program of information acquisition that is balanced: read a national newspaper, a national newsmagazine, several general interest magazines, some reference books, some non-fiction, and some fiction.

■■ FURTHER READING

Bloom, A. (1987). *The closing of the American mind*. New York: Simon & Schuster. (392 pages with index)

> This is a critique of the present state of higher education by a professor of social thought at the University of Chicago. His primary criticism is that universities no longer have a vision for what students should learn to be educated human beings. When curriculum decisions are left up to students, they decide to take easy, unchallenging courses and therefore graduate without having an understanding of the past or a vision for the future.

D'Souza, D. (1991). *Illiberal education: The politics of race and sex on campus*. New York: Free Press. (319 pages with index)

> In this criticism of higher education, D'Souza argues that the movement toward political correctness has led to an "anything goes" curriculum at most universities. As a result, students are not getting rigorous educations.

Hirsch, E. D., Jr. (1987). *Cultural literacy: What every American needs to know*. Boston: Houghton Mifflin. (251 pages with index)

> Hirsch points out that reading is more than recognizing words; it also requires the person to decipher the meaning of the words and stories. In order to do this, he argues, we need to educate students to have a core knowledge

about our world and our culture. He lays out a plan for doing this along with 63 pages of key terms and concepts that he feels every educated person should know.

Hirsch, E. D., Jr., Kett, J. F., & Trefil, J. (1993). *The dictionary of cultural literacy* (2nd ed.). Boston: Houghton Mifflin. (619 pages with index)

This is a dictionary of the "core concepts" of our culture. It is organized into 23 sections, such as life sciences, business and economics, world politics, technology, fine arts, and so on.

Wurman, R. S. (1989). *Information anxiety*. Garden City, NY: Doubleday.

This book contains many intriguing ideas about how much information has invaded our culture and how that is affecting us. The author has written it in a nonlinear manner so that the chapters and even the paragraphs can be read in any order.

EXERCISE 18.1

Thinking About a Plan for Real-World Knowledge

I. Make an assessment of your knowledge structures of the world.

   A. Start with a template of knowledge, such as Arts, Humanities, Social Sciences, and Physical Sciences. Then fill in the knowledge areas under each by looking at your college catalog's list of academic departments and courses. Or go to the library and look at how knowledge is organized there, whether by the Dewey Decimal System or the Library of Congress System. On a piece of paper, sketch a set of blocks to represent the different areas and sub-areas of knowledge. The big blocks (such as Physical Science) should be composed of smaller blocks (such as Physics, Chemistry, Biology, etc.). Some of the smaller blocks (such as Biology) may also be composed of sub-sets (such as Botany and Zoology). Don't spend more than a hour sketching this out. The goal is not to include every detail; instead, try to come up with a reasonable picture of how human knowledge is generally organized.

   B. Think back over the past 2 years and try to remember significant learning experiences you had during that time. A significant learning experience is something you remember as valuable to your learning, such as:

     1. A course that really challenged you and made you think

     2. An interest in something that made you read a series of books (or search out information in other media) and want to discuss the issues

     Write these significant learning experiences in the appropriate content blocks in your template in red ink.

   C. Think back over the past 2 years and remember the "just okay" learning experiences. These were courses where you learned something but not a whole lot.

     Write these "just okay" learning experiences in the appropriate content blocks in your template in blue ink.

   D. Look at the patterns on your template.

     1. Where are the blank areas where there is no red or blue ink? Have you been broadening yourself as a student in college or have you been playing it very safe so you don't experience new areas? What does this tell you about what you value in a college education and the kind of person you want to become as a graduate?

     2. Where are the red areas? Are they all in one small part of the template or are they sprinkled all over? What does this pattern say about you as a learner and what it takes to make something a significant learning experience?

3. Where are the blue areas? What do these have in common? How do these blue areas differ from the red areas? What does this pattern tell you about yourself as a learner; that is, to what extent were these experiences less than optimal because of outside forces (such as the teacher, the course materials, etc.) or because of something within you (such as motivation, previous knowledge structures, etc.)?

II. Think about your goals for overall learning.

    A. Do you have goals for depth? Are you building elaborate knowledge structures in a few particular areas so you can attain an expertise as a foundation for a career or further study in graduate school?

    B. Do you have goals for breadth? Are you building a string of knowledge structures across a variety of areas so you have strong contexts for interpreting the value of information throughout a wide range of topics?

CHAPTER

19

Key Idea: The journey to higher media literacy requires awareness and control.

The Media
Literacy
Perspective

Achieving higher levels of literacy is a life-long developmental process of building stronger and more elaborate knowledge structures by using a wide range of skills. How can we increase our literacy? This chapter and the next address this central question by synthesizing and extending the key points in the previous 18 chapters. This chapter asks you to be more self-aware by fully internalizing the media literacy perspective outlined in this book. The next chapter guides you in developing your strategies to increase your level of media literacy.

Increasing media literacy is best regarded as a journey to better perspectives from which to view the media. There is no one best perspective, so the journey does not have a single destination. Thus, becoming media literate is a continuous process. On your journey, you must take many steps. The steps alternate between awareness and control. The first step is to expand your awareness about some aspect. This expanded awareness gives you more options. The next step is control. With more options and with mindful decision making, you gain greater control over the effects. The exercising of this greater control leads you to a higher awareness, and this in turn leads to even greater control. Thus step by step—awareness and control—you make the journey to more and better perspectives on the media.

This chapter focuses on the awareness steps. Synthesizing from the information in the previous 18 chapters, the key domains for awareness are: your awareness of your own knowledge structures and your awareness about how your mind works. Each of these is discussed in more detail in the following sections. And each presents an exercise to help you diagnose your current level of awareness. The chapter concludes with some illustrations of various levels of media literacy compared on the learning ladders of cognitive, emotional, moral, and aesthetic development.

▊▊ AWARENE/S OF YOUR KNOWLEDGE /TRUCTURE/

Think back to the exercises in each chapter. How well did you do? Do you remember the main points of the previous chapters? Check this out by doing Exercise 19.1 now.

How did you do? How far along the media literacy journey are you in terms of having internalized some basic knowledge structures? If you have done well, then your exposure to more media messages will likely result in a more efficient acquisition of information. As your journey continues, you need to continue critically assessing media messages to decide if they are accurate, complete, and useful. If they are, then add them to your knowledge structures of the media and the real world. As your knowledge structures grow more elaborate, you will be developing more context that will help you make more efficient and more in-depth evaluations of future messages. It is important that you continually work on your knowledge structures. In our information-rich, fast-paced society, it is impossible to stand still. Information is perishable. Every day large pieces of information become obsolete as new facts replace old, as new research findings are reported, and as new perspectives emerge. Also, if you do not continually practice your skills, they will atrophy. If you do not work to improve, you will fall behind.

▊▊ AWARENE/S OF HOW YOUR MIND WORK/

It is important to develop an awareness of how your mind works in order to be media literate. This, of course, means that you pay attention to how well you handle the generic rudimentary skills as well as the more advanced skills of analysis, compare/contrast, evaluation, and synthesis.

In addition to our profile of using those skills above, we also have a unique profile of cognitive style. Your cognitive style is your approach to organizing and processing information (Hashway & Duke, 1992). We vary in our cognitive styles along several key dimensions that are delineated below.

Field Dependency

Perhaps the most important dimension in cognitive styles is the degree to which you are field dependent. Recall from Chapter 2 that this is a continuum from dependent to independent. You are positioned along this dimension in terms of your abilities to distinguish between signal and noise in any message. Noise is the chaos of symbols and images; signal is the information that emerges from that chaos. People who are highly field dependent get stuck in the field of chaos—seeing all the details but missing the big picture, which is the signal. Field independent people are able to sort quickly through the field to identify the elements of importance and ignore the distracting elements.

We live in a culture that is highly saturated with media messages. Much of this is noise, that is, it does not provide us with the information or emotional reactions we want. Field dependent people are passive and float along in this stream of messages, unable to do much of the conscious filtering that would help them focus on the signal and ignore the noise.

No one is purely field dependent, that is, perceiving every micro element in every message and totally incapable of sorting the signal from the noise. People vary by degrees. To estimate your position on the continuum, turn to Exercise 19.2.

Tolerance for Ambiguity

We continually encounter people and situations that are unfamiliar to us. To prepare ourselves for such situations, we have developed sets of expectations (schemas) about people and events. What do we do when our expectations are not met and we are put in an ambiguous situation? It depends on our tolerance for ambiguity. People who have a low tolerance for ambiguity find such situations very disturbing so they tend to ignore those messages. In contrast, people who have a high tolerance for ambiguity do not feel frustration. Instead, they are willing to stay with ambiguous messages and follow them into unfamiliar territory that goes beyond their preconceptions.

During media exposures, we try to look for patterns so we can make sense of the messages. But sometimes it is difficult to perceive a pattern. People with a low tolerance for ambiguity will become frustrated very quickly by something different and will avoid messages that do not fit their preconceptions. There is no analysis, and there is no formal or systematic comparing or contrasting of the message elements with those of other messages, because these people seldom recall any discordant elements that would be required to make a contrast. And these people are not in a position to synthesize, because they are not motivated to create new perspectives.

People with a high tolerance for ambiguity do not have a barrier to analysis. They are willing to break any message down into components and make comparisons and evaluations in a quest to understand the nature of the message and why their own expectations were wrong. People who consistently attempt to verify their observations and judgments are called scanners, because they are perpetually looking for more information (Gardner, 1968).

Conceptual Differentiation

People who classify objects into a large number of mutually exclusive categories exhibit a high degree of conceptual differentiation (Gardner, 1968). In contrast, people who use a small number of categories have a low degree of conceptual differentiation.

Related to the number of categories is category width (Bruner, Goodnow, & Austin, 1956). People who have few classification categories usually have broad categories that can contain all types of messages. For example, if a person has only three categories for all media messages (news, entertainment, and ads), then each of these categories contains a wide variety of things. In contrast, someone who has a great many categories would have narrow ones. For example, this person would not see all entertainment as the same—some is comedy and some drama. Within comedy there is situation comedy, stand-up comedy, cartoon comedy, and so on.

When we see a new stimulus, we must categorize it. Levelers tend to categorize new stimuli with previous types; they look for similarities, then match on them. They try to build cohesive cognitive schema. However, they fail to recognize small differences and gradual changes over time. In contrast, sharpeners focus on differences and try to maintain a high degree of separation between new stimuli and older stimuli (Pritchard, 1975).

Reflectivity-Impulsivity

This is a dimension that separates people in terms of how quickly they make decisions about messages and how accurate those decisions are (Kagan, Rosman, Day, Albert, & Phillips, 1964). People who take a long time and make lots of errors are regarded as slow/inaccurate; those who are quick and make few errors are fast/accurate; those who take a long time and make few errors are reflective; and those who are quick and make many errors are impulsive.

In summary, being highly media literate means being highly field independent (so we can quickly orient to the information and screen out the noise), having a high tolerance for ambiguity (so we like new experiences and information and thereby continually expand our knowledge bases), being high on conceptual differentiation (so we are driven to create more elaborate knowledge structures composed of a great deal of highly organized detail), and being fast/accurate (so we are able to cover a great deal of information and process it efficiently and effectively).

To help make you aware of differences in media literacy development, let's look at some examples of how people can react to different types of media content. These reactions are best understood when compared to positions on the learning ladders of cognitive, emotional, moral, and aesthetic development.

Learning Ladders

The learning ladders remind us that we can improve our degree of media literacy in four areas: cognitions, emotions, morality, and aesthetics. Progress up each of these ladders is accomplished by mastering the key skills of analysis, comparing/contrasting, evaluation, problem solving, and appreciation.

Cognitive Ladder. The first step is awareness, which is the ability to perceive information elements in media messages. This requires the use of the lower-order skills. The next step is understanding. This is the ability to perceive the relevant components in any messages, then to compare and contrast them in order to see how those elements are related to each other. The next step is evaluation, which requires a good deal of contextual information in order to have templates against which to compare current messages. In order to do this well, a person needs a great deal of context in the form of elaborate knowledge structures. At the highest step, people are able to appreciate a message by comparing it to their understanding of the constraints and resources of the people who produced the message. The more elaborate a person's knowledge structure is about the media industries, the more the person will be able to appreciate how difficult it is to produce certain messages.

Emotional Ladder. At low levels of emotional development, people's emotions control them. They get aroused and angry without being able to stop or control the emotion. They experience fear so strong they cannot shake it. Or they cry at a movie and cannot stop even though they are very embarrassed. Or they are unable to feel any emotion, even though they long to do so.

At higher levels of emotional development, people can use the media to shape and control their emotions. For example, stressed women watch more game and variety shows as well as more television in total, while stressed men watch more action and violent programming (Anderson, Collins, Schmitt, & Jacobvitz, 1996). Depressed people especially use television to escape unpleasant feelings and real-world stimuli that could exacerbate those feelings (Potts & Sanchez, 1994).

If people are aware of what they are doing, then the use of media to manage moods is a sign of high levels of media literacy, that is, people consciously use the media as a tool to satisfy a particular need. If, in contrast, people are depressed and they don't know what to do, they may watch television by default until they are tired enough to fall asleep. This is not an example of people controlling their exposure, so this is evidence of a low level of media literacy.

Moral Ladder. This requires the development of opinions about the acceptability of shows, people, and situations. Typically, we infer themes from shows by matching elements in the portrayals against our personal values. At the lowest level on this ladder, you develop your moral opinion of a message based purely on intuition or because someone else, whom you respect, gives you the opinion. You see the elements in the show as an undifferentiated mass or blur. You have quick intuitive reactions about whether the show feels right or not, according to your values. If there is a fit you are happy; if there is no fit, you have a negative reaction. You really can't articulate your reaction very well, because it is primarily emotional. For example, if a respected friend tells you that *NYPD Blue* is a morally reprehensible program, you will likely accept this opinion without watching the show. If you accidently find yourself exposed to it, you immediately have a negative reaction and turn it off.

At the middle levels of this ladder, you make a distinction among characters on their values and find yourself identifying with those characters who have the same values you do. If those characters are portrayed positively (rewarded, successful, attractive, etc.), then you are happy.

At the higher levels, you think past individual characters to focus your meaning making at the overall narrative level. You separate characters from their actions so that even if you don't like a particular character, but still you like his or her actions in terms of fitting in with (or reinforcing) your values. You do not tie your viewing to one character's point of view, but try to empathize with many characters so you can vicariously experience the various consequences of actions through the course of the narrative. During a narrative, you are able to assume different moral perspectives and more fully appreciate the action from all participants' points of view.

Aesthetic Appreciation Ladder. This development is oriented toward the cultivation of enhanced enjoyment, understanding, and appreciation of media content. At lower levels on the aesthetic ladder, people have a very simple categorical opinion—the show is good or it is bad. Not much reasoning goes into an intuitive decision, so viewers are not able to explain why they like something.

At the middle levels, people are able to distinguish acting from writing and directing. Viewers have the ability to perceive that one of these might be good while another is bad. Also, people are able to compare an artist's performance within this message with past performances and infer a trend in the artist's work.

At higher levels, there is an awareness of media content as a "text" that provides insight into our contemporary culture and ourselves. An awareness of artistry and visual manipulation is also needed. This is an awareness of the processes by which meaning is created through the visual media. What is expected of sophisticated viewers is some degree of self-consciousness about their role as interpreters. This includes the ability to detect artifice (in staged behavior and editing) and to spot authorial presence (style of the producer/director).

Learning about visual conventions is not a prerequisite for interpreting visual messages. However, learning these conventions can help heighten our appreciation of artistry; it also provides us with the ability to see through the manipulative uses and ideological implications of visual images. This helps to enhance critical viewing.

Can you make a quick assessment of your position on each of these four ladders? If you can, then your awareness is fairly high. But if you are unclear how to position yourself, then think about these ladders as you watch television or read a newspaper. As you reflect on your media exposures while they are happening, you will develop more insights into the levels at which you normally operate. Remember, you will move your positions on the ladders depending on the type of message and your mood. If you are simply looking for fantasy to help you relax, you are likely operating at lower levels. But you may be capable of operating at higher levels at other times. As you are exposed to media messages over a long period of time, develop a sense of where your "home position" is, that is, the level where you usually operate.

Now let's use these learning ladders as templates to examine some examples. This analysis will highlight important differences across levels of media literacy.

Examples of Levels of Literacy

There are many different reasons why people expose themselves to particular kinds of content, and there are many different benefits people can get from any given message. Because of this, it is not possible to analyze a message and assume that all those who are exposed will extract the same meaning or have the same experience from it. Below, we will explore several examples to illustrate this point.

Beavis and Butt-Head. There has been a great deal of criticism of the television show *Beavis and Butt-Head*. Many people find it offensive. However, it can be viewed in different ways, depending on how literate you are.

At one level you might really like the characters and identify with them. You feel that the characters see things the same way you do—something is either cool or it sucks. You think that finally there are characters who are not afraid to tell it like it is. You might watch the show and realize that they *are* you. You use them as role models and feel validated because there are other people like you, so it is okay to be the way you are. This reaction to *Beavis and Butt-Head* illustrates a low level of media literacy. The viewer demonstrates no real analysis of the show; the cognitive level is low. There is no evidence of moral or aesthetic development, but there is a moderate emotional reaction of liking for the characters. Overall, however, the pattern on the learning ladders is at or near the lowest level.

At a higher overall level of literacy, people would be aware enough to regard the characters as simple stereotypes. By comparing and contrasting Beavis and Butt-Head with other characters on television, it is clear that these characters are less developed. This might lead to an emotional reaction of frustration that the characters never change or learn from their mistakes. Also, it might lead to a moral reaction that the characters are reprehensible.

At levels of literacy that are higher still, the show could be regarded as a satire on the insipid values of the Generation X. It would require more cognitive efforts in analysis, comparing/contrasting, and evaluation to construct this conclusion. It would also require a broader knowledge structure about what the X-generation is supposed to be. This might lead to a strong humorous emotional reaction; however, the laughter is at the characters, not with them. This stance on laughter is evidence of an awareness of a moral position that abhors the values of the characters and in so doing finds them funny in their fool's paradise. An aesthetic analysis of the program would reveal the characters to be very flat from an artistic point of view. This could lead to an admiration of the producer's ability to keep things so consistently flat. The artistic perspective is flat. The character development is flat, that is, the characters do not change or mature. The dialog is flat; it does not develop into deeper levels of insight. This consistent flatness is not easy to sustain over many episodes. At this level, there is a strong aesthetic appreciation, along with strong cognitive, emotional, and moral reactions.

Soap Operas. Soap operas as a genre can appeal to viewers of all levels of media literacy. At a low level of literacy, people feel some kind of unarticulated attachment to the program. They cannot explain why they like the characters or the show, because they don't analyze it; they just let it be.

At a bit higher level of development, people will watch soap operas because they feel a personal identity with the characters and have substituted the soap world for their barren existence. This leads to a strong emotional reaction. Other people will watch soaps because they want to learn how attractive characters dress and behave; this leads to some cognitive processing and evaluation of how characters look and act.

At a higher level, some people view soaps in groups so they can discuss the action as it unfolds. Or they will call their friends later and use the action as an important topic of conversation. These people use the viewing to maintain a community of friends that they would not have without the soap opera. This requires a considerable amount of cognitive processing and emotional attachment.

At a higher level, the viewing includes an in-depth analysis of the aesthetic and moral elements that are displayed. Viewers marvel at the writing, directing, and acting challenges in mounting a multi-plotted program 5 days a week for an open-ended time period, sometimes stretching over decades. Also, the complexity of the changing moral sensibilities can be intriguing. It is a truly remarkable achievement that the creative people on these shows can sustain a sense of drama and suspense under such severe pressures in such a limited genre.

Nightly News. At a low level, looking at the news each night (whether in the newspaper, a magazine, on radio, or on television) can be nothing more than a mindless habit that provides people with a sense that they have been exposed to what is important each day. As a ritual, it provides structure to one's life, even if it does not provide any information of value.

At a higher level, people consciously monitor certain stories for new developments. They add new information to their existing knowledge structure on the story and feel some emotion as they derive a sense of satisfaction about learning more.

At the highest levels of media literacy, people use this regular exposure as a starting place for learning about the events of the day. They notice what is on the agenda and immediately use that information to elaborate their existing knowledge structures. But then they seek out alternative messages in other vehicles and other media to augment this information and to serve as confirmation of its completeness. They maintain a constant skepticism that there may be more to the story. They have developed a keen aesthetic awareness of the strengths and weaknesses of various reporters and news organizations and use these insights to evaluate the worth of each new story. Finally, they are very aware of the visual framing, the use of camera movement, the use (or lack of use) of graphics and other production techniques that subtly construct the tone of the stories.

Remember, it is not the types of shows you watch that make you media literate or illiterate. Instead, literacy is keyed to what you think and how you feel while you are being exposed.

▞ CONCLUSION

Media literacy is a perspective. In order to achieve this perspective, you need to increase your awareness and control. These are the two steps on the journey to higher media literacy. The exercises in this chapter are designed to help you make an assessment (and continue this practice over time) of your awareness about your own knowledge structures, about how your mind works, and about your ability to apply knowledge of the key elements in the effects process.

Media literacy is most clearly diagnosed when we compare people's patterns of thoughts and feelings to the positions on the learning ladders. Keep these ladders in mind during your exposures.

EXERCISE 19.1

Awareness of Your Knowledge Structures

Below is a list of chapters in this book. Each one presents a knowledge structure on its topic.

1. For each of these chapters, try to recall the structure of the content.

   a. Can you remember the key idea of that chapter? Can you remember major ideas or sections of the chapter?

   b. Then go back to the first page of that chapter and check your recall. If you remembered the key idea, give yourself 1 point, and give yourself another point for your recall of *each* major idea (the major points in the outline). Thus your score should be somewhere between 0 and 5 for that chapter.

   c. Enter your score in the left-hand column, which is labeled Book.

   d. Follow the same procedure for each of the chapters listed below.

Book	AdExp		
		Introduction	
____	____	Chapter 1	Definition: What Is Media Literacy?
____	____	Chapter 2	Developing Media Literacy
____	____	Chapter 3	Media Literacy Skills
____	____	Chapter 4	Importance of Knowledge Structures
		Knowledge Structures of Media Content	
____	____	Chapter 5	What Is News?
____	____	Chapter 6	What Is Entertainment?
____	____	Chapter 7	Commercial Advertising
		Knowledge Structures of Media Industries	
____	____	Chapter 8	Development of the Mass Media Industries
____	____	Chapter 9	Economic Nature
____	____	Chapter 10	Who Owns and Controls the Mass Media?
____	____	Chapter 11	Profiles of Media Industries
____	____	Chapter 12	What Is an Audience?
		Knowledge About Effects	
____	____	Chapter 13	Broadening the Perspective on Media Effects
____	____	Chapter 14	Immediate Effects
____	____	Chapter 15	Long-Term Effects
____	____	Chapter 16	HOW Do the Effect Processes Work?
____	____	Chapter 17	Effects on Institutions
		Putting It All Together	
____	____	Chapter 18	Importance of Real-World Information
____	____	Chapter 19	The Media Literacy Perspective

2. Next, think about additional reading you undertook after studying each chapter.

   a. For each book or article you read from the Further Reading list or from the reference list give yourself 2 points.

   b. For each additional book you have read relevant to the topic since studying the chapter, give yourself 1 point.

   c. For each significant experience you have had concerning that topic since studying the chapter, give yourself 1 point (a significant experience is an extended conversation you had with someone on the topic of the chapter, consciously trying to apply the principles in that chapter, etc.).

   d. Record your point totals for each chapter in the column labeled AdExp (Additional Experiences).

3. Look at the pattern of numbers across the chapters. What does this tell you about the state of your current knowledge structures?

   a. Look down the Book column. If you have mostly 4s and 5s, you have a very strong set of knowledge structures. If you have mostly 3s, you have a good beginning set of knowledge structures. If you have some zeros, you need to go back and re-orient yourself to the structure of information in those chapters.

      Remember that having strong knowledge structures does not necessarily mean you have a great deal of knowledge on that topic, but it does mean you are aware of the main ideas, and this will help you acquire additional knowledge much more efficiently.

   b. Look down the AdExp column. If you have 3s or above, you are showing a strong commitment to extending your knowledge and elaborating your knowledge structures. Look for any zeros and ask yourself why you were not willing or able to extend your knowledge on that topic.

   c. Look at the total pattern of numbers. Were you stronger on certain chapters than others?

      It is understandable that you may be more interested in particular topics than others, but remember that balance is important. Be proud of your accomplishments—now build on them to overcome your weaknesses.

EXERCISE 19.2

Awareness of How Your Mind Works

1. *Field Dependency:* Without looking back through this chapter, write down on a piece of paper the main idea in this chapter and several subsidiary ideas that amplify that main idea.

   If you were able to do this quickly, you are an active reader. You most likely previewed the chapter to determine its structure and main points. With that structure in mind you were able to navigate your way efficiently through the reading—adding detail to your structure at appropriate places. This is characteristic of a field independent cognitive style.

   If you instead struggled with this mini-exercise, you are less field independent. Perhaps you listed several points, but these were not the main points of the chapter. Perhaps you were able to list many relevant points (such as 10 or 12), but were not able to decide which were more important, that is, which were superordinate to others. Or perhaps you could not list any points, in which case you were forcing your eyes over each line of type but your mind was not distinguishing the ideas (signal) from the lines of type (noise).

2. *Tolerance for Ambiguity:* Expose yourself for 20 minutes to a television show on a topic about which you know nothing. For example, if you are *not* a sports fan, watch a hockey game. If you are not into high-brow art, watch an opera.

   During the exposure, did you continually look at your watch, wondering how time could go so slowly? Did you feel frustrated that you could not follow the action? If your answers to these questions are yes, you probably have a low tolerance for ambiguity.

   Instead, did you find the new experience fascinating? Were you intrigued as you began to see some patterns? If you answer yes to these questions, then you probably have a high tolerance for ambiguity.

3. *Conceptual Differentiation:* For this exercise, let's start with a general concept like a newscast, and break it down into its component parts, such as news, weather, and sports. Each of these can be broken down into its own sub-component parts. Think of this as a tree diagram. The trunk is labeled Newscast, and the top of the trunk splits into three main branches labeled News, Weather, and Sports. Each of these main branches can split off into sub-branches, and those sub-branches can themselves split off into smaller branches, and so on.

   a. Now try drawing a tree diagram for Books. Draw a trunk and label it Book, then split the top into two branches labeled Fiction and Non-Fiction. Now you're on your own. Continue with the splitting of branches. Label each branch.

   b. When you have finished, look at the overall pattern.

   On average, how many sub-branches come out of each split? In the newscast example above, the split produced three sub-branches. But it could have produced more, say six: National News, International News, Local News, Features, Sports, and Weather.

How many levels did you pursue? In our example above, there were only two levels: the newscast level and the level with types of stories. But there could have been a third level. For example, Weather could have been sub-divided into Today's Weather and Forecast. It could have been further sub-divided into a fourth level; for example, Forecast could be broken into Precipitation and Temperature.

If you had many levels and many branches at each split, then you are high on conceptual differentiation. This means that your cognitive style drives you to pay careful attention to structure and to acquire a good deal of information.

If, in contrast, you have only two or three levels and only a few branches at each split, then you are low on conceptual differentiation. Your knowledge structure about books is not as structured or as detailed as those of people who are high on conceptual differentiation.

CHAPTER 20

Key Idea: You have the power to develop media literacy strategies to influence society, other individuals, and yourself.

Strategies for Increasing Media Literacy

Congratulations on having worked on your knowledge structures in the previous chapters. By now you should have a fairly good awareness about what it means to be media literate and what your strengths and weaknesses are in terms of media literacy skills and knowledge structures.

You should now be asking yourself: How can I preserve the skills and knowledge structures I already have so that they don't erode? How can I overcome my weaknesses? Is there anything I can do to help with media literacy among other people and in society in general? These are very important questions.

The answers to these questions require you to think about developing some key strategies. You've probably been thinking about such development as you were reading the book. If so, you have already started. In this chapter, I can help direct your thinking, but I cannot give you THE STRATEGIES. You must develop them for yourself in response to your particular needs. So this last chapter will not give you a definitive list of strategies. Instead, think of this last chapter as a platform—a jumping off point for you to take greater control of the trajectory of your thinking as you glide through the rich atmosphere of media messages throughout the course of your life.

This chapter will attempt to stimulate your thinking in three areas: personal strategies, interpersonal strategies, and societal strategies. Use this information to guide the development of your own strategies to take control of your media exposure and the effect of those messages on you.

■■ PERSONAL STRATEGIES

The purpose of developing personal strategies is to shape the effects the media have on you by mindfully viewing and actively discounting or amplifying messages. Below are nine suggestions for you to consider when developing your own personal strategies.

Develop an accurate awareness of your exposure.

Periodically (maybe once a year) keep a diary of media usage for a week. Remember you did this in the exercise in this book's Preface. By repeating this exercise over time, you can monitor your changing interests in the media and their messages. As you monitor changes, ask yourself the following types of questions:

Am I broadening my exposure to different media or am I staying primarily with only one or two?

Am I broadening my exposure to different types of messages? (If you used to watch mainly sports and action/adventure on television, are you now spreading your viewing around to a wider range of genres?)

Am I planning my media exposures to serve specific goals of which I am aware, or am I just exposing myself to whatever comes along?

Variety and consciousness are important goals to achieve with exposure. Variety will broaden your interests and perhaps lead you to ask for different kinds of content from the media. Consciousness will lead you to move more of your exposure under your control, leaving less in the default area of passive exposure.

Continually practice literacy skills in mindful exposure sessions.

Try to reduce your amount of mindless exposure. But remember, mindless exposure is not necessarily associated with a particular type of content—any content can turn your mind off, and any content can potentially have value and engage your mind. For example, a bland situation comedy can turn our mind off, but so too can a great work of literature—but for different reasons. If we watch a Shakespearean tragedy, we might find our mind wandering because so much mental effort is required to follow the Elizabethan language, the poetic expression, the historical settings, and the many characters involved in multiple plots.

It is important to develop active media use habits and to avoid practicing bad habits. When you are passive, the media effects are uncontrolled. Remember that active processing and high involvement with media reduce unwanted effects. People who are conscious of what they are exposed to and actively interact with the content will retain control over the learning process. They will consciously discount certain messages and carefully encode other information for memory storage. People who are not active processors of information will let the media, especially television, happen to them.

The context of the exposure can also influence the activity of information processing. When watching a message, analyze the contextual elements. For example with ads, ask who the spokesperson is and whether he or she is credible and trustworthy. What are the product claims? With entertainment messages, look closely at the action. Is it rewarded? What are the character's motivations? What appear to be the producer's motivations? What values underlie this portrayal?

Beware of factors that increase mindlessness in exposure. Factors that distract your attention during exposure serve to move you into a state of low involvement. In this state you use peripheral modes of information processing, that is, your mind goes on automatic pilot. Advertisers rely on this to get their message into your subconscious without your defense mechanisms being aroused.

Acquire a broad base of useful knowledge.

The key to knowledge is that it is useful; acquiring knowledge that is not useful does not help. This means we must be consciously aware of our needs for knowledge. So when you see something unusual in the media, ask yourself: What additional information do I need in order to make sense of this? When you see something typical in the media, ask yourself: Is this really the way it appears?

There is always a gap between the knowledge we already have and the knowledge we need for understanding the world better. We can close the knowledge gap for ourselves, but we must do this on a topic-by-topic basis. The strategy for closing the knowledge gap on a topic is under our control, because the knowledge gap is influenced more by our interest in a topic than by our general level of education (Chew & Palmer, 1994). If we have high interest on a topic, we will search out information from many different media and many different sources. But when we have low interest on a topic, we allow the media to determine for us how much information we get.

Focus on usefulness as a goal.

There are different reasons for media exposure. All can be valid and highly useful. But uses vary. We need to be clear about what our goals really are during each exposure session. We should remember that we are placing ourselves at risk of unwanted effects if we expose ourselves mindlessly. With a little effort, we can increase our control over the content—and perhaps even increase our enjoyment of the content by experiencing a stronger emotional reaction or aesthetic appreciation on a new level of understanding.

Continually ask yourself what you want to get from this media exposure. If you want facts and information, then process the material actively to select those facts and categorize them well. If instead you want to be entertained by establishing a parasocial interaction with a particular character who is attractive to you, then be aware of the attraction and how it might be affecting you. Remember that this character lives in a world very unlike your own and is the product of a production system with particular goals and constraints.

Think about the reality-fantasy continuum.

Continually ask yourself the degree to which something is real or fantasy; this is a continuum. Some programs will be easy to spot as fantasy, such as *Looney Toons*. But other programs may not be so obvious. Some have a realistic setting and some realistic situations but are still fantasy, such as *Married With Children*. Others may have a fantasy setting but deal with situations in a realistic manner, such as *Star Trek*. Distinguishing reality from fantasy in the media is often a difficult task that requires you to think about the many different characteristics of a message. So you must think analytically and break a message down into its component parts, then assess which parts are realistic.

The argument here is not to avoid fantasy. Exposure to fantasy can have many positive effects. Such exposure can be very entertaining because of its imaginative or humorous appeal. It can stimulate our thinking creatively; however, we must realize that it is a stimulating tool, not a model to imitate. The important thing is to recognize when you are being exposed to fantasy so that you can process those messages differently. If you aren't sufficiently analytical, many messages with embedded fantasy elements might appear realistic.

Make cross-channel comparisons.

While media literacy is a generic concept that spans across all media, there are some special challenges presented by different channels. For example, reading a magazine article requires some skills not required when watching a situation comedy on television. This point, of course, is obvious, but the nature of the differences themselves is not so obvious. To illustrate this, watch a news story on CNN, then look for that story in your local newspaper. Analyze the similarities and differences—are they important?

These differences will become even clearer if you attempt to create a message for different channels. Try writing a news story for a radio station and for a magazine that comes out once a month. Try constructing a message that will make people laugh when they hear it in a song on a CD. Now translate that humor onto the computer screen for Internet browsers. Designing good media messages, especially humorous ones, is very difficult. Exercises such as these will help increase your aesthetic appreciation.

Increase your willingness to expend mental effort.

We all have expectations about the appropriate amount of mental effort necessary to read a book, listen to a lecture, or watch television. Compared to print, TV elicits lower expectations of mental effort. The amount of invested mental effort (AIME) while viewing is a voluntary matter (Salomon, 1981). Because we can control our mental effort, we can also control the degree of our learning. The greater the mental effort expended, the higher our comprehension, learning, and eventual recall.

Examine your opinions.

Ask yourself: Are my opinions well reasoned? For example, as Americans we say we are dissatisfied with materialism despite all the abundance in our society. In a recent survey, 82% of Americans agreed that most of us buy and consume far more than we need. And 67% agreed that Americans cause many of the world's environmental problems, because we consume more resources and produce more waste than anyone else in the world (Koenenn, 1997). The United States has less than 6% of the world's population but consumes nearly 30% of the planet's resources. Americans can choose from more than 30,000 supermarket items, including 200 kinds of cereal. Do we really need all these material products?

While people criticize television in general, their opinions are inconsistent. For example, The Roper Organization under the sponsorship of NBC in the early 1980s asked respondents in a national survey to express their reactions to 17 particular TV shows—16 of which had been the targets of complaints about sex and violence from religious organizations. Only 13% of respondents said there was too much violence on the *Dukes of Hazzard* and only 10% said there was too much sex on *Dallas*—these were the most negatively rated shows! But when asked about television in general, 50% of the respondents said there was too much sex and violence on TV (Roper Organization, 1981).

As can be seen in the above examples, we are not very systematic in gathering information and carefully assessing it in constructing our opinions. Instead, we operate fairly intuitively. As a result, we have a lot of superficial opinions.

Change behaviors.

To what extent do your behaviors correspond to your beliefs? For example, if you think society is too materialistic, do you avoid buying many material goods? If you do keep your consumption of material goods at a minimum, then there is a match between your behaviors and your beliefs. But there are people who continually complain about waste in our materialistic society, then go out and buy lots of new things they don't need. The first step in behavioral change is a realistic assessment of the match between your beliefs and your existing behaviors.

You could boycott advertisers, cancel subscriptions, and write letters when you see something you don't like in the media. This action, of course, will have almost no effect on the media themselves, unless large numbers of other people feel as you and do the same things. However, that is not a reason to stop yourself from doing these things. By taking action, you give yourself a sense of gaining control over the media.

Changing your behavior so it corresponds to your beliefs demonstrates a commitment to the moral responsibility of following through on your beliefs rather than simply blaming someone else and doing nothing, which has become a popular response to many of society's problems. For example, let's examine what has been happening in the area of the environment and pollution. The media have put the issue of pollution on the public agenda as the prominence and length of these stories has increased dramatically since the 1970s (Ader, 1995). During that same period, air pollution went down about a third, but solid waste went up about 25%. This shows us that as Americans become more concerned about pollution, we have put pressure on the government to clean up the air by regulating manufacturing plants and requiring emissions controls on cars. But solid waste reduction, which is under the control of individual citizens through voluntary recycling programs, has not been so successful. This means that individuals are not cutting back on their waste through lower consumption or recycling. Again, people are looking to the government or someone else to solve problems.

Interpersonal strategies orient you toward helping other individuals with their media literacy. You begin by identifying people who might be at risk for negative effects from the media and then work with them intensively. One example would be to work with children at a day care center, church, or other community group. Because of their young age, children are still at a low level of development and require special attention.

It is important that an adult guide young children's media exposure (Messaris, 1982). But among children 7 and older, 95% never watch TV with their parents, and even among children 2 to 7, 81% never watch with their parents. Also, about half (49%) of all children have no rules for TV viewing in their households. Among children 8 and older, 61% have no rules (Rideout, Foehr, Roberts, & Brodie, 1999).

When you have children, make time to watch TV with them and talk about what is happening on the screen. When parents actively mediate during television viewing, they can influence their children's interpretations (Austin, 1993). You can explain the meaning of words, pictures, narratives, and so on. You can make viewing active for them by continually asking questions about meaning and structure, such as: Who did what to whom? and Why? This gets them practicing making connections. Continually analyze messages, then move on to applying the other advanced skills as well. Actively ask questions such as: What are the categories (schemas) we have for characters? Are those categories thin and two-dimensional or are they richly developed? What are our expectations for scripts? Are they simple or complex? How do we make judgments about what is relevant in the plot—can we see the subtleties in the sub-plots that provide more texture to the main plot?

When working with children, be careful not to push them too hard before they are able to make the required connections to answer a particular kind of question. Remember, young children go through stages of cognitive development that cannot be rushed.

These strategies can move beyond cognitive aspects to include emotional and behavioral aspects. Children who experience emotional media messages when they are among peers or adults will exhibit a reduced likelihood and intensity of immediate emotional effects, especially fear effects from scary movies. Also, the probability of a child behaving aggressively when watching violence can be reduced if adults verbalize comments and interpretations while observing with the child—such as pointing out unrealistic and inappropriate behavior in programs.

Children are likely to model their behavior on attractive characters they see in the media. This modeling can be shaped by interpersonal strategies. For example, Austin and Meili (1995) found that children use their emotion and logic to develop expectations about alcohol use in the real world when they see alcohol used by characters on television. When children have both real-life and televised sources of information, they are more likely to develop skepticism about television portrayals of alcohol use when they rely on parents as primary sources of information and behavioral modeling.

When you become a parent, you will need to be careful in monitoring your children's experience with the newest of the media—computers and the Internet. People can (and do) put out lots of questionable information and entertainment services. There are primarily three types of risk for children or teens who use the Internet. One is exposure to inappropriate material, such as sexual matter and hate speech. A second is developing inappropriate relationships with strangers. The third is harassment ("Is Your Child Safe in Cyberspace?" 1995).

Parents therefore need to be careful to monitor the sites their children visit. Parents need to tell their children never to give out any identifying information such as address, phone number, school name, and so on, and they should never allow a child to arrange a face-to-face meeting with someone they have met online. Parents who find information that may be illegal (such as child pornography or hate speech) should report it to authorities. Parents should build skepticism in their children, because people on the Internet may not be who they seem; people can make up a persona in terms of gender, age, background, and the like. Parents should set time rules for access; too much contact can lead to addiction. And finally, surfing the Internet can be a fun activity for all family members to do together.

■■ JOCIETAL JTRATEGIEJ

With societal strategies, the focus is on exerting pressure on a particular part of the industry, the government, or some institution in order to increase public awareness about a problem or to bring about some particular change. To do this successfully, you will need a strategy supported by a great deal of commitment, money, and contacts. Your strategy will require many years of effort to effect a change. It will also require money. Often people will start a PAC (political action committee) or a consulting firm that will then apply for grants to support its work.

Contacts are also extremely important. By linking up with other powerful people and groups, you could become part of something that could potentially have enough power to get the attention of the large media companies. Look at

---

TABLE 20.1   Citizen Action Groups

Media Literacy Organizations

Center for Media Education
1511 K Street, NW, Suite 518
Washington, DC 20005
Telephone: (202) 628-2620
Fax: (202) 628-2554
Web site: www.cme.org/cme

Center for Media Literacy
4727 Wilshire Boulevard, Suite 403
Los Angeles, CA 90010
Telephone: (800) 226-9494
Fax: (213) 931-4474
Web site: www.medialit.org

Children Now
1212 Broadway, Suite 530
Oakland, CA 94612
Telephone: (510)763-2444
Web site: www.childrennow.org

Citizens for Media Literacy
34 Wall Street, Suite 407
Asheville, NC 28801
Telephone: (704) 252-0600

Cultural Environment Movement
P.O. Box 31847
Philadelphia, PA 19104
Telephone: (610) 642-3061

Foundation to Improve Television
60 State Street, Suite 3400
Boston, MA 02109
Telephone: (617) 523-5520
Fax: (617) 523-4619

Media Watch
P.O. Box 618
Santa Cruz, CA 95061
Telephone: (408) 423-6355
Email: mwatch@cruzio.com
Web site: www.mediawatch.com

Mediascope
12711 Ventura Boulevard, Suite 280
Studio City, CA 91604
Telephone: (818) 508-2080
Web site: www.mediascope.org

National Association for Family
  and Community Education
Children's Television Project
P.O. Box 835
Burlington, KY 41005
Telephone: (606) 586-8333
Fax: (606) 586-8348
Web site: www.nafce.org

National Telemedia Council
120 East Wilson Street
Madison, WI 53703
Telephone: (608) 257-7712
Web site: danenet.wicip.org/ntc

Parents' Choice
119 Chestnut Street
Newton, MA 02164
Telephone: (617) 965-5913

**Concerned Primarily With
Advertising**

Adbusters
1243 West Seventh Avenue
Vancouver, British Columbia
V6H 1B7 Canada
Telephone: (604) 736-9401
Email: adbusters@adbusters.org

Children's Advertising Review Unit
Council of Better Business Bureaus
845 Third Avenue
New York, NY 10022
Telephone: (212) 705-0124

Concerned Primarily With News

FAIR (Fairness and Accuracy in
  Reporting)
130 West 25th Street
New York, NY 10001
Telephone: (212) 633-6700
Email: fair@igc.apc.org

**Concerned Primarily
With TV and Movie Ratings**

Classification and Rating
  Administration
Motion Picture Association of
  America, Inc.
15503 Ventura Boulevard
Encino, CA 91436-3103
Web site: www.mpaa.org

OKTV (Alternative TV Ratings)
c/o Gaffney-Livingstone
  Consultation Services
59 Griggs Road
Brookline, MA 02146
Web site: www.aacap.org

TV Parental Guidelines Monitoring
  Board
P.O. Box 14097
Washington, D.C. 20004
Email: tvomb@usa.net
Web site: www.tvguidelines.org

the list of citizen action groups in Table 20.1. Contact those that are of most interest to you and ask them to send you information.

Changing media industry practices or content is very difficult. Remember that the industries have grown and developed in response to demands from the public. If an industry or a vehicle does not respond well to the demand, it loses money. Successful CEOs have confidence that their decisions will result in greater profits. So don't expect change when you ask them to ignore their experience and to change their practices when they might risk losing millions of dollars by making the changes you suggest.

This is why the public concern about television violence has resulted in so little change over the past 50 years. A more modest goal than to expect a change of content or practices is to expect a change in perceptions among some decision makers in the media industries. In explaining this non-action, Stuart Fishoff (1988), a psychologist who writes for television and movies, said: "Let's suppose the results, the conclusions, were incontrovertible—TV and film modeling of aggression and other anti-social values has significant effects on the viewing audience. Would it really make any difference to the gate keepers of media fare in Hollywood and New York? I submit the answer is not on your life!" (p. 3). He cites an important principle in psychology for his conclusion: "The more far-reaching and costly the consequences of accepting a message, the more facts needed before an audience will be persuaded as to the accuracy of the message—and the more energy will be expended in denigrating both the message and the messenger in order to maintain existing belief" (p. 3). Therefore, the media industries have been very slow in acknowledging the value of any of the research on negative media effects while using the research on positive effects to show that they are acting responsibly. This attitude has outraged many media critics and stimulated many members of the general public to want to do something to remedy the problem.

Another example of a societal strategy is to protect very young children from the effects of television advertising. In the early 1970s, some consumer groups were formed to protect children from what was seen as abuses by broadcasters. Prominent among these groups was Action for Children's Television, which found examples of children's programs that contained as many as 16 minutes of ads per hour—far above the industry's self-imposed limit of 9.5 minutes. And the products advertised were largely non-nutritious snacks and deceptively presented toys. Many products were being pitched by characters from the programs, thus making the distinction between the show and the ad indecipherable, especially for young children.

This pressure influenced the Federal Trade Commission (FTC) to hold hearings throughout the 1970s. The FTC considered banning certain types of ads. But in the end, the FTC concluded that although there was evidence that television advertising created risks for children, there were no practical effective remedies open to federal policy making. The primary problems were determining who is a child—that is, at what age is a person no longer a child? Also there was the fear that regulating advertising on children's television might cause broadcasters to stop programming for children.

Another example of a societal strategy took place in the fall of 1995 when some well-known political figures began a campaign to clean up talk shows on television. Headed by former Education Secretary William Bennett, Senator Joseph Lieberman (D-Conn.), and Senator Sam Nunn (D-Ga.), the campaign did not seek regulation of television content. Instead, it sought to influence public opinion and to shame certain television producers by characterizing the content of daytime talk shows as "lethal." These critics acknowledged that some of the 20 nationally syndicated talk shows dealt with serious issues of domestic abuse, drug abuse, and racism in a constructive way that enlightened viewers. But they pointed out that some shows had a circus atmosphere that included shouting matches, fist fights, foul language, and audience members yelling out unqualified advice. As an example of sleaze, they cited examples from the Sally Jessy Raphael show where she talked to girls who were sexually active at the age of 10, and Jerry Springer, who hosted a 17-year-old who had four children with her 71-year-old husband whom she called "Dad" (Hancock, 1995).

There are many other examples of people and groups who have tried to influence public awareness of problems with media content and to bring about change in the media industries. These efforts have been more successful in raising public consciousness about these problems than they have been in bringing about changes in programming. This leaves us with the question: Should we continue to try? The answer, of course, is yes. Look at the organizations listed in Table 20.2 and think about which ones should be targets for the societal change you would like to see. If you choose to target the federal government, the best way to make your views known is to contact your senators and congressional representatives directly. If you don't know who they are or how to contact them, you can obtain this information on the Internet:

House of Representatives Web site: www.house.gov

Senate Web site: www.senate.gov

With societal strategies, we should have modest expectations for change. And we need to have a long time frame. Societal change of this type moves at glacial speed—it takes decades to see change. But remember that a glacier is exerting constant pressure, and change is happening constantly—we just can't see it happening because it is happening very slowly. The same is true of societal campaigns. If we exert constant pressure, we will eventually be able to perceive changes. If you are impatient and want to see change happen more quickly, then try some interpersonal and personal strategies.

TABLE 20.2   Possible Targets for Beginning Societal Change

National Television Networks

ABC, Inc.
2040 Avenue of the Stars
Los Angeles, CA 90067
Telephone: (310) 557-6655
Web site: www.abc.com

CBS Entertainment
7800 Beverly Boulevard
Los Angeles, CA 90036
Telephone: (213) 460-3000
Fax: (213) 653-8266
Web site: www.channel2000.com

Fox Broadcasting Company
P.O. Box 900
Beverly Hills, CA 90213
Telephone: (310) 369-1000
Web site: www.fox.com

NBC Entertainment
3000 West Alameda
Burbank, CA 91523
Telephone: (818) 840-4404
Web site: www.nbc.com

Public Broadcasting Service
1320 Braddock Place
Alexandria, VA 22314
Telephone: (703) 739-5040
Fax: (703) 739-5295
Web site: www.pbs.org

Turner Broadcasting System
1 CNN Center
Atlanta, GA 30303
Telephone: (404) 885-4291
Web site: www.turner.com

Government Agencies

Federal Communications
  Commission
1919 M Street, NW
Washington, D.C. 20554
Web site: www.fcc.gov/vchip

Federal Trade Commission
Attention: Marketing Practices
Room 238
6th Street and Pennsylvania Avenue,
NW
Washington, D.C. 20580
Fax: (202) 326-2050

United States House of
  Representatives
Subcommittee on
  Telecommunications and Finance
2125 Rayburn Building
Washington, D.C. 20515
Telephone: (202) 225-2927
Web site: wwwhouse.gov/com

United States Senate
Subcommittee on Communications
227 Hart Senate Office Building
Washington, D.C. 20510
Telephone: (202) 224-5184
Web site: www.senate.gov/~
  commerce/

▀ CONCLUSION

This book is now ending. What kind of an effect have you let it have on you? Did you read it critically by analyzing the information and arguments? Did you compare and contrast the points made here with your existing knowledge structures? Did you evaluate my arguments and positions, agreeing with some and disagreeing with others? Did you synthesize the information you found most useful into your own perspective on media literacy and your own set of strategies to achieve that perspective? If you answered yes to these questions, then you have reacted well cognitively to the book. The key to a high-quality cognitive reaction is not whether you agree with me and accept all this information. Instead, the key is that your mind was continually active as you read the book.

Did you have some strong emotional reactions while reading the book? For example, were you upset by some of the information or arguments? Do you feel challenged and motivated to become more media literate? If you answered yes to these questions, then you have reacted well emotionally to the book. The key to a high-quality emotional reaction is not whether you have positive feelings about me or about the book. Instead, the key is that you were able to let your emotions become engaged by hating parts of the book and loving others.

Did you take moral positions throughout the book? For example, did you develop a sense of what is right about our culture (and what is wrong) because of the media? Did you make a strong commitment to yourself to do certain things to help yourself and others? If you answered yes to these questions, then you have reacted well morally to the book. The key to a high-quality moral reaction is not whether you agree with my positions. Instead, the key is that you are able to perceive a sense of right and wrong about certain conditions and to take a stand for yourself.

Finally, were you aware of aesthetic reactions to the book? Were there times where you appreciated the way I structured a chapter or the way I illuminated an important point? Did you find certain examples useful and creative? Did you feel that certain sections could have been written better? If you were able to answer these questions, then you were sensitive to the aesthetic features of the book. I, of course, hope that your aesthetic reactions were favorable. But whether favorable or not, the more aesthetic reactions you had and the more aesthetic awareness you exercised, the better for your media literacy development.

Most important, I hope you can see that you have achieved a significant degree of media literacy. You have many useful knowledge structures and many useful skills. As you continue developing these knowledge structures and skills, remember to be aware of what you are doing and stay in control of your progress. And make it fun!

FURTHER READING ■■

Adams, D. M., & Hamm, M. E. (1989). *Media and literacy: Learning in an electronic age: Issues, ideas and teaching strategies.* Springfield, IL: Charles C Thomas. (197 pages)

> This is a very applied approach to media literacy because the authors come from an educational technology background. They lay out some techniques that they suggest teachers can use to increase literacy in their students. While it is scholarly with its acknowledgment of some of the communication and education literature, there is little factual material or findings from research studies. There are chapters on teaching mathematics, computer literacy, and moral development.

Alvarado, M., & Boyd-Barrett, O. (Eds.). (1992). *Media education: An introduction*. London: BFI Publishing. (450 pages with index)

This edited volume contains 63 short essays organized into four sections: development and traditions of the subject of media education; key aspects of media education; analyzing classroom performance; and practical issues of practice, in-service training, strategies, and media education across the curriculum. All the contributors are British and their attention is on how media education should be incorporated into the curriculum in order to educate people between the ages of 4 and 18.

Brown, J. A. (1991). *Television "critical viewing skills" education: Major media literacy projects in the United States and selected countries*. Hillsdale, NJ: Lawrence Erlbaum. (371 pages including index)

Brown tries to inventory the range of systematic projects that have developed integrated curricula and long-range projects in media education with an emphasis on television. His audience is educators who are trying to design and implement their own media education projects at all levels: grade and high school, college, and adult education, as well as in local, regional, and even national interest groups.

Buckingham, D. (Ed.). (1990). *Watching media learning: Making sense of media education*. New York: Falmer. (234 pages with index)

This is an edited book of 10 chapters that deal with various aspects of media education in Britain. The main questions addressed are: What do students already know about the media? How have students learned what they already know? What should students know about the media?

DeGaetano, G., & Bander, K. (1996). *Screen smarts: A family guide to media literacy*. Boston: Houghton Mifflin. (206 pages with appendices and index)

Written by two teachers, this is a book for parents who are concerned about what their children are learning (or not learning) from television. They observe that "we are taught how to read and write, but we are not taught about visual images—how they work, how they affect us, and how we can use them for our purposes" (p. xv). The book is full of practical suggestions and exercises for parents and children. There are in-depth treatments of media violence, advertising, stereotypes, as well as news and talk shows.

Goodwin, A., & Whannel, G. (Eds.). (1990). *Understanding television*. New York: Routledge. (192 pages with index)

This contains 12 chapters, primarily by British cultural scholars who teach about television to college students. These essays comprise a text that the authors use to introduce their students to the history, social context, and textual interpretation of television.

Houk, A., & Bogart, C. (1974). *Media literacy*. Dayton, OH: Pflaum-Standard. (115 pages)

This was written for teachers who teach media literacy in public schools. The book offers many creative suggestions to teachers.

Kelly, M. R. (1983). *A parents' guide to television: Making the most of it*. New York: John Wiley. (129 pages)

This is a practical handbook that is very thin on information and research findings with only 17 research studies cited in the entire book. Instead, its focus is on providing parents with lots of suggestions about how to interact with their children while they are watching television.

Masterman, L. (1985). *Teaching the media*. London: Comedia Publishing Group. (341 pages including annotated bibliography and appendices)

Written for teachers of media, this book addresses the questions: Why teach about the media? What are the best ways to teach about the media? Why are media texts the way they are? It seeks to present a set of general principles for teaching about any mass medium.

McLaren, P., Hammer, R., Sholle, D., & Reilly, S. S. (Eds.). (1995). *Rethinking media literacy: A critical pedagogy of representation*. New York: Peter Lang. (259 pages)

This is an edited book of seven chapters by different college professors, concluding with an interview with the four authors on the topic of strategies for media literacy. The chapters are critical of the media and argue for activism.

EXERCISE 20.1

Awareness of Key Factors in Effects Processes

This exercise is similar to the one you did in Chapter 16. It is repeated here, because being aware of the factors that can increase the probability of an effect is so important. Also, this repetition will serve as a point of comparison with your performance several weeks ago to demonstrate how your learning has changed.

For each of the five scenarios below, think about the general factors synthesized in this chapter. Do not refer to them as you do this exercise; instead, see what you can recall and how you can apply what you recall.

For each scenario, write a brief profile that explains why the person is at risk for a negative media effect, that is, what factors are likely present to increase the probability of a negative effect. Also, make some specific recommendations for what this person should do to reduce the risk.

1. Bobby is a 5-year-old who loves to watch action/adventure cartoons on Saturday morning television. His mother is happy that the television serves as a baby-sitter for Bobby, freeing time up for her to work in another part of the house.

2. Jennifer is disgusted by watching political ads on television. She thinks all ads are negative and will not watch them. Also, she thinks all politicians are crooks and refuses to vote or pay attention to any news coverage of campaigns.

3. Cool Dude is a sophomore in college. For the past 4 years he has been closely following heavy metal and rap music. He also watches a good deal of MTV. He stays up partying all night every night and sees himself as the center of social life at the school because of his dress, his talk, and his style.

4. Four-year-old Alison has just watched Bambi's mother die in the movie. She is so grief stricken that she cannot take her nap.

5. Percy is a teenager who has seen every horror film made, but now the thrill is gone. Recently he has lost the ability to be scared while at the movies. Still he continues to go to every new horror film—hoping that there will be some awesome special effect or super-gruesome scene that can excite him.

EXERCISE 20.2

Fantasizing About Your Societal Strategy

Let's say that next year you win $10 million in the lottery. After you pay your taxes, pay off all your current debts, and splurge on all sorts of luxuries, you still have $3 million left. You decide to do something more worthwhile with your money and your life—you decide to set up a citizens action group that will help people become more media literate and change some of the things in society. Think about strategies as you address the following issues.

1. *Goals:* What would the goals be for your organization?
   a. List some interpersonal goals you would want to achieve
   b. List some societal goals you would like to achieve
2. *Targets:*
   a. In order to reach the goals set above, who would you target for change (see Table 20.2). List those targets.
   b. What specifically would you want each target to change?
3. *Strategies:* How would you bring about that change?
   a. What things would you do to get the people in your targets to understand your point of view?
   b. What things would you do to get the people in your targets to change their behaviors?
3. *Barriers:* What do you think the key barriers would be that might prevent you from achieving your goals?

References

A. C. Nielsen Co. (1990). *1990 report on television*. Northbrook, IL: Author.

Ad agency women hit TV stereotypes. (1996, May 20). *Los Angeles Times*, p. 10.

Adams, D. M., & Hamm, M. E. (1989). *Media and literacy: Learning in an electronic age: Issues, ideas and teaching strategies*. Springfield, IL: Charles C Thomas.

Ader, D. R. (1995). A longitudinal study of agenda setting for the issue of environmental pollution. *Journalism & Mass Communication Quarterly, 72*, 300-311.

Adler, R. P., Lesser, G. S., Meringoff, L. K., Robertson, T. S., Rossiter, J. R., & Ward, S. (1980). *The effects of television advertising on children: Review and recommendations*. Lexington, MA: Lexington Books.

Albarran, A. B., & Chan-Olmsted, S. M. (1998). The United States of America. In A. B. Albarran & S. M. Chan-Olmsted (Eds.), *Global media economics: Commercialization, concentration and integration of world media markets* (pp. 19-32). Ames: Iowa University Press.

Alexander, A., Wartella, E., & Brown, D. (1981). Estimates of children's television viewing by mother and child. *Journal of Broadcasting, 25*, 243-252.

Allman, W. F. (1985, October). Pesticides: An unhealthy dependence? *Science, 6*(8), 14.

Altheide, D. L. (1976). *Creating reality: How TV news distorts events*. Beverly Hills, CA: Sage.

Ammons, L., Dimmick, J., & Pilotta, J. (1982). Crime news reporting in a black weekly. *Journalism Quarterly, 59*, 310-313.

Anderson, D. R. (1985). Online cognitive processing of television. In L. F. Alwitt & A. A. Mitchell (Eds.), *Psychological process and advertising effects: Theory, research, application* (pp. 177-199). Hillsdale, NJ: Lawrence Erlbaum.

Anderson, D. R., Collins, P. A., Schmitt, K. L., & Jocobvitz, R. S. (1996). Stressful life events and television viewing. *Communication Research, 23*, 243-260.

Anderson, D. R., Field, D. E., Collins, P. A., Lorch, E. P., Pugzles, A., & Nathan, J. G. (1985). Estimates of young children's time with television: A methodological comparison of parent reports with time-lapse video home observation. *Child Development, 56*, 1345-1357.

Antunes, G., & Hurley, P. (1977). The representation of criminal events in Houston's two daily newspapers. *Journalism Quarterly, 54,* 756-760.

Arndorfer, J. B. (1998, December 21). A-B looking for women via daytime TV programs. *Advertising Age, 69*(51), 8.

Atkin, C. K. (1982). Television advertising and socialization to consumer roles. In D. Pearl, L. Bouthilet, & J. Lazar (Eds.), *Television and behavior: Ten years of scientific progress and implications for the eighties: Vol. 2. Technical reviews* (pp. 191-200). Rockville, MD: U.S. Department of Health and Human Services.

Audits & Surveys. (1991). *The study of magazine buying patterns.* New York: Publishers Clearing House.

Austin, B. A. (1989). *Immediate seating: A look at movie audiences.* Belmont, CA: Wadsworth.

Austin, E. W. (1993). Exploring the effects of active parental mediation of television content. *Journal of Broadcasting & Electronic Media, 37,* 147-158.

Austin, E. W., & Meili, H. K. (1995). Effects of interpretations of television alcohol portrayals on children's alcohol beliefs. *Journal of Broadcasting & Electronic Media, 39,* 417-435.

Average baseball salaries take rare dip. (1995, November 29). *Santa Barbara News-Press,* p. B1.

Aversa, J. (1999, May 5). Government employees get no respect on TV. *Tallahassee Democrat,* p. 3A.

Bagdikian, B. (1992). *The media monopoly* (4th ed.). Boston: Beacon.

Bagdikian, B. (1997). *The media monopoly* (5th ed.). Boston: Beacon.

Bandura, A. (1986). *Social foundations of thought and action: A social cognitive theory.* Englewood Cliffs, NJ: Prentice Hall.

Bandura, A. (1994). Social cognitive theory of mass communication. In J. Bryant & D. Zillmann (Eds.), *Media effects* (pp. 61-90). Hillsdale, NJ: Lawrence Erlbaum.

Barber, B. R. (1995). *Jihad vs. McWorld.* New York: New York Times Books.

Barnet, R. J., & Cavanagh, J. (1994). *Global dreams: Imperial corporations and the new world order.* New York: Simon & Schuster.

Barrett, M. (1996). Strategic behavior and competition in cable television: Evidence from two overbuilt markets. *Journal of Media Economics, 9,* 43-62.

Barwise, P., & Ehrenberg, A. (1989). *Television and its audiences.* Newbury Park, CA: Sage.

Bauer, R. A., & Bauer, A. (1960). America, mass society and mass media. *Journal of Social Issues, 10*(3), 3-66.

Bauder, D. (1998, January 15). NBC pays record price to keep ER. *Santa Barbara News-Press,* p. C3.

Bauder, D. (2000a, February 26). Fox network swears off spectacle TV—again. *Tallahassee Democrat,* p. 3E.

Bauder, D. (2000b, March 14). CBS to air two reality TV shows. *Tallahassee Democrat,* p. B1.

Becker, L. B., Kosicki, G. M., & Jones, F. (1992). Racial differences in evaluation of the mass media. *Journalism Quarterly, 69,* 124-134.

Berelson, B., & Steiner, G. A. (1964). *Human behavior: An inventory of research findings*. New York: Harcourt, Brace, and World.

Berger, P. L., & Luckmann, T. (1966). *The social construction of reality*. Garden City, NY: Doubleday.

Bimber, B. (1996, December 3). Study: 51 million Americans have Internet access. *93106 Newspaper*, p. 3.

Black, C. (1992, January). Fair and equal access. *Link*, p. 43.

Blankenburg, W. B. (1995). Hard times and the news hole. *Journalism & Mass Communication Quarterly, 72*, 634-641.

Bloom, A. (1987). *The closing of the American mind*. New York: Simon & Schuster.

Blumer, H. (1946). Collective behavior. In A. M. Lee (Ed.), *Principles of sociology* (pp. 185-186). New York: Barnes & Noble.

Book Industry Study Group. (1998). *Book industry trends 1998*. New York: Author.

Boswell, T. (1996, July 20). Between the commercials, waiting for the real show. *Washington Post*, p. G9.

Bowen, D. (1993, November 7). Multimedia is the message. *The Independent* (London), p. 3.

Brenner, L. (1996, June 23). What people earn. *Parade Magazine*, pp. 4-7.

Brouwer, M. (1964). Mass communication and the social sciences: Some neglected areas. In L. Dexter & D. M. White (Eds.), *People, society and mass communication* (pp. 547-568). New York: Free Press.

Brown, J. A. (1991). *Television "critical viewing skills" education: Major media literacy projects in the United States and selected countries*. Hillsdale, NJ: Lawrence Erlbaum.

Brownfield, P. (1999, July 21). As minorities' TV presence dims, gay roles proliferate. *Los Angeles Times*, p. A1.

Bruner, J. S., Goodnow, J., & Austin, G. A. (1956). *A study of thinking*. New York: John Wiley.

Buerkel-Rothfuss, N. L. (1993). Background: What prior research shows. In B. S. Greenberg, J. D. Brown, & N. Buerkel-Rothfuss (Eds.), *Media, sex and the adolescent* (pp. 5-18). Cresskill, NJ: Hampton Press.

Bureau of Justice Statistics (1994). *Uniform crime report*. Washington, DC: Author.

Buzbee, S. (1995, November 2). U.S. students score poorly in American history. *Santa Barbara News-Press*, p. A3.

Calfee, J. E. (1994). The 70% majority: Enduring consumer beliefs about advertising. *Journal of Public Policy & Marketing, 13*(2), 228-239.

Campaign '88: Assessing the media. (1988, November 14). *Broadcasting Magazine, 115*(21), 58-60.

Cantor, J. (1994). Fright reactions to mass media. In J. Bryant & D. Zillmann (Eds.), *Media effects* (pp. 213-245). Hillsdale, NJ: Lawrence Erlbaum.

Cantril, H. (1947). The invasion from Mars. In T. Newcomb & E. Hartley (Eds.), *Readings in social psychology* (pp. 619-628). New York: Holt.

Cassata, M., & Skill, T. (1983). *Life on daytime television*. Norwood, NJ: Ablex.

CBS headquarters, name taken over by Westinghouse. (1997, December 2). *Santa Barbara News-Press*, p. A6.

Chan-Olmsted, S. M. (1996). Market competition for cable television: Reexamining its horizontal mergers and industry concentration. *Journal of Media Economics, 9,* 25-41.

Chew, F., & Palmer, S. (1994). Interest, the knowledge gap, and television programming. *Journal of Broadcasting & Electronic Media, 38,* 271-287.

Christianson, P. G., & Roberts, D. F. (1998). *It's not only rock & roll: Popular music in the lives of adolescents.* Cresskill, NJ: Hampton Press.

Clark, E. (1988). *The want makers.* New York: Penguin.

Columbia Broadcasting System. (1980). *Network prime time violence tabulations for 1978-1979 season.* New York: Author.

Combs, B., & Slovic, P. (1979). Newspaper coverage of causes of death. *Journalism Quarterly, 56,* 837-843, 849.

Comstock, G. (1989). *The evolution of American television.* Newbury Park, CA: Sage.

Comstock, G. A. (1980). *Television in America.* Beverly Hills, CA: Sage.

Comstock, G. A. (1982). Violence in television content: An overview. In D. Pearl, L. Bouthilet, & J. Lazar (Eds.), *Television and behavior: Ten years of scientific progress and implications for the eighties: Vol. 2. Technical reviews* (pp. 108-125). Rockville, MD: U.S. Department of Health and Human Services.

Comstock, G. A., Chaffee, S., Katzman, N., McCombs, M., & Roberts, D. (1978). *Television and human behavior.* New York: Columbia University Press.

Cooper, R. (1993). An expanded, integrated model for determining audience exposure to television. *Journal of Broadcasting & Electronic Media, 38,* 401-418.

Currie, E. (1998). *Crime and punishment in America.* New York: Metropolitan Books.

Daly, C., Henry, P., & Ryder, E. (2000). The structure of the magazine industry. In A. N. Greco (Ed.), *The media and entertainment industries* (pp. 26-45). Boston: Allyn & Bacon.

Davidson, K. D. (2000). *Selling sin: The marketing of socially unacceptable products.* Thousand Oaks, CA: Sage.

Davie, W. R., & Lee, J.-S. (1993). Television news technology: Do more sources mean less diversity? *Journal of Broadcasting & Electronic Media, 39,* 453-464.

Davie, W. R., & Lee, J.-S. (1995). Sex, violence, and consonance/differentiation: An analysis of local TV news values. *Journalism & Mass Communication Quarterly, 72,* 128-138.

DeFleur, M. L., & Dennis, E. E. (1996). *Understanding mass communication: A liberal arts perspective.* Princeton, NJ: Houghton Mifflin.

DeGaetano, G., & Bander, K. (1996). *Screen smarts: A family guide to media literacy.* Boston: Houghton Mifflin.

Dennis, E. E. (1993, April 15). *Fighting media illiteracy: What every American needs to know and why.* Presented as the Roy W. Howard Public Lecture in Journalism and Mass Communication, Number 4, School of Journalism, Indiana University.

Dentzer, S. (1996, November 4). Delusions about deficits—and debt. *U.S. News & World Report,* p. 59.

Dervin, B., & Greenberg, B. S. (1972). The communication environment of the urban poor. In F. G. Kline & P. J. Tichenor (Eds.), *Current perspectives in mass communication research* (pp. 195-233). Beverly Hills, CA: Sage.

Dizard, W., Jr. (2000). *Old media new media* (3rd ed.). New York: Longman.

Dominick, J. R. (1999). *The dynamics of mass communication* (6th ed.). Boston: McGraw-Hill.

Donnelly, W. J. (1986). *The confetti generation: How the new communications technology is fragmenting America*. New York: Henry Holt.

Dorr, A. (1981). Television and affective development and functioning: Maybe this decade. *Journal of Broadcasting, 25*, 335-345.

Douglas, W., & Olson, B. M. (1995). Beyond family structure: The family in domestic comedy. *Journal of Broadcasting & Electronic Media, 39*, 236-261.

Douglas, W., & Olson, B. M. (1996). Subversion of the American family? An examination of children and parents in television families. *Communication Research, 23*, 73-99.

D'Souza, D. (1991). *Illiberal education: The politics of race and sex on campus*. New York: Free Press.

Dunn, A. (1999, July 8). Most of Web beyond scope of search sites. *Los Angeles Times*, Home Section, p. 1.

Dutka, E. (1995, January 27). A different Hollywood order. *Los Angeles Times*, p. D4.

Educational Testing Service. (1990). *Beyond high school: The transition to work*. Princeton, NJ: Author.

Elasmar, M., Hasegawa, K., & Brain, M. (1999). The portrayals of women in U.S. prime time television. *Journal of Broadcasting & Electronic Media, 43*, 20-34.

Eller, C. (1999, July 9). Literary manager built career by not following script. *Los Angeles Times*, pp. C1, C5.

Eller, C., & Bates, J. (1999, August 13). In Hollywood, more business than show. *Los Angeles Times*, pp. A1, A23.

Fabrikant, A. S. (1995, August 1). Disney to buy ABC for $19-billion. *Santa Barbara New-Press*, pp. A1, A2.

Farhi, P., & Shapiro, L. (1996, July 27). Sports as an afterthought on NBC. *Washington Post*, pp. A1, A14.

Federman, J. (1996). *Media ratings: Design, use and consequences*. Century City, CA: Mediascope.

Fedler, F., & Jordan, D. (1982). How emphasis on people affects coverage of crime. *Journalism Quarterly, 59*, 474-478.

Ferguson, D. A. (1992). Channel repertoire in the presence of remote control devices, VCRs, and cable television. *Journal of Broadcasting & Electronic Media, 36*, 83-91.

Fernandez-Collado, C., Greenberg, B., Korzenny, F., & Atkin, C. (1978). Sexual intimacy and drug use in TV series. *Journal of Communication, 28*(3), 30-37.

Fewer adults reading newspapers, watching news. (1995, April 6). *Santa Barbara News-Press*, p. A5.

Fico, F., & Soffin, S. (1995). Fairness and balance of selected newspaper coverage of controversial national, state, and local issues. *Journalism & Mass Communication Quarterly, 72,* 621-633.

Fishman, M. (1980). *Manufacturing the news.* Austin: University of Texas Press.

Fishoff, S. (1988, August). *Psychological research and a black hole called Hollywood.* Paper presented at the Annual Meeting of the American Psychological Association, Atlanta, GA.

Flanigan, J. (1999, July 30). There's no defense for NFL expecting more L.A. funds. *Los Angeles Times,* pp. C1, C2.

Foa, E. B., & Kozak, M. J. (1986). Emotional processing of fear: Exposure to corrective information. *Psychological Bulletin, 99,* 20-35.

Fore, W. F. (1987). *Television and religion: The shaping of faith, values, and culture.* Minneapolis, MN: Augsburg.

Friedson, E. (1953). The relation of the social situation of contact to the media in mass communication. *Public Opinion Quarterly, 17,* 230-238.

Fuller, L. K. (1997). We can't duck the issue: Imbedded advertising in the motion pictures. In K. T. Frith (Ed.), *Undressing the ad: Reading culture in advertising* (pp. 109-129). New York: Peter Lang.

Galician, M. L. (1986). Perceptions of good news and bad news on television. *Journalism Quarterly, 63,* 611-616.

Gardner, R. W. (1968). *Personality development at preadolescence.* Seattle: University of Washington Press.

Gellene, D. (1996, September 24). Seagram plans more TV ads for whiskey. *Los Angeles Times,* p. D2.

Gerbner, G., & Gross, L. (1976). Living with television: The violence profile. *Journal of Communication, 26*(2), 173-199.

Gerbner, G., Gross, L., Morgan, M., & Signorielli, N. (1980). The "mainstream-ing" of America: Violence profile no. 11. *Journal of Communication, 30*(3), 10-29.

Gerbner, G., Gross, L., Signorielli, N., Morgan, M., & Jackson-Beeck, M. (1979). The demonstration of power: Violence profile no. 10. *Journal of Communication, 29*(3), 177-196.

Gerbner, G., Gross, L., Morgan, M., & Signorielli, N. (1994). Growing up with television: The cultivation perspective. In J. Bryant & D. Zillmann (Eds.), *Media effects* (pp. 17-41). Hillsdale, NJ: Lawrence Erlbaum Associates.

Gerbner, G., Morgan, M., & Signorielli, N. (1982). Programming health portrayals: What viewers see, say and do. In D. Pearl, L. Bouthilet, & J. Lazar (Eds.), *Television and behavior: Ten years of scientific progress and implications for the eighties: Vol. 2. Technical reviews* (pp. 291-307). Rockville, MD: U.S. Department of Health and Human Services.

Gilligan, C. (1993). *In a different voice.* Cambridge, MA: Harvard University Press.

Glendon, M. A. (1991). *Rights talk: The impoverishment of political discourse.* Cambridge, MA: Harvard University Press.

Goldstein, D. (1999, September 25). Biggest-grossing movies gross in other ways. *Tallahassee Democrat,* p. B1.

Goleman, D. (1995). *Emotional intelligence*. New York: Bantam Books.

Goodman, E. (1997, October 27). Beauty industry on a rampage. *Santa Barbara News-Press*, p. A9.

Goodwin, A., & Whannel, G. (Eds.). (1990). *Understanding television*. New York: Routledge.

Goranson, R. E. (1970). Media violence and aggressive behavior: A review of experimental research. In L. Berkowitz (Ed.), *Advances in experimental social psychology* (Vol. 5). New York: Academic Press.

Graber, D. A. (1988). *Processing the news: How people tame the information tide* (2nd ed.). New York: Longman.

Graesser, A. C., Millis, K. K., & Long, D. L. (1986). The construction of knowledge-based inferences during story comprehension. In N. E. Sharkey (Ed.), *Advances in cognitive science 1* (pp. 125-157). New York: John Wiley.

Greenberg, B. S. (1982). Television and role socialization: An overview. In D. Pearl, L. Bouthilet, & J. Lazar (Eds.), *Television and behavior: Ten years of scientific progress and implications for the eighties: Vol 2. Technical reviews* (pp. 179-190). Rockville, MD: U.S. Department of Health and Human Services.

Greenberg, B. S., Edison, N., Korzenny, F., Fernandez-Collado, C., & Atkin, C. K. (1980). In B. S. Greenberg (Ed.), *Life on television: Content analysis of U.S. TV drama* (pp. 99-128). Norwood, NJ: Ablex.

Greenberg, B. S., Stanley, C., Siemicki, M., Heeter, C., Soderman, A., & Linsangan, R. (1993). Sex content on soaps and prime-time television series most viewed by adolescents. In B. S. Greenberg, J. D. Brown, & N. Buerkel-Rothfuss (Eds.), *Media, sex and the adolescent* (pp. 29-44). Cresskill, NJ: Hampton Press.

Greimel, H. (2000, February 5). Mannesmann agrees to buyout. *Tallahassee Democrat*, p. E1.

Grimm, M. (1996, June 10). Olympic grab bag. *Brandweek*, pp. 26-28, 30, 32, 24.

Gross, N. (1996, December 23). Zap! Splat! Smarts? *Newsweek*, pp. 64-71.

Guback, T., & Varis, R. (1983). *Transnational communication & cultural industries*. New York: Bernan.

Gulbransen, S. M. (1998, February 15). Best seller lists are numbers, power, money. *Santa Barbara News-Press*, p. D7.

Gunter, B. (1987). *Poor reception: Misunderstanding and forgetting broadcast news*. Hillsdale, NJ: Lawrence Erlbaum.

Hack attack. (2000, April 3). *U.S. News & World Report*, p. 7.

Hadly, S. (1997, April 27). 1 in 3 slayings in Ventura County remain unsolved. *Los Angeles Times*, p. A14.

Hancock, E. (1995, October 27). Culture cops take on sleazy TV talk shows. *Santa Barbara News-Press*, p. A1.

Hartman, T. (1999, March 22). Movie characters aren't reaping what they sow. *Tallahassee Democrat*, p. A1.

Hashway, R. M., & Duke, L. I. (1992). *Cognitive styles: A primer to the literature*. Lewiston, NY: Edwin Mellen Press.

Hawkins, R. P., & Pingree, S. (1982). Television's influence on social reality. In D. Pearl, L. Bouthilet, & J. Lazar (Eds.), *Television and behavior: Ten years of scientific progress and implications for the eighties: Vol. 2. Technical reviews* (pp. 224-247). Rockville, MD: U.S. Department of Health and Human Services.

Healy, J. M. (1990). *Endangered minds: Why children don't think and what we can do about it.* New York: Simon & Schuster.

Hiaasen, C. (1999, February 26). Lap dog of the NRA wants to outlaw suing of gun makers. *Tallahassee Democrat,* p. 11A.

Himmelweit, H. T. (1966). Television and the child. In B. Berelson & M. Janowitz (Eds.), *Reader in public opinion and communication* (2nd ed.). New York: Free Press.

Hirsch, E. D., Jr. (1987). *Cultural literacy: What every American needs to know.* Boston: Houghton Mifflin.

Hirsch, E. D., Jr., Kett, J. F., & Trefil, J. (1993). *The dictionary of cultural literacy* (2nd ed.). Boston: Houghton Mifflin.

Hoffner, C., & Cantor, J. (1991). Perceiving and responding to mass media characters. In J. Bryant & D. Zillmann (Eds.), *Responding to the screen* (pp. 63-101). Hillsdale, NJ: Lawrence Erlbaum.

Hofmeister, S. (1997a, February 19). $2.7-billion deal would create no. 2 radio group in U.S. *Los Angeles Times,* p. D1.

Hofmeister, S. (1997b, September 23). Seagram to buy USA Networks for $1.7-billion. *Los Angeles Times,* p. A1.

Holland, J. (1998, January 15). Internal records show tobacco firm targeted teen-agers. *Santa Barbara News-Press,* p. A2.

Hollander, B. A. (1995). The new news and the 1992 presidential campaign: Perceived vs. actual political knowledge. *Journalism & Mass Communication Quarterly, 72,* 786-798.

Hollenbeck, A., & Slaby, R. (1979). Infant visual and vocal responses to television. *Child Development, 50,* 41-45.

Holstein, W. J. (1999, September 20). MTV, meet 60 Minutes. *U.S. News & World Report,* pp. 44-46.

Holstein, W. J. (2000, April 3). And then there were five. *U.S. News & World Report,* p. 46.

Hoover, S. M. (1988). *Mass media religion: The social sources of the electronic church.* Newbury Park, CA: Sage.

Hoover's guide to media companies. (1996). Austin, TX: Hoover's Business Press.

Horowitz, D. (1996, June 24). Nowhere to hide from advertisers. *Santa Barbara News-Press,* p. B7.

Horsfield, P. G. (1984). *Religious television: The American experience.* New York: Longman.

Howard, H. H. (1995). TV station group and cross-media ownership: A 1995 update. *Journalism & Mass Communication Quarterly, 72,* 390-401.

Howard, H. H., & Carroll, S. L. (1993). Economics of the cable industry. In A. Alexander, J. Owers, & R. Carveth (Eds.), *Media economics: Theory and practice* (pp. 245-266). Hillsdale, NJ: Lawrence Erlbaum.

Hudson, T. J. (1992). Consonance in depiction of violent material in television news. *Journal of Broadcasting & Electronic Media, 36,* 411-425.

Huston, A., Wright, J. C., Rice, M. L., Kerkman, D., Seigle, J., & Bremer, M. (1983). *Family environment and television use by preschool children.* Paper presented at the Biennial Meeting of the Society for Research on Child Development, Detroit, MI. (Eric Document Reproduction Service No. ED 230 293).

Hyde, J. (2000, March 28). Auto industry's new credo: Partner up. *Tallahassee Democrat,* p. E1.

Intelligence Infocorp. (1996, May 22). *Nando.net release.* La Jolla, CA: Author.

Irvine, M. (1999, November 25). Married couples are the new endangered species. *Tallahassee Democrat,* p. 6B.

Is your child safe in cyberspace? (1995, December). *USAA Magazine,* pp. 28-31.

It's pretty hard to tell what's what these days. (1993, July 31). *Washington Post,* p. A12.

Iyengar, S., & Kinder, D. (1987). *News that matters.* Chicago: University of Chicago Press.

Jacoby, J. (2000, January 31). More politics on TV? No thanks. *Boston Globe,* p. A17.

Jamieson, K. H., & Campbell, K. K. (1988). *The interplay of influence* (2nd ed.). Belmont, CA: Wadsworth.

Jeffres, L. W. (1994). *Mass media processes* (2nd ed.). Prospect Heights, IL: Waveland.

Jensen, C. (1996). *Censored: The news that didn't make the news—and why: The 1996 Project Censored yearbook.* New York: Seven Stories Press.

Jensen, C. (1997). *20 years of censored news.* New York: Seven Stories Press.

Jensen, J., & Ross, C. (1996, July 15). Centennial Olympics open as $5 bil event of century. *Advertising Age, 67*(29), pp. 1-2.

Kafka, P. (2000, March 20). The power 100 (100 highly paid celebrities). *Forbes,* p. 199.

Kagan, J., Rosman, D., Day, D., Albert, J., & Phillips, W. (1964). Information processing in the child: Significance of analytic and reflective attitudes. *Psychological Monographs, 78,* 1.

Kaniss, P. (1996, December 19). Bad news: How electronic media muddle the message. *Philadelphia Inquirer,* p. A35.

Kantrowitz, B. (1993, May 31). An interactive life. *Newsweek,* pp. 42-44.

Katz, E., & Gurevitch, M. (1976). *The secularization of leisure: Culture and communication in Israel.* Cambridge, MA: Harvard University Press.

Kim, K., & Barnett, G. A. (1996). The determinants of international news flow: A network analysis. *Communication Research, 23,* 323-352.

Klapper, J. T. (1960). *The effects of mass communication.* Glencoe, IL: Free Press.

Koenenn, C. (1997, May 14). Let's get simple. *Los Angeles Times,* p. E1.

Kohlberg, L. (1966). Moral education in the schools: A developmental view. *School Review, 74,* 1-30.

Kohlberg, L. (1981). *The philosophy of moral development: Moral stages and the idea of justice*. New York: Harper & Row.

Koplovitz, K. (1990, March 12). Cable's cutting edge. *View*, p. 22.

Kubey, R., Shifflet, M., Weerakkody, N., & Ukeiley, S. (1996). Demographic diversity on cable: Have the new cable channels made a difference in the representation of gender, race, and age? *Journal of Broadcasting & Electronic Media, 39*, 459-471.

Kunkel, D., Cope, K. M., Farinola, W. J. M., Biely, E., Rollin, E., & Donnerstein, E. (1999). *Sex on TV: Content and context*. Menlo Park, CA: Kaiser Family Foundation.

Kunkel, D., & Gantz, W. (1992). Children's television advertising in the multichannel environment. *Journal of Communication, 42*(3), 134-152.

L.A. Times publisher errs, apologizes. (1999, October 31). *Tallahassee Democrat*, p. 5B.

Lacy, S., & Riffe, D. (1994). The impact of competition and group ownership on radio news. *Journalism & Mass Communication Quarterly, 71*, 583-593.

Larson, J. (1983). *Television's window on the world*. Norwood, NJ: Ablex.

LaSalle, M. (1996, July 7). Why overpaid stars aren't worth it. *Santa Barbara News-Press*, p. D9.

Lee, M., & Solomon, N. (1990). *Unreliable sources: A guide to detecting bias in news media*. New York: Carol Publishing Group.

The learning lag: You can't blame TV. (1996, December 2). *U.S. News & World Report*, p. 16.

Leo, J. (1996, August 19). The joys of covering press releases. *U.S. News & World Report*, p. 16.

Leo, J. (1999, September 27). And now . . . smut-see TV. *U.S. News & World Report*, p. 15.

Leovy, J. (1999, October 24). Online services open a new chapter in collegians' search for cheaper textbooks. *Los Angeles Times*, p. A4.

Lichter, L. S., & Lichter, S. R. (1983). *Prime time crime*. Washington, DC: The Media Institute.

Liebert, R. M., Neale, J. M., & Davidson, E. S. (1973). *The early window: Effects of television on children and youth*. Elmsford, NY: Pergamon.

Liebert, R. M., & Schwartzberg, N. S. (1977). Effects of mass media. *Annual Review of Psychology, 28*, 141-173.

Linz, D., Donnerstein, E., & Penrod, S. (1984). The effects of multiple exposures to filmed violence against women. *Journal of Communication, 34*(3), 130-147.

Linz, D., Donnerstein, E., & Penrod, S. (1988). Effects of long-term exposure to violent and sexually degrading depictions of women. *Journal of Personality and Social Psychology, 55*(5), 758-768.

Lippmann, W. (1922). *Public opinion*. New York: Harcourt, Brace, and Company.

Lorimer, R. (1994). *Mass communications: A comparative introduction*. New York: Manchester University Press.

Lowry, B. (1998, May 14). Seinfeld farewell: The death of nothing. *Los Angeles Times*, pp. A1, A26.

Lowry, B., Jensen, E., & Braxton, G. (1999, July 20). Networks decide diversity does-n't pay. *Los Angeles Times*, p. A1.

Luntz, F. (2000, March). Public to press: Cool it. *Brill's Content*, pp. 74-79.

Lyall, S. (1996, November 27). Penguin's deal to buy Putnam will create major publishing force. *Santa Barbara News-Press*, p. A6.

Maddox, K. (1998, August 3). Online advertising reaches $544.8 mil, new report says. *Advertising Age, 69*(31), 28.

Maddox, K. (1999, February 15). IAB: Internet advertising will reach new $2 bil for 1998. *Advertising Age, 70*(7), 34.

Makovsky, D. (1999, May 24). Getting into the ring: Wealthy American and other foreigners played a quiet role in Israel's election. *U.S. News & World Report*, p. 43.

Malamuth, N. M., & Check, J. V. P. (1980). Penile tumescence and perceptual responses to rape as a function of victim's perceived reactions. *Journal of Applied Social Psychology, 10*, 528-547.

Mandese, J. (1995, August 7). Is it Magic Kingdom or an evil empire? *Advertising Age*, p. 1.

Maney, K. (1995). *Megamedia shakeout: The inside story of the leaders and the losers in the exploding communications industry*. New York: John Wiley.

Manning, R. (1987, December 28). The selling of the Olympics. *Newsweek*, pp. 40-41.

Marcuse, H. (1964). *One-dimensional man*. Boston: Beacon.

Marin, R. (1996, July 8). Alien invasion. *Newsweek*, p. 48.

Material kids are on the march. (1994, April). *NEA Today*, p. 10.

Matthews, J. (1992, April 13). To yank or not to yank? *Newsweek*, p. 59.

Matzer, M. (1996, November 26). TV sponsors find more visible outlets for their plugs. *Los Angeles Times*, pp. D1, D4.

Maurstad, T. (1998, August 20). TV Land adds 60-second sitcoms to the lineup. *Tallahassee Democrat*, p. 7D.

McCarthy, M. J. (1991, March 22). Mind probe. *Wall Street Journal*, p. B3.

McDonald, M. (2000, March 27). L.A. is their kind of town. *U.S. News & World Report*, p. 45.

McGuire, W. J. (1973). Persuasion, resistance, and attitude change. In I. DeS. Pool, W. Schramm, F. W. Frey, N. Maccoby, & E. B. Parker (Eds.), *The process and effects of mass communication* (Rev. ed., pp. 216-252). Urbana: University of Illinois Press.

McLaren, P., Hammer, R., Sholle, D., & Reilly, S. S. (Eds.). (1995). *Rethinking media literacy: A critical pedagogy of representation*. New York: Peter Lang.

McLeod, J. M., Fitzpatrick, M. A., Glynn, C. J., & Fallis, S. F. (1982). Television and social relations: Family influences and consequences for interpersonal behavior. In D. Pearl, L. Bouthilet, & J. Lazar (Eds.), *Television and behavior: Ten years of scientific progress and implications for the eighties: Vol. 2. Technical reviews* (pp. 272-286). Rockville, MD: U.S. Department of Health and Human Services.

McQueen, A. (1999, November 19). Future voters come up short on knowledge of civics. *Tallahassee Democrat*, p. B1.

Meadowcroft, J., & Reeves, B. (1989). Influence of story schema development on children's attention to television. *Communication Research, 16*, 353-374.

Medrich, E. A., Roizen, J. A., Rubin, V., & Buckley, S. (1982). *The serious business of growing up. A study of children's lives outside school*. Berkeley: University of California Press.

Meisler, S. (1994, March 16). Poll: News media outclass churches. *Seattle Times*, p. A5.

Messaris, P. (1982). Parents, children, and television. In G. Gumpert & R. Cathcart (Eds.), *Inter/Media* (2nd ed., pp. 580-598). New York: Oxford University Press.

Messaris, P. (1994). *Visual "literacy": Image, mind, and reality*. Boulder, CO: Westview.

Metallinos, N. (1996). *Television aesthetics: Perceptual, cognitive, and compositional bases*. Mahwah, NJ: Lawrence Erlbaum.

Meyrowitz, J. (1985). *No sense of place: The impact of electronic media on social behavior*. New York: Oxford University Press.

Microsoft '99 revs up 29%. (1999, July 26). *Electronic News, 45*(30), 6.

Milgram, S. (1983). *Obedience to authority: An experimental view*. New York: Harper & Row.

Miller, S. (Ed.). (1989). *America's watching: 30th anniversary 1959-1989*. New York: Roper Organization.

Minow, N. N., & LaMay, C. L. (1995). *Abandoned in the wasteland: Children, television, and the First Amendment*. New York: Hill & Wang.

Multichannel News. (1993, July 19). p. 42.

Murray, J. P. (1980). *Television and youth: 25 years of research and controversy*. Boys Town, NB: Boys Town Center for the Study of Youth Development.

Myers, P. N., Jr., & Biocca, F. A. (1992). The elastic body image: The effect of television advertising and programming on body image distortions in young women. *Journal of Communication, 42*(3), 108-133.

Names & faces. (1995, September 11). *Santa Barbara News-Press*, p. B8.

National Football League 1999 salaries. (2000, May 23). *USA Today*, pp. 14C-15C.

National Television Violence Study. (1996). *Scientific report*. Thousand Oaks, CA: Sage.

NBC gambles on the future. (1996, January 22). *Santa Barbara News-Press*, p. A11.

NCTV says violence on TV up 16%. (1983, March 22). *Broadcasting Magazine*, p. 63.

Nelson, J. (1995, August 8). NBC gets Olympic TV rights in coup. *Santa Barbara News-Press*, p. A12.

Neuman, S. B. (1991). *Literacy in the television age: The myth of the TV effect*. Norwood, NJ: Ablex.

Newspaper Advertising Bureau. (1988). *News and newspaper reading habits: Results from a national survey*. New York: Author.

NFL teams dodge salary cap. (1996, January 2). *Santa Barbara News-Press*, p. B5.

Noelle-Neumann, E. (1984). *The spiral of silence: Public opinion—our social skin*. Chicago: University of Chicago Press.

Norris, V. P. (1983). Consumer valuation of national ads. *Journalism Quarterly, 60,* 262-268.

Numbers. (1999, August 16). *Time,* pp. 21, 76.

O'Brien, T. L. (1998). *The inside story of the glamour, glitz, and danger of America's gambling industry.* New York: Times Books.

Oliver, M. B. (1994). Portrayals of crime, race, and aggression in "reality based" police shows: A content analysis. *Journal of Broadcasting & Electronic Media,* pp. 179-192.

Ostrow, R. (1996, May 6). Violent crime in U.S. fell 4% in '95, FBI says. *Los Angeles Times,* pp. A1, A11.

Ozanich, G. W., & Wirth, M. O. (1993). Media mergers and acquisitions: An overview. In A. Alexander, J. Owers, & R. Carveth (Eds.), *Media economics: Theory and practice* (pp. 115-133). Hillsdale, NJ: Lawrence Erlbaum.

Pardun, C. J., & Krugman, D. M. (1994). How the architectural style of the home relates to family television viewing. *Journal of Broadcasting & Electronic Media, 38,* 145-162.

Parenti, M. (1986). *Inventing reality: The politics of the mass media.* New York: St. Martin's.

Patterson, T. (1980). *The mass media election.* New York: Praeger.

Perkins, K. (1996, November 27). Statistics blur image of American family. *Santa Barbara News-Press,* pp. A1, A2.

Perry, J. (2000, February 28). Only the cyberlonely. *U.S. News & World Report,* p. 62.

Petty, R. E., & Cacioppo, J. T. (1986). *Communication and persuasion: Central and peripheral routes to attitude change.* New York: Springer.

Pew Research Center for the People and the Press. (1998). *Internet news takes off.* Washington, DC: Author.

Picard, R. G. (1989). *Media economics: Concepts and issues.* Newbury Park, CA: Sage.

Picard, R. G. (1993). Economics of the daily newspaper industry. In A. Alexander, J. Owers, & R. Carveth (Eds.), *Media economics: Theory and practice* (pp. 181-203). Hillsdale, NJ: Lawrence Erlbaum.

Picard, R. G., Winter, J. P., McCombs, M., & Lacy, S. (Eds). (1988). *Press concentration and monopoly: New perspectives on newspaper ownership and operation.* Norwood, NJ: Ablex.

Pinker, S. (1997). *How the mind works.* New York: Norton.

Pipher, M. (1996). *The shelter of each other.* New York: Putnam.

Pizza pie in the sky. (1999, October 1). *Tallahassee Democrat,* p. B1.

Police cars to add advertisements. (1995, July 13). *Santa Barbara News-Press,* p. A4.

Pollay, R. W., Siddarth, S., Siegel, M., Haddix, A., Merritt, R. K., Giovino, G. A., & Eriksen, M. P. (1996). The last straw? Cigarette advertising and realized market shares among youths and adults, 1979-1993. *Journal of Marketing, 60*(2), 1-16.

Postman, N., & Powers, S. (1992). *How to watch TV news.* New York: Penguin.

Potter, W. J. (1987a). Does television viewing hinder academic achievement among adolescents? *Human Communication Research, 14*(1), 27-46.

Potter, W. J. (1987b). News from three worlds in prestige U.S. newspapers. *Journalism Quarterly, 64*, 73-79.

Potter, W. J. (1991). Examining cultivation from a psychological perspective: Component subprocesses, *Communication Research, 18*, 77-102.

Potter, W. J., & Ware, W. (1987). An analysis of the contexts of antisocial acts on prime-time television. *Communication Research, 14*, 664-686.

Potts, R., & Sanchez, D. (1994). Television viewing and depression: No news is good news. *Journal of Broadcasting & Electronic Media, 38*, 79-90.

Preston, I. (1994). *The tangled web they weave: Truth, falsity, & advertisers*. Madison: University of Wisconsin Press.

Pritchard, D. A. (1975). Leveling-sharpening revised. *Perceptual and Motor Skills, 40*, 111-117.

Procter & Gamble to cut advertising expenditures. (1996, February 19). *Santa Barbara News-Press*, p. B5.

Pulaski, M. A. S. (1980). *Understanding Piaget: An introduction to children's cognitive development* (Rev. ed.). New York: Harper & Row.

Quinn, J. B. (1996, April 1). Politics: Fable vs. fact. *Newsweek*, p. 62.

Radio Advertising Bureau. (1991). *Radio facts for advertisers 1990*. New York: Author.

Radio Advertising Bureau. (1993). *Why radio?* New York: Author.

Randolph, E. (1997, April 22). Journalists find little neutrality over objective reporting. *Los Angeles Times*, p. A5.

Rhodes, S., & Reibstein, L. (1996, July 1). Let him walk! *Newsweek*, pp. 44-45.

Rice, M., & Wartella, E. (1981). Television as a medium of communication: Implications for how to regard the child viewer. *Journal of Broadcasting, 25*, 365-372.

Rideout, V. J., Foehr, U. G., Roberts, D. F., & Brodie, M. (1999). *Kids & media @ the new millennium*. Menlo Park, CA: Kaiser Foundation.

Riggs, D. (1999, February 28). True love is alive and well, say romance book writers. *Tallahassee Democrat*, p. 3D.

Ritzer, G. (1993). *The McDonaldization of society: An investigation into the changing character of contemporary social life*. Newbury Park, CA: Pine Forge Press.

Roberts, D. R. (1973). Communication and children: A developmental approach. In I. DeS. Pool, W. Schramm, R. W. Frey, N. Maccoby, & E. B. Parker (Eds.), *The process and effects of mass communication* (Rev. ed., pp. 596-611). Urbana: University of Illinois Press.

Roberts, D. R., & Bachen, C. M. (1981). Mass communication effects. In P. H. Mussen & M. R. Rozenzweig (Eds.), *Annual review of psychology* (pp. 307-356). Palo Alto, CA: Annual Reviews.

Roberts, J. L. (1999, July 29). Main men. *Newsweek*, pp. 42-46.

Robinson, J. P., & Levy, M. R. (1986). *The main source*. Newbury Park, CA: Sage.

Roper Organization. (1981). *Sex, profanity and violence: An opinion survey about seventeen television programs*. Conducted for the National Broadcasting Company. New York: Information Office.

Roshier, B. (1981). The selection of crime news by the press. In S. Cohen & J. Young (Eds.), *The manufacture of news: Deviance, social problems and the mass media* (pp. 40-51). Beverly Hills, CA: Sage.

Rothberg, D. M. (1996, June 23). Group seeks increase in foreign aid budget. *Santa Barbara News-Press*, p. F2.

Rushton, J. P. (1979). Effects of prosocial television and film material on the behavior of viewers. In L. Berkowitz (Ed.), *Advances in experimental social psychology* (pp. 321-351). New York: Academic Press.

Salomon, G. (1981). Introducing AIME: The assessment of children's mental involvement with television. In H. Kelley & H. Gardner (Eds.), *Viewing children through television* (New Directions for Child Development, Vol. 13, pp. 89-112). San Francisco: Jossey-Bass.

Salovey, P., & Mayer, J. D. (1990). Emotional intelligence. *Imagination, Cognition, and Personality, 9,* 185-211.

Samuelson, R. J. (1992, April 2). I am a big lawyer basher. *Newsweek,* p. 42.

Sapolsky, B., & Tabarlet, J. (1990). *Sex in prime time television: 1979 vs. 1989.* Unpublished manuscript, Department of Communication, Florida State University, Tallahassee.

Schachter, S., & Singer, J. E. (1962). Cognitive, social, and physiological determinants of emotional state. *Psychological Review, 69,* 379-399.

Schrag, R. (1990). *Taming the wild tube: A family guide to television and video.* Chapel Hill: University of North Carolina Press.

Schramm, W., Lyle, J., & Parker, E. B. (1961). *Television in the lives of our children.* Stanford, CA: Stanford University Press.

Schultz, S. (1999, November 8). Why we're fat. *U.S. News & World Report,* p. 82.

Schwartz, S. (1984, Winter). Send help before it's too late. *Parent's Choice,* p. 2.

Scribner, S., & Cole, M. (1981). *The psychology of literacy.* Cambridge, MA: Harvard University Press.

Sessa, D. (1999, January 21). For college students, Web offers a lesson in discounts. *Wall Street Journal,* p. B7.

Shapiro, E. (1992, February 27). New marketing specialists tap collegiate consumers. *New York Times,* p. 16C.

Shaw, D. L., & McCombs, M. (1977). *The emergence of American political issues: The agenda-setting function of the press.* St. Paul, MN: West.

Shenk, D. (1997). *Data smog: Surviving the information glut.* San Francisco: HarperEdge.

Shoemaker, P. J. (1987). The communication of deviance. In B. Dervin (Ed.), *Progress in communication science* (Vol. 8, pp. 151-175). Norwood, NJ: Ablex.

Shoemaker, P. J., Danielian, L. H., & Brendlinger, N. (1991). Deviant acts, risky business, and U.S. interest: The newsworthiness of world events. *Journalism Quarterly, 68,* 781-795.

Shoemaker, P. J., & Reese, S. D. (1996). *Mediating the message: Theories of influences on mass media content* (2nd ed.). White Plains, NY: Longman.

Signorielli, N. (1990). Television's mean and dangerous world: A continuation of the cultural indicators perspective. In N. Signorielli & M. Morgan (Eds.), *Cultivation analysis: New directions in media effects research* (pp. 85-106). Newbury Park, CA: Sage.

Silverblatt, A. (1995). *Media literacy: Keys to interpreting media messages*. Westport, CT: Praeger.

Silverman, D. (1998, January 27). Compaq buyout industry's biggest. *Santa Barbara News-Press*, p. A6.

Simons, J. (1996, December 30). Waiting to download. *U.S. News & World Report*, p. 60.

Sinatra, R. (1986). *Visual literacy connections to thinking, reading and writing*. Springfield, IL: Charles C Thomas.

Singer, D. G. (1982). Television and the developing mind of the child. In D. Perl, L. Bouthilet, & J. Lazar (Eds.), *Television and behavior: Ten years of scientific progress and implications for the eighties: Vol. 2. Technical reviews* (pp. 39-52). Rockville, MD: U.S. Department of Health and Human Services.

Singer, D. G., & Singer, J. L. (1981). Television and the developing imagination of the child. *Journal of Broadcasting, 25*, 373-387.

Skidmore, D. (1999, March 2). Economy to start ninth year of expansion. *Tallahassee Democrat*, p. E1.

Slattery, K. L., & Hakanen, E. A. (1994). Sensationalism versus public affairs content of local TV news: Pennsylvania revisited. *Journal of Broadcasting & Electronic Media, 38*, 205-216.

Smith, P. K., & Cowie, H. (1988). *Understanding children's development*. Oxford: Basil Blackwell.

Smythe, D. W. (1954). Reality as presented on television. *Public Opinion Quarterly, 18*, 143-156.

Soley, L. C., & Reid, L. N. (1983). Satisfaction with the information value of magazine and television advertising. *Journal of Advertising, 12*(3), 27-31.

Standard & Poor. (1996, July). *Index to surveys*. New York: Author.

Stanley, B. (2000, January 25). Merger creates largest must business. *Tallahassee Democrat*, p. E1.

Statistical Abstract of the United States: 1999. (2000). Washington, DC: Congressional Information Service.

Steele, J. E. (1995). Experts and the operational bias of television news: The case of the Persian Gulf war. *Journalism & Mass Communication Quarterly, 72*, 799-812.

Sternberg, R. J., & Berg, C. A. (1987). What are theories of adult intellectual development theories of? In C. Schooler & K. W. Schaie (Eds.), *Cognitive functioning and social structure over the life course* (pp. 3-23). Norwood, NJ: Ablex.

Straus, N. (1995, July 10). Why do CDs cost so much? It's like this . . . *Santa Barbara News-Press*, p. B5.

Strauss, R. (1996, November, 29). The numbers game. *Los Angeles Times*, p. E4.

Stroh, M. (1999, October 9). From pulp to pixel. *Tallahassee Democrat*, p. E1.

Study links teen smoking to popular ads. (1996, April 14). *Santa Barbara News-Press*, p. A2.

Superbowl ad costs rise to $22-million. (1999, November 29). *St. Petersberg Times*, p. 6C.

Sutel, S. (1999, November 3). "Enquirer" owner buys rival tabloids. *Tallahassee Democrat*, p. E5.

Sutter, M. (1999, January 25). Marketers boost Pope's visit to Mexico with tie-ins. *Advertising Age, 70*(4), 14.

Tan, A. S. (1981). *Mass communication theories and research.* Columbus, OH: Grid Publishing.

Teen drug use soars. (1996, August 21). *Asbury Park Press*, p. A1.

Teen spending up again. (1996, March 31). *Parade Magazine*, p. 19.

Thomas, M. H. (1982). Physiological arousal, exposure to a relatively lengthy aggressive film and aggressive behavior. *Journal of Research in Personality, 16,* 72-81.

Timeline of major media mergers. (2000, March 13). AP Online, Financial section [Online]. Available: http://wire.ap.org

Top 300 magazines by gross revenue. (1998, June 15). *Ad Age*, p. S6.

Tuchman, G. (1978). *Making news: A study in the construction of reality.* New York: Free Press.

Turow, J. (1992). *Media systems in society.* New York: Longman.

USA Today. (1993, July 1), p. 2A.

Valkenburg, P. M., & Van der Voort, T. H. A. (1995). The influence of television on children's daydreaming styles: A 1-year panel study. *Communication Research, 22,* 267-287.

Vande Berg, L. R., & Streckfuss, D. (1992). Prime-time television's portrayal of women and the world of work: A demographic profile. *Journal of Broadcasting & Electronic Media, 36,* 195-208.

Vranizan, M. (1995, June 5). On-line junkie hooked on his screen. *Santa Barbara News-Press*, p. A11.

Walsh, D. (1994). *Selling out America's children: How America puts profits before values—and what parents can do..* Minneapolis, MN: Fairview Press.

Wartella, E. (1981). The child as viewer. In M. E. Ploghoft & J. A. Anderson (Eds.), *Education for the television age* (pp. 28-17). Springfield, IL: Charles C Thomas.

Watanabe, T. (1999, July 27). The crisis facing the Good Book. *Los Angeles Times*, p. A1.

Weiss, W. (1969). Effects of the mass media on communication. In G. Lindzey & E. Aronson (Eds.), *The handbook of social psychology* (2nd ed., Vol. 5, pp. 77-195). Reading, MA: Addison-Wesley.

Weiss, W. (1971). Mass communication. In P. H. Mussen & M. R. Rozenzweig (Eds.), *Annual review of psychology* (pp. 309-336). Palo Alto, CA: Annual Reviews.

Wharton, D. (1991, June 10). Let 'em eat junk? Fat chance, Solon says. *Variety*, p. 33.

White, M. (2000, March 14). Tribune-Times Mirror merger creates multimedia empire. *Tallahassee Democrat*, p. E1.

Whitman, D. (1996, December 16). I'm OK, you're not. *U.S. News & World Report*, pp. 24-30.

Whitman, D., & Loftus, M. (1996, December 16). Things are getting better? Who knew? *U.S. News & World Report*, pp. 30, 32.

Wicks, R. (1992). Improvement over time in recall of media information: An exploratory study. *Journal of Broadcasting & Electronic Media, 36*, 287-302.

Wildavsky, B. (1999, October 11). Kids don't have the write stuff. *U.S. News & World Report*, p. 28.

Will, G. F. (1991, September 23). Too much of a good thing? *Newsweek*, p. 68.

Will, G. F. (1996, April 15). Civic speech gets rationed. *Newsweek*, p. 78.

Williams, T. M., Zabrack, M. L., & Joy, L. A. (1982). The portrayal of aggression on North American television. *Journal of Applied Social Psychology, 12*, 360-380.

Williams, R. (1974). *Television, technology and cultural form.* New York: Schocken Books.

Wilson, B. J., & Cantor, J. (1985). Developmental differences in empathy with a television protagonist's fears. *Journal of Experimental Child Psychology, 39*, 284-299.

Wilson, B. J., & Weiss, A. J. (1992). Developmental differences in children's reactions to a toy advertisement linked to a toy-based cartoon. *Journal of Broadcasting & Electronic Media, 36*, 371-394.

Windhauser, J. W., Seiter, J., & Winfree, L. T. (1990). Crime news in the Louisiana press, 1980 vs. 1985. *Journalism Quarterly, 67*, 72-78.

Winn, M. (1984). *The plug-in drug: Television, children and the family.* New York: Penguin.

Witkin, H. A., & Goodenough, D. R. (1977). Field dependence and interpersonal behavior. *Psychological Bulletin, 84*, 661-689.

Wollenberg, S. (2000, May 13). Advertising deal done. *Tallahassee Democrat*, p. E1.

Woodward, K. L. (1990, December 17). A time to seek. *Newsweek*, pp. 50-56.

Wride, N. (1999, August 9). Children learn to say, "Buy, buy." *Los Angeles Times*, p. E1.

Wulff, S. (1997). Media literacy. In W. G. Christ (Ed.), *Media education assessment handbook* (pp. 123-142). Mahwah, NJ: Lawrence Erlbaum.

Wurman, R. S. (1989). *Information anxiety.* Garden City, NY: Doubleday.

Yang, D. J. (2000, January 17). Craving your next Web fix. *U.S. News & World Report*, p. 41.

Youn, S. M. (1994). Program type preference and program choice in a multichannel situation. *Journal of Broadcasting & Electronic Media, 38*, 465-475.

Zillmann, D. (1991). Television viewing and physiological arousal. In J. Bryant & D. Zillmann (Eds.), *Responding to the screen: Reception and reaction processes* (pp. 103-133). Hillsdale, NJ: Lawrence Erlbaum.

Index